VAN DIEMEN'S LAND

VAN DIEMEN'S LAND

JAMES BOYCE

Published by Black Inc.,
an imprint of Schwartz Publishing Pty Ltd
37-39 Langridge Street
Collingwood Victoria 3066 Australia
email: enquiries@blackincbooks.com
http://www.blackincbooks.com

Map of Van Diemen's Land (p. viii) is from the collection of The National Library
of Australia (*A new map of Van Diemens Land*, 1825, by James Tyrer).
Map of Tasmania in the 1850s (p. ix) © Royal Australian Historical Society.
Map of tribal boundaries of the Tasmanian Aborigines (p. x) is adapted from
The Aboriginal Tasmanians, Lyndall Ryan, Allen & Unwin, 1996.

Every effort has been made to contact the copyright holders of material in this
book. However, where an omission has occurred, the publisher will gladly include
acknowledgment in any future edition.

The National Library of Australia Cataloguing-in-Publication entry:

Boyce, James.

Van Diemen's land / James Boyce.

ISBN: 9781863954914 (pbk.)

Includes bibliographical references and index.

Tasmania--History--1803-1851.
Tasmania--Politics and government--1803-1851.

994.602

Book design: Thomas Deverall
Index: Garry Cousins

Printed in Australia by Griffin Press

Australian Government

Australia | Council
for the Arts

This project has been assisted by the Australian Government through the
Australia Council, its arts funding and advisory body.

CONTENTS

*   *   *

*To Emma who, with love, made
Van Diemen's Land home*

❦

MAP 1. *Van Diemen's Land*

MAP 2. *Tasmania in the 1850s*

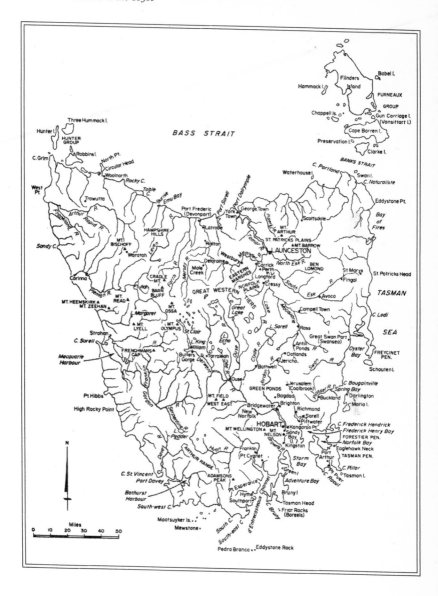

MAP 3. *Tribal boundaries of the Tasmanian Aborigines*

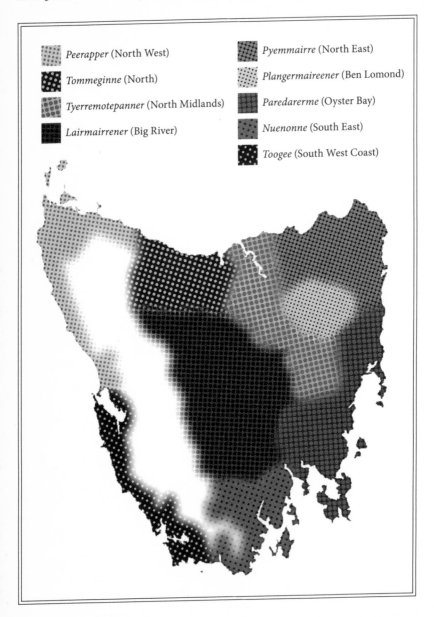

The stone that the builders rejected
has become the cornerstone.
—PSALM 118

INTRODUCTION

TASMANIA WAS ONCE KNOWN AS Van Diemen's Land. It was given this name by the Dutch explorer Abel Tasman in 1642, but it was only after the island became a penal colony in 1803 that the words attained wide notoriety. For 50 years Australia's southern isle was the dumping ground for convicted criminals from the largest empire the world has seen.

In 1856, fewer than three years after the final convict ship berthed in Hobart Town, the colony's name was changed to Tasmania. As Lieutenant Governor William Denison noted to London with polite understatement: "There is a feeling here that to the name Van Diemen's Land a certain stigma attaches."[1] Tasmania and Van Diemen's Land are the same place – this was a new name, not a new island – but even today it is easy to forget this. It remains hard to connect the abode of felons with the respectable, reserved and relatively crime-free "Tasmania" that it seemed spontaneously to metamorphose into. Yet, other than the cementing of the political power of a small group of large landowners, remarkably little changed after 1856 and self-government. At the same time that Victoria and New South Wales were reinventing themselves through the mass immigration brought about by the gold rushes, and England itself was experiencing massive cultural and economic change due to the accelerating industrial revolution, Tasmania became stagnant, a living economic and cultural museum of the pre-industrial era where convicts and their children were to remain the large majority of the population for decades to come. Van Diemen's Land never vanished, but by edict of an embarrassed ruling class, it went underground.

Popular images of Van Diemen's Land today largely reflect fiction, or more accurately, a single work of fiction. One nineteenth-century novel, *For the Term of His Natural Life*, has done more than any history book to shape perceptions of convict life.[2] Marcus Clarke claimed that the "tragic and terrible" events he narrated were all based on "events which have actually occurred."[3] This was true even of the infamous scene in which escaped convicts, driven beyond hunger to near madness by the harsh and inhospitable land, begin to eat their companions. The account was directly based on the confession of the convict cannibal Alexander Pearce, who escaped from Macquarie Harbour Penal Station on the isolated west coast of Van Diemen's Land in 1822.

There is one important difference, however, between real life and fiction. Pearce's journey was through country even the local Aborigines generally avoided, and that today only experienced bushwalkers, their packs heavily laden with supplies, occasionally traverse. Pearce's fictional substitute, Gabbett, escaped from Port Arthur in the south east of Tasmania and headed north up the east coast, journeying through one of the most hospitable and benign environments for human habitation anywhere in Australia. Clarke was a Melbourne journalist who only fleetingly visited Tasmania in 1870. He did not know the island, and it showed. But does the environmental mistake matter in what was after all a human drama? What if nature and empire were seen to work in harmony to crush the human spirit? Surely the all-powerful penal system, so vividly portrayed by Clarke, would ensure that the convicts' sorry fate was ultimately the same?

The hypothesis of this book is that the character of the island which became the enforced home of over 72,000 sentenced criminals (42 per cent of the convicts transported to Australia) *does* matter. The fact that protein-rich shellfish were there for the taking, that wallaby and kangaroo could be killed with nothing more than a hunting dog, and that abundant fresh water and a mild climate made travel by foot relatively easy, does change the story. The convicts' hell was, thank God, a human creation alone.

This book is about the tension produced by siting the principal gaol of the empire in what proved to be a remarkably benevolent land. It sees this paradox to be at the heart of early Tasmanian history, and to have important implications for the nation as a whole.[4] The dominant national narrative, which begins with the struggle of British settlers to come to terms with a "harsh and forbidding"[5] land, needs to be substantially qualified.

The environmental contrasts between Tasmania and the other place of early British settlement, New South Wales, remain obvious enough now, but in the early nineteenth century they were life-changing. Until the crossing of the Blue Mountains in 1813, the British in New South Wales were confined to poor coastal country where both introduced and indigenous foods were hard to obtain and pastoral pursuits were limited. John White, surgeon-general with the First Fleet, famously summarised the first settlers' predicament in April 1790: "much cannot now be done, limited in food and reduced as the people are, who have not had one ounce of fresh animal food since first in the country; a country and place so forbidding and so hateful as only to merit execration and curses ..."[6] Long after the immediate crisis was overcome, both hunting and farming remained difficult. The leading economic historian of early British settlement in Australia, Noel Butlin, has pointed out that "the colonists in New South Wales had chosen one of the worst locations in which to attempt to grow sheep and they continued to do so while they remained in a coastal environment."[7] The country around Port Jackson was equally deficient in game, and what there was proved very difficult to kill.

Unable to obtain food, and indeed clothing and shelter, from the new land, colonists found moving beyond the settlement a major undertaking. Except where rivers or sea aided travel, supplies had to be carried by horse or foot, restricting the time that could be spent away from supply depots. The Barrallier expedition travelled furthest and remained out the longest of any expedition conducted to that time, yet, as its November 1802 records show, the explorers still saw the environment as an obstacle to overcome rather than a potential resource on which to depend.[8]

Less than 12 months after that expedition, with the first settlement of Van Diemen's Land, a dramatically different encounter with the Australian bush began. Van Diemen's Land, even by comparison with the British Isles, proved to be a veritable Eden. Here was an abundance of fresh water, a temperate climate, reliable rainfall, density of game and many hospitable, largely uninhabited offshore islands. Most crucially, there were open grasslands – Aboriginal hunting grounds – close to the ports and estuaries of first settlement. It was the proximity of these rich pastures, adjacent to both Hobart Town and Launceston, and present in much of the land between, that long defined the British experience of the southern island.[9]

There was another factor of central importance. In 1803 Van Diemen's Land was one of the very few places of human habitation on earth where dogs were unknown. This conferred two major advantages on the new settlers. First, native herbivores were present in larger numbers than on the mainland, and second, the kangaroo and wallaby were not adapted to the imported hunting dogs, which were much faster than the indigenous thylacine (Tasmanian tiger) in open country. In an era when guns were of little use for hunting anything but birds – they did not become accurate enough for reliable killing of the wary nocturnal Australian marsupials until the middle of the nineteenth century – hunting proved a far more successful pursuit in Van Diemen's Land than in New South Wales or almost any other site of British colonisation.[10] What David Collins, second in command at Port Jackson until 1796 and from 1804 lieutenant governor of Van Diemen's Land, termed the years of "great despair" in Sydney were never replicated on the southern island.[11] From the commencement of settlement in September 1803 the British had fresh meat in abundance and the health of the population was far superior to that of the labouring classes of England.

The well-watered, almost predator-free grasslands (unlike in New South Wales, sheep were not even penned at night) allowed for a rapid increase in stock numbers. Meat was exported within a decade of first settlement, and by 1817 what the *Sydney Gazette* came to describe as "our sister island"[12] was home to more than twice as many sheep as New South Wales.

How the early British settlers of Van Diemen's Land experienced the Australian continent is thus greatly at variance with the standard opening of the national story. The hardships endured in Sydney were a local rather than a universal experience. Moreover, the widely assumed failure of early settlers to adapt to the new environment also needs to be re-examined in light of the rapid changes soon evident in the way of life of most of the population of the southern colony. The critical environmental difference was not the quantity of the bounty, but its availability to those without capital. Even when the open grasslands of New South Wales were belatedly settled, control was soon monopolised by a small elite. But in Tasmania two decades elapsed before free settlers occupied the lands first settled by convict hunters and shepherds, and even after this time Tasmanian topography, in which hills and mountain ranges invariably fringe the comparatively flat plains, ensured a sanctuary for the poor where a degree of independence and freedom could long be maintained. The back-blocks of Van Diemen's Land became the unexpected setting for an environmentally induced cultural evolution that was aided by the immigrants' too-often-caricatured British heritage.

Who were British Australia's first successful hunters, pastoralists and colonisers of the bush? Just as the natural world the convicts encountered has been overlooked, so too has the world-view the convicts brought with them. Their economic and cultural backgrounds have been pigeon-holed and homogenised in a way that precludes the possibility of a transformative encounter with the new land. Thus, D.N. Jeans suggests that Australia's late settlement meant "that the full power of the industrial revolution, lacking any sense of ecology, was brought to bear on the land."[13] Tom Griffiths claims that "Australia, unlike most other parts of the New World, experienced colonisation and industrialisation almost co-incidentally, a compressed, double revolution."[14] The fact that settlement occurred after the Enlightenment is seen to be almost equally significant. William Lines concludes that "Australian settlement advanced under the guidance of the modern outlook, a uniform way of thinking devoted to the simplification of life and thought and to the formulation of efficacious techniques for the conquest of nature. Reason and violence built, on Australian soil, a new empire."[15]

This is too simple. While Britain had achieved political unity and a greater degree of economic integration than any other European nation, many of its regions and peoples were, in the early nineteenth century, still only in the early stages of transition from a pre-industrial economy and society. Even London and other major urban centres remained very different from the industrialised cities of later mid-Victorian England. A profound gap had opened up between the classes in this respect. E.P. Thompson, in *Customs in Common*, argues that

> customary consciousness and customary usages were especially robust in the eighteenth century … Historians … have tended to see the eighteenth century as a time when these customary usages were in decline, along with magic, witchcraft, and kindred superstitions. The people were subject to pressures to "reform" popular culture from above, literacy was displacing oral transmission, and enlightenment (it is supposed) was seeping down from the superior to the subordinate orders. But the pressures of reform were stubbornly resisted, and the eighteenth century saw a profound distance opened, a profound alienation between the culture of patricians and plebs.[16]

Thus, while it is obvious and indisputable that British immigrants brought their economic and cultural background with them to Australia, it needs to be remembered that there was more than one Britain.

The resilience of pre-industrial society has many implications. Take, for example, the notion of absolute private property rights, a central tenet of the transplanted society that would eventually transform Australia. In the early nineteenth century, many smallholders, agricultural labourers and farm servants in Britain, as well as the itinerant poor, were still reliant on common land and communal rights over "private" lands to graze animals and gather food and fuel.[17] And in much of Ireland the "produce of the infields and outfields was primarily for home consumption," while livestock – grazed on more distant common lands – was the main commercial activity. The stock was watched over by summer herders who lived in basic huts, with each community utilising a designated territory.[18] Similar pastoral and land-use systems existed in parts of Scotland, Wales *and* Van Diemen's Land.

Early Van Diemen's Land saw two decades of largely shared land use, with convicts and small landowners using grasslands for pasture without seeking exclusive possession. Smallholders grew what they could consume and the little they could sell, but the major economic activity occurred in the unowned (according to British law) grasslands, where kangaroo was hunted and sheep and cattle thrived under the loose supervision of convict stockmen. With the arrival of free settlers with their modern private property claims in the 1820s, the progressive eviction of both black and white residents of the grassland plains commenced as part of a broader imperial struggle, the attempt to impose what are now "taken for granted" rights associated with the possession of land title. As John West lamented in his *History of Tasmania* (1852), "the English of modern times" did not comprehend "joint ownership, notwithstanding the once 'common' property of the nation has only been lately distributed by law." It was only because of this change, West suggests, that "the gradual alienation" of the hunting grounds of the Aborigines also meant "their expulsion and extinction."[19]

It has often been pointed out that the first settlers of Tasmania were unwilling invaders. Of greater significance, however, is that they were exiles – even the dream of going home was forfeit – and that most, including the urban majority, still held pre-industrial mores. Van Diemen's Land was not only the convicts' prison, it was their one source of hope. In this context, to gain freedom by obtaining the essentials of life directly from the new land became the chief motivation of their enterprise, and convicts showed themselves willing and able to make changes in clothing, diet, housing and social norms to achieve this.

The readiness of convict settlers to adapt was not a matter of heightened sensitivity, but rather a reflection of the fact that they were little buffered by either capital or privilege from a direct encounter with the demands of the new environment. As a consequence, their experience of the country was far more transformative than that of the wealthy free-settler minority, who were significantly quarantined by the technology of the Industrial Revolution and their very different needs and expectations. The common apprehension that "almost everything the settler did was a re-creation of the world which had been left behind"[20] reflects the experience of a relatively small elite. The fact that this articulate and literate group produced most of the written accounts of Van Diemen's Land explains, but does not justify, the assumption that their history was shared by the majority of the settlers. Indeed, the written accounts share a pervading concern: that in the convict districts a way of life very different from that in rural or urban England had emerged.

The convict exiles to Van Diemen's Land thus provide a remarkable human raw material for the study of Australian colonisation. At a time in Australian politics when there is political pressure to emphasise the contribution of the Enlightenment and British civilisation to the formation of national identity, Van Diemen's Land reminds us what a complex historical task this actually is. What does it mean to talk of the Enlightenment in the context of a society in which, as late as the 1850s, the majority of the population were convicted criminals, many thousands of whom had come from the most "primitive" country in Europe, where a million people were dying from starvation? Those convicts who were refugees from the Irish famine in the 1840s were the poorest group of immigrants to leave from anywhere in Europe in the nineteenth century, representing those who couldn't afford even the cheapest passage or call on even the most degrading forms of charity to save themselves and their families. But even for English convicts, criminality was usually closely connected with desperate poverty (the comparatively low level of serious crime in both Van Diemen's Land and Tasmania should be sufficient to quell finally the still-lingering nineteenth-century belief that convicts represented an inherently criminal underclass).

Tasmania's experience of being founded by convict settlers is not unique, but it is close to being so. Convicts were sent to other parts of the empire, but only in New South Wales did their numbers equal those transported to Van Diemen's Land. And nowhere else, including in New South Wales, did convicts, former convicts and their descendants constitute the majority of the population over such a long period of time.

Van Diemen's Land thus needs to be understood as a convict *society*. It is not best exemplified by the well-known penal apparatus – chain gangs, Port Arthur and hard labour – but by the everyday lives of the ordinary people of the colony. Convicts were simply, as David Collins used to say, "the people," and convictism the society they made. The penal system, intended to ensure subservience in all convicts, was an important part of the context in which this society evolved, but contrary to the picture presented by Marcus Clarke, and essentially reproduced by Robert Hughes in *The Fatal Shore*,[21] it did not determine its form.

The point has been made by a number of historians that, contrary to the popular perception, most convicts did not spend the majority, if any, of their sentence behind bars or in chains, an experience reserved for secondary offenders. Convicts are more accurately seen as servants (or unfree workers) than prisoners.[22] Nevertheless, the number that received various forms of harsh punishment was still very large, and the imminent possibility of joining them influenced, as it was intended to, the behaviour of every convict and former convict. It is not the horror of the penal system (at least as it operated from the late 1820s) that has been distorted, but its social impact. Demonstrations of submission (or the rarer acts of overt resistance) were not the only result of a culture of fear. Material security and, in the early years, existence itself, were frequently risked in pursuing a life of comparative freedom far from the degrading institutions of authority. Even under the comparatively relaxed early penal system, freedom proved to be a powerful motivator to "go bush." Surely this was, and remains, a powerful expression of resistance to the dominant social and economic order. These convicts and their descendants were not merely passive victims of imperial design, and if we are to understand the alternative way of life they forged, it is the land, more than Port Arthur, that holds the key.

The home-making undertaken by Van Diemonian Britons, and the achievement this represents, does not mean, of course, that there were not negative consequences. The impact on the environment and on the land's first people was immense, and the suffering and brutality associated with invasion and conquest must forever remain central themes of any truthful account of life in Van Diemen's Land.

In 2003 the publication of Keith Windschuttle's *Fabrication of Aboriginal History: Volume One, Van Diemen's Land 1803–1847* gave national prominence to the topic of Aboriginal–settler relations in Van Diemen's Land. The irony of this was that the chosen locale for debate happened to be the one place in Australia where the work of contemporary historians had actually moderated, not increased, previous estimates of violence. In *Fate of a Free People*, Henry Reynolds had argued that the massacre of Aborigines, far from being ignored as in many other regions of Australia, had previously been *exaggerated* because earlier historians underestimated Aboriginal advantages in the conflict.

In assessing the level of violence (the only question most of the politically motivated commentators in the so-called history wars seemed to take an interest in), this book essentially defends the conclusions of nineteenth-century writers such as James Bonwick and John West, whose work was based on a considerable body of settler testimony. It argues that Reynolds, and even Lyndall Ryan in *The Aboriginal Tasmanians*, have, far from exaggerating the number of Aborigines killed by the British, probably underestimated fatalities. Their analysis, and most debate to date, has been distorted by the unusual abundance of documentary sources relating to the final stages of the war between 1828 and 1831. This rich collection of documents, first put together by Lieutenant Governor George Arthur, records small groups of survivors engaged in a guerrilla-style resistance in which they proved highly adept. By the time these documents were written, however, most of the Aborigines were already dead. What of the years before, when whole communities, not small bands of warriors, were Britain's enemy?

The argument that massacres were limited, now almost universally accepted, is closely tied to the assumption that settlers were strangers to the new land and thus unable readily to kill the indigenous people in an environment where the horse and gun did not confer the same advantages as in much of mainland Australia. But this analysis ignores the two decades of comparatively peaceful shared land use that preceded the free-settler land-grab, and the extent to which this equipped Van Diemonian bushmen to undertake the expulsion and mass killing of Aborigines on behalf of their masters in the years immediately before the final guerrilla war. Massacres were, as most nineteenth-century historians believed, likely to have been commonplace. Equally horrific, and almost unscrutinised, were the government-sponsored ethnic clearances conducted on the west coast *after* the fighting was over.

These and other aspects of Aboriginal–settler relations are important subjects of this book (and are considered in some detail in the appendix), but nevertheless this is not Aboriginal history, nor even general history. It does not pretend to describe Aboriginal culture, strategy or political organisation. Furthermore, unlike in previous histories of Van Diemen's Land, notably those by John West in the nineteenth century and Lloyd Robson in the twentieth, government policy and actions, along with free-settler concerns, provide the context for the discussion, not its primary object.[23] The focus is on the convicts and the life they made in the southern isle of Australia in the first half of the nineteenth century. The book can thus best be described as environmental history, not because it explores how convict settlers changed the environment but because its primary interest is how the environment changed *them*. In exploring this question, I have sought to put to one side an oddly resilient obsession with passing moral judgment on convicts and their society. Of course convict culture was usually rough, and it could be brutal. More seriously, it is undeniable that convicts and their descendants were implicated in environmental destruction and a human tragedy of almost unimaginable proportions. The argument made here is not intended to qualify this, but rather to demonstrate that the implications of the invasion were not only one-way. Southern Australia's convict founders were changed by their exile to a bountiful but defended land, the home of an ancient and distinct people. They too were changed by conquest. This book is intended to be their history, the history of Van Diemen's Land.

PART I

THE EARLY YEARS
1803–07

[1]

VAN DIEMONIAN SEA-WOLVES

THE CONQUEST OF VAN DIEMEN'S LAND began without flags, cannon, prayer, proclamation or military display. Van Diemen's Land was invaded by the British in much the same way as their own land had been by Viking raiders over a millennium before – coastal forays for plunder followed by gradually expanding periods of settlement and interaction with the native peoples. The first colonisers have become known (somewhat misleadingly) as "sealers" and, like the Nordic traders and raiders, widely caricatured. Sixty years ago, Leslie Norman presented a picture of "rude, rough, wife-snatching" men, who were "wreckers, pirates, freebooters, slave-drivers, murderers, rum-swillers, sea-wolves, and sea-rats – ragged drunken beasts."[1] It is a view that still has wide currency.

The Bass Strait islands were the sealers' primary base. The seal colonies there were discovered after the vessel *Sydney Cove*, returning to its home port from a Calcutta trading run, ran aground near Preservation Island in February 1797. The entire crew was landed safely, along with a speculative cargo that included 7000 gallons of spirits, and some of the often-inebriated men were to live on Preservation Island for 12 months. A long boat was sent to Sydney and two of the 17 sailors manning it survived to raise the alarm. The rescue and salvage boats sent from Port Jackson noted the quantity of seals available on the islands, and by October 1798 commercial sealing had begun.[2]

Sealskins were the first significant export item from British Australia. Joseph Banks' complaint that Britain had by then "possessed the country of New South Wales more than ten years and not one article has hitherto been discovered by the importation of which the mother country can receive any degree of return for the cost of founding and maintaining the colony" was at last to be answered.[3] By 1803 the value of sealskins taken was reported as £303,046, involving the slaughter of 57,560 seals. In 1804, the peak year of plunder, 107,591 seals were killed, but a price drop, due to over-supply, meant that the total value of the hunt increased only marginally. Most skins were exported to China.[4] These figures were many times higher than the collective annual budgets, or the total agricultural output, of all the British settlements in Australia combined until the mid 1820s. Wool exports did not reach a similar value until the late 1820s. But such "mercantile greed," as the French naturalist François Péron noted in December 1802, could not fail "to cause a noticeable and irreparable reduction in the population of these animals,"[5] and from 1805 the number of seals killed dropped dramatically.[6]

Far more sustainable than the large seal colonies were the human communities that developed around them. The 1804 Sydney muster listed 123 "free" men in the "islands at the southward," and Governor Philip King reported that 180 people in all were known to be on the islands that year.[7] As the most accessible seals were killed, and the big profits disappeared, a different form of sealing emerged. Men lived on the islands for months, sometimes years, at a time, and gradually began to form permanent settlements. They killed what seals remained, as well as wallaby, wombat and emu, selling the skins and eating the meat, and many even had gardens and small farms with crops and goats. As the *Sydney Gazette* reported, the sealers lived in a "curious state of independence."[8]

The small islands were attractive sites for settlement for men, a large proportion of whom were former convicts, who sought freedom and distance from the penal establishments. The native animals had never known dogs or humans, and were easily killed (and in some cases, like the King Island emu and wombat, soon wiped out). An even greater attraction than the abundance of animals was the absence of people. There had been no human occupation of the Furneaux Group in the Bass Strait for thousands of years, and the islands were thus safe to colonise without resistance from the Aborigines.

Sealer colonisation proceeded virtually independently of official sanction and, except in a nominal sense, was not under imperial control. Some attempts were made – indeed, securing the seal resource was one of the reasons Governor King gave for sending a settlement party to Van Diemen's Land in September 1803 – but little power could in practice be exercised until official colonisation extended into sealer territory in the mid to late 1820s. As seal numbers declined, most of the bigger Sydney-based merchant capitalists left the industry, and what the *Hobart Town Gazette* called "an extraordinary number of small colonial craft" largely supplanted them.[9] Often boat-owners would hire their boats to those without capital in return for a significant percentage of the takings.[10] A Sydney businessman, W. Stewart, wrote to the colonial secretary in 1815 urging that what had largely become an unregulated Van Diemonian industry be controlled:

> There is a custom ... of whale boats from 25 to 30 feet long, who clear out from the Derwent or Port Dalrymple each with two or three people on board, and after their departure amount to six or seven in number, then go equipped with arms and dogs to hunt for their living, and save the kangaroo skins as well as what seal skins they can; the elephant they kill and destroy for their tongues ... The people are a banditti of bushrangers and others who are carried ... after committing robberies and depredations on the industrious settlers and depriving them of their arms, dogs, boats and other property ... they encourage men belonging to vessels to desert and leave them in distress ... and likewise to rob and plunder them.[11]

Sealers were not the only unofficial colonisers. Whales had been hunted in the waters south of Van Diemen's Land since 1775, when the Enderby company pioneered whaling in the south seas. Crew-members spent extended periods ashore gathering food, fuel and water.[12] From the early nineteenth century through to the 1840s, bay whaling was also conducted in small boats from stations established in sheltered waters around the eastern and southern coast of Van Diemen's Land, such as Adventure Bay, Oyster Bay, Recherche Bay and Southport, well before the official settlement of these regions commenced.[13]

Before 1825 it was these predominantly Van Diemonian sealers and whalers, rather than the land-hungry squattocracy or official settlement parties, who were the major instrument of territorial expansion by the British in Australia. Within Van Diemen's Land, sealers soon moved beyond the Furneaux Group to King Island and Robben's Island in the north-west, and Schouten Island and Waub's Boat Harbour (now Bicheno) on the east coast. Kangaroo Island became a major sealing centre as early as 1806, and permanent sealing communities were also established on many other South Australian islands in Spencer's Gulf.[14] Sealers also lived at Portland Bay, Port Fairy, Westernport and Phillip Island in what is now Victoria, and King George Sound and various West Australian islands[15] – all well before official settlement of these areas. After a large colony of seals was discovered at the remote sub-Antarctic Macquarie Island, sealers even established themselves there, although the harsh environment made for a different, more provisional, form of community.

As official colonisation extended during the mid 1820s, the new wave of settlers encountered these men. Major Lockyer, sent from Sydney to King George Sound to found the first settlement in Western Australia, found sealing parties already resident, and noted that sealers had also traversed the Swan River. Lockyer complained that "alongside this legitimate and profitable though officially uncontrollable industry there was another association entirely illegal and objectionable: the existence of bands of runaway convicts."[16] Similarly, the expedition sent to found a settlement at Westernport in 1826 found a party of sealers who "hailed from Port Dalrymple, they were living in Phillip Island and moreover had a couple of acres of wheat and some maize growing well."[17]

Nor were sealer communities isolated fringe settlements, as is often assumed. Before the 1820s the sealers were not at the periphery of colonisation but were its economic and cultural heartland, with ties that extended far into, and beyond, New Holland (as mainland

Australia was called). Sealing was integral to a web of trading relations that encompassed New Zealand, Mauritius and the Pacific Islands, with most of the sealing communities adjacent to the main sea highway connecting Europe and India with the Pacific.[18] Moreover, the sealers were closely integrated with the still-dominant culture of the Aborigines. From their small settlements on offshore islands and in coastal bays they developed complex economic and cultural ties with the peoples whose land and resources they took for their own. Violence was never absent from this encounter, and it eventually came to dominate it. But, as will also be discussed, it was not the only or, at least in the early years, the major theme.

These Van Diemonian "sea-wolves" are not easy founding fathers to come to terms with, but whatever judgments are made about their way of life it certainly cannot be characterised as one which sought to reproduce a Little England. Through the labour and crimes of these "rude wife-snatching men," Van Diemen's Land had been born.

[2]

THE SETTLEMENT OF
THE DERWENT

URING 1803 AND 1804 THREE DIFFERENT British parties
were sent to Van Diemen's Land. Each was made up of convicts, soldiers, civil and military officers, and a few free settlers. Two
were sent from Sydney and one – by far the largest of the three – came
from London via a short-lived stay at Port Phillip. Two settlements
were established on the Derwent River in the south of the island –
Risdon Cove and Sullivans Cove – and the last of the three (to be considered in the next chapter) was formed at Port Dalrymple in the
north.

These were not journeys into the unknown. Although it was not
visited for well over a century after the Dutchman Abel Tasman
briefly landed at Blackman Bay on the Forestier Peninsular in 1642
and named the new land after the governor of the Dutch East Indies,
from 1772 Van Diemen's Land had become an established refuge for
explorers of the southern seas needing a safe harbour, fresh food,
water and fuel. Adventure Bay on Bruny Island and the sheltered
waters of the D'Entrecasteaux Channel were the preferred localities to
sojourn, but by 1803 much of the coast of Van Diemen's Land was well
mapped, and its birds, animals and people documented in various
annals of discovery. Many visitors, particularly the French, had been
sensitive observers,[1] although the largest of the scientific expeditions, led by Nicolas Baudin, had, from an Aboriginal perspective, a
disastrous consequence. Governor King, fearing (with some reason)
that the French had territorial ambitions, attempted to formalise the

British claim (through what Baudin described as a "ridiculous" and "childish ceremony"[2]) on King Island in December 1802. Baudin wrote to King:

> I have never been able to conceive that there was justice or even fairness on the part of Europeans in seizing, in the name of their governments, a land seen for the first time … it appears to me that it would be infinitely more glorious for your nation, as for mine, to mould for society the inhabitants of its own country over whom it has rights, rather than wishing to occupy itself with the improvement of those who are very far removed from it by beginning with seizing the soil which belongs to them and which saw their birth.[3]

But the raising of the Union Jack in the midst of the French camp was not considered sufficient to confirm the British claim, so in early September 1803 King established a small military outpost on the Derwent River near present-day Hobart, manned by soldiers from the New South Wales Corps under the command of John Bowen, a 23-year-old officer newly arrived from England.

Risdon Cove

The first encounter between the Aborigines and the British at Risdon Cove after the arrival of HM Brig *Lady Nelson* is the subject of obscure and conflicting accounts. Bowen, whose report to King is the only surviving record of the first weeks of settlement, was on the whaler *Albion*, which arrived some days after it occurred.[4] The new commandant noted merely that Aborigines were "seen" before he arrived, but "I have not made any search after them, thinking myself well off if I never see them again."[5] In his 1852 *History of Tasmania*, John West gave the following account, presumably on the basis of oral testimony:

> The party dispatched from Sydney, to take possession of the island, who landed in September 1803, on their arrival at Risdon saw nothing of the natives. A solitary savage, armed with a spear, after-

wards entered the camp, and was cordially greeted. He accepted the trinkets which they offered, but he looked on the novelties scattered about without betraying surprise. By his gestures they inferred that he discharged them from their trespass. He then turned towards the woods, and when they attempted to follow, he placed himself in the attitude of menace, and poised his spear.[6]

However, an Aboriginal recollection recorded in the diary of the government-appointed conciliator and emissary to the Aborigines, George Augustus Robinson, in July 1831, suggests a less pacific first encounter. Woorady, an elder of the Nuenonne people of Bruny Island, told Robinson that

> he saw the first ships come to Van Diemen's Land when they set-
> tled at Hobart Town, called Niberlooner; that the Py.dare natives
> speared some white men who landed in a boat, one man in the
> thigh; that white men went after the natives, the natives see them
> come but did not run away, saw their guns and said white men
> carry wood; that by and by white men shoot two blacks dead, when
> they all became frightened and run away.[7]

An early hostile exchange is also suggested by the oral testimony of the convict Edward White to the government-appointed Aborigines Committee in 1830, and a written account by an American whaler, Amasa Delano.[8] Both claimed that a young Aboriginal child was abducted in the early days of the settlement. And in mid May 1804 David Collins wrote of a "former affair" having soured relations.[9]

It is likely that the long-term significance of the new settlement was at first missed by the Aborigines. Whalers had already joined explorers as regular visitors to the Derwent – the estuary being a well-known source of food, water and timber – and 49 Britons setting up their "tent huts," collecting water, lighting fires and doing some hunting could reasonably be assumed to be more of the same. However, by the end of September, when Bowen reported that prisoners and soldiers had got "very comfortable huts," the different nature of this settlement would have been clear.[10] Moreover, the settlement party might have been small, and its immediate territorial impact modest, but this motley collection of 29 prisoners, eight soldiers, seven free settlers and a small civil department[11] now occupied a prime Aboriginal hunting ground.

Risdon Cove, on the eastern shore of the Derwent, was a site recommended by the explorers Bass and Flinders following their 1798 visit. Both the explorers and the commandant emphasised the rich pasture on hand, Bowen describing the area as "more like a nobleman's park in England than an uncultivated country ... very little trouble might clear every valley I have seen in a month."[12] Grasslands extended north from the valleys behind Risdon Cove for about 200 kilometres to the locality of present-day Launceston, with the first settler guide to be published in 1820 noting that this whole length of country could be traversed on horseback (or foot) "with almost as much facility as if the island had been in a state of civilisation and cultivation for centuries."[13]

The island's open grassland plains had been developed and maintained as hunting grounds through regular seasonal burning by Aborigines. Although the archaeologist Rhys Jones coined the term "fire-stick farming" in 1969,[14] the systematic nature of Aboriginal land management was recognised much earlier. Edward Curr junior, a Van Diemonian pioneer emigrant to Port Phillip, believed there was an "instrument in the hands of these savages which must be credited with results which it would be difficult to overestimate. I refer to the fire-stick ... he tilled his land and cultivated his pastures with fire." Curr suggested that "it may perhaps be doubted whether any section of the human race has exercised a greater influence on the physical condition of any large portion of the globe than the wandering savages of Australia."[15]

The British were adept at living in grasslands and clearly appreciated having settled, for the first time on the Australian continent, in a comparatively familiar environment. They were to experience nothing like it in New South Wales until the celebrated crossing of the Blue Mountains in 1813 by an expedition led by three large landowners – Blaxland, Wentworth and Lawson[16] – and the lands then discovered were to be used primarily for grazing by a small elite, not as the hunting-pastoral common which Van Diemen's Land was at the time.

The grasslands of Van Diemen's Land abounded in game, especially the forester or eastern grey kangaroo, the larger Bennett's or red-necked wallaby and the distinctive Tasmanian emu. One of the convicts, Edward White, recalled that "there were hundreds and hundreds of kangaroo about Risdon then."[17] But they were notoriously difficult to shoot: "so watchful is that gentle, inoffensive creature," it was reported, "that it is almost impossible to get within gun-shot of it."[18]

In consequence of this, of all the luggage brought by the invading Europeans none was as significant as their hunting dogs. For the next two decades, the dog would be central to a rapid change in the way of life of both British and Aboriginal residents of Van Diemen's Land.

The British were fortunate indeed that colonisation had proceeded in the last days of the widespread use of hunting dogs in the British Isles.[19] Such dogs, used mainly by this time to kill deer, were variously known as the deerhound, the Irish wolfhound, Irish greyhound, Highland deerhound and Scottish greyhound. The large "boomers" and emus of dingo-free Van Diemen's Land had been familiar with no predator faster than the persistent but slow thylacine and so found the introduced carnivore a formidable foe.[20]

Killing by the neck a full-grown kangaroo or emu was a difficult and dangerous affair, even for such powerful canines. Speed was of the essence, which led to the wolfhounds being crossed with greyhounds. One immigrant reported on the outcome of such breeding: "the dogs used here to hunt the kangaroo have the shape and general character of the greyhound, but are very much larger in size, and coarser all together, uniting great strength with speed."[21]

Most of the civil and military officers administering the new penal settlement had one or more hunting dogs, and kangaroo and emu were soon being killed in large numbers. The "greyhounds" belonging to the surgeon at Risdon Cove, Jacob Mountgarrett, for example, were reported to have killed "six or seven [kangaroos] ... in a forenoon."[22]

The meat was considered excellent. One convict thought that kangaroo flesh was "equal in quality to most foreign – not English – roast beef."[23] A comparison with venison was more often made.

Kangaroo and emu were not the only indigenous foods readily available. Shellfish, especially mussels and oysters, were easily accessible, while swans congregated in large numbers a short distance up the river. Such bounty ensured that there would be no repeat of the disastrous first few years at Port Jackson, and that the health of Britons living in the empire's newest outpost would soon be far better than that of their countrymen in almost any other part of the globe.[24]

Port Phillip

In early 1803, during a brief interregnum in the interminable 20-year war with France, the British government sent a very much larger party to consolidate the British claim to southern Australia. This expedition of over 400 men and women was under the command of an officer of the marines and former judge advocate of New South Wales, David Collins.

Marjorie Tipping, in *Convicts Unbound*, studied the individual lives of all but five of the 308 convicts who left London with Collins on 24 April 1803 on board the *Calcutta*. Her analysis supports Hamish Maxwell-Stewart's conclusion that convicts were "broadly representative of the early nineteenth-century working population of the British Isles."[25] Tipping concludes that they were handpicked, with almost all having trades suitable to begin a new colony. There were, for example, a dozen shoemakers, nine sawyers, four carpenters and five fishers. This was in marked contrast to the first fleet to New South Wales (although the more illuminating fact is that few practised their trade after being transported,[26] perhaps indicating that their carefully selected knowledge had limited application in the new land).

The *Calcutta* convicts were a multicultural lot. There were six or seven Jews from the East End of London, a Pole, a German, a Portuguese, two Dutch, an Afro-American – the violin player William Thomas – and a French confectioner, Nicholas Piroelle. There were also 17 Irish (although all were arrested in England), at least eight Scots, and the same number of Welsh. Their ages when convicted ranged from two boys aged nine, William Steel and William Appleton, to the 57-year-old Romani (Gypsy) Robert Cooper.[27] A few educated convicts were on board, and at least one of these was a wealthy man. James Grove left England with his wife "without a sigh" and reported that the governor and chaplain treated his family kindly.[28]

Of great subsequent use to Collins were seven recently disgraced soldiers who had been involved in the Gibraltar mutiny. These prisoners were hastily taken on board as part of a cover-up to protect their commanding officer, the King's son, the Duke of Kent (later to become the father of Queen Victoria), against whom they had mutinied on Christmas Eve 1802.[29]

Although males were overwhelmingly predominant, there were some women. Seventeen wives left England with their convict husbands, including two de facto partners, and journeyed with their six sons and five daughters. There were also the wives of eight male settlers. Finally, there were two individual women settlers, including Mrs Hobbs, a naval widow with five children.

This expedition had the benefit of antipodean experience, most significantly through Collins, but also James Carrett, a convict who was to become a man of some notoriety in Van Diemen's Land, who had illegally returned to England from New South Wales.[30] Given the lieutenant governor's time in Sydney, it is not surprising that hunting dogs were on board. The surveyor, G.P. Harris, lamented the loss of his dogs on the journey out, "as a good dog is invaluable at New South Wales both as a guard for our tents and to hunt kangaroos."[31] Collins had better luck with his "large staghound, intended to keep him supplied with fresh game in his new home."[32]

The expedition put ashore in Australia, after a five-month voyage, in September 1803, just after the settlement at Risdon had begun. The first choice for a settlement was Port Phillip, at the approximate site of present-day Sorrento on the Mornington Peninsula. As he had earlier at Port Jackson, the lieutenant governor was soon complaining of hunger, illness and hostile Aborigines. He wrote to London in November 1803: "I have been much disappointed in my hope of saving the salt provisions by the issuing of fish and kangaroo occasionally, but of the latter not one has yet been killed, and of the former but very few taken."[33] And for his part, Surveyor Harris complained that "no quadrupeds of any kind have been seen except native dogs and two kangaroos which I saw while surveying."

After the long voyage, this failure to hunt or fish with any success was a very serious matter – there were never less than 30 people under medical treatment and scurvy remained rampant. John Pascoe Fawkner, a convict's son who was later to return to Port Phillip as a founder of Melbourne, recalled that their rations were "salt pork, not of the very best quality at times, and a hard, almost black substance, served out as beef, but commonly called Old Horse."[34] Collins later reported to London that there had been 18 deaths during the three months at Port Phillip.[35] Surveyor Harris was moved to describe the land, in "appearance truly delightful," as "the most deceitful I ever saw."[36]

Lack of fresh food was a serious problem, but it was Aboriginal resistance to an under-manned and rebellious British military that explains why Collins chose to evacuate so soon. Relations with the Aborigines were strained from the beginning. A missionary, William Pascoe Crook, was horrified that when the first landing party was met by a native brandishing a shield and a spear, they had responded by firing at and pursuing the Aborigines, burning down their huts and stealing goods. Three other Britons shot and killed another Aborigine and took ornaments and weapons. It was only when Collins' ship arrived that negotiations belatedly commenced and blankets and biscuits were exchanged.[37] It was probably already too late. Soon afterwards the first survey party, led by one of the Royal Navy officers, James Tuckey, and Harris, had a serious fight at Corio Bay, involving an estimated 200 Aborigines. Tuckey acknowledged that two Aborigines were killed, including the "chief," who seemed "to despise the superior effect of our arms."[38]

The Britons became increasingly frightened after these incidents, fearing vengeance for the deaths. Large groups of Aborigines were believed to be gathering in the north, and noises that the settlers feared were war cries could be heard across the water. The fires all around them were seen to be a particularly ominous sign.[39] Collins issued an order on 20 November 1803 warning against travel even in the vicinity of nearby Arthur's Seat, as it was believed large groups of natives were gathering there. Convicts were forbidden to go to the seashore for crayfish from sunset to sunrise. All outlying huts were destroyed and everyone was required to concentrate in the vicinity of the main compound.[40]

Collins knew there was better land and ample fresh water available nearby. The Scottish convict, David Gibson, one of the first runaways, first alerted him to the river at the head of the bay, where over three decades later Melbourne was to be founded.[41] However, Collins informed London that "were I to settle in the upper part of the harbour, which is full of natives, I should require four times the strength I have now."[42]

Collins had requested a garrison of 100 marines, but received only half this number.[43] More than this, though, it was their unreliability for the task at hand that limited his options. Collins' challenge, one that was to prove a recurring one for lieutenant governors, was to assert effective control over the military. The rank and file were from a similar social background to the convicts. Moreover, they too were to some extent under "sentence," generally seeking little more than to survive a prescribed period of poorly rewarded service. If pushed too hard, there was the possibility that they would identify a shared interest with the convicts and, if not swap sides, at least withdraw from active risk-taking. To achieve rank and file co-operation, the provision of a liberal rum ration was essential. This, however, produced its own discipline problems, especially as the military often drank with the convicts.

At Port Phillip the tensions soon reached a head.[44] By the end of the year, Collins, faced with threats from Aborigines, an "improper spirit" among the military and "a large sick-list," decided, like similarly suffering European explorers had before him, to leave for the well-known refuge of Van Diemen's Land. He chose to follow Bowen to the Derwent, he wrote, because of the "addition of strength" which would come from the New South Wales Corps troops and because "its position at the southern extremity of Van Diemen's Land gives it a [commercial] advantage over every other harbour yet discovered in the straits."[45]

In one sense at least, Port Phillip had been what its political masters intended: a prison without walls. Of the 27 convicts who absconded, 20 returned, six died and only William Buckley survived with the help of the Aborigines (with whom he was to remain until the founding of Melbourne in 1835).[46] On New Year's Eve 1803, Collins portrayed the fate of these men as a warning to all:

> We cannot but pity the delusion which some of the prisoners labour under in thinking that they can exist when deprived of the assistance of Government. Their madness will be manifest to themselves when they shall feel too late that they have wrought their own ruin. After those who have absconded we shall make no further search certain that they must soon return or perish by famine.[47]

Runaways, he warned, "lived in constant fear of the natives by whose hands it is now more than probable they have by this time perished."[48]

At this time the British authorities still did not need to build gaols to keep their antipodean convicts confined. A "country which nowhere affords a supply to the traveller"[49] was a far more effective prison than any man-made construction. But in Van Diemen's Land the environmental walls were to be quickly broken down and the convicts' "deluded" fantasy that they could "exist when deprived of the assistance of Government" would be realised to an astonishing degree.

Sullivans Cove

The approach of the Port Phillip evacuees up the Derwent in mid-February 1804 was recorded by Surveyor Harris: "we are now riding snug, about two miles from as beautiful a country in appearance as I ever saw … From the great number of fires we see all around it appears to be tolerably well inhabited."

Harris's appreciation of the new land was no doubt aided by a satisfied stomach. Even before arriving at Risdon Cove, he ate mussels and oysters gathered by the party in nearby Frederick Henry Bay. Now the surveyor looked forward to even better things to come: "I am in hopes we shall want no supply of game in this new settlement. We know kangaroo to be in great abundance." He was not disappointed, finding that the "woods abound with kangaroos and emus." The black swan was also present in "astonishing numbers," and Harris considered it "excellent food, as white and good as any geese that I ever eat in England." Not surprisingly, Harris concluded that there was a stark contrast between the "barbarous shores of Basses Strait" and the "noble and fertile banks of the Derwent."[50]

A day after arriving at Risdon, the settler William Collins (no relation to the lieutenant governor) and Harris selected a site for a new settlement at Sullivans Cove, on the western shore of the Derwent.[51] Harris described the location of "the camp," as it was colloquially known until the 1820s:

> our settlement is formed about 16 miles from the mouth of the Derwent, one of the finest rivers I ever beheld ... deep enough and large enough to admit the whole navy of Great Britain at once. The shores rise gradually into hills covered with fine grass and noble trees – we are settled on the left hand side going up in a small cove where there is an island and an excellent run of fresh water – the town is built on a fine gently rising plain.

The decision to transfer to the western shore of the Derwent came at a cost. The main hunting grounds were now less accessible, with potentially dangerous boat trips (especially for the majority who could not swim) across the river required to reach them. The extensive tree cover, hilly terrain and generally poor soils also made the land around "the camp" largely unsuitable for agricultural and pastoral pursuits. So limited was the land available for farming that the few free settlers soon opted to move up-river to "New Town," ensuring the first physical divide between the lands of the convict and the free.

The main advantages of Sullivans Cove were the improved water supply and – ironically, given the reasons for choosing the Derwent – the distance from the troublesome, aggressive and mutinous New South Wales Corps. Despite his expressed need for military reinforcements, Collins never made any use of their services and made no attempt to bring the Risdon Cove settlement under his direct command until forced to do so by a direct order from Governor King in May 1804.

Soon after moving to Sullivans Cove, another advantage from the move across the Derwent would have become apparent to the lieutenant governor. The river was a tribal boundary, and there was therefore an opportunity to begin diplomacy anew. The first contact with the Aborigines on the western shore was recorded by one of the civil officers of the establishment, the chaplain, magistrate and diarist Robert Knopwood, on 9 March 1804: "many of the natives were about the camp ... Cap. Merthow and Mr. Brown had an interview with them on the shore near the *Ocean*."[52]

Relations with the Aborigines on the western shore remained comparatively peaceful for many years, and Collins must be given considerable personal credit for this. He had studied and reflected on Aboriginal–settler relations at Port Jackson, and his *Account of the Colony of New South Wales* includes extensive sections on Aboriginal customs. Collins' biographer, John Currey, notes that "none of his other activities ... were recorded in such detail or with such a sense of involvement."[53] Inga Clendinnen has observed that Collins matured "into an absorbed observer of native conduct, and a man capable of recognising, indeed of honouring, a quite different way of being ... our best and most sensitive informant on Australian ways of life and thought, especially in matters of justice and rights."[54]

David Collins can thus legitimately be described as the European expert on Aborigines in the 1790s, despite the obvious limits to such expertise. Even so, John Currey is critical of the lieutenant governor's failure to pursue his study of Aborigines and promote cross-cultural contact in Van Diemen's Land, believing he "was not the man he had been at Sydney Cove" and was "often tired" and "sometimes showed a mood of depression."[55] However, British policy toward Aborigines in Van Diemen's Land seems more a reflection of learnt wisdom than physical or mental exhaustion. The mature Collins saw little value in promoting extended contact between Aborigines and settlers because he believed this had neither promoted peace nor benefited the Aborigines in New South Wales. Collins noted in his *Account* that such cultural exchange "had not been yet able to reconcile these people to the deprivation of those parts of this harbour occupied by the English; but while they entertained the idea of the English having dispossessed them of their residences, they must always consider them as enemies."[56]

As lieutenant governor, Collins did not prevent contact between Aborigines and the settlers at the Derwent. At the same time, close and ongoing relations were not encouraged (a contrast with Port Jackson). Perhaps the English did know less of Aboriginal culture as a result, but it is also true that during Collins' tenure there were few Aboriginal children separated from their parents, no Aborigines struggling to survive in the town, no parallel to the 1789 smallpox epidemic that devastated the Aboriginal population around Port Jackson and Botany Bay, and no outbreak of sustained violence such as at the Hawkesbury from January 1795. Van Diemen's Land was fortunate indeed to have as its first lieutenant governor a man who at least understood that, whatever the legal claims of the British, the Aborigines "also have their real estates."[57]

Some contact, mainly on the western shore, did occur. The *Sydney Gazette* noted that the Aborigines were "very friendly to small parties they meet accidentally." One settler even recalled that "the children were often left" with the Aborigines.[58] Perhaps it was the same woman the historian James Bonwick met late in her life, who remembered as a child setting off from New Town to Mt Wellington with her brother, getting lost and falling in with some Aborigines by whom she was "kindly treated … She furthermore told me that when a girl she often met them in the camp, as Hobart Town was then called."[59]

We cannot be sure which of the south-eastern peoples these early encounters involved. It is likely that most involved the Nuenonne, whose home territory was Bruny Island, rather than the Mouheenenner, whose territory encompassed Sullivans Cove. Both clan groups moved regularly between the Derwent and Bruny, but by 1804 it was the Nuenonne who were the most experienced at dealing with Europeans because of the frequency with which explorers and whalers had visited Adventure Bay for food, water, timber and shelter. Only the previous year the Baudin expedition had spent a month anchored there.[60]

On the eastern shore, though, relations remained more tense. In February 1804 James Meehan recorded that while surveying to the north of Risdon Cove, "a considerable body of natives ... endeavoured to surround us" and he was "obliged to fire on them." On the following morning,

> the natives again assembled in a large body on a hill over us – all around with spears and in a very menacing attitude. They followed us a short distance and then stopped. They appear to be very dexterous at throwing stones. Them who surrounded us yesterday in such multitudes had no arms but a few waddys, but several of them picked up stones.[61]

Nevertheless, relations were generally peaceful, and given this and the abundance of fresh food, after the hardships of the hulks, the long voyage out and the difficulties at Port Phillip, the first few months at the Derwent must have been something like an adventure holiday. Harris wrote that, "were it not the great distance from home and the great expense paid for all the little comforts of life, a single man might live very contentedly and comfortably at least for a few years."[62] James Grove wrote that "our health has been continued beyond calculation ... it's being so contrary a life to that which we have been used to, that I am – as must anyone be – astonished at it." He recorded with relief that "my good, my merciful, my gracious God has made this thorny bed a bed of roses" and confessed to being "unaccountably indifferent" to going home.[63]

Grove was a privileged prisoner, and the deprivations of servitude would have been much less for him than for other convicts. Nevertheless, the contrast between the living standards of the poor in Britain and in Van Diemen's Land at this time was undoubtedly marked. In 1803 Patrick Colquhoun published his *Treatise on Indigence*, which measured the increase in pauperism in England caused by the price rises, especially of wheat, associated with the long French war. Matters were so desperate, it was argued, that "the state of everyone who must labour for subsistence" had been reduced to what was termed "indigence" – defined as "the state of those destitute of the means of subsistence." Colquhoun's analysis is substantiated by the fact that in 1803 over a million people – one in nine of the English population –

were said to be in receipt of poor relief, casual or permanent.[64] For these men and women, wheaten bread, let alone fresh meat, was a luxury, and hunger an almost daily sensation.

By contrast, in Van Diemen's Land the main challenge for the authorities was how to restrict food supply. Control of the island's abundant natural resources was recognised as essential to the maintenance of social order and penal discipline. The native animals of the new land were, as in England, assumed to be the property of the Crown. English game laws restricted hunting to those with an annual income of £100 from a freehold estate, and this principle was carried over to Van Diemen's Land, where only the civil and military officers and their designated "gamekeepers" could legally hunt.[65] The game laws were seen as integral to a stable social order. In Van Diemen's Land during 1804, convicts ate emu and kangaroo, but they had to work for it.

The officers used their monopoly of fresh meat to employ convicts outside designated government work hours. Harris informed his mother in 1804 that he was building a little place at a farm "about a mile from the town" by "employing workers (convicts) after Government hours and paying them ... which I easily do at no cost to myself, in kanguroo flesh."[66]

The spirit of the game laws, as well as the need to preserve a valuable food resource, was reflected in the colony's first conservation order. In March 1804 Collins prohibited the killing of the swans and reiterated the instruction (as Christmas lunches were being planned) on 22 December. This restriction, however, did not affect the right of officers to hunt. Knopwood, for example, continued to eat swan regularly.[67]

The colonists also had access to plentiful supplies of fresh water. It is easy to take this resource for granted – and therefore to miss its importance – but easy access to clean water was unknown to most of the English population for much of the nineteenth century. The presence of fresh water in the bush also made possible overland journeys and hunting expeditions. Few horses were available until well into the 1820s and those that existed were the monopoly of the elite, but with water came access to the far-flung bounty of the land. "Thank God, there is water in the country, plenty and sweet enough," noted the "kangaroo man" in Charles Rowcroft's *Adventures of an Emigrant*.[68]

Collins well understood the importance of clean water for the colonists' health, cautioning "the people against polluting the stream, by any means whatsoever" and "positively forbid[ding] their going into, or destroying the underwood adjacent to the water, under pain of being severely punished." Like the swan protection orders and the measures to protect the local timber resource (no "timber whether young or old near the encampment" was to be cut down without permission),[69] such conservation laws have been described by Tim Bonyhady as "predictably utilitarian."[70] But the British were not wholly blind to ethical questions concerning the exploitation of their new environment. Chaplain Knopwood's first sermon called on the officers, soldiers, free settlers and convicts to pray that

> God would bless and prosper all our undertakings in this infant
> colony, and increase the fruits of the earth, by which through his
> blessing, our lives and those around us, the natives of the land, may
> be amply supplied … let us give God thanks for the grass of the field
> … let us take notice of the great variety of those creatures which are
> made for our use … at the same time let us remember that our right
> in these creatures is not absolute, we hold them for God … Thou
> has created all things and for thy glory they are and were created.[71]

This was a prayer that looked to the new land and its native people with a surprising degree of gratitude and hope. To the invaders' surprise, there had been much to be thankful about. The "fruits of the earth" had been supplied with a generosity beyond their imagining.

Even so, as welcome as fresh food and clean water were, not even Eden itself could assuage the feeling of loss produced by permanent exile to an island six months' travelling time from home and family. The pain of exile was to grow during the autumn of 1804 into a fear-filled sense of abandonment as the newest imperial outpost was comprehensively neglected by London. By May 1804, the adventure holiday was well and truly over.

[3]

HOW SHALL WE SING THE LORD'S
SONG IN A STRANGE LAND?

FOR MONTHS THAT TURNED INTO YEARS, the residents of the
Sullivans Cove camp waited in vain for supply ships and further shiploads of convicts from London. James Grove had not believed
any more convicts would be sent to Sydney and that all would now
come to the Derwent. He noted the general disappointment when it
was learnt that the next convict ship had berthed in Sydney, as indeed
all were to do until after Groves' death in 1810.[1]

Knopwood's sermon of May 1804 acknowledged the growing
despair. He compared the people's experience with that of Old Testa-
ment Jewish prisoners who, also lamenting enforced exile, sat down
and wept by the rivers of Babylon. The chaplain then asked the assembled convicts and soldiers the same question posed by the Jews: "How
shall we sing the Lord's song in a strange land?" The answer, their
pastor suggested, was to never forget your homeland: "If I forget thee,
O Jerusalem, let my right hand forget her cunning."[2]

England had now supplanted the new environment as the focus of
the chaplain's prayers. But in the homeland itself, it seemed that no
one remembered Van Diemen's Land. The Colonial Office did not
even reply to the regular correspondence it received from David Collins, carried on faithfully until his death in 1810.

Almost the only person of influence who showed an interest in the
new settlement was the eminent naturalist Sir Joseph Banks. Collins
tried valiantly to tempt him with news of natural resources that might
increase the colony's value. He wrote of an abundance of whales,

suggesting that the government should equip convict transports as whalers.[3] He sent plants and animals to London, including a keg containing the uteri of two kangaroo "and a live animal known as the Devil," and he supported the endeavours of the botanist Robert Brown.[4] The latter's work was sponsored by the navy, but no one in the imperial government showed interest in the potential of local timbers, let alone in his landmark botanical study published in 1810 as *Prodromus Florae Novae Hollandi ae et Van Diemen 1802–5*. It was not until the Naval Board Inquiry of 1819 that there was official follow-up to this early scientific work, and by then the imperial government's knowledge of Van Diemen's Land's timber resources seemed to have gone backwards.[5]

To be fair to the British government, war with France had resumed in 1804, meaning that few goods or ships could be spared, and Van Diemen's Land was the administrative responsibility of Sydney. The difficulty was that the mother colony lacked the funds and rations to maintain a settlement the size of Hobart Town – which after all had been the initiative of London. Occasionally a few secondary offenders and even some provisions were sent south, but there was remarkably little movement of people or goods, heightening an already overwhelming sense of isolation.

The lack of provisions became a pressing issue as the weather got colder and the nights longer. The winter of 1804 was, Collins informed the uninterested secretary of state, "severely felt by the people."[6] The settling party was still reliant on cotton clothing of limited efficacy in keeping out rain or cold, and supplies of even these garments were running low.[7] Much more appropriate were animal-skin clothes and rugs, but even though a technique for tanning leather using an extract from wattle had been developed in New South Wales in 1803, these were still not much used, with the notable exception of kangaroo-skin shoes, a pair of which was issued to each convict at the end of 1804.

Cold weather was not the only problem faced by the settlers in the winter of 1804. Relations with the Oyster Bay Aboriginal people had broken down in the late autumn following Van Diemen's Land's first documented massacre.

37

The Risdon Massacre

In early May 1804 the peculiar administrative and military separation between the two British settlements on either side of the Derwent River continued. Sullivans Cove remained under the command of Collins and the protection of the marines. Risdon Cove was still the responsibility of John Bowen, who maintained only a tenuous authority over his senior military officer, Lieutenant Moore of the New South Wales Corps. On 3 May 1804, during Bowen's temporary absence from the settlement, a violent confrontation with the Aborigines occurred. The details of what became known as the "Risdon massacre" have been hotly debated for over 200 years. What is definitively known is that the soldiers under Moore's command opened fire on a large group of Aborigines that included women and children. Muskets and a carronade (a ship's gun then being deployed in the settlement) were used. The shooting started at about 11 o'clock in the morning and continued for three hours until the carronade was fired and the Aborigines finally fled.[8] Three bodies were eventually collected by the British, but a precise fatality figure is impossible to estimate as it is not known how many of the dead or fatally injured were removed.

Most of the evidence concerning the massacre was compiled by a committee that reviewed the events nearly 27 years after they occurred. Moore's claim, in his official report on the incident, that the soldiers acted in self-defence following an Aboriginal attack on the settlement was contradicted by the one direct witness available to the 1830 enquiry, the convict Edward White, who claimed that the Aborigines approached peacefully and that there were "a great many of the Aborigines slaughtered and wounded; I don't know how many."[9]

The fact that the assault went on for so long is the most difficult and terrible aspect of the tragedy to understand. In later violent encounters, the Aborigines invariably fled for cover when shooting began. Were the Aborigines fighting back at Risdon? Or did the volleys of the still unfamiliar musket engender such chaos that the group – which included young children, the frail and the elderly – did not know where to run?

Four hours after the shooting stopped, the surgeon, Jacob Mountgarrett, wrote a note to Knopwood:

Dear Sir,

I beg to referr you to Mr Moore for particulars of an attack the natives made on the camp today, and I have every reason to think that it was premeditated, as their number farr exceeded any that we have ever heard of. As you express a wish to be acquainted with some of the natives, if you will dine with me tomorrow, you will oblige me by christening a fine native boy who I have. Unfortunately, poor boy, his father and mother were both killd. He is about two years old. I have likewise the body of a man that was killd. If Mr Bowden wishes to see him desected I will be happy to see him with you tomorrow. I would have wrote to him, but Mr Moore waits.

Your friend

J. Mountgarrett, Hobart, six o'clock

The number of natives I think was not less than five or six hundred – J.M.[10]

Collins soon ordered that "that the child be returned to his own people, who might if they never saw it again, imagine we had destroyed it," but with the Oyster Bay people not surprisingly keeping their distance, it seems that this was impossible to arrange. The *Sydney Gazette* on 2 September carried a follow-up report, noting that "in compliment to his native soil and in remembrance of the month upon which it was the will of fate that he should be released from a state of barbarous insignificance, he has been baptised Robert Hobart May."[11]

What has been often missed in analysing the Risdon massacre is the deep sense of vulnerability felt by the British in the first year of settlement. The notion that white settlers with guns and technology swept into Aboriginal territory without fear or constraint bears little relation to the experience of the soldiers and convicts clustered along the banks of the Derwent in 1804. By May of that year, the British had lived though a Van Diemonian spring, summer and much of an autumn, and had been regularly exposed – in the heart of a major hunting ground – to the main tool of Aboriginal land management, fire. This was a frightening experience for men and women whose background led them to assume that the firing of the bush was probably targeted at them. Arson had long been the ultimate means of popular protest in England and Ireland.

Furthermore, the British knew that they were occupying Aboriginal land, and that a response was likely. In September 1804, Collins admitted to King that he had never informed "the whole, that the Aborigines of this country are as much under the protection of the laws of Great Britain, as themselves," even though "this essential point, having formed an article in my instructions, I should have issued a general order at Port Phillip ... [and] repeated it here." Collins told King that he would "wait until my numbers are increased" before doing so.[12] King's reply is also pertinent. He acknowledged receipt of the despatch, but never commented on it, thus avoiding sanctioning or censuring Collins' lack of action. After many years in New South Wales, the governor-in-chief knew well the difficulty of reconciling London's instructions for the protection of Aborigines with the invasion of Aboriginal land and all that was consequent upon it.

The likelihood of Aboriginal resistance may have led a sensitive observer like David Collins to do what he could to avoid provocation, but the seasoned veterans of the New South Wales Corps had become accustomed to a different approach. The aggressive response at Port Jackson to Aboriginal resistance from the mid 1790s is well documented, and in Van Diemen's Land the corps operated virtually independently of the civil authorities. Relations between the corps and Bowen were particularly fraught throughout April, and on 23 April mutiny had even threatened, with Collins forced to intervene.[13]

The confluence of all these factors made it unsurprising that a few fearful, poorly disciplined and possibly drunk men guarding the small British outpost at Risdon Cove viewed with alarm a large group of Aborigines approaching the settlement on 3 May 1804, although the attitude of Edward White, who watched the Aborigines arrive and quickly concluded that this was no war party, stands as permanent testimony that there was nothing inevitable about the terrible response that followed.

What would its impact be for the two settlements? "I well know these indiscriminating savages will consider every white man as their enemy," Collins told King, "and will if they have opportunity revenge the death of their companions." His fears were confirmed within a few days when men sent to the eastern shore to collect oysters were beaten off with clubs and stones.[14] The next few years saw several violent incidents with the Oyster Bay people, including an attack on sealers in Oyster Bay in early 1805, the destruction of the Ralph's Bay lime kilns in June 1806 and regular skirmishes with kangaroo hunters.[15]

The lieutenant governor responded promptly. On 8 May he implemented the recent order from King to take command of Risdon Cove and advised that it would be evacuated as soon as the *Ocean* returned from Port Phillip with the final evacuees from the settlement there. The niceties of consultation with Bowen on this significant step were ignored. Moreover, despite his own troop shortage, likely now to be even more acute, Collins chose to send all members of the New South Wales Corps back to Sydney, noting that "the trouble, which might attend bringing the remainder into a proper state of discipline, induced me to send the whole away."[16] The same shipping problems that delayed the evacuation of Port Phillip meant, however, that it was not until 9 August that Risdon Cove returned to Aboriginal control.

What seemed eminently sensible – settling on a major Aboriginal hunting ground where game was abundant – had proved to have major drawbacks. Collins had reason to be grateful for being based on the comparatively less attractive, but also less populated, western shore – even more so for it being the territory of another tribe. The tribal boundary provided by the Derwent River meant that even after the Risdon massacre, peaceful encounters continued with the Mouheneenner and Nuenonne people. Knopwood records that Aboriginal men were in the camp on 2 November 1804 and that a large meeting occurred at Brown's River.[17]

Port Dalrymple

By the end of 1804 the Derwent settlers were not the only official British residents of Van Diemen's Land. A small party commanded by William Paterson, the senior officer of the New South Wales Corps, arrived at Port Dalrymple in the north of the island on 5 November. Paterson chose a hill site, which he saw as "well situated for the protection of the settlement," near present-day George Town, and recorded that

> on the 12th a body of natives consisting of about 80 in number, made their approach within about 100 yards from the camp; from what we could judge they were headed by a chief, as everything given to them was given up to this person ... from this friendly interview I was in hopes we would have been well acquainted with them ere this, but unfortunately a large party (supposed to be the same) attacked the guard of marines, consisting of one sergeant and two privates ... the Guard was under the unpleasant act of defending themselves, and fired upon them, killed one and wounded another; this unfortunate circumstance I am fearful will be the cause of much mischief hereafter, and will prevent our excursions inland, except when well armed.[18]

Paterson had already shown a readiness to use force against Aborigines in New South Wales. According to Collins, after Governor Arthur Phillip's departure Paterson had ordered a party of the New South Wales Corps to be sent from Parramatta "with instructions to destroy as many as they could meet with of the wood tribe (Be-dia-gal) and, in the hope of striking terror, to erect gibbets in different places, whereon the bodies of all they might kill were to be hung."[19] Perhaps this background helps explain his early use of arms at Port Dalrymple. Nevertheless, like Collins, Paterson seems to have well understood the practical advantages of peace as, despite the violence, negotiations continued and there was a friendly meeting with 40 Aborigines, involving the exchange of more goods, on 9 December.[20]

Paterson also followed Collins' strategy of enthusiastically selling the potential of the new settlement to Sir Joseph Banks. In January 1805 he sent six tons of iron to England, "and if it proves serviceable any quantity may be had." He also sent some green earth that he hoped might be copper and various birds and animals.[21] Paterson also reported favourably on the timber: "there remains no doubt but that most of it will be found superior in quality for ship building to any hither yet discovered in this part of the world."[22]

One early find was of more immediate benefit. Paterson told Banks that "the pigs turned out on Green Island have dug out a farinaceous root which may be valuable, for the soldiers of the guard used it as a substitute for potatoes."[23] *Gastrodia sesamoides* (native potato or potato orchid) was certainly a useful find, its roots being rich in starch and very nourishing.

Fresh meat was, however, hard to obtain at first. In January 1805 Paterson reported that "although the kangaroos are here in numbers, there has not been more than four large ones killed; and the smaller sort is hardly worth the expense of keeping a dog."[24] King was anxious that the new settlement be as self-sufficient as possible, and the difficulty of obtaining fresh meat may have been one factor in Paterson's decision to move the settlement twice: initially to York Town, on the western side of Port Dalrymple, in 1805; and then, during 1806, to present-day Launceston, immediately adjacent to some of the finest hunting grounds on the island.

Kangaroo Hunting

Paterson, more familiar with the coastal scrub surrounding Port Jackson, was ecstatic about the country bordering the North and South Esk Rivers. He informed King that the ground on the North Esk extended "on both sides into considerable plains without a tree, and in many places farther than the eye can reach." It was "superior, both for grazing and tillage" even to the excellent land on the South Esk, "which I did not think could have been surpassed."[25] In August he told London that "where I have fixed our principal agricultural settlement is the centre of the most superior tract of arable and grazing ground I have witnessed," describing it as an "immense tract of one of the most beautiful countries of the world."[26] Such country abounded in game, and from 1805 kangaroo largely fed the small northern settlement.[27]

In the south the shift to indigenous foods was more gradual because of the two years' supply of imported food that the expedition carried when it left London. However, with the arrival of the last of the evacuees from Port Phillip in June 1804, and the incorporation of a few from Risdon, the British settlement on the western shore of the Derwent comprised 433 Europeans, and providing these people with the legally prescribed ration became more and more difficult. Although most people could obtain supplementary fresh meat for themselves or purchase it from others through labour or barter, Collins faced a dilemma when it came to those who were ill and thus totally dependent on the ration, which comprised flour, sugar and salted meats of little enough nutritional value in March 1803, but was now decomposing into a substance scarcely recognisable as food. In August 1804 he told London that they had had "no less than 467 people under medical treatment since we first landed at Port Phillip."[28] Between July 1804 and the end of the year there were 18 deaths, adding to the 30 lost since the departure from England. It was clear that a diet exclusively consisting of poor-quality imported fare was the main reason why so many convicts and soldiers had not recovered from the scurvy and other hardships associated with the voyage and sojourn at Port Phillip.

To avoid further deaths, on 10 September 1804 Collins took what was to prove a momentous policy decision. He ordered the first government purchase of kangaroo meat: "the number of scorbutic patients increasing daily, the commissary is directed to receive kangaroo at 6d per pound from any person who may deliver such at the Public stores."[29]

A large cash market for kangaroo was immediately created, and, in direct consequence, the foundation for a new society was laid.

[4]

A KANGAROO ECONOMY

THE KEY DECISION TO PURCHASE KANGAROO meat having been taken, it was not long before its scope was expanded. Late in September 1804, Collins announced that

> The principal surgeon having stated to the lieutenant governor that the scorbutic patients under his care have considerably benefited by the fresh animal food ... he requests that all those gentleman who have dogs will exert themselves in procuring an ample supply of kangaroo for the hospital. The numbers of this animal are at this time fortunately for us abundant.[1]

Collins understood that creating a cash market for a product so easily procured from the surrounding bush had the potential to undermine social control, but he had good reason to believe that the risk could be managed. At this stage hunting rights were still controlled, dog ownership restricted and convict hunters remained assigned gamekeepers. At the end of 1804 no convict could survive long in the bush and men gained access to its resources only with official help and permission. With profit and plunder concentrated and controlled, the full implications of the new market for kangaroo thus took some time to become apparent. During 1804, only officers directly profited from the government purchases, and at the end of that year Collins was able to advise that with the "number of patients ... so reduced ... fresh animal food is not longer required ... [and] the

Commissary will discontinue receiving [it] into the public store."[2] Scurvy had been comprehensively beaten – banished from Van Diemen's Land for a generation.

Matters were not so straightforward at Port Dalrymple where, with so few supplies coming from Sydney, Paterson had no option but to purchase large quantities of kangaroo and emu merely to provide the legally prescribed ration to which virtually all residents, including convicts, soldiers, officers and the few free settlers, were entitled.

In January 1805 Paterson gave an early warning to Governor King of the danger of relying on kangaroo meat to feed the settlement, asserting that unless the "Government was to have proper people who could be trusted constantly for no other purpose [than hunting], it [kangaroo] will never answer for serving as a ration."[3] Almost a year later he again warned the governor-in-chief that

> such a spirit of buying and selling dogs exists, and hunting kangaroos, if a stop is not soon put to it, it will in the end be the cause of much idleness, and consequently the neglect of cultivation. I have now restricted the settlers from having more than one dog between two, which I believe is considered arbitrary.[4]

King was unmoved. His response revealed how different life in the two colonies – Sydney and Port Dalrymple – had become. He ordered that kangaroo only be purchased from "individuals who have leisure to hunt that animal."[5] But the prospect of the officers doing their own hunting on Aboriginal territory rather than sending convict servants to do it for them, or purchasing it cheaply from men in the woods for profitable resale, was unlikely. Convicts were prepared to risk danger for freedom, but the officers preferred to stay closer to home.

By the autumn of 1805 the supply of imported food was also fast running out in the southern settlement, and in May the rations of flour and sugar were cut. Collins advised that, given "the supplies which the lieutenant governor has been for some time in expectation of receiving not having arrived … it is necessary to make every possible saving of the salted provisions now remaining in store," and the commissariat "will therefore receive kangaroo at eight pence per pound ... and issue the same at the rate of one pound of fresh meat for one pound of salt meat."[6] A dependency on kangaroo skin had also developed. Kangaroo skin and fur were increasingly employed in place of imported clothing, footwear and rugs.

The surveyor, G.P. Harris, wrote to his mother in October 1805 that "two to three thousand (lbs) weight a week" of kangaroo were being "turned into the store by the officers," and poignantly contrasted the place of hunting with nascent agriculture and pastoral pursuits:

> I have got about 1 acre of wheat in this year (which considering is doing wonders) – My stock consists of 1 cow and calf – 1 ram 2 ewes – 2 ewe lambs 1 He goat – 4 females 2 female kids – 4 geese – 10 goslings – [?] fowls – Besides which I have a pack of Kanguroo dogs as good as any in the whole country – namely Lagger, Weasel, Lion, Boatswain, Brindle etc etc – & with those dogs I scarcely ever go out or send out (for I have two huntsmen) but get 3 4 5 or sometimes 8 kangaroos in a day or two – Some of the kanguroo stand 6 feet high and weigh from 100 to 130 or 150 lbs and fight the dogs so desperately so as sometimes to kill them and very frequently to wound them sadly – Sometimes we get emus (a large bird species of the ostrich) which are hunted in the same manner as kanguroo and make a worse resistance. They frequently weigh 80 or 90 lb and run (for they cannot fly) amazingly swift, so that the swiftest greyhound can get up with them – They are much coarser food than the kanguroo, which when young, is nearly as good as venison – it only wants fat.[7]

The most significant difference between the northern and southern settlements was the seasonal arrival of whalers at the Derwent. Knopwood reported in July 1805 that there were four whalers close by and "a great many whales" in the "river beyond town." Some ships spent months at a time in the estuary.[8] Nevertheless, while the whalers lessened the isolation of Hobart Town and brought occasional supplies, on balance they probably increased the demand for kangaroo by providing another market.

It was the government store, however, that was the principal engine for the development of a kangaroo-based economy. It provided a consistent and reliable cash market for a product freely available in the immediate environs of the settlement, ensuring certain profits that could be further supplemented with the sale of skins and demand from whalers. An officer of the marines, Edward Lord, was already well on the way to becoming a very wealthy man on the back of his assigned convict gamekeepers and a growing number of hunting dogs.

Unable to sell direct to the government store, convict hunters accumulated little capital themselves. But in 1805, in both the northern and southern settlements, a development occurred that was to have profound consequences: the monopoly ownership of dogs was surrendered. Hounds were too easily stolen and bred too fast to remain a restricted possession. In March, Knopwood reported that he was "fearful that my kangaroo dogs should be taken away. It was the intention to rob me of my dogs." It seems even the chaplain's own servants could not be trusted to protect them, as he prevented any theft through staying home himself "the aft and eve."[9]

The Bush Becomes Home

The possession of a single dog, stolen or purchased, meant a convict could live independent and free in the bush. In 1805 Knopwood recorded the return of five convicts who had been absent for nearly three months despite the colder weather (they also provided the first sighting of a "tiger"), and by the next year convicts were living in the bush right through the winter months.[10]

The association of the bush with freedom was a dramatic, and largely unrecognised, moment in Australian colonisation. Collins had only been stating the facts at Port Phillip when he warned that the armed runaways "must soon return or perish by famine." Even in the first year in Van Diemen's Land, the five prisoners that "got off into the woods" with muskets and gunpowder surrendered quickly.[11] Without dogs, the bush was a site of probable death, but with them, the grassy woodlands of Van Diemen's Land became, within two years of settlement, a hospitable refuge. With no man-made walls to keep the few hundred prisoners contained (there was not a secure gaol on Van Diemen's Land until the early 1820s), many convicts simply wandered off to live a life of quiet freedom in the well-watered, game-rich bush, well away from the supervised labour, dependency and potential for harsh punishment integral to a convict's life in a penal colony. With what seems extraordinary speed, a motley collection of British criminals made the bush home.

Those who stayed in the bush without authorisation as hunters were listed as absconders – the first bushrangers. Sixty-eight of the *Calcutta* convicts (those who arrived with Collins) would be listed as having absconded at some time, several of them more than once.[12] The settler and trader James Gordon summarised the origins of bushranging at the British government's Commission of Inquiry into New South Wales and Van Diemen's Land undertaken by John Thomas Bigge:

> I think that it originated from a practice that prevailed as far back as the time of Govr. Collins, who, when provisions were not to be had, allowed the convicts to repair into the country and hunt for the kangaroo. In this they were joined by the officers' servants, who went to hunt for their masters. By this means, they got habits of wandering and obtaining subsistence. No outrages were committed by these men, but still Govt. cd. not call them in.[13]

How quickly the convicts came to be at ease in the bush is revealed in Knopwood's description of a holiday he took in the new year of 1806 with Collins, Harris and the surgeon, Mathew Bowden. Imported tents and food were discarded, with the officers' servants instead supplying all their masters' needs from the environment. Knopwood records that they left Hobart at 4.30 a.m. on 2 January, and after breakfast at the government farm headed 40 miles up-river where they "had two huts built." One of Knopwood's men then supplied the kangaroo and "at half past six" they "sat down to a very excellent dinner." The party arrived back on the evening of 4 January after what the chaplain described as "one of the pleasantest excursions I ever took."[14]

"Famine" and Its Implications

Though they had lost their dog monopoly, and despite the growing number of bushrangers, hunting continued to be very successful for the officers through most of 1805. From 3 August until the year's end, Knopwood sold 66 kangaroos to the government store, earning the chaplain £107, considerably more than he received in wages.[15]

Yet despite this abundance of fresh meat and the ready source of profit it provided, the officers began to describe tough times in their letters and journals and even made reference to a "famine" in the settlement. A careful reading of their comments shows, however, that there was no hunger or general food shortage, and that these sentiments merely pertain to the exhaustion of familiar foods from home. In a letter home to his mother, Harris wrote that "we have lately and are now almost in a state of starvation," but also pointed out that as "we have such abundance of kangaroo here we can never want."[16]

It was the shortage of the British staple, bread, that most led to the exaggerated descriptions of near starvation that have persisted in the historical literature and cultural memory. To "break bread" was not simply to partake of food for early-nineteenth-century Britons; to receive their daily bread was their most basic request to God. As E.P. Thompson puts it, if "the labouring people in the eighteenth century did not live by bread alone … many of them lived very largely on bread … Britain was only emerging from the … periodical visitations of famine and of plague, and dearth revived age-old memories and fears. Famine could place the whole social order on the rack." As recently as 1801 the poor had rioted when bread shortages caused large price rises and widespread hunger.[17]

Given the significance of what a later free settler, George Meredith, called "that first of all earthly acquisites,"[18] it is not surprising that Harris informed his brother in 1806 that "a famine prevails in this land" solely on the basis that he had "not tasted bread … for a fortnight." Similarly, in 1807 he wrote that the settlers were facing starvation because they had been reduced to eating "kanguroo fried in rancid pork in lieu of bread."[19]

There is no doubting the anguish many Britons experienced in the absence of familiar provisions – especially flour, but also tea, sugar and alcohol. In October 1805 Knopwood recorded the arrival of supplies on the *Governor Hunter*: "I may truly say that the colony was in a very dreadful distress and visible in every countenance. Had it not have been for the good success in killing kangaroos, the colony would have been destitute of everything. We had only three weeks flower [*sic*] in the colony and five weeks pork."[20] The relief was only temporary, and by the new year the supply of almost all commodities had again run out. Harris wrote that they were "as far as the deprivation of almost every comfort will allow, tolerably well – We have neither tea sugar coffee soap candles oil wine spirits beer paper cheese butter or money and if we had the latter those things are not to be procured."[21]

The most significant impact of these shortages was not on officer comfort, but on the social order as a whole. This is because the relations between convicts and authorities were governed by customary expectations, rights and responsibilities as much as by regulation and formal authority, as were all social relations in the rigidly hierarchical early-nineteenth-century English society.

The Rights of Servants

In early 1805 Collins articulated his view of the place of convicts, it being in his view "not clearly understood." They were under the "protection of British laws," and "while under sentence of the laws the prisoners are to be considered as the servants of the crown to be employed under the direction of the person in whom his majesty has been pleased to visit that trust, the lieutenant governor of this settlement."[22] Collins consistently described the convicts as "the people" or "servants of the crown," drawing on customary expectations of master–servant relations to ensure a degree of order in a society where, although almost the entire labour force were prisoners, gaols did not exist. "Servant" (which was the term used for what we would now describe as a "worker" or "employee") continued to be the standard official language to describe convicts until at least 1820, with "prisoner" reserved mainly for those who had committed a secondary offence in the colony. Convicts were thus offered, on the condition of not re-offending, the status of servant with its rights and responsibilities. As E.P. Thompson has shown, similar labour systems were common in England in the late eighteenth century, with masters clinging "to the image of the labourer as an unfree man, a servant in husbandry, in the workshop, in the house" and the "masterless man as a vagabond to be disciplined, whipped and compelled to work."[23]

Nor was the idea that convicts were servants rather than prisoners a mere ideological ploy. It was the everyday reality. In a society largely made up of convicts and soldiers, convicts did almost all the work of the colony. They formed the majority of civil servants, clerks, carpenters, bakers, labourers, teachers and, of course, hunters. The small number of free men not employed by the government as part of the civil or military establishment were mostly self-employed (particularly smallholders). Even the free labour market was mostly made up of convicts selling their labour as they were encouraged to do after the designated hours of work for their assigned master had been completed.

In this context, Collins' inability to provide the set ration was widely seen as a violation of the rights of servants and an abrogation of responsibility that (no matter how unavoidable) had certain consequences. If the regulation ration could not be provided, nor would regulation working hours be fulfilled. Collins acknowledged the legitimacy of this claim and reduced hours of work when tea, sugar, salted meat and other essentials were unavailable.[24] A similar form of contract existed with the military, and even with the early bushrangers. Before mid 1805 (when the ration had not been compromised), Knopwood used the word "deserted" to describe convicts who went into the bush (pointing to the abandonment of the individual's responsibility to society), but later the chaplain would write of those who had "absconded" or were merely "absent."[25] When supplies arrived and the full ration was temporarily restored, Collins would often issue a general amnesty, and those who came in from what was still officially described, and even believed to be, the inhospitable world beyond received paternal forgiveness if they confessed the error of their ways. The Irish political prisoner Joseph Holt recalled how Collins dealt with early absconders at Derwent: "'Well,' he would say to them, 'now that you have lived in the bush, do you think that the change you made was for the better? Are you sorry for what you have done?' 'Yes Sir.' 'And will you promise me never to go away again?' 'Never sir.' 'Go to the store keeper then ... and get a suit of slops and your week's ration.'" [26]

The Exhaustion of the Local Hunting Grounds

The shortage of imported foods had social implications, but while kangaroo remained in abundant supply, no one was left hungry or malnourished. However, during 1806 the British confronted a more genuine food crisis, one with potential to cause a level of death and suffering comparable with the early years of New South Wales, or even to force an evacuation. For the first time since the invasion commenced, there was a shortage of kangaroo.

More than a hundred forester kangaroos a week had been needed just to supply the ration in the southern settlement alone,[27] and probably more than double this number were killed when those taken for animal food, private consumption, barter and sale, and to meet the demands of the whalers, are included. No doubt dogs mortally mauled a large number of additional animals that could not be salvaged, and fear of the new predator drove even more away. In short, it is not surprising that by 1806 the supply of kangaroo available within a day's walk of either settlement had been greatly reduced. The progressive evacuation of almost the whole population of Norfolk Island – ex-convicts and their descendants – to Van Diemen's Land from November 1805 exacerbated the problem by eventually doubling the mouths to be fed. Almost the entire population was still entitled to a government ration, with only ten of the 475 people in the southern colony on 30 June 1806 not "victualled from the store."[28] Domestic animals made no contribution to the government's food reserves (in June 1806 there were only 96 cows, 127 ewes and one breeding sow in the southern colony, and the emphasis was on breeding rather than killing stock to eat), and imported supplies remained as precarious as ever.[29]

To maintain a supply of kangaroo, the price paid by the government was increased on 21 April 1806 from six pence a pound to a shilling. The price adjustment had an instant effect, and two months

later purchases were temporarily halted because of "the great surplus of kangaroo at present in hand." Whalers then kept the southern
settlement supplied in large part with other products over the winter
of 1806, but the crisis deepened again in the spring. When Knopwood reported on 4 October 1806 that there is "scarce any provisions
for the marines and prisoners," he also meant, for the first time, kangaroo. That month Collins issued an order:

> Every person who possesses the means, will use the utmost exer-
> tions in furnishing the public stores with kangaroo … The officers
> who have had the services of several men for this purpose, will
> inform their people that if they continue to exert themselves in this
> season of distress their conduct will be noticed and rewarded.[30]

Nevertheless, kangaroo remained in alarmingly short supply.
On 13 October Knopwood wrote that "it is truly lamentable to see the
distress that the people are in. Not a man able to do any work."[31] At
the end of the month the price for kangaroo and emu was raised to
one shilling and sixpence (1s 6d) per pound, but even then supplies
were limited.[32] On 8 December the kangaroo ration had to be reduced
and, for the first time, its provision could not be guaranteed: "the
commissary will issue 7lbs therefore to each person as far as the quantity he has received will enable."[33]

In the northern settlement, Paterson justified the extraordinary
expenditure of £2114 (mainly for kangaroo and emu) by the price
rises caused by the exhaustion of local hunting grounds:

> Such was the slaughter of kangaroo necessary actually to preserve
> the lives of the people that the difficulty of procuring them in suf-
> ficient quantities became gradually so much greater, and they
> were daily driven to such increasing distances from our camps …
> that 1s 6d per lb was at last necessary to be given for such as could
> be tendered.[34]

The kangaroo shortage must be kept in context – this was still no
famine and the convicts' health remained excellent. In November

1806 Knopwood reported that there had been only one burial in the last 12 months, "and that an infant three days old."[35] And in *Convicts Unbound* Marjorie Tipping documents only six deaths in total from 1805 to 1808 (and none from malnutrition or disease) compared with 48 deaths in the first 18 months after leaving England when all had received the full prescribed ration.[36] Van Diemonian Britons, even at the height of the food shortages, remained very healthy.

The main impact of the food crisis was not on health but on land occupation. It became obvious that the British were in an increasingly vulnerable position, and to ensure food supplies authorities had no option but to encourage convicts to hunt in territory far from even a semblance of official control. There was no prospect of policing the increasingly remote grasslands given the low number and poor quality of troops available. Securing meat would require convict hunters to negotiate land access for themselves in the face of potent threats from both whites and blacks.

Bushrangers

Bushrangers with stolen hunting dogs presented the most immediate obstacle to achieving a secure supply of food and profit. Knopwood observed that "it is generally believed that the prisoners which are in the bush had taken many of the gentlemens dogs."[37] The subtleties of this change in dog control were shown in Knopwood's description of the theft of his bitch "Miss." Knopwood's assigned convicts were twice sent after the missing dog, as were Mathew Bowden's men (the surgeon had also had a dog "taken from him by the bushrangers"). The animals were not to be found, presumably because, beyond the official gaze, the boundary between servant and bushranger blurred. In what was to become a Van Diemonian tradition, a reward was the key to property recovery. A Norfolk Island settler, William Williams, claimed the ten pounds promised for the return of Miss.[38] This was significant money, a year's income for some English labourers and about a fortnight's wages even for the chaplain. Many had been transported for stealing less.

Stolen dogs were even more expensive to replace. Harris reported that the four he lost were valued at 25 guineas (or £26-5s) each.[39]

Henry and Mary Hayes had sold eight "greyhound" pups, still nursing, for £80 in 1805, and in 1807 Knopwood paid £25 for a dog.[40] As more dogs were bred the price dropped, but one purchased late in October 1807 still cost Knopwood £8.[41]

With such a high capital outlay, and given the animal's vulnerability to loss, the economics of kangaroo hunting for some officers became marginal. Those who wanted large profits needed to ensure that their dogs were protected and game access guaranteed. This required deals with bushrangers. The basis of such negotiations is clear: the officers could offer access to the one large cash buyer – the government – while the bushrangers offered protection, land access and a guaranteed meat supply. In September 1807 Collins gave notice of two convictions for buying or receiving kangaroo and emu from the servants of two officers and advised that he was

> determined to punish in the most rigorous manner any prisoner, officer, servant or otherwise, who shall be known to procure kangaroo or emu from any of those miscreants now at large in the woods, or from any employed in hunting, or who shall supply the above with provisions.[42]

But the convicts who were living for extended periods in the bush legally hunting kangaroo were inevitably in contact with bushrangers, and the incentives for private arrangements were great. The officers who tacitly sanctioned their gamekeepers to negotiate deals became direct beneficiaries of the new order through the elimination of less savvy (or less corrupt) competitors, and profited from price increases caused by the reduction in supply. The result was that men like Edward Lord built fortunes while more honest hunters, such as Harris, Bowden and Knopwood, had increasing difficulty in supplying any meat to the store at all.

While the authorities depended on the convict hunters, there was little they could do to bring them under official control. On 17 August 1807 Knopwood reported that the price of kangaroo had again reached 1s 6 d per pound. It is surely no coincidence that two days earlier Knopwood had listed 14 current bushrangers who were "all armed and have plenty of dogs" (and the numbers of convicts who were living independent of any authority for extended periods in the bush hunting kangaroo was much greater again).[43] Only the arrival of imported supplies could temporarily restore negotiating power to the lieutenant governor. The purchase of kangaroo was immediately stopped when a ship arrived in late October and "full rations" were restored with, on 30 November 1807, an amnesty offered to those in the bush.

The threat posed by bushrangers was even more evident in the northern settlement, where, with no visiting whalers to trade with, the dependence on indigenous foods was compounded. Paterson warned London of the consequences in April 1807:

> From last January the colony has existed entirely on the precarious chance of the chase, and kangaroo was the only food they depended on. In consequence labour stood still, and the inhabitants became a set of wood-rangers; and I much fear it will be some time before they are brought to the industrious habits which an infant settlement requires.[44]

In August he made it clear that his worst fears had been realised:

> In my last letter I anticipated the evil consequences that was likely to arise from the necessity of making kangaroo the principal part of our animal food, which is now realised; for not less than ten prisoners have absconded with their master's dogs, firearms etc, and are living in the woods and mountains, where (from their knowledge of the country) there is little chance of their being apprehended … It is but a few days since that two of these runaways (who have been absent for 16 months) seized two of the soldiers … robbed them of everything.[45]

More details of "the dangerous consequences of our being under the necessity of employing convicts to furnish the colony with kangaroo" were provided by Paterson in a letter to Sir Joseph Banks a few months later. Nine convicts had "absconded with dogs and firearms" and become a "desperate banditry" which Paterson was powerless to pursue: "I must give up the chase … my little force is so scattered." Available troops were "barely sufficient to protect our stores and livestock."[46]

The livestock Paterson referred to were predominantly the survivors of the 612 Bengal cattle shipped to the settlement in the autumn of 1805, which he had described as "perhaps the most fortunate circumstance that ever happened to a new settlement."[47] Although over half the cattle had died initially,[48] by 1807 Paterson could inform Banks that the livestock "thrive better than any I ever saw … but we are in daily dread of the bushrangers, as they are called, committing depredations on them. I am under the necessity of having two soldiers with each flock."[49]

The risks posed by bushrangers were great, but an even more serious threat to the colony's essential food supply emerged during 1806. That year Aboriginal groups began systematically to resist white access to the remote hunting grounds on which the future of both settlements depended.

Aboriginal Resistance to Hunters

Aborigines had sought to remove kangaroo from British hunters from at least March 1804, when Collins' own gamekeeper, Henry Hacking, was confronted by them. The *Sydney Gazette* recorded that Hacking and the "Sydney native" who "attended him" ("John Salamander," probably the first mainland Aborigine to travel in Van Diemen's Land in 12,000 years) had successfully hunted a kangaroo, only to be confronted by Aborigines who "made use of every policy to wheedle Hacking out of his booty."[50] Comparatively peaceful confrontations of this sort probably continued, but as British plunder escalated, so did the Aboriginal response. The threat was increasingly plain from mid 1806, and corresponded with the penetration by Europeans into hunting grounds that were a greater distance from the settlements.

Knopwood chronicled the growing crisis in his diary. A hunter was speared on June, with two dogs being killed and the kangaroos taken. In December three prisoners, after being "absent in the wood for five months," reported that "the natives took from them nine kangaroos while they were hunting and their boat." On 14 February 1807 a kangaroo hunter was speared in a manner which sounds like a formal punishment: a convict hunter was taken some distance from his hut "and one of the party throwd a spear at him." On 18 February the Aborigines were reported to be "very troublesome to the men out a-kangarooing" and before the month was out kangaroo was again reported as having being taken and another hunter was speared. By 24 February Knopwood observed that "the distress of the colony is great," and at the height of the crisis on 2 March, when "the natives have been very troublesome for a long time but not so desperate as lately," the chaplain admitted that his men had killed two Aborigines. Another fatal skirmish was reported on 19 May:

> My man Richardson came home, having been absent 19 days. He gave information that the natives had nearly killed him and dogs. The governor's people were out and fell in with them when a battle ensued and they killed one of the natives. The natives killed one of the dogs. It is very dangerous to be out alone for fear of them. They are so hardened they do not mind being shot at.[51]

Knopwood's private journal was not intended to be a complete record of the killings of Aborigines that occurred at the time. With one possible exception, Knopwood only records killings done by, or in the presence of, his own servant. To assume that these were the only violent encounters is to assume that the many gamekeepers assigned to other officers avoided the Aboriginal resistance witnessed by Knopwood's man, and that contemporary observers who documented, in general terms, high levels of conflict with Aborigines, were mistaken.[52]

Knopwood's journal entries also attest to the critical fact that convicts killing Aborigines to protect the interests of their masters was tacitly accepted by the government. Robert Knopwood was a magistrate as well as a priest. Why then did he not investigate or even report the death of two British subjects at the hands of his own servant? Similarly, why did the lieutenant governor not investigate or report the killing of an Aborigine by his own gamekeepers? Why is a *private* journal the only record we have of these killings?

The challenge faced by the officials of Van Diemen's Land at that time was how to motivate convicts to carry on hunting in remote country without any military protection. It is clear that the officers had little choice but to turn a blind eye to the conflict and, moreover, that they did their best to prevent any inconvenient interference from either Sydney or London. Convicts were given guns (which were not needed to hunt) and complete freedom outside of the settlements, provided they returned with meat.

Given Aboriginal advantages in remote regions, however, force was unlikely to prevail. How access to the grassy woodlands of Van Diemen's Land could be secured had become the most critical question facing the nascent British settlements. Whether sufficient supplies of kangaroo would be maintained as the white population increased, given the exhaustion of the local resources, the growing power of runaway convicts and a vigorous defence of more remote hunting grounds by their Aboriginal owners, was as yet an open question.

As the Napoleonic War continued unabated, the contest for control of the major resources of this far-flung outpost of the empire was by no means resolved, and the securing of food supplies for the island's thousand or so European residents far from guaranteed.

PART II

THE MAKING OF
VAN DIEMEN'S LAND
1808–23

[5]

ACCESS WITHOUT CONQUEST

I N EARLY 1808 THE BRITISH IN Van Diemen's Land were more vulnerable than at any point since 1803. The invaders were, for the first time, experiencing the pangs of hunger that had been so familiar to many in their homeland. Hunting grounds within a day's travel of the settlements had largely been exhausted, threatening not only the officers' profits but what was now the colony's principal food supply. Knopwood's diary chronicles the crisis: from May 1808 the chaplain regularly reported "no success" in hunting.[1]

The British knew that wallaby, kangaroo and emu were plentiful in the extensive grassy woodlands of the midlands. The colony's surveyor, G.P. Harris, wrote to his brother in May 1808 of his "march of ten days" from Hobart Town to Port Dalrymple "thro the finest country in the world ... the quantities of kanguroos, emus and wild ducks we saw and killed were incredible."[2] The problem for the colonisers was how to gain reliable access to these remote lands.

Between 1808 and 1810 this challenge was answered with extraordinary success. In what was the most dramatic expansion of British settlement anywhere in Australia since 1788, in just two years the convict kangaroo-hunters of Van Diemen's Land successfully occupied the whole midlands region, stretching about 200 kilometres from the northern to the southern settlements. So successful were they that by 1810 the price of kangaroo had dropped from one shilling and sixpence a pound two years before to only four pence a pound. The crisis of 1807–08 had been overcome with astonishing speed.

Given the Aboriginal control of these prime hunting grounds, and the effectiveness of earlier resistance to trespassing kangaroo hunters, how was this remarkable access to both the land and its resources so quickly achieved?

Were the Pasture-lands Already Empty?

One possible explanation is that – as in some parts of mainland Australia – the pasture-lands had already been vacated as Aborigines died from European diseases. However, there are sufficient recorded observations of large groups of Aborigines, including infants and the elderly, to suggest that before 1820 deaths from disease were limited. The fact that there is not one recorded Aboriginal death by disease in Van Diemen's Land before the mid 1820s does not mean that there were no such deaths, but that Port Jackson-style epidemics seem not to have occurred.[3]

What little information there is suggests that Aboriginal immune systems, aided by the long period of European contact before settlement began (a period which may have seen a much higher death toll from disease), had adapted to British germs. The small, stable and healthy British population living on the island during the two decades after 1803 also helped. The extended sailing time from England, during which germs could be "burnt out," the fact that only one more convict ship and few free settlers arrived before 1816, an effective smallpox vaccination program, the ready availability of clean water and an excellent protein-rich diet made Van Diemen's Land one of the healthiest outposts of the British empire before 1820. Surgeon Mountgarrett told Commissioner Bigge – who was conducting an inquiry into the colony of New South Wales on behalf of the British government and held extensive hearings in both Hobart Town and Launceston during 1820 – that at Port Dalrymple there was little disease and that his main work was treating the old war wounds of ex-soldiers and sailors.[4]

Asked about diseases among the Aborigines, Surgeon Luttrell in Hobart Town told the commissioner: "I don't know any other than the cutaneous [skin] eruption I have just mentioned."[5] Luttrell ran a temporary hospital specifically for Aborigines in late 1819, when a number were ill with this skin condition. However, none seems to have died, and Lieutenant Governor Sorell told the surgeon he wanted the hospital closed. A later medical officer, John Barnes, who lived in the colony from 1823 to 1828, noted in a paper to the Royal College of Physicians that "in the earlier period of colonization the natives of Van Diemen's Land are said to have been mainly free from disease," with the exceptions of gonorrhea and, again, the unnamed skin disease, which may have been a severe allergic reaction to canine scabies, caused by the Aborigines' enthusiastic adoption of the dog.[6]

Aborigines never mentioned large-scale epidemics in their recorded discussions with George Augustus Robinson during his extensive travels with them from 1829 to 1834. Once confined to detention, they became very familiar with the ravages of introduced disease, but this seems to have been a new and unfamiliar experience. The Aborigines Robinson met with in the bush as late as the early 1830s seem to have been remarkably healthy.

The Trade in Dogs

A more likely explanation for the convict hunters' largely peaceful access to Aboriginal hunting grounds lies in trade. Van Diemonian Britons had a major advantage over their mainland contemporaries seeking access to land – they possessed a product of immediate and obvious utility. Aborigines in both New South Wales and Van Diemen's Land used other British goods, including sugar, tea, tobacco, flour, blankets and even potatoes as they became available, but in the first years of settlement the supply of these products was limited and they were not much valued by the Aborigines. Dogs, however, were another matter. Although dogs were still being commonly speared in 1807–08, Aborigines living in the grassland regions soon began using them as their main hunting tool. Rhys Jones has argued that the Aboriginal adoption of the dog "happened in Tasmania so quickly that ... the process would seem to have been instantaneous," and that it was likely that dogs "entered the traditional exchange systems."[7] Some dogs were forcibly taken, but as numbers built up, puppies and even adult dogs would have been traded in exchange for peaceful relations and access to land. In August 1832, George

Augustus Robinson conducted negotiations with the Aboriginal people of the north-west. Ever careful with his purse, he spent four pounds buying three dogs to cement a new relationship with the Aborigines.[8] Similar negotiations may have occurred in the midlands a generation before.

The rapid spread of hunting dogs enabled the Aborigines to obtain meat more efficiently in the open grasslands, which in turn would have made for more peaceful co-existence with the white settlers. Both cultures now relied on similar hunting methods. As long as the total population remained small, Indigenous people with dogs were assured of an abundant supply of fresh meat, despite increased competition from the colonists.

Co-existence

Whether due to the trade in dogs or not, Aboriginal resistance to British kangaroo hunters peaked in 1807–08 and probably declined thereafter. In 1811, Governor Lachlan Macquarie, on his first tour of Van Diemen's Land from Sydney, noted the change: "several years having elapsed since anything like a principle of hostility has been acted upon, or even in the slightest degree exhibited in the conduct of the natives, it must be evident that no deep-rooted prejudice exists in their minds."[9] It is possible that Macquarie's informants had a vested interest in exaggerating the peacefulness of their unsanctioned (but highly profitable) expansion of the settlement. John Murray, the commandant at Port Dalrymple, recorded in September 1810 that bushrangers were committing cruelties against "natives and others," and even Macquarie acknowledged that "male convicts ... betoken into the woods or bush ... continually molest the natives of the country."[10]

Nevertheless, while few whites would have refrained from acting in self-defence, most convict hunters would have had little incentive to confront the Aboriginal owners of the land. The musket was frightening (at least while it was still novel) but inaccurate, and the Aborigines' skill in bush warfare became obvious over subsequent decades. Isolated white hunters still learning bushcraft would have been no match for them in a sustained conflict. While some of the more deranged bushrangers (and there were always a few of these) attacked Aborigines indiscriminately, this was an unlikely course of action for ordinary convicts trying to survive in the bush. Most who took this path probably suffered the fate of William Russell and George Getley, who "ill used the blacks" before being killed by them.[11]

While the evidence available is too sparse to be definitive, it strongly suggests that violence abated after 1808. Some British residents of the grassy woodlands, like Edward White who lived near the Great Western Tiers for three years, were not even armed.[12] The nineteenth-century historian James Bonwick, who detailed the extensive frontier violence of other periods, recorded a number of personal accounts of peaceful relations with Aborigines between 1814 and 1822: "others have told me that they were able to travel about the bush in perfect security between that period … several elderly ladies have narrated circumstances showing more geniality and friendly intercourse; as, the playing of their children with the Aborigines, and their boys going to hunt with the dark skins."[13] Settlers taking up land grants after 1818 also recorded peaceful exchanges in their journals and letters.[14] Knopwood noted that Aborigines even came into Hobart Town during 1815–16 and again in 1818. Some visited his foreshore land around present-day Salamanca Place to collect shellfish and receive bread, meat and potatoes.[15] They do not seem to have displayed any of the obvious signs of dependence and degradation that had followed Aboriginal dispossession in Port Jackson, although by 1820 there was a "town mob," which probably comprised dispossessed Aborigines. The seasonal firing of the bush continued around Hobart Town until at least 1818.[16] Other Van Diemonian writers and early historians, many of whom, like Henry Melville, lived through these events, also claimed that, after the early forays, there was no major violence until the 1820s.

A true picture of the frontier before 1820 is extremely difficult to establish. There was no government supervision, very few free settlers and only occasional second-hand newspaper reports. All that can be said with confidence is that although sporadic violence continued, access to Aboriginal hunting grounds had been achieved without outright conquest. This was a period of uneasy co-existence: and for the British, the successful occupation of Aboriginal territory soon meant far more than an abundance of kangaroo. Between 1810 and 1820 stock numbers multiplied, and the grassy woodlands of Van Diemen's Land became the site of Australia's first large-scale pastoral industry.

Australia's First Pastoral Economy

In 1810 the surveyor-general, John Oxley, had predicted that "this rich interior country will ... contain at no distant period flocks and herds not inferior in size or number to the celebrated plains of Paraguay."[17] His vision was realised with remarkable speed. The extraordinary increase in sheep and cattle numbers preceded a similar expansion in New South Wales by over a decade. The Derwent muster of May 1809 showed there to be only 489 privately owned cattle and 1091 sheep.[18] By 1813, numbers had increased to 3894 cattle and 24,691 sheep, and the government was able to stop buying kangaroo meat. Four years later there were about 11,000 cattle and 100,000 sheep, and by 1820 the muster tally of 182,000 sheep was more than twice that of New South Wales.

For the stock-keepers and shepherds who watched over them, pastoralism did not replace hunting but supplemented it. The Bengal-cross cattle and tough traditional meat breeds of sheep were let loose to wander. Controls over both the animals and their guardians remained very weak; moreover, this form of pastoralism could co-exist with (and indeed benefit from) traditional Aboriginal land management.

Cattle in particular, Curr noted, "receive little attention from their proprietors ... they are suffered to range about uncontrolled." Moreover, they "breed very fast" and thus "are kept at very little expense."[19] Sheep may have been, as Semmens has argued, "very badly managed"[20] compared with the coddled merinos of the next generation, but they were hardy and self-sufficient breeds. The climate was mild and they did not need to be penned at night; there was no threat from dingoes, and indigenous carnivores such as the devil and the thylacine inflicted only minimal losses. One settler noted in the early 1820s that it was "really astonishing how fast the latter [sheep] increase: you may calculate on five young lambs in two years from one ewe."[21] Curr observed that a single shepherd could supervise over a thousand animals.[22] Given this, it is not surprising that many older colonists remained loyal to the traditional breeds long after the wool trade was developed and newer breeds introduced. The land commissioners observed in May 1828 that "the lower order of settler consider the merinos as a curse to the colony, that they are eternally scabby, require much attention, and that they diminish in size. They therefore keep up the blood of the Bengal and Teeswater sheep."[23]

As with the animals they watched over, the pioneer pastoralists of Van Diemen's Land were a very different breed from those, like John MacArthur, who were to develop the industry in New South Wales. Given that they were the first to run sheep on a large scale, these men merit a central place in the history of Australia. Yet even in Tasmanian historiography, credit for the development of the pastoral industry is given to later free settlers. The distinguished economic historian R.M. Hartwell did not even include the period before 1820 in his classic account of *The Economic Development of Van Diemen's Land*; before this, he reasoned, the colony was merely a "prison farm on a subsistence basis."[24] Lloyd Robson similarly dismissed early Van Diemen's Land as "a rum economy."[25]

Another eminent economic historian, Noel Butlin, acknowledged early pastoralism in Van Diemen's Land but largely dismissed its importance on the basis that "even though livestock increased rapidly, wool from sheep was almost entirely wasted."[26] Yet while the wool had almost no market value, the meat most certainly did. Meat was sold both fresh and salted to the government store, to whalers and to a variety of export destinations, including New South Wales. For example, one merchant claimed in the Christmas 1819 edition of the *Hobart Town Gazette* that in the previous four months he alone had "slaughtered no less than 120,000 weight of meat for the consumption of Port Jackson." There was even a live export trade, with the *Gazette* reporting in July 1818 that one ship carrying 1200 sheep and 12 cows, and another with 48 cows, had gone to Mauritius.

The free-settler immigrants of the early 1820s recognised the economic value of sheep meat. When Curr wrote in 1824 that "in the flocks of Van Diemen's Land its true riches will always be found to consist," he did so on the basis of the "high price which has been given, and the constant demand which has existed, for meat."[27] The first official settler-landowner of the Shannon region, James Ross, wrote that he bought his sheep from an unauthorised long-term hunter-pastoralist, "Dennis," because they were good meat animals. "At that time there was no thought of sending wool to England," he explained; and "if it were not necessary to clip the wool from the sheep annually for the sake of the animal's health, sheep owners at that time would never have troubled themselves to shear the fleece."[28]

Butlin's statistics confirm the importance of sheep and cattle to the colony's economic development. The pastoral industry in 1817 accounted for 39.8 per cent of GDP in Van Diemen's Land, compared to 22.1 per cent in New South Wales. Pastoral expansion meant that GDP went from less than 10 per cent of the New South Wales total in 1810 to nearly 30 per cent in 1820, and was much higher than New South Wales on a per capita basis.[29] As Abbot and Nairn point out:

> With only a quarter of the population the satellite dependency of Van Diemen's Land after 17 years of settlement had half as many cattle, half as many acres of wheat and half as many sheep again as the parent colony. That is six times the productivity (in these sectors) per head of population with an average income at 32 pounds, or about twice that of New South Wales.[30]

If this is considered, Butlin's claim that "Van Diemen's Land farming was highly inefficient" seems to miss the point.[31] In terms of a return on the capital and labour employed it was a very productive and efficient enterprise indeed. The costs of this form of farming were minimal. Almost nothing was paid for access to the native grasslands and little labour was needed in proportion to the numbers of animals involved. As one contemporary observer pointed out, "Van Diemen's Land was aught beyond a vast common."[32] Van Diemonian pastoralists had free and unrivalled access to well-watered grass-lands, and under these circumstances there was no incentive to invest capital in more intensive, but less efficient, forms of farming.

The "Thirds"

In 1823 the newly arrived settler T.O. Curling suggested that there was "no drawback" to pastoral pursuits in Van Diemen's Land "except the loss by sheep stealers."[33] "Robbery is not confined as in England to a single sheep or cow," the settler William Williamson observed in 1820. Instead, "whole droves are driven off at once and slaughtered."[34] Curr warned prospective immigrants that stock theft was "organised into a most complete system."[35]

Settlers' fortunes were largely determined by the extent to which they adapted to this system. The frontier pastoral lands were largely outside official control, but this does not mean that there was anarchy. In the period between 1810 and 1820, a rough and ready breed of local capitalists came to prominence. This new establishment included some surprising recruits. David Gibson and James Lord, founding patriarchs of establishment dynasties, were both pioneer *Calcutta* convicts.[36] And there must have been some irony for William Field, who was one of the largest stock-owners in the north of the island, in recalling that his sentence in England was for receiving stolen sheep.[37]

These men understood that the most effective stratagem for mini-mising stock theft and motivating and managing labour was to hand over ownership of a portion of stock to the convict stock-keepers. Under the "thirds" system, the Van Diemonian elite offered their con-vict workers economic independence and social freedom in return for free, motivated labour and guaranteed returns. Stock owners, often resident in the towns, handed over a flock or herd to a worker pre-pared to risk frontier life and payed him a portion (usually a third) of the natural increase in lieu of wages. The custodian took the animals to the leased or granted land or, more commonly, to unallocated grasslands, where he watched over the animals, doing the necessary deals to minimise losses from bushrangers and Aborigines while making extra money for flour, tea, sugar, tobacco and rum by selling kangaroo skins. Curr described this as "common practice" and it remained widespread until the late 1820s, mainly because it was the most effective way "to ensure the care and fidelity of their convict shepherds."[38]

The thirds system largely explains why, although there were some very large livestock holdings, there was much more diffusion than in New South Wales. The historian Hamish Maxwell-Stewart calculated that in 1817, 46 per cent of cattle and 52 per cent of sheep in the southern settlement were owned by emancipists or convicts. That year there were even 113 men and women recorded as running stock but possessing no land.[39] Even these figures, based on official returns, are likely to be conservative, for ownership was not always easy to establish or readily declared, and early government musters probably underestimated the number of sheep and cattle owners dispersed across the remote interior.

Small landowners also ran their stock on the grasslands. James Gordon told Commissioner John Bigge that many placed their stock "in the interior of the country and at a distance of 40 and 50 miles from the settlement ... [with] a ticket of occupation describing in very general terms the tract of land that he is to occupy."[40] The 102 tickets issued in 1817 provide the first official descriptions of how extensive such pastoral "runs" had become. For example, the ticket of occupation granted to Stines and Troy extended from Prosser's Plains (near present-day Orford) to Oyster Bay.[41] By 1819 settlers were disputing rights of access to grazing land at York Plains (nearly midway between Hobart Town and Launceston).[42] This situation began to change in the early 1820s as the best sheep country was granted to a small elite of free settlers. Nevertheless, as late as 1826 the *Colonial Times* noted that in contrast to New South Wales, "here almost every settler keeps a flock of sheep, more or less."[43]

In the lands outside official British control, convicts enjoyed a surprising degree of individual liberty. The new pastoral economy also had broader social and political implications. After the death of David Collins in 1810, the foundation existed for a collective convict uprising that would pose a potent challenge to imperial power.

[6]

THE LIEUTENANT GOVERNOR
OF THE WOODS

O N 3 APRIL 1810 THE SHORT-LIVED *Derwent Star and Van Diemen's Land Intelligencer* reported the sudden death of David Collins at the age of 54, describing him as "truly a father and a friend. His humanity to the unfortunate victims under his care was most conspicuous, being ever more ready to pardon than punish the offender."[1] The death of Collins left a vacuum in which the customs that had moderated relations between convicts and the authorities seem to have broken down.

Part of the problem was the calibre of Collins' replacements. Captain Murray, who was commandant from 1810 to 1812; Edward Lord, who filled in between times; and Thomas Davey, who finally took up his posting as the new lieutenant governor of Van Diemen's Land in 1813 – all lacked the wisdom and administrative skills to fulfill their challenging task. At least, this was how it seemed to the governor-in-chief in Sydney: Lachlan Macquarie was scathing in his assessment of the character and competency of these men.

Another factor was the lack of a local higher court. John West recorded that "crimes of less magnitude than murder, or burglary under aggravated circumstances, were punished in a summary manner. To prosecute [by going to Sydney] was to encounter ruin: the person despoiled, while pursuing the robber, lost the remnant of his property; and returning to his dwelling, found it wrecked and pillaged."[2]

The first convicts to come direct from England, who arrived on the *Indefatigable* in 1812, also played a disproportionate role in the

growing discontent. These were joined by larger numbers of secondary offenders from Sydney. Both groups had experienced a level of
institutional brutality unknown to the *Calcutta* convicts. They also
lacked the personal ties that had helped to forestall the resort to violence in the small founding community.

The most important factor underlying what soon escalated into a
serious convict revolt, however, was more fundamental. Given the
number of convicts and former convicts living independently in the
bush, the bushrangers had a solid social and economic foundation on
which to base their growing power. In his *History of Tasmania*, John
West summarised the desperate situation that emerged:

> Towards the close of 1813, the daring and sanguinary violence of
> bushrangers reduced the colony to utmost distress: the settlers,
> generally of the lowest class, received their plunder, and gave them
> notice of pursuit. Their alliance with stock-keepers, who them-
> selves passed rapidly, and almost naturally, from the margin of
> civilised to a lawless life, was well understood; nor could they read-
> ily refuse their friendship; the government, unable to afford them
> protection, left them no other source of safety. The division of the
> colony into those who had been convicts and those who controlled
> them, naturally ranged all of loose principles on the side of the
> outlaws. Nor was their mode of living without attractions: they
> were free: their daring seemed liked heroism to those in bondage.
> They not infrequently professed to punish severity to the prison-
> ers, and like Robin Hood of old, to pillage the rich, that they might
> be generous to the poor.[3]

The threat posed by bushrangers is not nineteenth-century hyper-
bole. Lloyd Robson has argued that "during the period of Davey's
administration the bushrangers nearly took over Van Diemen's Land,"
and even parts of Hobart Town were not safe.[4] The authorities held
genuine fears that many more convicts would join the bushrangers
and that real power and effective government would pass to them.

Such was the urgency of the situation that in mid 1814 Governor
Macquarie proclaimed that all bushrangers would be pardoned of all

crimes apart from murder if they surrendered by 1 December 1814. Predictably, a six-month crime spree followed.[5] James Gordon, in evidence to Commissioner Bigge in 1820, described how this "promise of indemnity was injurious to the colony." "They almost all came in," he observed, "but not till the time granted was nearly expired," and there were "a good many" robberies committed during the intervening period by those who proudly proclaimed themselves "free booters by authority of Governor Macquarie." Moreover, says Gordon, "all but one or two of the bushrangers and several others went out soon after receiving the pardon, and the practice of bushranging became worse than ever."[6]

On 25 April 1815, Davey declared martial law. He did this in open violation of Macquarie, who wrote: "I have *ordered* Lt Govr Davey to revoke and annul his order for martial law as being illegal and unwarrantable; but I doubt very much whether he will obey my orders."[7] Later that year Davey took personal charge of a military expedition into the very heart of bushranger territory: the Central Plateau.[8]

Davey also sought to undermine the economic foundation of bushranging. The purchase of kangaroo meat by the government store – which Macquarie felt had been "a great encouragement to these bushrangers who are in the habit of supplying the inhabitants with it [to sell on]"[9] – had already ended. Now, Davey banned traffic in kangaroo skins and apparel made from undressed skins, and even ordered that all kangaroo dogs be destroyed.[10]

These instructions were widely ignored. Carlo Canteri has argued in *The Origins of Australian Social Banditry: Bushranging in Van Diemen's Land 1805–1818* that the bushrangers outmanoeuvred Davey by shifting their focus to domestic livestock.[11] Many stock-owners were willing to sell stolen meat to the government store rather than cull their own animals, as quotas to supply the store were issued in proportion to stock held. Moreover, the thirds system made it easy to conceal stolen animals on crown lands.[12]

Bushranger connections permeated colonial society. The commandant at Port Dalrymple, Captain McKenzie, wrote to Davey in 1814 that "almost everyone here is, I firmly believe, more or less, a villain." His concern was well founded. One rebel was the former acting deputy surveyor-general, Peter Mills, who joined the bushrangers to escape his creditors. He escaped again after capture, probably with the help of the assistant surgeon, John Smith; the desperate McKenzie reported that "Thomas Hobbs the sentry has also absconded with him." Both Smith and his superior, Mountgarrett, were tried and acquitted in Sydney on charges of participating in stock stealing with bushrangers.[13]

According to Canteri, bushranging groups came under the protection of private interests.[14] In the case of the most powerful bushranger of this or any other era, this was almost certainly true. From 1815 to 1818, the British authorities in Van Diemen's Land were engaged in what amounted to a civil war with a convict gang led by the well-connected "Lieutenant Governor of the Woods," Michael Howe.

Michael Howe and the Van Diemen's Land Elite

Michael Howe, a Yorkshireman who arrived on the *Indefatigable* in 1812, was the only Australian bushranger to pose a genuine alternative to the colonial government's political authority. Unlike later, more famous bushrangers, he was much more than a celebrated outlaw. His chosen titles, "Lieutenant Governor of the Woods" and "Governor of the Ranges," were not baseless presumption. He corresponded with both Sorell and Davey "as though he was their equal" – and in terms of local power and influence, between 1814 and 1817, he was.[15] Howe controlled access to the most valuable resources of the colony; he was a leader to be taken seriously by all those who wanted to travel through, reside in or make money from the grassy woodlands of Van Diemen's Land. There is little doubt that some of the most powerful men in Hobart Town and Launceston had arrangements with him, and that the most profitable of these partnerships was with the colony's wealthiest individual, former marine officer Edward Lord.

Although Lord's land holdings were dispersed across the interior grasslands, including Howe's home base in the Central Plateau, his property was never attacked by Howe. The first attack upon Lord's principal residence, his 35-room mansion at Orielton Park, was made in May 1817 – shortly *after* Howe had negotiated a settlement and was residing in Hobart Town.[16] While the bushrangers preyed on his competitors, Lord's empire expanded so rapidly that by 1821 he owned three ships, 35,000 acres, 6000 cattle and 7000 sheep. In 1823 he told London that his Van Diemen's Land assets were worth £200,000 and that he was owed another £70,000 (by contrast, Sorell's annual salary as lieutenant governor was £500).[17]

This is not to suggest that there were direct negotiations between the two men, but rather that understandings were reached between the groups they led. In this, the role played by Lord's wife and business partner, Maria Lord, may have been crucial. Maria not only ran the merchant business but also had the major responsibility for her husband's interests during his six trips to England before 1825. It was Maria who, as a former convict, had the contacts and the cultural knowledge to ensure that an understanding was reached with the bushrangers.

One hundred men were supposed to have been members of Howe's gang at some time, and from 1815 his authority seems to have been accepted by all the bushranger gangs. Most stock-keepers, shepherds and hunters in the frontier lands had no option but obeisance, since it was he, not the colonial government, who exercised real power in these regions.[18]

Those who were targeted by Howe often faced ruin. Gordon told Bigge that he could not live on his land for four years before 1818 for fear of bushrangers. John Wade, chief constable, informed the commissioner that he resigned his post "on account of the losses I sustained by the bushrangers."[19] A.W.H. Humphrey may have regretted becoming a justice of the peace in 1810, as in 1815 he wrote to London that his "exertions to suppress and bring to justice these daring offenders" had resulted in his sheep being "taken way from their grazing ground ... fifty and a hundred at a time and either destroyed or driven to distant parts," and the corn stack on his farm at Pitt Water being "wantonly set fire to in the dead of night," involving a loss of "upwards of £700." On another occasion, eight bushrangers broke into his house and "after plundering it of every portable article of value, wantonly and maliciously destroyed everything that they could not take away."[20] Even Lieutenant Governor Davey's own farm at Coal River was twice raided.[21]

Michael Howe and the Aborigines

Howe also reached understandings with the owners of the land. James Kelly reported that he had an alliance with "Tolobunganah" and his people, and according to the *Hobart Town Gazette*, Howe's gang included "two black native girls armed as well as the men."[22] West and Calder both reported that Howe meted out severe corporal punishment to any of his men who assaulted an Aborigine, although neither was sure if this was due to "policy or humanity."[23]

Critical to Howe's negotiations would have been his Aboriginal partner, known to the British as "Black Mary" or "Mary Cockerill." This is highlighted by the fact that his power largely ended with the breakdown of their relationship, after Howe reputedly shot Mary during a pursuit in early 1817 in a failed attempt to prevent her being captured alive. Following this betrayal, she is said to have led a military party to his hide-out. Almost immediately after, Howe wrote directly to Lieutenant Governor Sorell offering to give himself up and provide information to the authorities concerning his associates in exchange for a pardon. Sorell conditionally agreed to this and Howe came in to Hobart Town, being held under only limited supervision while Governor Macquarie in Sydney, who backed Sorell on the matter, forwarded the request for a full pardon to London.

The official investigation into the information provided by Howe never went far. Howe's depositions to Sorell and the magistrates, if they were ever recorded, are no longer available; nor has any other record of their content survived. There is also no evidence of any action having been taken on the basis of the testimony other than an investigation of Chaplain Knopwood, who was accused of "improper intercourse with people living in the woods" but later cleared.[24] It was not in Howe's interests to betray his partners, and if the authorities were serious about getting him to do so, they would surely have removed him to the comparative safety of Sydney, as was done with other bushranger informers. As Canteri surmises, Sorell seems soon to have realised what the magistrates would have already known, that "a complete exposure of all the bushrangers, interconnecting linkages would shake Van Diemen's Land to its very rum-cellars."[25]

As far as British officialdom was concerned, the question of Howe's probable partnership with the Van Diemonian elite was closed when he walked out of Hobart Town in early 1818. Given the number of powerful men Howe could still inform on, he was very vulnerable, and it is not surprising that without the promised speedy pardon and leave to depart from the island he had been promised, he chose to return to the bush. He did so alone, and with his authority largely surrendered. Moreover, the Hobart Town and Port Dalrymple elite were now united – for the first time – by the common cause of killing him. One of Edward Lord's stock-keepers was a principal agent of their eventual success.

During his last desperate year of freedom, Howe became a conventional outlaw, with a hundred-guinea reward (later doubled) and free pardon and passage to England offered to any "crown prisoner" who killed or captured him.[26] With Macquarie keeping Mary in Sydney, "lest she should renew her intercourse with Howe and be the means of protracting the terms of his submission,"[27] Howe's most dangerous pursuer became Musquito, a New South Wales Aborigine captured by the British in 1805 and sent to Port Dalrymple in 1813, who tracked Howe and other bushrangers in an attempt to secure a passage home.

The *Hobart Town Gazette* reported in September 1818 that Howe had been seen near Fat Doe River and was pursued, "losing his dogs, knapsack and all that he had … from a paper found in his knapsack it appears that he has been much harassed by the natives and had been very nearly cut off by them several times." And in the first book of general literature published in Australia, *Michael Howe: The Last and Worst of the Bushrangers of Van Diemen's Land*, printed in Hobart Town in 1818, Thomas Wells gave the details of his final betrayal:

> In the month of October a person named Warburton, in the habit of hunting kangaroo for skins, who had occasional opportunities for seeing Howe, communicated to a crown prisoner, named Thomas Worrell, stock-keeper to Edward Lord Esqe. a scheme for

taking him. Worrell agreed to the trial, and with Private William Pugh of the 48th Regt. a man of known courage … determined to lay in wait at a hut on the Shannon River, likely to be visited by Howe for supplies … On 21st of October Howe met Warburton near the place already mentioned … a severe encounter ensued; and finally, from well-directed blows on his head with their muskets, fell and expired without speaking.[28]

Worrell (like Howe, a former soldier in the Napoleonic wars) claimed that the bushranger, who was "covered with patches of kangaroo skins and wore a black beard," cried out "Black Beard against Grey Beard for a million!" as he fired for the last time. Pugh then "ran up, and with the butt end of his firelock … battered his brains out."[29] Howe's head was brought to Hobart Town and displayed by the authorities as public proof of imperial triumph, and Knopwood noted that "a great many people" went to see it.[30] His body was "interred on the spot where he fell,"[31] its return to the earth probably hastened by carrion-loving Tasmanian devils.

As a reward for their efforts, Worrell was given a free pardon and Pugh (known as "Big Bill") a free discharge, and both, along with Warburton, received a share of the reward money. There was to be no recognition, not even a passage home, for Musquito. He was left to defend himself against the taunts and probable violence of those who considered Howe a hero, and the British of all social classes were to pay dearly for this betrayal. Mary, too, received no reward – except the right to victuals from the government store. She died in the Hobart hospital the following winter, less than nine months after her former partner.[32] During his bushranging career, Howe was reported to have been loyal to only two of his associates – Mary and his kangaroo dog "Bosun."[33] Given the realities of Van Diemen's Land, these relationships were well chosen. It is telling that the bushranger's loss of power in frontier regions coincided with the end of his relationship with Mary, and his final capture was precipitated by the taking of his dog.

The power wielded by Howe had made him a hero to the convict and ex-convict population of Van Diemen's Land. Even after his death, those who betrayed him were ostracised by the majority. The defeat was, to an extent, "the people's defeat – the defeat of their hope."[34] The year after his beheading was the first since Collins' arrival in which there were no armed bushrangers fighting the authorities. The hope of direct resistance had suffered a mortal blow.

Thomas Wells, in his short book, captured some of the archetypal and mythical aspects of the Howe legend:

> In his knapsack was found a sort of journal of dreams … From this little book of kangaroo skin, written in kangaroo blood, it appears that he frequently dreamt of being murdered by natives, of seeing his old companions … of being nearly taken by a soldier; and in one instance … his sister. It also appears from this memorandum book, that he always had an idea of settling in the woods; for it contains long lists of such seeds as he wished to have, of vegetables, fruits, and even flowers![35]

West noted that the plants were intended "to adorn the seclusion which he contemplated," and described Howe's retreat in the Upper Shannon: "the site was chosen with taste, in an open undulating country, stretching to the western mountains: the spot was secluded from observation, was covered with a large honey suckle, and on a rise sloping to the stream."[36]

The Howe legend is thus distinctive among early bushranging stories in its emphasis on the freedom that it was possible to create within the Australian environment. Unlike the early escapees from Port Jackson and Port Phillip or later runaways from Van Diemonian convict hellholes, Howe seems to have had no plans to walk to China or steal a boat to South America. His dreaming place was the heart of Van Diemen's Land itself.

Such mythically potent stories ensured that Howe was not forgotten. James Ross reported that while on his 1823 expedition to the Great Lake, the wife of one of Edward Lord's stockmen told him, on being asked if she was lonely, that "sometimes at night 'my cow' came to her."[37] Ross interpreted this to mean that terrifying memories of Howe haunted her, but given what the Lieutenant Governor of the

Woods had represented to this class of settler, such a vision could just as well have provided solace from the dangerous, isolated and possibly hopeless circumstances of that unknown woman's life.

Bushranging Controlled

Sorell's negotiation of generous terms of surrender directly with individual bushrangers proved to be highly effective – a far more sophisticated approach than the general amnesty of 1814, it undermined the bonds of solidarity on which the bushrangers' influence depended. The bushrangers' own preference for collective bargaining had been expressed in a November 1816 letter to Davey, signed by 11 of them and written in kangaroo blood, seeking a clear position from the lieutenant governor, "full and satisfactory – either for us or against us."[38] Howe was reported to have made his gang swear an oath on the Church of England Prayer Book to abide by their collective position,[39] but such solidarity broke down when Sorell offered clemency to individuals who gave information and used their knowledge to assist the authorities.

For those bushrangers who did not return voluntarily, Sorell enlisted Van Diemonian bushmen to capture them. There was nothing new in this approach. Ever since early bushrangers Lemon and Brown were caught by experienced bushman Michael Mansfield in May 1808 after two years of dodging the soldiers, the authorities had sought to employ the bush skills of hunters and stock-keepers by offering rewards and indulgences. The skills of these men meant that Aboriginal trackers were never as important in Van Diemen's Land as in New South Wales, although during the height of the emergency, when few Van Diemonians could be motivated to betray Howe or other rebel leaders, they were called upon. The most important tracker of Howe was Musquito, but an Aboriginal man the British called Dual also seems to have been transported to Van Diemen's Land in 1816 to help with the chase (unlike Musquito, he was returned in 1818 when the job was done).[40]

Soldiers continued to be of limited use against bushrangers, although individuals and small parties usually guided by convict bushmen could prove effective as long as they were offered sufficiently generous rewards. Key personnel, including convict informers, were employed in designated "secret service," presumably to avoid being targeted for retribution.[41] Equally crucial to Sorell's success was his attempt, for the first time, to regulate access to the grasslands and bring their occupation under some form of official sanction. The *Hobart Town Gazette* noted in late 1817 that the "tickets of occupation for grazing grounds" were ready. The only requirements were that a small annual fee be paid and a stockyard be erected, but the fact that tickets or licences had to be renewed annually gave Sorell the potential power to remove access to pasture-lands if he suspected a ticket-holder of stock theft or providing support for bushrangers.

These measures meant that by the end of 1818 the convict uprising was over. Sorell's victory was not, however, all that it seemed. While there was no longer any threat to the political authority of his government, stock theft remained rife, and it was to be another generation before the grassy woodlands were brought under the effective control of the crown.

CROSS-CULTURAL ENCOUNTERS

C OLLINS' PREMATURE DEATH in 1810 was momentous in other ways. Not only was it the precursor to a serious convict revolt, but it marked the end of official attempts to restrict cross-cultural contact. This was first evident in the lifting of the bar on keeping Aboriginal children. The change under Collins' temporary replacement, Captain Murray, is confirmed by the fact that a number of the children baptised between 1810 and 1812 seem to have had the names of soldiers of the 73rd regiment, which had replaced Collins' marines. One of them, "Lucy Murray," even took the surname of the commandant.[1]

In 1810 one couple, the McCauleys, became the guardians of an infant boy who was to become "Black Robert," one of the first Aborigines to be engaged by George Augustus Robinson for the conciliation expedition over 20 years later. Mrs McCauley later recalled that "my late husband Sergt McAlley found him at the Cross Marsh ... and brought him home to me to nurse. He then appeared to be about 18 months old."[2] There is no government record of this child, despite Sergeant McCauley's official status. Nor does Knopwood ever mention Robert in his diary, despite his close friendship with the family and his broad pastoral responsibility to "illegitimate" (as he classified Aborigines in his baptismal records) children. Both the chaplain and the government he served seem to have taken the presence of Aboriginal children for granted.

In consequence, it is not clear how many Aboriginal children lived with the British. By 1820, of the 685 children who had been christened by Knopwood, 26 were Aborigines,[3] but many Aboriginal children lived with white settlers without being baptised. We have little more than glimpses into their lives. In February 1809 Captain John Brabyn wrote to Paterson that "Fanny the native girl has walked out on Mr Dry and had not been seen since."[4] In December 1817 the *Hobart Town Gazette* reported that "we understand that a native black boy, late stock-keeper to Mr B Reardon at Pitt Water, has been found dead there, and is at present supposed to have been murdered." A week later the paper reported on the inquest into the death of "Paddy," which found that he had in fact "drowned by accident" while hunting ducks with his dog. An almost simultaneous inquest in the northern settlement reported on a "black native girl ... drowned in South Esk River."[5] And in 1821 the paper reported on "George Van Diemen," an Aboriginal child who had been "found in the woods near the River Plenty about 2 ½ years ago and has been since under the protection of the lieutenant governor," had recently gone to England "in the care of William Kermode," and was "supposed to be almost nine years old." The boy returned to Van Diemen's Land in 1827, having become literate and reasonably well educated, in the forlorn hope that he might be given colonial government employ, but died soon after.

Many of these children left white families at adolescence, presumably because they desperately wanted to return to their families and communities, and did so as soon as they were able. In 1818 the *Gazette* recorded the fate of a young Aborigine who had presumably absconded from his master. He had been "charged with wandering in the woods without any visible means of obtaining a livelihood" and was sentenced to 12 months in the chain gang.[6]

Desertion was often taken as proof that the innate "savagery" of Aborigines could never be removed (the main reason for Collins arguing, in his *Account*, that there was little long-term philanthropic benefit in removal), or, more sympathetically, seen as prompted by the search for a partner. Certainly it was very rare for Aboriginal youths brought up with whites to find long-term partners within the British settlements. Catherine Kennedy and William Ponsonby, or "Black Bill," who married in St John's Church, Launceston in 1830, are the best-known exceptions.[7]

It generally took an act of violence for Aboriginal young people to be much noticed by white officialdom. The first record of a serious incident was when "three civilised black natives" with "guns and dogs" were deemed responsible for "depredations" in March 1817.[8] In November 1818 two Aborigines were even sentenced to transportation. The *Hobart Town Gazette* reported that

> Two black natives who have been long among the inhabitants, named James Tedbury and George Frederick, were charged with robbing Robin Gavin of several articles, and James Goodwin of a musket at Coal River; after which they escaped to the woods, and were there apprehended, both armed. They were each sentenced to be transported to such part of this territory as His Honor the Lieutenant Governor may be pleased to direct for the term of three years.[9]

It is likely that some of the Aboriginal children who had lived with the British were by this time reaching young adulthood and making their primary loyalties known. Perhaps they were even exacting revenge for the circumstances of their capture.

Why were Aboriginal children kept by the British? For some there was a religious and philanthropic dimension. The "salvation" of Aborigines was to be a persistent nineteenth-century (and indeed, twentieth-century) theme. George Augustus Robinson, for example, told Arthur in mid 1829 that the Aboriginal children of the Bruny Island establishment "appear to be destined by providence as a foundation upon which the superstructure of Your Excellency's benevolence is hereafter to be erected."[10]

Philanthropic motives notwithstanding, the most important reason for procuring Aboriginal children was the unpaid labour they could provide, with settler expectations conditioned by centuries of exploitation of "native" workers.[11] The value of Aboriginal children to the British was particularly significant in the period before 1818, when there was a pervasive labour shortage. Only one convict ship from England arrived before 1816, and the sentences of many of the first arrivals had expired. Former convicts demanded higher wages than many small settlers could afford. Meanwhile, the move into remote grassland regions exacerbated the demand for labour, while increasing access to Aboriginal children. The children's bush knowledge and potential ability to liaise between the settlers and the Indigenous landowners would also have been valued. Furthermore, unlike most former convicts, Aborigines were allowed to travel without restriction, making them attractive recruits for sealers, whalers and merchants. Tasmanian Aborigines were employed on missions that took them to Mauritius, New Zealand and many islands in Oceania and the Pacific.

Older children were more immediately useful, thanks to their capacity to work and their knowledge of the bush. Even once "civilised," however, these older children generally retained their tribal identities and relationships. Babies and infants usually lost their community ties and consequently had fewer options as they grew up. Black Robert, for example, stayed with the McCauleys and provided free labour until he was engaged by Robinson in 1829; McCauley reported to the government that "he has ever been a faithful and trusting domestic to me" and was the "best servant I have."[12]

Removed infants were almost certainly refugees from armed conflict, their families having fled or been killed. The circumstances by which older children came to live with the British, at least during the 1808–20 period when Aboriginal control over their ancestral lands remained largely intact, may have been more varied. Did Aborigines see advantages in having some of their children spend time with the British? It is even possible that fostering arrangements were seen to bind the newcomers into reciprocal obligations. Simple curiosity about British life and access to British food and products may also have played its part.

Nevertheless, kidnapping was probably prevalent. Certainly this seems to have been the view of Lieutenant Governor Davey, who, concerned at the "very marked and decided hostility has lately been evinced by the natives in the neighbourhood of the Coal River," issued a proclamation in mid 1814, expressing his "most extreme concern" that the "probable causes" of this were a most barbarous and inhuman mode of proceeding acted upon towards them, viz. the robbery of their children! Had not the lieutenant governor the most positive and distinct proofs of such barbarous crimes having been committed, he could not have believed that a British subject would so ignominiously have stained the honour of his country and of himself; but the facts are too clear, and it therefore becomes the indispensable and bounden duty of the lieutenant governor thus publicly to express his utter indignation and abhorrence thereof.[13]

The next lieutenant governor, William Sorell, also made reference to the "occasional outrages of miscreants," who

sometimes ... pursue the women, for the purpose of compelling them to abandon their children. This last outrage is perhaps the most certain of all to excite in the sufferers a strong thirst for revenge against all white men ... With a view to prevent the continuance of the cruelty before-mentioned, of depriving the natives of their children; it is hereby ordered that the resident magistrates at the districts of Pitt Water and Coal River, and the District Constables in all other Districts, do forthwith take an account of all the native youths and children which are resident with any of the settlers or stock-keepers, stating from whom, and in what manner they were obtained ...[14]

Sorell advised that children removed without "the consent of the parents ... will be removed to Hobart Town," but there is no evidence that this occurred or that the practice of child abduction ceased. Indeed, as the balance of power on the frontier moved against the Aborigines, kidnapping probably became more common. In October 1830, one young Aboriginal woman told Robinson that she had been forcibly taken when little more than a baby:

Asked Bull.rer alias Jumbo who took her from her people. Said Munro [a leading member of the sealing community in the Furneaux Group] and others rushed them at their fires and took six, that she was a little girl and could just crawl; said she had been with Munro ever since.[15]

At Richmond gaol in the same year Robinson met with another captured Aboriginal women who was in "extreme distress" at the loss of her son. Robinson noted that "this is not the first time I have had occasion to deplore the pernicious custom which prevails of separating children from their parents."[16] This "custom," it seems, was by then longstanding.

White Men and Aboriginal Women

Relationships between white men and Aboriginal women became both more common and more open between 1810 and 1820. One *Calcutta* convict and former bushranger, Archibald (or Richard) Campbell, even established a home with his Aboriginal partner at South Arm, near Hobart Town. Knopwood and the *Sydney Gazette* record that the couple facilitated visits by Aborigines to the settlement before the woman died at Coles Bay in January 1820 while guiding an official party seeking an overland route to the east coast.[17]

However, most such relationships still occurred in remote regions. Commissioner Bigge heard contrasting views about their prevalence in 1820. James Gordon believed that "intercourse … between the female natives and the stock-keepers in the interior … is very rare if ever, and then only with such female natives as have frequented the towns." By contrast, Henry Barrett, the long-term resident of York Town, claimed that "the black women frequently live with the English, and they quarrel and the women are turned away. I have heard the black men say sometimes that the English take their wives."[18] Much of the apparent contradiction probably reflects regional difference. In the north-east a greater number of Aboriginal women lived with whites because of the influence of the sealers.[19]

The subject of these men's relations with the Aborigines is one of the most complex and sensitive issues in Tasmanian history. At an early period, sometime before 1810, the sealer communities included Aboriginal women and their children, most of whom were from the north-east of the island. Lyndall Ryan estimates in *The Aboriginal Tasmanians* that by 1820 there were about 100 Aboriginal women living with 50 sealers.[20] Rebe Taylor has calculated that 22 named Aboriginal women from Van Diemen's Land went to Kangaroo Island alone, but "there were possibly many more who cannot be accounted for."[21] The French navigator D'Urville, who met the sealers of Westernport, noted that five Aboriginal women from Van Diemen's Land were with them.[22] Robinson accounted for 74 women in the Bass Strait alone in 1831 and also gave the names of 14 others still on Kangaroo Island.[23]

Sealers were often brutal men, capable of extreme, wide-ranging violence against the women and their communities, but they also offered a refuge of sorts from the British conquest of mainland Tasmania that accelerated from the mid 1820s. The sealers, as Ryan put it, both helped save "Aboriginal society from extinction" and were "instrumental in the destruction of a number of Aboriginal tribes."[24] That the women were widely regarded as slaves – the personal property of the sealers – is perhaps the least surprising aspect of this complex encounter. Slavery had a long history in the British empire and was not officially abolished until 1833.[25] The assumption that native people could not only be forcibly employed, but become for all practical purposes private property persisted even longer.

In the first period of contact, many sealers had close ties with Indigenous communities, and there is evidence to suggest that some even learned Aboriginal languages and participated in tribal life. But as the sealing community grew after 1820, and white settlement spread, friendly relations largely ended, especially in the north-east. Robinson documents many examples of violence, including the testimony of "Mary":

> The Aboriginal female Mary informed me that the sealers at the straits carry on a complete system of slavery; that they barter in exchange for women flour and potatoes... they took her away by force, tied her hands and feet, and put her in the boat; that white man beat black woman with a rope.[26]

Before the 1830s, it is somewhat misleading to talk of the sealers as if they were a distinct group. Many men moved regularly between the offshore islands, coastal bays and interior hunting grounds. Two of the best-documented relationships between European men and Aboriginal women in Van Diemen's Land, those involving James Carrett and George Briggs, are examples of this. Carrett was first named by Knopwood as an absconder in 1807. He became notorious for cruelty to Aborigines after James Hobbs repeated a sadistic boast made to him by Carrett, probably while they were on a north-west exploratory trip together in 1824. Hobbs alleged that Carretts had "told him that he had once cut off a native man's head at Oyster Bay, and made his wife hang it round her neck, and carry it as a plaything" and "from Carrott's manner he credited the story."[27]

New South Wales-born George Briggs is remembered for less horrifying exploits. He lived with several Aboriginal women in Van Diemen's Land and fathered a number of children with them. One of them, Dolly, later married Thomas Johnson at Meander River and had seven children, becoming the matriarch of a large clan. In the summer of 1815–16, he also accompanied James Kelly on his remarkable circumnavigation of Van Diemen's Land in an open whaling boat. Kelly's report of this voyage provides by far the most comprehensive account of Aboriginal–British relations before 1820, and deserves to be considered in detail.

James Kelly's Expedition

In the summer of 1815–16 James Kelly, accompanied by four experienced Van Diemonians, set off to circumnavigate Van Diemen's Land. Kelly's report of the journey is of unique value because the men were not in a conventional vessel sailing far out to sea, but an open five-oared whaling boat which hugged the coast. Kelly met Aborigines right around the island. The attitudes and responses of the expeditioners are also of particular interest because they were not explorers from distant lands or privileged urban chroniclers, but men whose home was now Van Diemen's Land, and who already had many years' experience of living in Aboriginal lands. James Kelly was born in Parramatta in 1791, the son of a convict. Among his companions, John

Griffith and George Briggs were also native-born[28] and connected with sealing. William Jones and Thomas Tombs were *Calcutta* convicts, long-term kangaroo hunters and sometime bushrangers, as well as experienced boatmen.[29] All four had spent most of the previous decade outside the British settlements. Kelly's report of the expedition thus provides a rare insight into the view of Aborigines held by resident Britons of the convict class.

The first contact with Aborigines occurred on the day after setting out, 13 December 1815, when Kelly reported "we attempted to haul the boat up on the south side of Recherche Bay, but were prevented by a large body of natives giving us a tremendous volley of stones and spears."[30] Recherche Bay, since Bruni D'Entrecasteux's prolonged and peaceful encounter with the Aborigines in 1792, had been a frequent resort of Europeans, especially whalers, and this probably explains the local Aborigines' hostile reaction to the party's arrival.

On the following day, in the still largely unvisited south-west, Kelly recorded a more pacific encounter:

> in a small sandy bay to the northward of De Witt's Isles ... we had a friendly reception from a large number of natives. We made them a few presents, consisting of sugar and biscuit ... They seemed ... to behave as if at a rejoicing, on account of their seeing new visitors ... they brought down their women and children to see us, a token which shows friendship amongst these savages.[31]

Kelly then spent three days at Port Davey, which was "discovered" and named on this expedition, and on 21 December the explorers saw two Aborigines who "seemed very much alarmed at seeing us ... We gave them two black swans, of which we had a good stock in the boat. They seemed delighted with the present." Kelly and his crew could well have been the first Europeans they had ever seen.

At the entrance to what they were to name Macquarie Harbour, Kelly documented the nervousness of the expeditioners as they travelled the unknown, but well-populated, west coast. The fact that the "whole face" of the coast was on fire was, he thought, a lucky circumstance for us. The smoke was so thick we could not see a hundred yards ahead of the boat. On pulling into the narrows, at the small entrance island, we heard a large number of natives shouting and making a great noise, as if they were hunting kangaroo. It is highly fortunate that the smoke was thick, for had the natives seen the boat pass through the narrow entrance, it is possible they would have killed every person on board, by discharging in their usual way volleys of spears and stones. In the afternoon the smoke cleared off a little, and we found ourselves in a large sheet of water near a small island where we landed, and found plenty of black swans on their nests, and plenty of their eggs. We remained for the night upon the island, thus keeping safe from the natives.[32]

North of Macquarie Harbour, Kelly had an unplanned rendezvous when after a day getting very wet and having

just got a large fire made to dry ourselves ... to our great astonishment, we were accosted by six huge men, black natives, each of them above six feet high and very stout made ... They had one spear in their right hands, and two in their left ... Our men were greatly alarmed ... it was thought best to make gestures to them to come closer to us ... Our arms all wet and no means of defending ourselves, we were indeed in a very perplexing situation. Fortune ... was still on our side. We had nine or ten black swans and a large wombat in the boat, that we had brought from Macquarie Harbour as fresh provisions. On our showing them one of the swans they seemed delighted, and came nearer to the boat ... each of them had a spear between the great toe of each of their feet, dragging them along the ground. We supposed they had never seen a white man before. It was thought best to try to barter with them for their spears, so that if we got possession of them they could not hurt us. We luckily succeeded in giving them four swans and the wombat for them all. They appeared very much pleased with the bargain they had made, and went away holding up one hand each as a sign of friendship. A great number of smokes were made along the coast, which we believed were intended as signals to the tribes. We remained on the beach that night, and drying our arms brought them into firing order, keeping – apprehensive of another visit from the natives – incessant watch.[33]

Not for the first time, British vulnerability enabled a productive and peaceful exchange to occur.

On 4 January, Kelly landed at Hunter's Island off the north-west tip of Van Diemen's Land. Seeing "a great many fires along the shore," he "kept the boat and the arms ready, in case of an attack from the natives." An armed group of "at least fifty in number" soon approached and "began to advance slowly towards us near the fire." The British held up their guns and made "signs to them not to come any closer." The Aborigines, however, were not put off and forced a meeting, mocking the British pretension:

> They held up their spears in return, accompanying their movements with loud laughing. They jeered at us … We thought it desirable to retreat to the boat, when suddenly they laid down their weapons in the edge of the bush, and each holding up both hands as if they did not mean any mischief, at the same time making signs to us to lay down our arms, which we did to satisfy them – for if we had retreated quickly to the boat, it was probable they would have killed every one of us before we could have got out of range of their spears. The natives then began to come to us, one by one, holding up both hands to show they had no weapons … there were twenty-two came to the fire. We made signs to them that no more should be allowed to come … When the chief came he ordered all to sit down on the ground, which they did, and formed a sort of circle around the fire. The chief ordered the old man to dance and sing, as if to amuse us …

What followed is something of a mystery. The experienced Briggs "brought two swans from the boat, one under each arm," presumably to cement the peaceful exchange. But Kelly reports that

When the chief saw them he rushed at Briggs to take the swans from him, but did not succeed. He then ordered the men to give us a volley of stones, which they did – he giving the time in most beautiful order, swing his arm three times, and at each swing calling "Yah! Yah! Yah!" and a severe volley it was. I had a large pair of dueling pistols in my pocket … and seeing there was no alternative I fired amongst them, which dispersed them; the other I fired after them as they ran away … We found several marks of blood on the stones in the direction that the natives ran away when the pistols were fired. Some of them were most probably wounded. We then got into our boat. Just as we were pulling away we received a large volley of stones and spears from the natives … but luckily no one was hurt. We landed on a small rock covered with birds. They were laying, and we got six bucketfuls of eggs – a good supply. This seemed to offend the natives as a number of women came down on a point of rocks and abused us very much for taking their eggs.[34]

Why Briggs resisted the swans being taken is not clear. More certain is that the British were saved by their boat. The hidden pistols temporarily dispersed the unarmed Aborigines, but without a ready boat to flee in, there would have been little hope against such a large group.

The next meeting with Aborigines was on the north-east coast, where contact between the British and Aborigines, through the sealers, had been the most extensive. Kelly's record gives a unique insight into the established cross-cultural exchange and the extent to which Briggs at least had assumed some identity and responsibilities in Aboriginal society. It also shows Briggs' willingness to ignore these when it suited. At noon on 13 January, the party

landed on Ringarooma Point; here we suddenly fell in with a large mob of natives, who, upon their first appearance, seemed hostile – but on seeing Briggs, whom they knew particularly well, the chief, whose name was Lamanbunganah, seemed delighted at the interview, and told him he was at war with his own brother

Tolobunganah, a most powerful chief, and then on the coast near Eddystone Point. Tolobunganah was also one of Briggs's acquaintances. Briggs had left two wives and five children upon the islands during his absence at Hobart Town, and had taken this trip round the west coast thinking he might fall in with some of his black relations near Cape Portland. One of his wives was a daughter of the chief Lamanbunganah, whom we had just fallen in with, and he generally called his father-in-law Laman for shortness. The chief made enquiry after his daughter, and was told that she and her children were safe over at Cape Barren. Laman said he knew that, for he saw her smokes every day.

"Laman" sought Briggs' aid in an internal conflict. He "had heard that five or six white men well armed were with his brother Tolobunganah at Eddystone Point, and that they intended to come and attack his [Laman's] tribe and kill them all." These were assumed "as a matter of course" by Kelly to have been the bushranger Michael Howe and his party. When Briggs was reticent, Laman "told Briggs in a very hostile tone that he had often before gone with him to fight other tribes when he [Briggs] wanted women." The situation became very tense when

> Laman gave a loud cooee, and in two minutes we were surrounded by above fifty natives ... We now got very much alarmed at the dangerous situation we were in, and as an excuse, Briggs told Laman that we would go over to Cape Barren and fetch Briggs's wife, that we would also get five or six of the sealers to join us with plenty of firearms, and come over and fight Tolobunganah. Laman was much pleased ...[35]

Kelly confirms that Briggs "had acquired the native language of the north-east coast of Van Diemen's Land fluently" and that he often went "over from the island to Cape Portland to barter kangaroo skins with the natives, as also to purchase the young grown-up native females ... whom they employed, as they were wonderfully dextrous in hunting kangaroo and catching seals."[36]

Rather than head north to Cape Barren Island as Briggs had promised, Kelly went south. After landing on a small island he articulated the two reasons why offshore islands were favoured European refuges. On the island, the party was "safe from native attack," and found "a number of seals lying on the rocks basking in the sun." On this occasion, "having no salt with us to cure the skins we thought it useless to kill them," but the next day, forced "to lie idle with a foul wind, and being all old hands at sealing," an alternative technique (commonly used to cure skins in North America) was employed:

> we commenced killing and flinching the skins from the bodies, stretching them out upon the grass with wooden pegs. They were dried in the sun, and in one day became perfectly cured. This day we killed and pegged out thirty skins. The following day, 16th January, we killed, flinched and pegged out twenty-five seal-skins.[37]

A "large number of natives" had by now gathered on the beach opposite the island, and on 17 January, when the expeditioners found "the seals getting shy of coming up on the rocks," they "gave them a rest" and went to communicate with the Aborigines:

> We did not go closer to the beach than musket shot for fear of being surprised by Howe's party. Briggs stood up in the boat and called out to the natives in their own language to come to the waterside. They seemed shy until he told them who he was, when an old man rushed up to his middle in the water. Briggs called to him to swim to the boat, which he did, and we hauled him in. It turned out to be the old chief, Tolobunganah. Tolobunganah was overjoyed at seeing Briggs ... Tolobunganah stood up in the boat and called to the natives. About 20 of them came down to the waterside; they all knew Briggs, and seemed glad to see him. We made Tolo a present of the four dead seals and the live pups, at which he seemed highly gratified. Immediately after they had obtained the seals six women came down, each with a dead kangaroo on their shoulders. Tolo ordered them to be brought to the

boat ... We felt obliged to ... extract all the friendly information we could from the Aborigines relative to Howe and his party, as we were still of opinion ... that they were close at hand, but the natives assured us that they were gone a long distance to the southward, towards St Patrick's Head.[38]

Kelly's crew and the Aborigines agreed to continue the exchange, and both parties spent the next day hunting – the British for seals and the Aborigines for kangaroo. On the following morning "the whole tribe came down on the beach; there were about two hundred men, women and children, and at least fifty dogs." But Kelly's party stayed wary, and

Tolo seemed much displeased at this evident want of confidence. The natives asked if we would bring over more seals on the following day. Briggs informed them that they were getting scarce and shy of being caught. Tolo considered that we had better take some women over to the island to assist in catching them. This course being agreed on, Tolo ordered six stout women into the boat. They obeyed with alacrity, evidently delighted with the prospects of the trip.

Over the next few days, mainly through the seal-hunting skills of the Aboriginal women, which Kelly describes in some detail, a total of 122 sealskins were obtained (worth, he claimed, a pound each in Hobart Town) and in exchange for the seal carcass, a further 246 kangaroo skins from the Aborigines. The trade was closed with a dance around the dead seals involving about 300 Aborigines, including many children.[39]

Before completing the circumnavigation, Kelly recorded that a "large number" of Aborigines were seen at Schouten Island and "several" at Maria Island. The latter "ran along the beach calling us to go ashore, which we declined."

What can be made of these varied encounters? First, there is the extent and diversity of the cross-cultural contact that had by then occurred in different regions of Van Diemen's Land.

Second, a pervading nervousness is evident among those who had lived in Aboriginal-controlled lands, including in places where contact had been most extensive. Even in the north-east, despite the personal links between Briggs and the Aboriginal leaders, Kelly's account suggests that, for one side at least, profit drove the cultural exchange and mistrust remained pervasive.

Third, it seems that in 1816, abduction of Aboriginal women by whites acting alone was rarely an option, as the risk of Aboriginal retaliation was very real. Briggs remained accountable to the Aboriginal elders for the women on Cape Barren Island, who communicated with their people through smoke. It is significant that his wife was the daughter of a senior man, and that the marriage had brought with it customary ties and obligations (even if Briggs disregarded these by not returning to Cape Barren as agreed).

Some have cast doubt on Kelly's credibility.[40] He, like Briggs and the other expeditioners, was certainly no innocent – a number of Maoris were to die on a sealing voyage he led, and Robinson later expressed concern about the "improper conduct towards the natives" at Kelly's farm on North Bruny Island.[41] But character assessments do not go far towards explaining frontier relations. Kelly's account suggests that the balance of power and the promise of profit probably limited the sealers' use of violence against Aborigines before 1816. At the same time, the foundations of the increased conflict of the 1820s were being laid. In some areas, violence had already become endemic, and sealers were forcibly abducting Aboriginal women when they could enlist the help of rival clans to do so.

The fourth significant theme to emerge from Kelly's report concerns the vulnerability of the British. They were clearly aware that the whole coast, apart from the small outpost at George Town, was under Aboriginal control. Kelly's estimates of the Aboriginal population were consistent with prevailing opinion, including the official census, which estimated the Aboriginal population as twice that of the whites. For the 1818 census, officials put the Aboriginal population at 7000 when the white population was 3240. Many settlers believed numbers were even higher. Williamson wrote in December 1820 that "the blacks are supposed to be about 10,000 in number but they have been driven mostly into the interior."[42] There was no basis for such estimates, but they do indicate that both the government and settlers believed they were outnumbered and had seen no evidence of any significant decline in the Aboriginal population.

Kelly's account also suggests that the impact of disease and violence on Aboriginal communities remained moderate. There is no evidence that there were few children or old people (who were most vulnerable to disease), or that, even in the north-east, Aboriginal groups had yet lost a critical mass of their young women. The circumnavigation of the island provides further proof that this was not the empty land that awaited the British in some areas of the mainland, where smallpox and other epidemics sometimes cleared the path for conquest. In Van Diemen's Land, 13 years after official white settlement began, and 18 years after the unofficial invasion commenced, Aboriginal political, economic and social structures were intact.

[8]

THE "SAVAGE LIFE" OF THE
VAN DIEMONIANS

WHAT WAS THE INFLUENCE OF the increasing cross-cultural contact evident between 1810 and 1820? How, for example, did red ochre – one of the most traded items in pre-settlement Aboriginal society – come to be so widely used by Europeans (in home decoration) that by early 1832 two Aborigines are recorded buying it from a Launceston store?[1]

The Aboriginal impact was twofold. First, the Aborigines, like the bushrangers, provided a "safety buffer" behind which hunters, shepherds and other itinerants could avoid regulation and supervision. Officers and masters, wary of the Aborigines, tended to keep their visits to remote regions brief, and not to take up permanent residence. Second, there was a degree of convergence in diet, clothing and housing (which will be considered in the next chapter). The difficulty for historians considering this cultural exchange is that only the outcome, not the process, can be described with confidence. While there was on occasion direct transfer of specific skills and technologies, in most cases the process was more complex. British customs and knowledge were gradually adapted to the new environment through, in part, observation of the Aboriginal way of life.

The sealing communities are the best documented example of the cultural melting pot of the Van Diemonian back-blocks. The *Sydney Gazette* described Captain Hammond's meeting with European men and Aboriginal women living on Kangaroo Island in a "curious state of independence" in 1817:

They are complete savages, living in bark huts like the natives, not cultivating anything, but living entirely on kangaroos, emus and small porcupines, and getting spirits and tobacco in barter for the skins which they capture during the sealing season. They dress in kangaroo skin without linen and wear sandals made of seal skin. They smell like foxes.[2]

John Boultbee, who stayed with one of the sealers' leaders, James Munro, on Preservation Island in September 1824, wrote that the women were "clothed in a kind of jackets made of kangaroo skins" and that the men's "general appearance is semi-barbarous ... They wear a kangaroo skin, coat, caps of the same and moccasins (a kind of sandal fastened with thongs of hide)."[3] Even a common dialect developed on the islands, which Robinson termed "island slang."[4]

Aboriginal influence was of course not confined to Bass Strait. Consider the use of fire, so central to both communities' lives. This example is particularly pertinent, for the Aborigines' supposed inability to make fire, an implausible but persistent hypothesis, is commonly cited as evidence of their "primitiveness."[5] As it did for the Aborigines, fire shaped the British use of the land and the emerging economy and society. By discouraging investment in permanent homes, farm buildings, fences or high-value breeding stock, the threat of fire made for a flexible, more provisional form of settlement and fostered semi-nomadic pastoral and hunting pursuits. Furthermore, it redistributed power from those with flammable property – and there was not much that didn't burn – to those without. The wife of George Meredith, for example, wanted a servant taken to Hobart "as she had suffered much abuse from her and was afraid she would burn the place."[6] Not surprisingly, it was the bushranger Michael Howe who made the most ambitious claims, informing Lieutenant Governor Davey in 1814 that his gang "could set the whole country on fire with one stick, and thrash in one night more than could be gathered in a year."[7] For all the dangers it posed, fire was a friend of the poor, and underpinned their social and economic freedom beyond the main settlements.

Fire was also essential for survival, and Aboriginal fire-technology was soon appropriated by the British. "Lucifer" matches were not invented until 1835, and even then, as the settler James Fenton noted, they could easily get wet, especially in winter when starting a fire could be vital for survival.[8] The established alternative, using flint and steel to light imported tinder (which was expensive and even harder to keep dry), did not make fire-making easy. The British residents of the bush sought out local substitutes and followed the Aboriginal example of keeping fires alight. James Ross wrote that "a settler should never be without his tinder box or substitute for it – the large perennial fungus, that grows sometimes to an enormous size on the trunks of the gum trees, commonly called punk, when dry serves as an excellent tinder, and as a match that will smoulder and hold fire for many hours."[9] William Thornley (the pseudonym of settler Charles Rowcroft) also "lighted a piece of charred punk," which he considered "as good for the purpose as the German tinder brought to the colony by some settlers." Others described using "two pieces of lighted stick, or charcoal" that "crossed and in contact will keep alight," and recognised that "the settlers have borrowed this trick from the natives."[10]

Controlled burns were integral to both hunting and farming in the grassland plains. Aboriginal burning regimes were more cost-efficient than the labour-intensive cultivation of introduced grasses, and as a consequence the latter was virtually unknown until the 1830s.[11] Early pastoralism relied on Aboriginal techniques, but in areas where Aborigines had been dispossessed, the British were forced to set the country on fire themselves. The east-coast settler Louisa Meredith noted in the 1830s that sheep owners "generally arrange to burn portions of their sheep runs at different times, so as to have a new growth about every three years. When this is neglected for a length of time … such a body of fuel forms that when a fire does reach it, the conflagration is thrice as mischievous in the destruction of fences as it otherwise would have been." Meredith was well aware that this approach did not originate "with the colonists," but that the Aborigines "practised it constantly."[12]

Historical Perspectives on Frontier Culture

The convergence in the ways of life of immigrant and Indigenous residents of Van Diemen's Land has been noted by historians. John West, in his *History of Tasmania*, pointed out that Britons living outside the settlements had a "way of life somewhat resembling that of the Aborigines." Drawing largely on oral memory, he painted a vivid picture of the Van Diemonian frontier:

> The agriculture of this colony was long trifling: the convicts were chiefly employed as stockmen and shepherds: from the banks of the Derwent to the district of Launceston, the land in general was a wilderness, unfenced and untenanted: the men, stationed 40 and 50 miles from their master's' dwellings, were rarely visited, and were under no immediate control. They were armed, to defend themselves from the natives, and clad in skins: they lived in turf huts, thatched with long grass, and revived the example of savage life.

West believed that the "degeneration" of Van Diemen's Land into savagery became pronounced after 1810: "while Governor Collins lived, some order was maintained: it was during the rule of his successor that the British standard covered a state of society, such as never before possessed the official sanction."[13]

West's emphasis on the wildness of Van Diemonian life was reiterated a century later by M.C.I. Levy: "The back areas of granted lands were peopled by stockmen and shepherds – a breed of folk as wild as the wastes around them."[14] More recently, Lloyd Robson recognised that "a subculture developed in the persons of those who found a hunting and wandering life to their taste." He viewed bushrangers as "consummate bushmen" who "dressed completely in kangaroo skins from cap to moccasin" and "swam easily in the sea of convict and ex-convict stockmen, hut-keepers and genial servants."[15]

But neither West, Levy nor Robson explored this sub-culture in any depth – its "savagery" both defined and marginalised it. Such neglect is often underpinned by the assumption that the evolving culture was a fringe phenomenon, confined to those isolated in the bush. What is missed is the extent to which this new culture permeated the settled districts, in an era when small farmers were as much hunters and nomadic pastoralists as agriculturalists.

Van Diemen's Land Farmers

By 1810 convicts who had left England in 1803 with seven-year sentences were free, and with only one convict ship coming from England before 1816 (the *Indefatigable* in 1812 with 149 male prisoners), those under sentence were reduced to 16 per cent of the population. Some secondary offenders were sent from Sydney, but in 1817 serving convicts made up only 17.7 per cent of the population. (By contrast, from 1818 through to the 1850s the proportion never again fell below 30 per cent.)[16] Before 1820 most former convicts were eligible for small land-grants and were largely free to live and work where they liked, provided they did not leave the island.

Most free immigrants who arrived during this period were also former convicts or their descendants. The Norfolk Islanders who arrived in Van Diemen's Land after 1805 were provided with small land-grants, mainly in Norfolk Plains (in the Longford area) and the Derwent Valley (around New Norfolk). The surveyor, G.P. Harris, was kept busy, writing in May 1808 that

> At the Derwent we are rapidly increasing in population and consequence as a settlement – the evacuation of Norfolk Island will when completed bring about 900 free persons into the colony … We have already about 300 arrived & I have been fully employed these last 6 months in measuring out … farms of 20 or 30 acres each.[17]

Because of their background, these new settlers did not have the impact one might expect from such a large influx. They had lived a simple, largely subsistence life on Norfolk Island, and most nineteenth-century historians and commentators remarked on their cultural affinity with the Van Diemonian lower orders. West's view was that "their hopeless and dissipated state is remarked in every document of the times: their frail dwellings soon exhibited all the signs of decay and their ground was exhausted by continued cropping." These views echoed those of the elite and have been widely reproduced by historians ever since.

Once the Norfolk Island evacuation was complete, there was very little further immigration, convict or free. The overall population increased relatively slowly, from 1321 in 1810 to 1933 in 1815,[18] and this meant the home-grown culture had many years to consolidate before immigration once more became a significant force for cultural change.

Farmers and the Bush

Although the island's economy at this time was based predominantly on the supply of meat and skins from the grassy woodlands, the smaller agricultural sector was closely integrated with this bush-based enterprise.

Although almost every crop grown in Britain did well in Van Diemen's Land (even some which were to disappear in years to come, such as hemp and grapes),[19] wheat was the main cash crop, and was "amply sufficient" in Port Dalrymple as early as 1810.[20] A drought in New South Wales in 1815 prompted the *Sydney Gazette* to declare that it was "a happiness to know that the Derwent crops are likely to be luxuriant, as from their redundancy we shall derive useful supplies." In June the following year, the *Hobart Town Gazette* reported that 25,000 bushels of wheat had been exported to Port Jackson, and remarked proudly that "nothing can show more the fertility of Van Diemen's Land, than the exuberance of our late harvest."[21]

Van Diemen's Land was in fact celebrated for its agricultural output, even as its farmers were widely condemned. The "problem" was that agricultural output seemed to bear no relation to the effort expended or the technology employed. Farmers were judged harshly because of their perceived failure to fulfil an English ideal of "real" farming and "honest" labour. Edward Curr warned potential immigrants in the early 1820s to "beware how he places himself amongst these people, for they are in general as poor and as flagitious as idleness, encouraged by the almost spontaneous fertility of their lands can make them."[22] Even Governor Macquarie's recognition of a "plentiful and abundant harvest" during his tour of the island in 1811 was qualified by an exhortation to farmers to strive for "industry, honesty, sobriety and morality."[23]

It is true that the agricultural revolution accelerating at this time in Britain had little effect on its faraway colony. In June 1816 the

Hobart Town Gazette reminded readers that "'Ye generous Britons venerate the plough,' is the exhortation of the melodious bard," but few were listening. Land clearing, artificial grasses, fencing, manuring and crop rotation were also ignored. Commissioner Bigge complained that he had seen no sign of any attempt to implement "any system of improvement," and that "the cultivation of artificial grasses in the southern part of Van Diemen's Land seemed to be altogether neglected." Furthermore, he found that "the cultivated lands of each farm are entirely open, and except upon an estate of Col. Davey and one of Mr Lord, I did not observe a single fence."[24] Curr lamented that "the beautiful appearance of a hedge … is unknown in Van Diemen's Land,"[25] while the author of another settler guide described a farm at Newtown as having "been in a state of cultivation during 12 or 13 years *without ever having been manured*." By some "miracle," the guide grudgingly acknowledged, "the sown ground has constantly averaged at the rate of 35 bushels of wheat per acre."[26]

The practice of "chipping in" wheat to unploughed, uncleared, unfenced and unmanured land has been used to condemn Van Diemonian smallholders for 200 years. However, contemporaries and historians are wrong to assume that these farming methods were inefficient. On the contrary, they met market demand with a low input of labour and capital – the usual definition of efficiency. The "slovenly" smallholders adopted a pragmatic approach, growing what they needed with the minimum of effort. [27] Even the free settlers had to acknowledge that in Van Diemen's Land, "those who were farmers at home" had no significant "advantage over their less experienced neighbours."[28]

There was in any case little incentive for producers to increase production. The domestic and export markets were limited, and the ever-present hazards of fire and wandering cattle, which could reduce a year's work to ashes or trampled fodder, made it foolish to over-invest. The 1820s free settlers had to discover this for themselves. At the Shannon, James Ross was "on all sides surrounded" by Edward Lord's cattle, which caused such damage that Ross "wished Mr Lord's cattle and himself … a hundred times back at Lawrenny or anywhere else in the remotest and most miserable part of Wales."[29]

Even more significantly, the market was becoming increasingly monopolised, with more and more farmers excluded from supplying the government store.[30] A farmer's viability in Van Diemen's Land was not determined by the size of his farm, but by the level of access enjoyed to the main cash market – the commissariat. The typical 30- or 60-acre farm[31] was not small even by late nineteenth-century English standards, and Surveyor Evans informed Bigge that Van Diemonian farms of this size were "fully capable of affording support to any person who cultivates it." Indeed, given the technology available, larger land-holdings could not achieve economies of scale; most of the recently arrived wealthier settlers with bigger land grants, Evans believed, had "done nothing," while, of the smaller landowners, "all those who have been industrious have been successful."[32]

Increasingly, however, many of these farmers were denied the opportunity to sell their product direct to the government. John Wade, a large farmer with 900 acres at Pitt Water, told Bigge that in 1819 "the whole of the settlers at Pitt Water were unable to send any wheat to the store on account of the distance from Hobart Town, the stores being filled before the settlers could arrive with it." Anthony Fenn Kemp, a leading merchant, told Bigge that "when ... grain is wanted, it has been the practice for the commissary to advertise and to state that the stores are open for the reception of wheat, and when they have the quantity they want, the stores are shut."[33] It is not surprising that the 12 dealers who mainly supplied the store in 1820 were merchant-farmers with warehouses near the commissariat.[34] Others were left with no option but to sell their crop at reduced prices to these same merchants, who then sold it on at inflated prices. Many farmers were forced into debt, with credit supplied by the same small group.

The dubious character of those in power exacerbated the problem. Thomas Archer, in charge of the store from 1813 to 1817 at Port Dalrymple, discriminated against small farmers in both wheat and meat purchases, and in doing so enriched his own pocket, laying the foundation for his subsequent fortune. Archer admitted that when he began to employ tenders, he "took respectability into account." He also acknowledged that there were frequent deficiencies in what was tendered and what was needed, and that "of those who supplied deficiencies ... Mr Lord supplied very large quantities." Archer sometimes even supplied goods to the store himself, explaining to the commissioner that "Mr Lord lent me the meat," and that this was "part of the patronage of the Commissariat Department."[35]

There were few safeguards in place against such abuses. As their debts to the merchants increased, many small farmers were forced to use their land and stock as security to obtain goods on credit. And the merchants proved to be a litigious and unforgiving lot when a bad harvest or low prices meant repayments fell behind schedule. The lieutenant-governor's court spent much of its time giving legal sanction to the seizure of the assets of the poor. Three-hundred-and-five suits ended in the issuing of writs, almost all to small farmers, and many led to properties being forfeited.[36] By early 1824 Barnes believed that "half the small farmers are ruined ... The merchants are selling them up every day."[37] As one historian concluded, "large merchant graziers obtained improved agricultural land by extension of credit and foreclosure."[38]

The concentration of land and profit had one unexpected consequence. It meant that for most farmers, agriculture was largely focused on self-sufficiency – they relied on the resources of the bush and unallocated pasture-lands beyond the settled districts to generate a cash income. Both those who clung to their small holdings and the growing class of landless poor were dependent on the unallocated "common" land, with the result that frontier culture permeated far beyond frontier regions. Whether hunters, shepherds or farmers, Van Diemonians relied on the bush.

Products of the Land

On 8 October 1823 two ships left Sullivans Cove with characteristic and illuminating cargoes. The *Lusitania* took on board 26 bundles of kangaroo-skin, five tons of wattle bark, one bale of possum fur and one bale and two cases of sundry skins, 52 bolts of whale bone and 61 casks of oil. The *Regalia* had sealskins, wool, wattle bark (for tanning leather), Huon Pine, "cedar" (probably blackwood or sassafras), possum fur and black-swan skins.[39] These products were being exported by a small number of settlers, and the profit was concentrated in their hands, but a large number of ordinary Van Diemonians had supplied them.

Nor should the level of domestic demand be underestimated. The fact that Van Diemen's Land was a penal colony, with a high proportion of the population in the employ or service of government, provided an engine for economic growth that even significantly larger British colonies lacked. According to Hamish Maxwell-Stewart,

> Small-scale settlers used their land to provide timber for the Hobart market. Other settlers combined farming with ship and boat building, brewing, baking, flour milling, inn keeping, transport services, tanning and shoe making, to name but a few ... in a majority of cases the land continued to supply the raw materials upon which other activities relied, for example, flour, barley, wood, stone, hides, meat, brick earth, charcoal, bark and shells.[40]

Before the early 1820s, nearly everyone – even convicts in Hobart Town – had ready access to unallocated land, and thus to resources that could be traded with little or no capital investment. This meant that bush-based enterprise was not only the prerogative of the free. Convicts were encouraged to engage in self- or paid employment outside the hours set for government labour. Furthermore, before the early 1820s, those working in lime kilns or harvesting timber usually had government quotas to fulfil rather than set hours of work, and thereafter could work for themselves. Some assigned convicts before the mid 1820s were set free by their masters to pursue economic independence in return for a weekly fee.

What almost all workers had in common was a dependence on the resources of the bush. By 1820 a complex economy had emerged, closely integrated with agriculture and pastoralism and directly based on the natural bounty of the land. With little start-up capital, former convicts and even those still under sentence could achieve a significant degree of economic independence. Although markets, and thus profits, were concentrated and controlled, access to the land's resources was not. To take advantage of this natural wealth, however, a degree of environmental adaptation was required. In the bush surrounding the two settled districts, across the grassy woodlands that stretched between them, and in the accessible coastal bays, estuaries and offshore islands, a distinctively Van Diemonian way of life was born.

FOOD, CLOTHING AND SHELTER

FOR MOST CONVICTS TRANSPORTED TO Van Diemen's Land before the mid 1820s, their new home had at least one advantage over England: the food. There was an abundance of high-protein indigenous foods – shellfish, swan, seal, emu and, above all, kangaroo – and, from 1810, mutton and beef. Back in England, the recession that began after the Napoleonic wars continued into the 1820s, and many labourers went hungry. Hunger riots occurred in 1816, and an 1826 government report found that in many rural regions wages were "utterly insufficient to supply that population with those means of support and subsistence."[1] Fresh meat remained a rare luxury for large segments of the population until living standards finally began to rise consistently in the mid nineteenth century.[2] The settler William Williamson might have exaggerated, but the contrast he drew in 1820 between "our starving countrymen in England" and Van Diemonians who "grumble excessively if they don't have three fresh joint meals a day" was nevertheless a legitimate one.[3]

Kangaroo continued to be the leading indigenous food source. It was eaten in different ways, although the most characteristic and enduring "national dish" became the "steamer," which probably emerged from the pre-1813 convict ration – which often combined fresh kangaroo with salted pork. Jeffreys described the first meal of his assigned convicts at his new property as the hind-quarters of a kangaroo cut into mince-meat, stewed in its own gravy, with a few rashers of salt pork. This dish is commonly called a steamer, they add to that a sufficient quantity of potatoes, and a large cake [damper] baked on the spot.[4]

The steamer was enjoyed by all classes. In 1823, the newly arrived free settler Samuel Guy declared that kangaroo "is beautiful roasted or steamed in its own gravy with a piece of pork – tis astonishing what a quantity of rich gravy it will produce." The poet and novelist Mary Grimstone called the "kangaroo steamer" a "Van Diemen's Land luxury."[5] Kangaroo soup, made using the tail, was also standard, and much enjoyed, fare.

Later historians who dismissed kangaroo as "not even as good as mutton" would find few to back this claim in Van Diemen's Land.[6] Williamson's opinion that kangaroo was "as good as any venison" was more typical.[7] When the first Australian cookbook was published in the 1860s in Tasmania, Edward Abbot included in it a number of long-established recipes for cooking 'roo.

Seafood, especially the familiar oyster, was another excellent source of protein, so easily procured that it scarcely seems to have been traded until it became a significant export commodity in later decades. As Williamson observed, "Oysters and other shell fish are got for the trouble of picking them up at low water."[8]

A few new indigenous meats also entered the colonists' diet, especially in areas where larger native animals were no longer to be found (which was much of the settled districts by 1830). Evans noted that "wattle bird is here reckoned a great delicacy."[9] Kelly and his crew in 1816 ate wombats, seals, swans and a variety of eggs. In 1839 Thomas Lempriere, a public official, diarist and keen naturalist, wrote that the "the echidna is common and in the absence of fresh meat makes an excellent dish," noting that "when properly stuffed with sage and onion and roasted" it had "all the flavour and taste of a goose." He also recommended young wombat roasted like sucking-pig, but warned that "the older animal is only fit for soup."[10]

The short-tailed shearwater, or mutton bird, was perhaps the most important new indigenous meat source from 1810. Although particularly associated with sealers of the Bass Strait, both fresh and salted birds (along with their eggs, feathers and eventually oil) were also consumed on the mainland of Van Diemen's Land. The hunting and use of mutton birds reflected both Aboriginal and British traditions, and the impact of the cross-cultural encounter. As Irynej Skira and others have pointed out, eating and preserving sea birds and their eggs had long been a part of life in coastal regions of the British Isles.[11] Indeed, some offshore British islands, such as St Kilda, were almost totally dependent on sea birds like the fulmar. As with the mutton bird, the fulmar chicks were harvested "when the young birds are at their fattest, but just before they have learnt to fly."[12] They too had to be caught by hand and quickly killed by twisting their neck lest the oil – used for various purposes, including medicinal – be lost before it could be drained out. In both hemispheres feathers were plucked for down.

Despite this heritage, however, the early British hunting of the mutton bird had more in common with Aboriginal practices and focused on the birds' value as fresh food. Only after the Aborigines were permanently confined to offshore islands on or near major rookeries were British traditions drawn on and the birds put to more varied use.

Shearwaters, wattle birds, wombats and even kangaroo notwithstanding, by 1820 mutton had once again become the main meat consumed by the British residents of Van Diemen's Land. The traditional British meat was eaten both fresh and salted. Good quality salt was imported from Kangaroo Island, although a rougher variety described by Williamson as "very coarse indeed" and by Rowcroft as "blackish and gritty" was available locally from the heart of the pastoral and hunting region at Salt Pan Plains.[13] Virtually unlimited mutton became a right of workers, convict and free, in the grassy woodlands until well into the 1830s. This was in contrast to the mother colony at Port Jackson, where, as Curr noted, it was "not usual to allow farm servants anything beyond what is required to be given to them by government regulations."[14] Even as late as 1834, one settler, Ellen Viveash, complained of having to kill 400 sheep a year to feed "our numerous fencers and builders."[15]

Apart from meat, the only foods much eaten were wheat and potatoes. The convict John Broxup, who was marched for eight days from Hobart Town to Launceston, wrote of his journey:

> We made large fires of wood and bark, and when the wood and bark had burned down we would open the ashes and put the dough in and then cover it with the ashes from the wood and it produced as good bread as ever was eaten.[16]

The making of damper reflected cultural heritage as well as environmental necessity. The "open-hearth baking of breads" was traditional to both the Scots and the Irish.[17]

Potatoes were not as important during this era – their weight made them difficult to transport – but they were grown by smallholders; according to Oxley, they were produced "in great perfection."[18] Knopwood reported in March 1808 that there were two tons of potatoes in the store and that no more were needed.

A noticeable change from the English diet was the almost complete absence of dairy foods before the 1830s. In July 1831, a newly arrived free settler, Mrs Fenton, could not find any milk for her baby even near the comparatively densely settled New Norfolk, and asked her servant what the children lived on. "Please mam, fried meat and tea," came the response.[19]

Comparatively little use was made of indigenous plant foods, although, as Lempriere observed, the "native potato" and "native bread" were eaten:

> The *gastrodia sessamoides* or native potato … is in general to be found among the roots of decayed trees and is parasitical … They eat best roasted or if after being boiled, they are fried. The native bread is a tuber which grows to the size of a man's head, the rind of which is a very dark brown. When cut the inside bears an exact resemblance to rice boiled hard and in flavour and taste, is nearly the same. It has been found at Port Arthur weighing as much as 27 pounds.

Fern root, the most widely available plant food in Tasmania, and another Aboriginal staple, was also eaten or drunk. Even Alexander Pearce, the runaway cannibal from Macquarie Harbour, did not survive on human flesh alone, but "boiled some fern and drank it."[20] Evans cited a few edible plants, including *scheffleria* ("a new species of parsley, good to eat"), *plantago trienspedita* ("good to eat in salad, and one of the most useful plants this island furnishes") and "a new species of ficoide, the fruit of which the natives eat" (although Evans' natural history observations must be treated with caution. He quotes the French naturalist Labillardiere as saying that kangaroos lived "in burrows like a rabbit"!).[21] Lempriere also wrote of "the *solanum macinatul* or kangaroo apple … a very handsome plant and the fruits, when perfectly ripe, pleasant to taste," and the "*polygonum adpressum* or Macquarie Harbour grape," which he described as one of the "greatest ornaments in most of the gardens of Hobart Town in covering arbours, fences, etc." It produced "a fruit of a sub-acid taste, excellent for tarts and preserves," and "leaves and branches [that] taste like sorrel and have been used as an anti-scorbutic medicine."[22]

A number of plants were drunk as tea. Jeffreys noted that the bushrangers "drunk a decoction of the sassafras and other shrubs, particularly one which they call the tea-tree bush."[23] Most invigorating of the indigenous beverages was a mildly intoxicating drink made by replicating the Aboriginal custom of tapping the sap of the cider gum (*Eucalyptus gunnii*) in the Central Highlands.[24] Lieutenant William Breton reported that

> The shepherds and stock-keepers which tend the flocks and herds on that elevated region are in the habit of making deep incisions wherever an exudation of the sap is perceived upon the bark. The holes are made in such a manner as to retain the sap that flows into them, and large enough to hold a pint. Each tree yields from half to a pint daily during December and January, but the quantity lessens in February and soon ceases.[25]

George Augustus Robinson found most of the Central Plateau trees had been tapped in late 1831. "In some of these holes," he wrote, "I observed upwards of a quart of this juice," which "my people greedily partook of." Robinson himself, evangelical Methodist and stalwart of the Bethel Peniel Mission, also enjoyed the drink, finding it to be "exceedingly sweet and well flavoured."[26]

Because of the difficulty of establishing which plants were potential food and medicinal sources by any other means, it is almost certain that the knowledge of them – so much more widespread then than in contemporary Tasmania – initially came through observation of, and interaction with, the Aborigines. The *Hobart Town Gazette* provides a rare record of this:

> On Saturday afternoon as some labourers were employed in ploughing a small allotment of ground in Argyle St, the plough unexpectedly came in contact with a large root of a fungous nature. Several natives being on the spot, eagerly ran after one of the men … exclaiming 'Bringally' (for bread-root); they quickly devoured large pieces of it. The owner of the ground (William Aston in Liverpool St) has some of this extraordinary production of nature in his possession, where it has been viewed and tasted by several persons, who esteem it is palatable.[27]

The other significant elements of the Van Diemonian diet were tea and sugar. These products were consumed in prodigious quantities. As Williamson wrote, "fine sugar is got from the East Indies 4d per pound which in England would cost 1s … tea [is] also cheap."[28] Tea and sugar were often supplied to stockmen and shepherds, including convicts – not only at levels well above the official ration but often without any restrictions whatsoever – and formed a substantial part of the employer's total costs. William Barnes wrote from Launceston in May 1824 of the "very foolish custom prevalent in both these colonies of giving servants tea and sugar morning and evening" amounting to "three ounces of tea and a pound of sugar every week."[29] Such generosity may have reflected the fact that the workers traded these products with the Aborigines in exchange for land access. Tea and sugar had, along with flour, been integrated into the diet of Aborigines on the grassy woodlands by the early 1820s, with regular visits to stock huts to obtain supplies an accepted part of life.

Clothing

From about 1808 until well into the 1820s, European clothing was rarely seen outside the two main settlements. This had less to do with availability and expense than with preference: animal-skin clothing proved far warmer and more water-resistant than clothing made of cotton or hemp, and had the added advantage of being easily obtainable for those living in the bush.

Jeffreys recorded that bushrangers "construct their clothing of kangaroo skins, which they make into jackets, waistcoats, trowsers, shoes, hats and rugs to sleep in. Their thread is made of the sinews of the leg and tail of the same animal."[30] Wells wrote in 1819 that Howe "wore at the time of his death a dress made of kangaroo skins."[31] Their pursuers soon followed suit. James Ross wrote of an encounter in the Central Highlands in the mid 1820s:

> we surrounded the hut, I peeped through the crevices between the logs, and there I saw not four but five men in bush dresses, but three of them [were] soldiers of the 48th, whose faces were well known to me, guarding two bushrangers who they had apprehended near the Lakes the day before.[32]

David Burn confirmed the widespread military preference for clothing made from native animals:

> When the military were detached in pursuit of bushrangers, they were rarely, if ever, in uniform; their dress consisting of a grey jacket and trousers, trimmed with fur, kangaroo-skin knapsack, opossum-skin cap, and kangaroo cartouch-box. This garb the bushrangers closely copied; hence mistakes constantly arose.[33]

One such mistake occurred in 1816 when James Kelly and his fellow expeditioners arrived at George Town and were rushed by eight other Europeans "dressed in kangaroo skin." These men proved to be soldiers who had, in turn, thought that Kelly and his party were bush-rangers.[34]

Even in the main settlements, British-made clothing was worn only by a minority: the officers, senior government officials and the few better-off free immigrants. James Dixon, who visited in 1820, reported that "servants generally make kangaroo-skin jackets, and shoes of something of the same sort. Many of the settlers who are poor, frequently dress in articles of the same description."[35] And kangaroo- and possum-skin rugs were widely used, even by the social elite. By the late 1830s Lempriere could distinguish between the fur of the wallaby and the kangaroo and expressed a preference for the former:

> The fur of these animals is far superior in colour and softness to that of the kangaroo, but the skins are smaller. Wallaby rugs and cloaks are much esteemed for the bush. Every person who had occasion to travel through the uninhabited parts of the colony can testify to the comfort of a good fur rug. They are in general about seven feet square, one half is laid under the body as a mattress, the other serves as a blanket.[36]

Kangaroo-skin knapsacks were also common, being the standard means of carrying essentials in a land where most journeys were still made on foot (horses were uncommon before the 1820s, and remained out of reach of most Van Diemonians throughout the convict era). Surveyor and explorer John Helder Wedge recorded in April 1828 that before setting out on an expedition he "purchased 60 kangaroo skins," and that his men spent that day "employed making knap-sacks."[37] A Victorian squatter noted as late as the 1840s that Van Diemonians could be distinguished from Sydneysiders by their kangaroo knapsacks or "Derwent drums."[38]

The growing similarity of British and Aboriginal clothing and accessories is striking, but it was only in the widespread adoption of Aboriginal "thongs" that indigenous garb was exactly reproduced. The Aborigines' use of pieces of kangaroo-skin fixed to the feet with sinew was first recorded by Cook,[39] and Van Diemonian Britons soon recognised their usefulness. Wells recorded that in May 1817 a military party chasing bushrangers had been "reduced to eat the skin mocassons from their feet."[40] Howe's gang had reportedly been making replacement moccasins when surprised by an ambush.[41] Such footwear, however, remained largely confined to bushmen and bushrangers, and in April 1823 the east-coast settler Adam Amos equated it with a "suspicious appearance."[42]

Shelter

A vernacular Van Diemonian architecture emerged early and developed two main forms: temporary structures designed for ease of movement through the grassy woodlands, and more permanent huts for long-term use.

Tents were of little use as temporary shelters because they were too heavy to carry without horses, in short supply and ineffective in extreme weather. They were thus almost never used, although probably for appearance's sake the officers and free settlers occasionally sheltered under them.

As in the first years of settlement, the easiest option was to seek out natural shelter: caves, rock overhangs and the hollowed-out trunks of large trees. The land commissioners came across a man "whose abode was a cave in the rocks," and three men who lived in a cave near Baghdad.[43] George Augustus Robinson, while in the northwest, "saw several large hollowed stringy bark trees, some of them 12 feet in diameter, which had been burnt by the natives."[44] With "the natives playing at snow balls," Robinson took his "abode" in one such shelter and "though the weather was excessively cold … we felt no ill effect." Later a Van Diemen's Land Company official showed Robinson "the hollow trees the men had dwelt in at the commencement of this establishment."[45]

Temporary huts, not dissimilar to those constructed by Aborigines, were the most common form of short-term accommodation. These, in fact, were integral to the semi-nomadic lifestyle of kangaroo hunters, stockmen, sealers, bushrangers and even small farmers. The style of these "brush huts" or "break winds" varied, but they were usually variations on the distinctive Van Diemonian A-frame, formed, as Burn described, "of the boughs of trees and sometimes thatched in a rude manner with long grass" or strips of bark.[46]

It is likely that they were inspired by similar designs already dotting the landscape. Aboriginal architecture at this time was not derided as it would be in later years: Jeffreys believed that "the houses, or huts, are much better formed than those of the Port Jackson natives" and "the huts made by the natives of Van Diemen's Land approach nearer the principles of regular architecture."[47]

The details of housing construction were rarely described. Robinson, for example, stayed in these temporary huts most nights when in the bush over a period of nearly five years, but never once bothered to describe their construction in his lengthy journal (despite giving details of the Aboriginal equivalents). It is clear, however, that they were erected by Robinson's convict assistants, not the Aborigines, who left mundane labour to these men and showed a reluctance to construct the emissary a shelter even when no servants were available.[48]

James Ross provided the best description of hut design. On arrival at his new land grant at the Shannon River, his men

> proceeded to cut down some poles, of which we formed the skeleton of a temporary hut or shelter. These poles, the sprouts of young trees, grew around us, as they do in almost every part of Van Diemen's Land, tall and straight as a May pole. By tying two together within a few inches of the upper end, and fixing the others about three yards apart in the ground, we formed a good gable. The same was repeated a few yards off to form the other end of our intended wigwam, and by laying a pole with its extremities resting in the forks which the points of these gable pieces formed, the ridge was erected. We then cut some thick, umbrageous boughs and laid all round, leaving an opening at one end for a door or window.[49]

More sophisticated versions took a day or so to build and were more durable. Jeffreys described how his men built "a house rendered watertight" before sunset.[50]

In the settlements and on outlying smallholdings, somewhat grander huts were built. By 1820, English wattle and daub techniques had largely been supplanted by less labour-intensive and more environmentally effective methods. Log huts became the norm, made of split timber, with shingles usually replacing reeds as roofing. Guy wrote in 1823: "the stringy bark is in general used for building timber and the peppermint for shingles – they are extremely hard and durable when seasoned." The shift to shingles was in part because of their resistance to fire.[51]

Ross described the process of constructing a more permanent log hut that began with chopping down a nearby stringy bark. A 12-foot piece was then selected and

> we rolled it out with the handspikes or small wooden levers which we cut down from the bush beside us, and began to divide and subdivide it with wedges. It split with great ease in the straightest form, and with surfaces almost as smooth as if they had been planed. We obtained from it 50 to 60 logs, or planks of from 8 to 12 inches wide, and about one and a half or two inches thick.[52]

To construct the hut itself, which was "generally of two apartments, an eating and a sleeping-room," Burn noted,

> four strong corner posts were sunk, then a somewhat lighter sort were up reared, into which were afterwards inserted the doors and windows. Strong wall-plates are then laid along; these are, in some instances, grooved; a heavy log, with a corresponding groove, being partially sunk in the earth beneath. Split gum or stringy bark slabs are then inserted and hammered close together, until the wooden wall becomes complete. Where the groove is unused, the one end of the slab is nailed against the wall-plate, the other being sunk some six or eight inches in to the soil, in either case one of the gables is left for the chimney, whose ample dimensions and primitive masonry fills up the entire of this space. The tie-beams, connecting the wall-plates, are frequently adzed; and these, being laid with boards, serve as excellent bed-chambers for the juvenile branches. Thatch was the usual covering, until the hostile blacks rendered shingles necessary, as a precaution against their blazing fire-spears.[53]

The American influence, particularly the "midland tradition" – which evolved from Finnish and Scandinavian influences – is strongly evident in this Van Diemonian architecture. The British traditionally knew nothing of log-hut building, and it was not until the mid eighteenth century that the English, Scots and Irish in North America had generally adopted midland designs. Whole log huts, using notches rather than nails, were the most common, but there was "a second less common American pioneer method" which involved "split-log" construction – whereby the timber was split lengthways as with fence rails – and it was this technique that became standard in Van Diemen's Land. Huts with interstices between the slabs, made airtight by "daubing," were also characteristic of the midland tradition. British influences on American log cabins had included the square shape, with centred front and rear doors and the chimney centrally positioned in the gable wall,[54] and this style also became the norm in Van Diemen's Land.

This vernacular architecture was widely employed in Tasmania until the 1950s, and even today the skills have not been entirely lost. Its great virtue was its accessibility. Those without capital were able to build their own huts without borrowing money or paying rent; the building materials were freely available in the bush and could be obtained with nothing more than an axe. Moreover, easy to replace, these huts were well suited to the Van Diemen's Land environment, especially to the ever-present threat of fire.

Even in Hobart Town, convicts commonly constructed their own accommodation until the mid 1820s, and some even received the indulgence of an allotment of land to build on. These were not legal land grants but, as Surveyor Evans explained, "the convicts look upon them as property and treat them as such, for they dispose of them in their life time and by will."[55] The usual block size was a quarter acre[56]; consequentially, as Boyes wrote in November 1826, Hobart Town was spread over "three times the space of ground" as an equivalent-size English village.[57]

Before the early 1820s, there was little official control exerted over the type of house built by the convicts. The most common style was referred to as a "skilling":

When a person of small means can procure an order (which is not only given to emancipated convicts, but also the prisoners of the crown) for an allotment of ground in the town, he usually commences by building what is called a *skilling* or *lean-to*, which composes the rear of his future house, and as his means improve he erects a front. The same method is pursued in all parts of the colony.[58]

George Thomas Lloyd, who arrived in 1820, recalled that Hobart Town then had only about "15 or 20 buildings in it worthy of the designation of dwelling houses." The remainder, "in number about 250," were constructed "of various materials, such as split palings, wickerwork bedaubed with clay, and log and turf cabins of all orders of low architecture."[59]

The authorities hoped that these homes would give convicts a motive to conform. Humphrey informed Bigge that convicts "become correct in their behaviour when they are possessed of a house and a small piece of land ... for if such persons are punished ... they are obliged to leave their property and to forego all the comforts it afforded them."[60] He believed that "allowing the unassigned convicts to find their own lodgings ... tends to their moral improvement more than that of locking them up all together."[61] Such were the philosophical origins of Australian suburbia.

Despite its practical advantages, Van Diemonian architecture has generally been measured against the neatness and order of the English countryside and found lacking. Governor Macquarie noted during his 1811 tour that "the habitations of the settlers are wretchedly mean."[62] Nearly a decade later, Bigge expressed similar sentiments, reporting that "habitations are small, and in a state of great dilapidation."[63] Curr, while more positive about Hobart Town, described the 250 houses at Launceston as "hovels" and warned prospective immigrants that "the mention of a farmhouse" must not "mislead," as these were

so opposite to the comfort, neatness, convenience and frugality, which are conspicuous on the first approach to houses of a similar class in England. Though it would be too much to expect the economy, good order, and comfortable appearance in a new colony, where there has as yet been time for little more than what is necessary for existence; yet we too frequently see in the cottages and fields, much to remind us of the idleness and profligacy in which a great proportion of the inhabitants have been brought up, and but for which they would never have been colonists in Van Diemen's Land.[64]

"Progress" meant a move from a rough bush structure to a stone and brick residence. At least, that was the well-documented experience of a small group of wealthy immigrants. The Meredith family on the east coast, for example, moved in 1822 from their first "turf cottage" to a "more substantial" wattle and daub home and finally, in 1836, to the substantial stone residence that was intended as the permanent family "seat." The daughter of another family, Mary Morton Allport, sketched the move from "Our winter quarters" in 1832 – a bush A-frame hut – to, ultimately, one of the large Georgian-style stone dwellings that remain a familiar feature of the midlands today.[65] This was not, however, the experience of most people. Prominent observers believed that people *should* be seeking to build English-style farmhouses and cottages, but there is little evidence that, outside a wealthy minority, many did so.[66] In fact, the large majority of the population were felt to be disturbingly satisfied with what they had. Macquarie, Curr and the land commissioners all echoed James Atkinson's sentiment that far too many Van Diemonians had grown accustomed to living in bark huts.[67]

[10]

WINE, WOMEN AND SONG

I N 1822 THE NEWLY ARRIVED CATHOLIC chaplain, Phillip
Connolly, wrote to Bishop Poynter in London that there was a
"degree of unusual levity and wildness" about the native-born, "which
some persons say, I think with justice, they derive from their intercourse with the indigenous inhabitants."[1] According to John Henderson, who spent a year in the colony in 1829–30, it was "extraordinary
that the removal of a native of England from his own country to
another, peopled by British subjects, should occasion an alteration in
his national disposition; such, however … is the case … The descent
of mankind towards a savage life is easy and rapid." For Henderson,

> the free low-born European soon acquires a thorough acquaint-
> ance with the evil practices of the convict, and speedily becomes
> as little worthy of confidence; while at the same time he imbibes
> such ideas of liberty, equality and independence … that he is
> found to be afterwards completely incapacitated for the situation
> of a subordinate. [2]

Some visitors were more positive about the emerging local character. Hospitality was highly valued, and Ross reported that "the
traveller was sure to meet with a kind reception wherever he went."
Thornley observed that a visitor would be "quickly shown into the
house and, according to the custom of the colony, food and drink
were placed before him ere he was troubled with any questions."

And Louisa Meredith wrote home that "the unfailing mark of hospitality" in Van Diemen's Land was "a steaming tea-pot of gigantic capacity."[3]

For 200 years, however, observers have generally maligned the morals of the men and women of Van Diemen's Land. Their love of the pub, the roles assigned to women and their lack of religion have been both condemned and caricatured. But how fair is this assessment, and how did the unique economic and social conditions of the new land contribute to its distinctive moral climate?

Marriage and Morality

Much of the condemnation of the moral degeneracy of Van Diemen's Land has its origin in the nineteenth-century evangelical revival, with its rigid belief in the evils of sex outside marriage. But, as we have seen, to a significant extent Van Diemonian society reflected the values of an earlier era – the late eighteenth century, which had quite different norms.[4] Even John West acknowledged this: "the tastes of society have since that period been mollified, even in Great Britain; and that character can never be fairly judged when separated from the circumstances in which it is developed."[5] Nevertheless, negative judgments have persisted. One historian has described Van Diemen's Land as a "great mass of vice and corruption;"[6] another has argued that "the moral tone of the settlement was appallingly low; every kind of immorality thrived;"[7] and still another that "convicts and officers lived in a sort of moral anarchy."[8]

There may be some truth to these allegations, but the pattern of relationships between men and women in early Van Diemen's Land provides little evidence of it. Society in this era was in many respects more respectful of women and children than in later years. Children born out of wedlock, and the women who bore them, were not automatically shunned. Many unmarried couples lived openly together in committed relationships. Dr Bowden and Maria Sergeant, the wife of a marine, were examples of the extent to which an "adulterous" relationship could nevertheless be a loving and stable one. Their partnership lasted from the voyage from London in 1803 until Bowden's death in 1814. On his tomb in St David's Park, Hobart, Maria had inscribed that their two children were left "with a disconsolate mother to lament the loss of their dear protector who fulfilled the duties of an affectionate father, a tender husband and a faithful friend."[9]

Even the governors' relationships reflected the moral norms of Van Diemen's Land. Sorell's relationship with his partner, Louisa Kent, was a marriage in all but name. Collins' two relationships were more akin to serial monogamy than degraded vice, and the children he had with Margaret "Peggy" Eddington were publicly acknowledged, provided for and given his name. Bowen's two daughters with Martha Hayes were similarly treated.[10] While the age and power gaps between the governors and the 14- and 15-year-old Eddington and Hayes are disturbing to modern sensibilities, at least Bowen and Collins did not hide their relationships or abandon their illegitimate children.

Even the implications of a documented wife-sale in 1817 – commonly cited as proof of moral depravity[11] – are not straightforward. The *Hobart Town Gazette* reported that a wife had been sold for a gallon of rum and 20 ewes. E.P. Thompson argues that wife-sales became more common in the late eighteenth century and puts them in the context of divorce and remarriage, with the purchaser often the wife's lover. In a society with no legal means of divorce except for the rich, and "in a plebeian culture which … had a high regard for rituals and forms," the public nature of the exchange was important for both parties, although the gender power-imbalance and the potential for abuse remained.[12]

The customs of "plebeian" England are a better guide to Van Diemonian sexual norms than the judgments of a later era and a different social class. John Pascoe Fawkner, himself the son of a convict, was one of the few commentators to put the moral character of early Van Diemen's Land in context, and his recognition of "the prevalence of so much good moral conduct in the face of all this evil" seems a balanced one.[13]

The Status of Women

Violence and oppression were widespread for women, and Robson's view that "the few adult females were extremely vulnerable"[14] is indisputable. Yet a relatively relaxed morality and the small number of women in the colony also carried certain advantages. Although "the need for a protector ... characterised the female convict experience and marked out its difference from that of the male convict,"[15] the gender imbalance at least gave women some degree of choice. Female-initiated separations – criminal behaviour in England – were reasonably common. The *Hobart Town Gazette* regularly carried notices from men advising that their wives had deserted them and that they would not be responsible for any debts incurred.[16] Sometimes separation was amicable: Charles Fletcher advised in July 1819 that no credit was to be provided to his wife, a "mutual separation having taken place between us."[17] But antagonism was more common, and the husband's legal right to prosecute anyone who harboured his "stolen property" was occasionally brandished, though with little apparent effect. For example, in May 1819 William Ashton publicly advised that his wife, Elizabeth, had left him and that "person or persons harbouring, concealing or maintaining her after this notice will be prosecuted ... and who ever will give me information where she is ... shall receive on conviction of the party or parties, the above reward [ten pounds]." In the same edition, John Cummings also gave notice that he would prosecute anyone concealing his wife Anne or helping her to leave the colony after "absenting herself for some years."[18]

The bush could be a refuge from angry and vengeful husbands, especially if the husband wielded official power. Josepit Martin, constable, advised in February 1818 that his wife had "withdrawn herself from her home without any just provocation and absconded into the woods with Benjamin Gibbs, an absentee."[19] She returned, but on Boxing Day 1818, Josepit warned that "whereas my wife Jane Martin is again walked away ... and I hear has taken with a fellow who looked after cattle in the neighbourhood of the Macquarie River ... I will not pay for bite or sip or for anything she may contract on my account to man or mortal and that I am determined to prosecute with the utmost rigour the law will admit any person or persons who may harbour or conceal or maintain the said runaway Jane Martin."

One *Hobart Town Gazette* account suggests that some jilted husbands were more distraught than angry, with the bush a refuge from their hurt and shame. In July 1816 Thomas Frisk was reported to have disappeared; it was feared he had killed himself in consequence of his partner leaving him. A week later he returned, "after several days wandering in the woods barefooted," although he soon left again, "taking with him his whole flock of sheep."[20]

Even when women stayed with their partners, the possibility of leaving must have given many women greater bargaining power and some level of protection from abuse. Certainly, whatever the perils of relationships, most Van Diemonian women seemed to prefer them to the often more dangerous servitude of domestic service – the main alternative for poor women in Britain. Former convicts, the native born and even sponsored immigrants consistently avoided domestic service. The settler Thomas Parramore advised his fiancée in England that "the women are very independent and are almost sure to be married before the end of their service. Never think for a moment of bringing one out; the only benefit you would receive from it would be paying her passage."[21]

The shortage of free domestics meant many middle- and upper-class families had to rely on assigned convicts instead. This gave rise to a common complaint: "It is almost impossible for those families who study the quiet and morality of their children to endure the female convicts," wrote Elizabeth Leake in 1835.[22] The implacably anti-transportationist John West lamented that in Van Diemen's Land could be found "all the advantages of opulence, except what money could not procure – a comely and honest-hearted woman servant."[23]

In the early years, even convict women could sometimes avoid domestic service. Until the mid 1820s, women regularly left their assigned positions to marry or live with a man and often, especially if that man was a soldier or official, little was done about it. George Hull complained in 1824 that his servant, Mary Higgins, had left his home in George Town to live with a soldier. He conceived it "to be almost absurd to keep any female in the home while any inducements are held out to them to act as Mary Higgins had done – and while they are afterwards allowed to go unpunished and live without restraint."[24] Evidence given to the Bigge Inquiry in 1820 confirmed that virtually all the female convicts at George Town and Port Dalrymple lived with soldiers or settlers.

Punishing female convicts was in any case not a straightforward matter. Flogging, road gangs and places of secondary punishment were ruled out by regulation, and Sorell's request for a female factory (gaol) was knocked back by Macquarie because of the expense (he suggested that recalcitrant women be sent to Parramatta, and a small number were). Few punishments were legally available before the female factories were eventually constructed in the late 1820s and early 1830s, although the iron collar (literally a large collar of iron placed around the neck) was occasionally, if illegally, used[25] and stocks were erected for a time in Launceston.[26]

Women lost many of their legal rights after marrying (although they had more customary legal rights than in England, including the right to be independent parties to legal actions[27]) and often preferred to stay in de facto relationships. John Henderson was critical of the number choosing not to marry in order to keep their independence: "females feel and act far more independently ... their continuance, therefore, in an unmarried state, is exceedingly injurious." He wanted women convicts to be compulsorily married off, "to get rid of an enormous expense and troublesome charge."[28]

Marriage rates do seem to have increased from the mid 1820s, but unique Van Diemen's Land legislation passed in 1837 that provided for the maintenance of de facto partners reveals that many couples continued to live together without marrying – and suggests that, for mothers particularly, there were also risks associated with this should their partner abscond.[29]

Whether they married or not, living without a man was rarely a realistic option for convict and ex-convict women in what remained a fiercely patriarchal society. Samuel Guy met a woman convict in Hobart Town in 1823 whom he recognised from his home town, noting that

> she is doing well here, she told me that she had a house of her own, she is living with a man but does not wish her husband should be informed of it, indeed I do not blame her altogether, as women are scarce – that if they do not live as a wife – they can scarce avoid doing worse.[30]

Whether convict or free, old Van Diemonian or new immigrant, childbirth limited women's choices and posed the usual dangers. The first known Van Diemonian midwife was Sarah Morney, a convict who arrived in 1818. She had a very good reputation and no doubt for many women was literally a life-saver.[31] But the *Hobart Town Gazette* of 2 October 1819 gave notice of impending changes that were to sideline such midwives and their expertise, advising that: "W.M. Boston DM, surgeon and man-midwife, from the University of Edinburgh … means to settle here and has assumed Mr Brannen as assistant partner in the surgical and midwifery profession." No doubt middle-class women, unhappy to have a convict deliver their children, would have provided Boston's main market. In this instance, however, the more privileged were probably disadvantaged as a result. Such quacks possessed little of the midwife's traditional knowledge or experience, and they were also expensive. Sutherland recorded in 1824 that the fee for a doctor's attendance at his daughter's birth was the considerable sum of 20 Spanish dollars. Whatever type of help they received, some women and many babies died. The first European triplets known to be born in Van Diemen's Land, to Catherine O'Neill in 1818, were three of these. They were born prematurely at Catherine's home in Herdsman's Cove (now Gagebrook) just eight months after she had given birth to her last son.[32] Any visitor to an old graveyard is poignantly reminded just how common maternal and infant death continued to be throughout the nineteenth century – regardless of class, marital status or wealth.

The path to economic and social freedom for women remained narrow and difficult, but it was probably wider in Van Diemen's Land before the mid 1820s than in England. Women ran a range of businesses.[33] Sarah Piroelle was one of the four licensed bakers in 1806, and Mary Hayes ran her hotel from as early as 1808. There were female landowners, mostly the wives of convicts with their husbands assigned to them as servants, and they employed labour and supplied the government store.[34]

The wealthiest and most powerful woman in Van Diemen's Land was a former convict. As we have seen, Edward Lord's relationship with Maria Risley, who had been transported to Sydney in 1804 for stealing, was a key reason for his economic success. After moving to Hobart Town in 1805, Maria ran the couple's merchant business, and they married in 1808.[35] In 1809, an appeal to Maria's class loyalties grew into the most overt example of protest by convict women in early Van Diemen's Land. Edward Lord, in his capacity as magistrate, had detained the convict Mary Granger, and some of the other convict women had gone to Maria to ask her to intercede. When she declined to do so, Martha Hudson abused her. Lord had Hudson flogged; according to G.P. Harris, "some of the women who were spectators of the punishment rather loudly expressed their disapprobation and threatened revenge," which was probably what led Lord to instruct the "drum beating to arms" (the emergency response signal for the military).[36] Women were not normally flogged, and Lord may have feared that if other convicts and soldiers sympathised with the women's anger, the protest would spread.

It was not until free immigration increased after 1818 that the divide between convict and free became rigid, and Maria's past as a former convict became a political and social liability to Lord. This occurred precisely at the same time as economic changes were undermining the value of her convict connections. Williamson voiced the prejudices of the new immigrants towards Maria: "she pretends to set up for a fine lady but neither her manners or language are lady-like."[37] Janet Ranken, in a letter to her sister in December 1821, was even more pompous: "the society here is abominable. Mr Lord a man worth half a million money is married to a convict woman ... Mrs Lord sent her daughter Miss Lord and her sister Mrs Simpson to call upon me when I came here but I have never returned the call yet nor shall I."[38]

Edward Lord divorced his wife in 1824. William Parramore, who was present throughout the divorce proceedings, believed that Lord's aim was to secure "a divorce from a wife whom he is now ashamed of, because she can't read and *can* put herself into the most *original* passions and curse and swear."[39]

Religion

Christianity permeated popular culture, but as in both England and pre-famine Ireland, this did not necessarily entail acceptance of the teachings, authority or customs of the churches. Christian baptism and burial were the rituals that most connected church and people.[40] And most, including condemned men, seem to have favoured repentance and reconciliation before facing their maker. Even one of the victims of Macquarie Harbour cannibal Alexander Pearce sought and was granted half an hour to prepare himself with a prayer book before being eaten.[41]

Many 1820s observers claimed that Van Diemen's Land was "pagan," but such accusations were frequently levelled by those whose rigid Christianity scorned traditional popular expressions of faith. The Celtic Christianity of rural Ireland and the western isles of Scotland, along with the Gaelic language in which it was expressed, was forcibly suppressed during this era by Roman and Calvinist arms of the institutional churches. Even among English convicts in the early nineteenth century, long-held "superstitions" permeated popular religion, not as an alternative to Christianity but as an integral part of it.

It is easy to forget that Van Diemen's Land was predominantly settled by a people still influenced by the world-view of the pre-industrial age. The prevalence of herbal medicines and sacred charms,[42] the search for indigenous plant remedies, the primeval fear of the woods and of the haunting screams of the "Devil" emanating from them,[43] and the mythical descriptions of Aboriginal "giants" all suggest that the settlers' experience of Van Diemen's Land was influenced by inherited traditions and beliefs. But this did not, at least from the perspective of the people themselves, make them any less Christian.

By downplaying the extent of religious faith among the ordinary people of Van Diemen's Land, secular historians have uncritically reproduced assumptions about what qualified as "true Christianity" without recognising the extent to which these were based on class and culture.[44] Wariness of formal religion may have reflected resistance to institutional structures rather than to Christianity per se; individual missionaries could be well received if they were prepared to meet outside the confines of formal worship. The Quaker visitors Backhouse and Walker found a receptive audience for their spiritual message in the early 1830s, and the open-air preachers who later ministered to isolated, mainly ex-convict smallholders also found considerable support.

Music and the Pub

What Henry Mayhew referred to in his record of the street life of London as the "underground of the ballad singer" found almost immediate expression in Van Diemen's Land. G.P. Harris mentioned a convict who "wrote some very scurrilous verses on the Gvr and some of his officers" and, threatened with a court of inquiry, "escaped to the woods."[45] Convict verses about resistance and exile were also put to music – usually to the tunes of well-known folk songs.[46] The best-remembered ballad-maker of Van Diemen's Land was Francis McNamara, or Frank the Poet, well known to fellow convicts in the 1830s and 1840s.

As with the slaves of North America, songs sustained the spirit and gave voice to sentiments of resistance. At the Launceston women's factory, "singing, telling stories and dancing took up much of the women's time," while the man in charge of the Hobart factory, John Price (later the infamous commandant of Norfolk Island and the inspiration for the character of Maurice Frere in *For the Term of his Natural Life*), confirmed that the female inmates spent much of their time composing songs ridiculing the authorities.[47] On occasion women were punished for singing "obscene" songs in the factory.[48] According to Mrs Nixon, wife of the bishop of Tasmania, matters were worse at the Brickfield factory, which held over 400 women in Hobart Town in the mid 1840s. The women were left "in total idleness; they dance, play, dress up for acting" in what Mrs Nixon believed amounted to a "sink of iniquity."[49]

Singing also occurred at executions. By celebrating the life of the condemned man and expressing solidarity with him in his final fearful moments, the music undermined the intended function of the gruesome public spectacle. The custom in Britain was that songs about the condemned individual were composed by professional balladmakers and sold to the crowd. In Van Diemen's Land such was the number of executions after 1825, and no doubt the shortage of composers, that a song described by Gray as "The Song of Death" – which she believes was a traditional English prison song – was widely sung. At the execution of Mathew Brady and his gang, "the whole gathering took up the singing and by the time the fourth verse had concluded five bushrangers were dead."[50]

Singing together was also a convict response to other external threats. Jorgen Jorgenson, the Danish convict adventurer and leader of one of the roving parties pursuing Aborigines, reported that in July 1829 the Aborigines "had the audacity to threaten Mr Meredith's men, and when they [the convicts] began to sing in defiance, the natives re-echoed their song in derision from the rocks, and told them they would come soon and take them all."[51]

Whenever possible, singing was accompanied. One of the *Calcutta* convicts, the Afro-American William Thomas, was known as a violin player. The settler Alex Laing described being ordered to play by Michael Howe after the bushranger visited his master's house at Pittwater in November 1816. The instrument was often played in public houses, but convicts in harsher circumstances could make do without it. A surgeon in the 1820s noted how convicts turned the jingling of their chains into music "whereto they dance and sing."[52]

Unfortunately, most of these songs and ballads, and even the dialect used to compose them, have been lost. There is one well-known exception. In 1852 John West noted that convicts still sang about the capture of the brig *Cyprus* by convicts nearly two decades earlier:

> The prisoners who wage war with society, regarded the event with exultation; and long after, a song, composed by a sympathising poet, was propagated by oral tradition, and sung in chorus around the fires in the interior. This version of the story made the capture a triumph of the oppressed over their oppressors.[53]

No site was more important for music – or, for that matter, dance, betting and games – than the public house. The freedom of all ranks of society, including convicts and soldiers, to visit pubs – virtually unrestricted until the mid 1820s – is one of the most remarkable aspects of early Van Diemen's Land. Until the evening curfew (in Hobart Town in 1820 this was eight o'clock in winter and nine o'clock in summer), ordinary Van Diemonians – male and female, bonded and free, sailor and settler, policeman and prisoner – got drunk together, usually on rum imported from India. There were 11 pubs in Hobart Town by 1818, and three others nearby – at Herdsman's Cove, Kangaroo Point and Clarence Plains, and the number kept pace with population growth thereafter; one establishment was maintained for every one to two hundred people. Most of these pubs escaped much official interference or elite patronage, serving as a place apart where the people's culture was let be, and where daytime distinctions between prisoners and their gaolers – who were, after all, generally from a similar class background – were loosened. Such slackness seems extraordinary from the perspective of even a decade later, but this was a time when there was no barracks for the soldiers and no gaol for the convicts. Appeals to Sydney to fund public buildings were ignored, and it was not until the island became a separate colony in 1825 that secure gaols and barracks were built. In these circumstances, having prisoners (and the almost equally intractable rank-and-file soldiery) concentrated each evening in recognised public houses probably aided after-hours supervision. More importantly, it also aided public and private finance. The colonial government had almost no source of revenue other than the excise on rum, and its sale was also an easy source of profit for the merchant capitalists of the town.

Even in those districts where there were no accessible pubs, rum was still consumed in large quantities. Securing willing labour from everyone from convict shepherds to military guards depended on the provision of a liberal supply of alcohol. As the land commissioners observed: "wheat, the staff of life, is the standard for wages in other countries, here rum is the alpha and omega."[54]

Naming the Land

One reason for the endurance of the myth of Van Diemen's Land as a Little England is the fact that so many contemporary Tasmanian place names remember Britain. However, this was not true before 1820, when most geographical features were named by the ordinary people, especially the kangaroo hunters, stockmen and bushrangers who first visited them. This has been obscured because many of the major geographical features were subsequently renamed as part of the broader attempt to remake the land and its people.

Explorers, immigrants, writers and mapmakers of the 1820s provide a record of the old names and the changes already under way. Names of a number of geographical features, like the Fat Doe River (now the Clyde) and Dick Brown's River (now the River Dee), had already been changed, but examples of the older nomenclature survived, generally in less prominent landmarks, including Native Hut Plains, Kangaroo Point, Black Bob's Rivulet and Tooms' Lake. John West acknowledged that "the popular names of places denote the character or tastes of their early visitors and heroes" and gave as colourful examples "Murderer's Plains, Killman Point, Hell Corner, Murderer's Tiers, Four Square Gallows, Dunne's Lookout, Brady's Lookout, and Lemon's Lagoon."[55] One apparently classical name probably also has humble origins. Burn believed "the reader may probably suppose" that the Styx River

> owed its title to old and endearing classical associations: such, however, is certainly not the case. Like many other things in the colony, it took its name from circumstances. Flowing through a rich and fertile valley, its banks are heavily timbered with huge superb trees, which from time to time have fallen into its channel, and nearly impeded its course. Time has stripped these trees of their bark and verdure; and as the bleached and tortuous boughs lie basking in the summer's sun, the impression upon the unlearned convict's mind is obvious – resolving itself in the *river of sticks*, which a corrector taste has since metamorphosed into a more antique and more distinguishable appellation.[56]

Official exploration parties were responsible for some of the name changes. It is ironic that the "explorers" were commonly guided by Van Diemonians who already knew and had named the sites. The first official explorer of the Lakes Country was unusually honest about this process: "although the country visited had been discovered by bushrangers and hunters and the expedition was accompanied by a guide with previous knowledge of the country, yet this journal by

J. Beamont is the first available account of the country in the neighbourhood of the Great Lake."[57]

Macquarie's 1811 and 1821 visits to Van Diemen's Land represented the most systematic attempts to rename the land. The names of powerful Britons and British geographical features were imposed without any regard for established nomenclature. Only occasionally did Macquarie even acknowledge the change – as when he named "York Plains in honour of HRH the Duke of York … The name these plains have hitherto been called by is Scantling Plains, from an outlaw runaway convict of that name having been killed there."[58]

Macquarie's efforts to rename Van Diemen's Land were resisted, and many of his efforts – especially those that commemorated his Hebridean homeland, such as Ulva, Staffa and Ormaig – have not survived.[59] Bigge was informed that after new place names were decreed by Macquarie, "particular pains were taken by putting up boards with the names painted on them, though lately they have been taken away."[60] This opposition was confirmed by Edward Curr: "I speak of these places by their local names. We cannot bring ourselves to be Highlanders and Shetlanders in a moment, not withstanding our late governor-in-chief would seem to desire it." Curr claimed that the new names

> remain confined almost to the proclamations which published them. There is already a degree of nationality in Van Diemen's Land; people begin to talk of the good old times with which the old names are connected; and a governor might as well abolish the English language by proclamation, as the names which are associated with former days. We still talk of the Fat Doe River, Gallows Hill, Murderers Plains, and Hell's Corner. These names were principally bestowed upon them by bushrangers and the hunters of the kangaroo, who in fact have been the discoverers of all the good districts of the island.[61]

The conflict continued for some time. In early 1827 the land commissioners called for a renewed effort: "in preference to naming lakes and rivers after individuals, we conceive that it would be better to suit the name to the situation, or in remembrance of places in Europe,"[62] but this was never fully achieved.

The result was what a later governor of Van Diemen's Land, William Denison, described as an "extraordinary nomenclature," involving an "absurd mixture of common place names with sacred, historic or romantic ones."[63] Poorly represented, however, in part *because* of the role played by ordinary people in their discovery, were Aboriginal names. The kangaroo hunters and their ilk may have had more contact with Aborigines than most explorers and first settlers of Australia, but they named geographical features out of their own experience and lacked the sensibility or detachment to appropriate the language and culture of the Indigenous people in doing so.

A New Type of Immigrant

After conflict with the French formally ended in 1815, and especially from 1820, Van Diemen's Land became an attractive destination for a small but influential group of wealthy free settlers. During the 1820s, legal title over the grassy woodlands was granted to this elite group, who made the dubious but ultimately accepted argument that this extinguished all prior claims.

West believed that this new class of "respectable" settler was dismayed by what they found on arrival in Van Diemen's Land, although the beauties of the "empty" native grasslands offered hope for a more prosperous future:

> The settler, whose imagination pictured the rustic beauties and quiet order of the English farm, saw unfenced fields of grain, deformed with blackened stumps: a low cottage of the meanest structure, surrounded by heaps of wool, bones and sheepskins; mutton and kangaroo strung on the branches of trees; idle and uncleanly men, of different civil condition, but of one class; and tribes of dogs and natives. No green hedges or flowering meadows, or notes of the thrush and nightingale; but yet there was the park-like lands, the brilliant skies, the pure river and untainted breath of the morning.[64]

This view of ordinary Van Diemonian life is strikingly similar to the judgments passed on the highland Scots and rural Irish during the same period. In all three cases, unfavourable contrasts with both "old" England (with its hierarchical rural society) and "new" England (with its improved and efficient agriculture and industry) were drawn. In both cases the people were seen to be, if not quite "savages," at least not fully "civilised." And in the penal colony, just as in Scotland and Ireland, this was used to justify a mass eviction that would deliver exclusive control of the most productive land to a powerful and privileged elite.

PART III

VAN DIEMEN'S LAND CONQUERED
1824–38

[11]

THE COMING OF LITTLE ENGLAND

OR MUCH OF THE 1820S, free-settler immigrants preferred Van Diemen's Land to New South Wales. The principal attraction of island life was the easily accessible native grasslands: according to an early settler guide, "the colonist has no expense to incur in clearing his farm" and "is not compelled to a great preliminary outlay of capital, before he can expect a considerable return."[1] In the early nineteenth century, it was also widely believed that "the climate of Van Diemen's Land is perhaps the most salubrious of any on the globe for a European."[2] Drought and flood were comparatively rare. In all, it made for an enticing package.

By 1830, of the 71,000 non-Aboriginal people in Australia, over 24,000 were in Van Diemen's Land. Moreover, the southern colony had 60,000 of the 126,000 acres in cultivation, more than half the sheep, more than half the customs revenue and more than half the exports.

Credit for the colony's rapid economic development in the 1820s is usually given exclusively to the "first shoals of free immigrants." They ensured, according to the colony's first historian, Henry Melville, that "Van Diemen's Land had arisen from a wilderness ... The seeds of industry had been sown."[3] John West agreed, arguing that "it is from the date of emigration that progress has been conspicuous."[4] James Fenton's later *History of Tasmania* (1884) continued with this theme: the original settlers "lived in the free indulgence of their vicious propensities. The new settlers were men of intelligence and character."[5] These early historians and commentators were concerned to establish that although Van Diemen's Land had always been a penal colony, real development only began with, and could be directly attributed to, *free* settlers. They, not prisoners, were to be the founding fathers of the new, convict-free "Tasmania."

Land Grants

As early as December 1820, William Williamson wrote that he would have to go at least 30 miles, "perhaps nearly 50," to get a land grant, "as all the best lands in the intermediate distance are granted." In 1823 Samuel Guy advised that a new settler "will now have some difficulty in obtaining good land except he gets into the infrequent parts of the colony – among wild natives." In the next year William Parramore confirmed that "it is indeed incredible how many people are searching for land in the interior; within five months have arrived five ship loads of immigrants from England and Scotland. At this rate Van Diemen's Land will be completely colonized in a very short time."[6]

Government statistics, even allowing for a couple of years' lag caused by delays in processing grants, confirm how quickly the grasslands were alienated in the 1820s. From 1804 to 1822 only 132,550 acres of land had been granted, but from 1823 to 1831 (when free land grants ended) 1,899,332 acres were given away.[7]

By June 1831, when the new Ripon land regulations (which introduced the sale of crown lands) came into effect, almost all the profitable land had been granted. Lieutenant Governor Arthur had made sure of this by handing over nearly 250,000 acres of what remained to new and existing settlers in the first half of 1831, including the long-coveted 100,000-acre grazing reserve near Ross, which was seen as "the finest tract of land in the island."[8]

Very little of the land alienated in the 1820s went to ex-convicts or their children. Governor Macquarie had fought a rearguard action for residual land rights for the ordinary people of New South Wales and Van Diemen's Land, arguing in early 1820 that

> it must never be forgotten that this is, at present, a convict country, originally established for their punishment and reformation; that

at least 9/10 of its present population consist either of convicts, persons who have been convicts; or the offspring of convicts ... Consequently some consideration appears to be justly due to so very large a portion of the population of the country.[9]

Such sentiments were rejected by Commissioner Bigge and given little consideration after Macquarie's departure. Bigge recommended that land grants be restricted to free immigrants with a minimum of £500 capital. The supposed maximum grant became 2560 acres, or four square miles, but this was not strictly applied until 1827,[10] and, as James Fenton noted, "exceptions to the rule were freely admitted."[11] For example, William Effingham Lawrence arrived in 1822 and received, with Lieutenant Governor Sorell's support, 12,000 acres as well as having 2000 acres reserved for his son.[12]

Contrary to what is often assumed, however, small land grants did not totally disappear. They were an integral part of the reward system, a powerful means of conscripting ordinary Van Diemonians to the struggle against both black and white threats to the property of the elite. In the bushranger emergency years of 1825–26, the total number of grants under 500 acres reached 264 (compared with 124 grants over 500 acres). Nevertheless, smaller grants were an insignificant proportion of the total land granted.[13]

Along with the change in land policy went any notion of concentrated settlement. While the geographical boundaries of the settled districts had never been firmly set – there was no equivalent of the 19 counties of New South Wales which were meant to define the limits of settlement – before 1820, land grants were only made in a few surveyed areas. But thereafter the land rush in the midlands began. In 1821, Macquarie marked out the sites of Perth, Campbell Town, Oatlands and Brighton (although they remained little more than the names of districts for some years). In his *Narrative of a Trip to Van Diemen's Land*, the governor noted that these prospective towns

are arranged with a due consideration to the accommodation and convenience of new settlers, they being all seated in the midst of

extensive tracts of rich land, and forming at the same time, a regular chain of stations between Hobart Town and Launceston whereby the journeying between these places will be rendered both safe
and convenient.[14]

While the guidebooks pointed out that the permission of the
Colonial Office was not needed to immigrate, London's sanction was
undoubtedly an advantage, and most of the wealthiest settlers
secured it. The official letter carried by approved immigrants reflected
the British government's land policy, instructing the governor to
make "a grant of land in proportion to the means ... of bringing the
same into cultivation."[15] But as the colonial secretary, Lord Bathurst,
noted in April 1827, "in the various orders and instructions from
home respecting land, the use of the word 'cultivation' seems scarcely
to have been duly regarded." Bathurst was prepared to be flexible
about the type of investment appropriate to "a farm in the interior,"
but he wanted the regulations tightened to ensure that land was
clearly held on "conditional tenure," with the settler obliged to spend
the "full estimated value of the land" before "being freed of its conditions." Bathurst sought to confirm the long-established principle
that "any settler who keeps large tracts of land uncultivated" risked
losing it.[16]

Despite such specific instructions, no notion of conditional land
ownership was ever accepted in Van Diemen's Land. The settlers
fought for, and in practice won, an absolute right over their property
that commenced with the first approval of the land grant, regardless
of the regulations and laws that ordered otherwise. The settlers did
what they liked with the land – sold it sight unseen, left it "waste," or
sat on it as speculative capital. Curr wrote in 1824 that "until of late,
grants of land were sold and exchanged ... without being actually
located by the settler," and observed that, although a recent clause
supposedly prevented sales within five years of the grant,

> there are various ways of evading the clause: but indeed in most
> cases no evasion has been practiced; for, in defiance of it, they
> have been sold in the most public manner possible, and have

been bought without fear or scruple, in the confidence that such matters, would never be investigated.[17]

The settler William Barnes informed his brother, also in 1824, that "it is understood that you either cultivate or put stock upon your farm within five years, otherwise the government can take it back; but I believe this regulation is never enforced."[18]

The rapid appreciation in land value meant that a grant was a financial windfall, well worth the lobbying and scheming often necessary to secure it. Barnes estimated he could sell his 1000-acre grant for £800 in the same year he received it. This breach of regulation was not only common practice but, on occasion, rewarded. George Hobler was not the only favoured settler who, after selling his free land grant for what he described as a "handsome profit," sought yet another handout.[19] No taxes were received on this misplaced state benevolence. Even quit-rents – an annual property tax legally levied on land grants – were hardly ever paid. Governor Arthur tried to enforce the payment of the large amounts owed in 1831, but the solicitor-general found that any attempt to resume land would be denied by a jury (which would comprise other free settlers), and payment could not therefore be enforced.

No land was ever resumed. Even when settlers had lied about their personal capital to ensure the maximum grant, their absolute ownership rights were never questioned – perhaps because most of the land in the colony had been so acquired. Arthur told London in 1828 that "the schedule of property which settlers exhibit on their arrival in order to gain land is faithless to a proverb."[20] Robson was more generous – he estimated that "probably half the entire land granted in Van Diemen's Land to 1830 was obtained by evasion of the law."[21]

Such widespread deceit is confirmed in settlers' private letters. Hamilton Wallace wrote to his father in 1825 that "I was only entitled to 500 acres however I managed to get 1280" (for which he was "repeatedly offered £700").[22] William Williamson, who told his sister that he now sought to "do my duty to all as a truly honest man," nevertheless boasted of having "given in a fictitious capital" in order to receive his expected 1000 acres.[23]

The land grab almost came unstuck in 1828 when Chief Justice Pedder found that "all the grants in the name of the governor are void in law, and that none are good but those purport to be made by the King … it is plain that the commission does not convey any estate or interest in the lands to the governor."[24] As all land grants in Van Diemen's Land had been made in the name of the governor, the attorney-general confirmed in 1829 that all grants were "utterly void." Settlers used this confusion to avoid quit-rent – claiming they lacked "secure title to their lands" in a resolution at a public meeting in May 1831 – but new legislation soon confirmed the status quo.[25] Then, as Levy noted, "the whole disreputable business was, as a matter of policy, glossed over."[26]

A belated change in policy came from London in 1831, after the new Whig broom at the Colonial Office, Lord Howick, described the Australian land system as "entirely contrary to both reason and experience."[27] The essence of the Ripon regulations was that free land grants were replaced by land sales at public auction with a floor price of five shillings per acre.[28] A preference for concentrated settlement underpinned this change, influenced by the writings of Edward Gibbon Wakefield who, partly based on the Australian experience, believed that the "essence of civilization is concentration," as "to permit a people to spread thinly is to invite a descent into barbarism."[29] The hope was to subsidise unemployed labourers to emigrate with the proceeds of land sales – they were meant to provide both labour and a market for the new concentrated farming settlements.[30] But the new regulations came too late to have a significant impact in Van Diemen's Land, where the best of the land was already gone and the continued supply of convicts meant that the demand for free unskilled labour was, by then, largely met. The land still available was usually poorer country surrounded by existing grants. Moreover, getting access to roads, water and markets could be difficult for a new settler surrounded by established and often proprietorial settlers. The main practical effect of the new regulations was to cement the power of large landowners, who usually outbid less privileged purchasers in what, until the late 1830s, remained a highly speculative and rapidly appreciating land market.

Critics of the Give-away

The government's land policy had a number of contemporary critics. The land commissioners, who journeyed across all the settled districts of Van Diemen's Land from mid 1826 to the end of 1828 delineating land boundaries, were the most influential of these.[31] They were particularly critical of the older-style cattle barons. Edward Lord, by then owner or lessee of 75,000 acres, and David Lord (no relation) who, through small grants, had secured water sources and thus effective control of a vast territory around them, were harshly judged because of the impact of their unsupervised wandering cattle on bona fide agriculturists.[32] But most of the newer land grantees were also criticised, principally because they invested so little, still preferring to make easy profits by placing sheep on unfenced and unimproved native pastures to developing farms on the English model.

The commissioners argued, for example, that the land surrounding Oyster Bay on the east coast had been "most injudiciously granted away." By "having allowed such a man as Mr Meredith to cut and carve it out as he thought proper," they reported to Lieutenant Governor Arthur,

> one of the finest corn districts in the colony has been condemned at his option either to remain a wilderness of wild cattle to roam over, or to be leased out to a set of wretched tenantry, instead of being the property of an independent industrious community who would have cultivated and improved their own estates.[33]

It should be pointed out, however, that the principal author of the commissioners' reports, Roderick O'Connor, aided by his close relationship with Arthur and official appointments, was himself estimated by the *Colonial Times* to own 30,000 acres of land. By the time of his death in 1860, he owned over 65,000 acres of Van Diemen's Land across 11 properties and was one of the largest landholders on the island.[34]

The Van Diemonian Dispossession

As the free settlers moved onto their newly acquired estates, or had their retainers do so for them, they met and confronted not only the Aboriginal owners of the land, but also the white Van Diemonians who had occupied the grasslands during the previous two decades.

A detailed account of such an encounter was given by James Ross, the "first" settler of the Shannon River. Ross found his land already occupied, recording that "the sheep which this man tended, belonged to three or four different proprietors, one of whom had put them under his charge, and without further license or ceremony he had set himself down with them in this secluded spot." Ross "never saw a finer set of sheep than his flock appeared to be. The lambs ... were thriving and numerous." A rare glimpse into the personal story of one of the pioneer convict pastoralists also resulted from this encounter:

> I saw that he was a shrewd fellow and had not forgotten the cunning that he had learned in the old world ... He was moreover now an old man, near 60 years of age, had been many years in the British navy (by his own account) and as many a fisherman or rather a smuggler at Deal, the accidents of which uncertain occupation had finally led to his visit to this colony – to his exchanging the busy scenes of a sea port town, or the racket of a crowded ship, for a silence and solitude that were not interrupted from months end to months end. He had been three years in his present retirement ... His name was Dennis.[35]

While Dennis was not moved on by Ross, there can be no doubt that as scores more free settlers followed during the next few years, he would have been. As Curr advised immigrants, although "extensive tracts of good country" were "generally overrun by the flocks of herds of other proprietors," they "are bound to remove them immediately upon receiving notice from any person who has located himself on the land on which they feed."[36] T.W. Birch advertised in the *Hobart Town Gazette* that, "having authority from the lieutenant governor to occupy the tract of land adjoining Col. Davey's farm near the mouth of the Coal River," he was giving "notice to all persons who have stock grazing thereon ... to remove the same without delay; as all cattle and sheep found trespassing on the said land ... will be impounded."[37] This area was previously the common pasture of the small farmers at Pitt Water.

It is not surprising that such dispossessions were rarely recorded – since the occupation was usually not official, the dispossession could not be either. The exceptions were when people resisted the land takeover on the basis of established custom or the existing residents had some legal basis for their claims.

Sorell accorded a rare recognition of the rights of established graziers when he defended their interests in one dispute. The lieutenant governor advised one land claimant that "the Macquarie Plains being the chief grazing run for the stock belonging to the settlers of New Norfolk ... can not be interfered with in the occupation thereof beyond the limitation of your grant."[38] However, customary usage weighed little with the authorities in the 1820s, and even legal title could be disputed. William Kersall, who came to Port Dalrymple with Paterson as a convict, petitioned Arthur in 1828 for the return of his home. Kersall reported that for more than 20 years he had lived on a piece of land that he understood had been granted to him by Macquarie, but was now facing eviction by a new land-grantee. He testified that

> The General told me ... to take my land where I had always resided – on the west side of the river and Port Dalrymple near opposite George Town ... I have no other land but what is here stated neither have I sold or tried to sell any of the said land. I came to this country for life and if this is taken from me where is my inheritance.[39]

Kersall's claims were dismissed when Surveyor Frankland found no title or land order to back up his claims, noting, furthermore, that the land was not cultivated. Given the large number of missing land orders and titles – the land commissioners confirmed that many of the transactions in the early years were oral – and that only a small proportion of all grants were cultivated, such logic consistently applied would have led to the forfeiture of many bigger land grants. But none of the rich were evicted for similar reasons. Kersall lacked official support because of who he was, not because of the justice of his claim.[40]

Despite the power of legal authority and the political clout of the new landowners, "squatting" proved to be a difficult practice to stop. The land commissioners were positive about Arthur's efforts, but also documented, in November 1828, how widespread the practice remained:

> Many ... have not thought proper to avail themselves of the government regulations which were evidently intended to prevent idle and "bad" characters from "squatting," thereby giving such extreme annoyance to all around them. The government having held out such inducements to respectable settlers, it is now their duty to assist in so important a work. They are all eager enough to assist upon the removal of an obnoxious character, but, they should go farther, they should pay a little towards completing a work so happily begun.[41]

Squatting on the "common" and "waste" lands (such as forests and fens) had been a traditional practice for those without land for many centuries in England. Although the opportunity and right to do this had largely ended with the private enclosure of over six million acres of common field pasture and waste land through some 4000 acts of parliament, and perhaps half as much again by "agreement" between 1760 and 1815, cultural views and custom were slower to change.[42] Dispossessing the poor, in both England and Van Diemen's Land, proved to be a long, and resisted, process.

One of the ironies of the Van Diemonian dispossession is that the new landowners were commonly told about, and guided to, their granted lands by the same class of men whom they were ultimately to evict. Ross, with three fellow passengers, followed standard practice and "clubbed together in hiring a ticket-of-leave man ... who was acquainted with the country and would serve us as a guide."[43] Curr advised prospective settlers to dispense altogether with the expense of hiring a guide, "as stock-keepers and other persons will be willing to direct him."[44] Ross found this to be true enough, as beyond the

Clyde he was "fortunate enough to meet with a constable, who had been formerly employed in collecting the herds of wild cattle that roamed at large through that part of the country, and who undertook to conduct us to the most inviting spots."[45]

George Meredith, "pioneer" settler of the east coast, was equally fortunate. He was led to Oyster Bay by Henry Rice, *Calcutta* convict and former bushranger. A shepherd joined Meredith's party at Spring Bay, guiding one of the group, Adam Amos, overland, while the others continued rowing. This man and another local stock-hand kept the whole group supplied with kangaroo.[46]

The Vision of a Little England

The new immigrants differed from the Britons who had come to Van Diemen's Land in the first two decades not just in their freedom, wealth and privilege, but in the nature of their connection to England. They could, if they wished, "go home." For many free settlers, life in Van Diemen's Land was seen as temporary – a means of making enough money to live a comfortable life in England. Jane Williams, who travelled out to Van Diemen's Land in 1821–22, recalled that her fellow passengers spent much of their time "talking over the readiest and shortest mode of making their fortunes – displaying their love of country by always taking it for granted that in a certain given number of years they would return to spend their wealth in their native land."[47] Janet Ranken wrote to her sister in December of 1821 that "we all came here to make money and make money we will by hook or by crook."[48]

But while many fulfilled this goal, the plans of others were modified by experience and time. Many settlers came to realise that they were better off in Van Diemen's Land than in England, as, gradually and often imperceptibly, the new land became home. As Boyes reflected in 1830, "to this country our children must look, sooner or later, for their patrimony."[49]

It is often assumed that the English struggled to see beauty in the natural environment of Van Diemen's Land, and such an assumption is understandable given the vigorous attempts free settlers made to modify the landscape. But in fact almost all of the settlers found the country, particularly the open grasslands, picturesque. To William Barnes in 1824 it was "certainly a most beautiful country," and to G.W. Evans, "one of the most beautiful landscapes imaginable."[50] John Maule Hudspeth, who arrived in 1821, noted in his personal journal that the "beautiful and rich valley of Jericho" seemed "more like a gentlemen's park in England, laid out with taste, than land in its natural state."[51]

That such comparisons with the homeland were commonly made was not surprising: most of the settlers had no other reference point. But this did not blind the observers to what was new. Ross observed that while "mother earth" was, "in general appearance, the same," it was

> specifically different. Indeed, upon close examination, I do not think there is a single indigenous plant or animal in the whole island, that is not essentially different from the old world, and even the fishes of the sea, which forms the connecting medium between all parts of the terraqueous globe, are equally distinct.[52]

A considerable number of the settlers studied, painted, planted and wrote about indigenous plants and animals. Natural history was a popular hobby, while native shrubs were well known and widely planted in gardens, usually in combination with English plants. In Hobart Town, Mrs Fenton observed in 1830 that "gardens surround almost all" houses and included "hedges of scarlet geraniums, stocks, wallflowers and an unknown variety of native shrubs." [53]

Responses to the forests of Van Diemen's Land were more ambivalent. Samuel Guy wrote that "the timber is very different from England," but he enjoyed the change:

> It is awfully grand to take a walk into the forest and see nature in all its beauty, the beautiful black wattle all in bloom – the tall and majestic peppermint and gum of immense size with strips of bark peeling from them and floating in the wind. Trees of every size torn up by the roots from the trade winds and others dying with old age – in every direction is a sight beyond description.[54]

Mrs Fenton, too, found much pleasure in the novelty of the forests: "I come as often as I can possibly find a time. The birds, the trees, the wild flowers, the lovely weather, are all strange. Oh how delightful it is to me …"[55] While some found it difficult to appreciate the "dark charred stumps" and "long strips" of bark, Ross argued that they "serve to create in the wilds of Van Diemen's Land, a sort of spectral mythology of its own."[56]

The response to the less accessible wet sclerophyll forests is harder to gauge – they were admired from a distance but most Britons were fearful of closer contact. After two millennia of forest clearing in Britain, by the early nineteenth century wild woods had become unfamiliar places and the dense forests of Van Diemen's Land were generally avoided. Not until the 1840s did land hunger drive the landless into their midst.

For almost all resident whites up to 1840, Van Diemen's Land meant reasonably open country – the grasslands, grassy woodlands, coasts, open highlands and some areas of dry sclerophyll forest in the eastern half of the island – and this country was much appreciated. As the land commissioners put it, "were it not foreign to the nature of an official report here we would expatiate on the beauty and magnificence of the scenery of the island generally."[57]

It was not the environment that the free immigrants of the 1820s generally had trouble accepting, but the convicts. The beauty of the land was widely contrasted with the ugliness of its humanity. William Williamson wrote that "the inhabitants are like a set of vultures … defacing one of the finest countries in the whole world."[58] Mary Leman Grimstone wrote that the convict, "like an ugly nose, spoils the face of the country."[59] Mrs Fenton found in her new home at Macquarie Plains, "not one individual in the neighbourhood I either could or would associate with." Her solace was the natural world: "the banks of the rivers are so endless in rich variety of shrubs. I go miles along them with undiminished interest and never meet a human face."[60]

The "contrast between the natural beauties" and "the moral turpitude of their inhabitants" led Curr to "exclaim with the poet":

Strange that where nature loves to trace
As if for gods a dwelling-place;
There man, enamoured of distress
Should mar it into wilderness.[61]

Two Societies: Van Diemen's Land and Tasmania

"Tasmania" represented the new society the free immigrants sought to superimpose on the convict homeland of Van Diemen's Land. The first printed use of this nomenclature (other than in an 1808 atlas[62]) was, appropriately enough, contained on the first page of the first settler guide, Charles Jeffreys' *Van Diemen's Land* (1820).[63] The name achieved greater prominence through the title of a subsequent guide – *Godwin's Emigrant's Guide to Van Diemen's Land More Properly Called Tasmania*, published in 1823, and from the middle of the decade it achieved widespread use in print and in various clubs and associations,[64] including a Launceston newspaper and the Turf Club. Giblin has concluded:

> the colonists began about the turn of the quarter-century, to associate this new expression ... with their conception of the colonial homeland they were striving to build up from the wild hills and dales ... a fitting name, one worth contending for, had been found for a country that had no rigid relation with the degrading character sought to be imposed upon it.[65]

Nevertheless, few of the free settlers were yet anti-transportationists. Convict labour, along with the markets and the possibilities for patronage and high office in a penal colony, were far too profitable for a felon-free island to be more than a far-off dream. Rather, during the 1820s, there developed a society in which convict and free, broadly corresponding with the old "Van Diemen's Land" and the new "Tasmania," co-existed in what were almost entirely separate social worlds.

As Melville described it, the new free settlers "never by any chance mixed with either the emancipists or the prisoners."[66] Their exemplar was Arthur himself who (unlike all previous lieutenant governors) "always refused to meet convicts and emancipists socially."[67] By 1830, this social division had become so ludicrously rigid (even by the standards of British culture) that Van Diemen's Land is perhaps best seen as a caste-based society, with an untouchable majority barred from almost all contact with their "betters." In 1834 John Montagu was outraged that the wife of the chief justice, Mrs Pedder, would even write to a woman whose grandfather was a convict. Such distinctions were upheld even after death. An ex-convict was not allowed to build a vault over his dead wife's grave, the Catholic chaplain, Philip Connolly, believing that "it is my duty to hold moral rectitude in such respect as to make some distinction … between the meritoriously conducted and those of a different class."[68] Bushrangers mocked this free-settler snobbery. One of them, Martin Cash, liked to arrange for convict servants to smoke and drink in their master's presence during his hold-ups of rural estates, with one particularly sensitive settler once placed "at the foot of the table, between two of his own men." Cash noted that this was "enjoyed exceedingly" because "of the notions of exclusiveness entertained by the former."[69]

David Burn, arguing for the free settlers of Van Diemen's Land "to regain their rights as Britons," highlighted why the social divide between convicts and free settlers was more rigid in Van Diemen's Land than in New South Wales:

> The emancipist, that is, the conditionally pardoned class, are people of money and means in the former, whilst in the latter they possess no consideration – the tide of emigration which set up in 1820 having thrown all the power into the hands of the free people of Van Diemen's Land.[70]

The desire of free immigrants to differentiate themselves had many unfortunate implications, including the petty snobbery and superficiality that came to pervade the society of the elite. In 1828 Boyes advised his fiancée "to come as respectably as you can – remember that, you don't know and can't conceive the value of a first impression in such a colony as this," and he further warned that "if they were to suspect that any of their intimates had sprung from a lowly origin – the cut direct would be spotted."[71] Two years later, Mr Fenton warned his newly arrived spouse not to visit the house of his agent, for "as a merchant he is not visited by the first class, you would lose caste."[72]

The obsession with status, even among many of those who had been born and educated in a lower social class, could cause much embarrassment. Edward Lord divorced his ex-convict wife, while George Meredith kept his wife, the former governess of his children, confined to Oyster Bay. His reasons for doing so were acknowledged in a letter written during one of his frequent excursions to Hobart Town:

> You express your regret not to be with me in Town and your apprehension that you shall never enjoy that pleasure … circumstances do not exactly conspire in favour of your visiting Hobart Town for the first time just now … when Mrs Meredith appears in the metropolis I hope … to see her only support the character of the lady but also enjoy the comforts and accommodations benefiting her rank and station in society … I only hope that you do not fail to remember all I ever saw and wrote to you about in qualifying yourself for moving in the circles for which you are ultimately destined.[73]

Meredith believed that "at Swanport we may ruralize and live and appear as plain as we please – but in the world the case differs."[74] To Meredith and his ilk, the "world" was Hobart Town, and by the mid 1820s Hobart "society" was taking itself very seriously, becoming, William Parramore wrote in 1824, "very good. We have a great many gentlemanly men and hardly ever see a dag, except in the sea captains and the farmers."[75] But change was slower in Launceston which still lacked "society comfort,"[76] and outside the two towns, "dags" were still everywhere.

In his 1824 guidebook, Curr warned free settlers away from the many disreputable regions in the north of the colony, noting that although "nothing can surpass the native beauties and excellence in soil" of the districts "of Honeysuckle Banks, Patterson's Plains, Norfolk Plains on the South Esk, and the settlement on the North

Esk … their possessors have done little beyond making them cele-brated for their crimes."[77] In the south it was a similar story. Curr directed prospective immigrants to select areas like "the district of the Coal River … The greater part of it has not been so long settled … and a majority of the inhabitants are respectable free settlers, with large grants of land located during the last three years."[78]

During the 1820s the free settlers' land takeover expanded their geographical influence. Not only the midlands, where most land grants were taken, but also many of the established regions of concen-trated small farms changed in character as ex-convicts were evicted or sold up.

The most obvious change in the late 1820s was undoubtedly in Hobart Town, which had been transformed from the rough convict village of self-made skillings of a decade before. When Mrs Prinsep arrived in November 1829, full of apprehensions about what the in-famous penal colony would be like, as she "walked up the High Street … she enjoyed a thousand English associations … carts and cottages, ships and shops, girls in their pattens, boys playing at marbles; above all the rosy countenances, and chubby cheeks and English voices."[79] But even in the capital the old co-existed with the new. An 1830 visi-tor reported: "Hobart Town is straggling, and looks more so than it really is, from the great variety of its buildings; the inferior houses of some of the first settlers still remaining by the side of the smart shops of later residents."[80] Nevertheless, by 1832 Arthur was reporting on the old way of life in the capital in almost nostalgic terms:

> A taste for expensive houses and furniture is prevalent and gaining ground; and, but for the alternation of costly houses of recent con-struction with such of the primeval huts as are still permitted to stand as memorials of the infancy of the colony, I do not know there is anything in the appearance of Hobart Town, or in the manner of living of the inhabitants that would suggest in the mind of the newly arrived emigrant that where Hobart Town stands, there was, 30 years since, nothing but a wilderness.[81]

[12]

CONTROLLING THE CONVICTS

WHILE THE INFLUENCE OF FREE SETTLERS grew dramatically in the 1820s, they remained only a small proportion of the population. Van Diemen's Land was still overwhelmingly a convict society, and so long as this remained the case, the values and pretensions of the new Tasmania would remain a minority concern.

In 1824, a highly capable and uniquely powerful administrator had arrived in Van Diemen's Land: Lieutenant Governor George Arthur. The challenge facing him was to discipline and control a growing labour force. The proportion of convicts still under sentence had risen from its all-time low of 17.7 per cent of the population in 1817 to 40 to 50 per cent in the early 1820s, where it stayed until 1839.

Convicts were meant to be unfree labourers, not peasant smallholders or bush entrepreneurs with their own stake in the land. To achieve the desired transformation in the face of an unruly Van Diemonian culture and the economic system that underpinned it would prove a significant challenge, one that dominated government policy and preoccupied the free settlers until the mid 1830s.

The penal system that resulted from Arthur's reforms eventually became a sophisticated and wide-ranging enterprise that could punish, reward and, if necessary, brutalise to ensure the subservience of the many thousands of prisoners exiled to the island. But resistance to the reforms was also wide-ranging, and this both delayed and shaped their implementation.

Many of Arthur's reforms had their origins in Lieutenant Governor Sorell's term of office from 1817 to 1824. Sorell had established a regular weekly muster for convicts (including those with tickets of leave), travel passes and better rewards and protection for informers, withdrawn labour from settlers who co-operated with bushrangers, and ensured that an increasing number of convict indulgences were linked to good behaviour. And, most famously, he had established the penal settlement at Macquarie Harbour on the isolated west coast.[1]

What a focus on official policy can easily overlook, however, is actual results – how effectively the reforms were translated into action. In the frontier regions, which in 1824 still encompassed most of the territory occupied by the British, they had almost no impact at all. Consider, for example, Sorell's 1821 prohibition of a raft of common practices.[2] Sorell decreed that sheep be yarded "at least once a week ... for the purpose of keeping the stock-keepers in check," and prohibited stock-keepers from keeping dogs. He even banned "the common practice with owners of flocks to allow their shepherds to acquire and keep sheep, which, indeed, in many cases form the medium of payment for their services [the thirds system]." Sorell was explicit: the masters were not to "permit their servants to be at all owners of stock."[3]

What is most revealing about this order is not its logic or intention, but the complete failure to implement it – it is almost impossible to discern any resulting change in practice. When Sorell left the colony in 1824, stock was still not regularly mustered,[4] most stockmen were still hunting with dogs, and payment through the thirds system was common. In August 1825 Arthur complained to Bathurst that "a more pernicious practice than ... the Thirds cannot possibly exist in any country ... It is the system on which sheep stealing, which is carried to such an alarming extent in this island ... derived its origins and is still encouraged and perpetrated."[5]

Arthur himself concluded, soon after his arrival, that the convicts had only been "kept passive by a system of extreme indulgence, which I am sure the comprehensive mind of Colonel Sorell would never have suffered to exist had he not been cramped in all his measures and unable to follow the dictates of his own judgment."[6] It would be more than two years before the new lieutenant governor was able to change this.

Arthur was the most powerful political leader the island has ever known, and enjoyed a level of personal authority arguably unmatched by any leader in Australian history. Van Diemen's Land formally became a separate colony from New South Wales in 1825 and power was then concentrated in one office – that of the lieutenant governor – to a greater extent than at any other period. Even appointments to the executive council and other government offices were largely within Arthur's personal control.[7] This unparalleled formal authority was combined with the relative trust and subsequent autonomy Arthur received from London and the capacity for patronage which the convict system and land grants made possible. Why, then, given the authority vested in Arthur and his clear instructions to act, was reform so slow?

The most obvious point, quickly made by Arthur in correspondence to London, was that he lacked the military capacity to counter anticipated resistance:

> In resigning the command into my hands, Colonel Sorell expressed the opinion that the period had now arrived when measures of coercion and restraint might in greater safety be enforced towards the convicts; my predecessor, however, had not himself ventured to take any step, and the only one I have presumed upon has convinced me that more rigid discipline cannot be introduced without opposition, and therefore with the present military force I cannot feel justified in attempting it.[8]

This issue was dealt with in 1826 when a full regiment (the 40th Regiment, with 607 rank-and-file soldiers) was posted to Van Diemen's Land, but other constraints were far more difficult to address. In an 1825 letter the lieutenant governor was candid about the complexity of the issue: "I am beset with difficulties and quite at my wits end ... The convicts have too much liberty and great evils result from it ... if my hands are strengthened, I hope to make transportation a punishment which, at present, it certainly is not."[9]

The link between convict laxity and the preservation of settler profit is the key to understanding Arthur's dilemma. Any challenge to the liberty of the stockmen-hunters who roamed the frontier grasslands threatened the property of the elite. With almost no formal British authority existing in these areas, sheep and cattle could just as easily disappear as multiply. From the perspective of the lieutenant governor, the masters were "in many respects, but especially as regards the safety of their property, quite at their [assigned servants'] mercy, [and] are reduced by self interest, or perhaps in self defence, to adopt a system of indulgence, which it is not in the power of the governor to control entirely."[10] Settlers and convict labourers co-operated, tacitly or otherwise, in ignoring regulations that impinged on established custom, and until the increase in wool exports and the rapid alienation of land changed pastoral practices and the reach of official power, there was very little the lieutenant governor could do about it. As Arthur put it in January 1827, "where master and servant have an interest in deceiving, it is almost next to impossible to detect their scheme."[11]

Malcolm Smith, the police magistrate of Norfolk Plains, highlighted the policy conundrum in the winter of 1827. Smith advised Arthur that "the present system of stock huts ... being removed from any controul, and the keepers being mostly prisoners, are rendezvous for runaways and bad characters, as well as receptacles for stolen property or stock." Arthur agreed: "the strong persuasion of my mind is that these stock-keepers not only continually insulted and ill-used the natives but they have harboured, aided and assisted the bush rangers. These men are in fact a most intractable evil." But, he lamented, "what is to be done? ... if this is not allowed, the settlers will declare themselves injured and ruined – if it is, the evil is apparent."[12]

It was only when settlers' economic interests came to correspond with the government's policy objectives that the frontier labour force was brought into line. The critical change came with the dramatic shift to a wool-based economy, evident from the mid 1820s but dramatically accelerating after 1828. Farming merinos for wool required the separation and daily supervision of valuable flocks and their protection from fire, theft, interbreeding and predators. The much tougher meat breeds had thrived on indifference, casual supervision and Aboriginal land-management regimes, but a successful wool property involved a significant capital investment that had to be managed and protected. "Trespassers" – white and black – were a threat, and lax labourers a major problem. Authorities and settlers were therefore by the late 1820s increasingly united: the independent hunter-shepherds must be replaced by a supervised and controlled convict labour force.

Before this could happen, however, a more immediate threat from the convict bushmen of Van Diemen's Land had to be countered. Between 1824 and 1826 the colony faced its last serious bushranger insurrection, and defeating this became the first priority of the government.

The Last Bushranger Emergency

The most powerful of the bushranging gangs was led by Matthew Brady. Born in Manchester of Irish parents and sentenced to seven years' transportation for forgery in 1820, Brady had arrived in the colony in 1821. He was subsequently sentenced to Macquarie Harbour for two years for twice trying to stow away to England, but escaped by boat with a gang of 14 in 1824, landing in Storm Bay where they found food and welcome in a sawyer's camp. From then until his capture in April 1826, Brady launched a series of daring raids that became legendary.[13] Although the economic and social changes already in train meant that Brady's power never approached that of Michael Howe, bushrangers still posed a serious challenge to imperial authority, thanks to what the *Hobart Town Gazette* described as the "silent understanding which so barefacedly subsists between these abominable wretches ... and the distant stock-keepers."[14] Chaplain Connolly wrote in April 1826 that the bushrangers were "frightfully formidable":

> A wild forest country, with which they were better acquainted than their pursuers, afforded them easy retreat, which they secured in great measure, by dividing their spoils with shepherds, herdsmen

(chiefly of the convict class) and others of bad character who were best acquainted with their hiding places … hundreds of men were unable to catch them.[15]

George Meredith was one settler who seriously considered quitting Oyster Bay for a more "secure asylum,"[16] and his sympathetic Hobart Town agent documented how the impact of the crisis was being felt even in the capital:

I was exceedingly sorry to hear of the extent of the mischief done by the Banditti at your house … In the town we are all soldiers and also special constables and do duty on guard every night thereby allowing all the military to turn out in quest of the rascals.[17]

The rebels' power was also felt in the north. Wallace wrote from Port Dalrymple in September 1825 that "the country at present is in a most deplorable state with the bushrangers. It is impossible to travel from one township to another without being robbed."[18]

Ann Horden, passing though on her way to Sydney in 1825, described the "awful state of Van Diemen's Land," where there were "dreadful robberies and murders continually." Hobart Town evoked in her "a kind of disgust … We landed most of the passengers at Van Diemen's Land but they would most of them have been glad to have gone back again to London if they had enough to have gone back with."[19] In the following year, the number of free settlers arriving in Van Diemen's Land dropped dramatically, and the fear of bushrangers was an important factor in this. Even the colonial secretary, Lord Bathurst, privately recommended to a Gloucestershire neighbour, William Lyne, that Van Diemen's Land had so many problems with bushrangers and Aborigines that he was better off going to New South Wales.[20]

Matthew Brady famously targeted the social pretensions of the free settlers and the symbols of state oppression, with aspiring gentry forced to assume the roles of their servants, and soldiers being gaoled in their own cells. Little England was being effectively mocked, and the enormous popular support Brady received, and the speed with which his exploits became legend, reflected how deeply this challenge to the pretensions of the elite resonated in popular culture. As early as 1827 a drama based on the gang's confrontation with their oppressors, *The Van Diemen's Land Warriors*, had to be banned and copies destroyed.[21]

Much of Arthur's penal reform agenda was put on hold while Brady was at large. Arthur explained to Lord Bathurst in June 1826, two months after Brady had finally been captured (100 guineas reward and free pardon and passage to England for each convict involved in the capture had been offered as an incentive):

> The troublesome times I have described, when the prisoners were excited by a most mischievous faction, and when a daring band of their associates was in open arms, was no season to introduce reforms by the imposition of greater restraints. I cannot therefore gratify your Lordship by representing that the wise and salutary system so often inculcated by His Majesty's Government to be observed in the treatment of convicts, has been introduced to any extent. The most that could be done was to prevent matters from becoming worse.[22]

Brady was captured and executed in 1826. With that, Arthur's policy of restraint ended and the colonial government embarked on an unparalleled two-year killing spree that was explicitly designed to shock the population into submission.

The Gallows

In 1822 James Ross had complained of the capital of Van Diemen's Land that "the whole appearance of the town was dull and saddening … Even that ancient mark of civilization, the gallows, was then wanting in Hobart Town."[23] Capital offences (including stock theft) still had to be tried in Sydney – a strong disincentive, as we have seen, against bringing charges because of the time and costs involved.

It was only with the establishment of the supreme court in 1823 that people could be sentenced to death by a court in Van Diemen's

Land. The legal historian Alex Castles argues that Arthur's subsequent use of capital punishment was unprecedented in the colonial experience in Australia – there were 103 hangings in 1826–27 alone and 260 during his term of office.[24] Bodies were left in the open for months at a time, no doubt plucked at and slowly mauled by the many Van Diemonian carrion-eaters. Arthur knew that it was not dying, but the desecration of the body after death, that was the most dreaded punishment in the popular mind.

Most executions were not for murder – this remained an uncommon crime in Van Diemen's Land – but for crimes against property, overwhelmingly stock theft. Although the law had been changed in England in 1823 so that the theft of sheep (along with about 100 other crimes) was no longer a capital offence, Arthur's "sheep-stealing act" ensured there would be no such leniency in his jurisdiction. Without an end to systematic stock theft, there could be no hope of obtaining a subservient convict labour force; zealous masters across the island would continue to find their sheep and cattle disappearing when they attempted to enforce discipline. Arthur liberally used bribes (indulgences) to break down convict solidarity and bring men before the courts. The alleged receivers of stolen animals – particular the small landowners – were also executed. George Farquharson, who was convicted of this crime in 1826, complained that "there was so strong a link of villany between the whole of the shepherds in the neighbourhood ... that to discover sheep after they had once been stolen was utterly impossible." True enough, perhaps, but he was hanged anyway.[25]

New Forms of Punishment
After 1827 the number of hangings dropped off somewhat, although the substitutes developed by Arthur as part of a sophisticated seven-layered hierarchy of penal punishment were scarcely more humane. By 1834, 14 per cent of male convicts were on road gangs, 6 per cent were in irons and 7 per cent were at the newly built Port Arthur – that is, one in four were in "some form of work-orientated punishment."[26] Furthermore, while the majority of convicts were still assigned servants, and usually another 10 per cent or so had tickets of

leave, convicts were regularly moved up and down the punishment/ reward hierarchy so that the terrors of the new punishments were widely experienced and universally feared. Even ticket-of-leavers could quickly find themselves back in a public work gang for a minor breach of regulations, while a repeat offence was likely to see them placed in a penal institution. The terror of punishment greatly increased the masters' power to extract work and subservience from their assigned servants. In earlier, less stringent times, a return to government labour had sometimes been welcomed as an escape from a tyrannical master; now, it was universally dreaded. In these circumstances, convicts were far more likely to accept brutality from their masters. In October 1826, George Hobler "thrashed" his assigned servant "with a stick to save myself the pain of flogging him legally."[27] Few convicts would see much point in complaining to a magistrate about such criminal assault when the arbiters of justice were themselves largely drawn from the ranks of landowners.

Though some free settlers differed with Arthur on questions of patronage, land and labour allocation, and the restriction of political rights, most applauded the new discipline regime. The first measure to have a substantial impact was the chain gang, trialled in 1826 (as soon as Brady and his gang were safely dead) and permanently introduced in the following year.[28] Chains had been used on a small scale in earlier years, but it was Arthur who made them a dreaded, and common, part of convict life. A correspondent wrote to Meredith in late August 1826 that "the chain gang is one of the best things that has been projected in this reign, never were men better worked, better flogd and better managed than they are in the gang."[29]

A few of the more sensitive settlers worried about the depths to which British civilisation had sunk. The government official G.T.W.B. Boyes was appalled at the conditions of the four to five hundred convicts who laboured on the Bridgewater causeway for well over a decade from 1829 as they slowly forged a crossing across the Derwent:

> Here the convicts labour, and with short intervals of refreshment and repose it may be said incessantly. They quarry stone, break it, shape it – or not as required, wheel it to the causeway and apply it

either to form a foundation or in the erection of piers upon foundations already formed. The work is almost of an endless description – from the extent and depth of the mud in which it is constructing, and the unhappy labourers are therefore not even cheered by viewing the progress of their daily toil.[30]

Boyes also reported that "modifications of punishment" could be "produced by varying the weight of and length of the chains." "The shortest are the most painful and embarrassing by affording the least possible space for the motion of the legs," he explained, and he had "heard a man after receiving the cat o' nine tails" say "that he would rather be hanged than forced to work in short chains." Nor was there much respite after the day's work was completed, with convicts being confined to cells seven feet long by only two and a half feet high. Boyes believed the horrific conditions must have been devised by "some modern Phalaris" (a notoriously cruel sixth-century BC tyrant of Sicily).[31]

Even Arthur thought the chain gangs as "severe a punishment as may well be inflicted upon any man."[32] The aim was to break the source of convict resistance, with, as the lieutenant governor informed London in 1833, "idleness or insolence of expression or even of looks, anything betraying the insurgent spirit" leading "to the chain-gang or the triangle or to hard labour on the roads."[33]

Accompanying the new rigours of public labour were secure prisons and barracks, including female factories.[34] The administrative oversight of New South Wales had greatly curtailed the amount of public building, and Arthur, arguing to a budget-conscious London in 1826 that "nothing effectual can be done until proper places for the accommodation and confinement of the prisoners with substantial gaols etc are erected," used his independence to build secure places of confinement.[35] No convicts were free after dark in Hobart Town from this time, excepting those who had earned this privilege through good behaviour. One prominent Hobart Town resident, James Grant, wrote to the colonial secretary in June 1827, urging that there should be no compromising with the rigorous new system:

For heavens sake let not the governor ever be persuaded to depart from his own excellent system which has worked so well ... not a man, who has not proved himself a good character, should be suffered on any pretence to have the disposal of himself after dark in this place. Otherwise the old system, which has been suppressed by the extraordinary exertion of the governor, will recur with only its positive horrors.[36]

Barracks took a little longer to build, but were seen as equally important to the cause of civil order. Lieutenant-Colonel Balfour wrote to Arthur in August 1826 that "without means to confine soldiers at night, and potential to punish them by confinement ... it is almost impossible to take effectual measures for the prevention of crimes." But over a year later, in November 1827, Arthur was still lobbying London in an attempt to convince the imperial government of the importance of this issue in Van Diemen's Land:

the consequence of troops being dispersed ... remote from their officers and lodged in unenclosed buildings is most destructive to discipline anywhere, but in a convict colony it leads to a connexion and intimacy between the soldiers and prisoners which is attended with the very worst consequences.[37]

By the early 1830s, even this issue had been largely resolved and an almost impenetrable wall descended between the world of the prisoners and the soldiers who watched over them.

Paradoxically, the new regime of penal discipline involved the closure of the infamous Macquarie Harbour penal station. At the executive council meeting of 28 January 1833, Arthur reported that the English parliament wanted "to convince criminals in England that the mere fact of being transported to the colonies will be by no means operate as an extinction of their crimes but that they are to expect on their arrival here a life of slavery and privation." To this end, resources would be concentrated at Port Arthur, where convicts could more "easily be secured, classified and put to work suitable to their strength and the degree of punishment it is intended to inflict upon each." This would be aided by the fact that "vessels may go and return within 24 hours, [and] troops may be withdrawn and reinforced speedily" (by contrast the trip to Macquarie Harbour was "scarcely of shorter duration than ten days" and one vessel had taken four months to get there from Hobart Town!).[38]

Port Arthur's horrors are the best known and best documented aspect of the convict experience in Van Diemen's Land.[39] Nearly one in six convicts would spend some time there, and even those who never saw the empire's largest gaol were greatly affected by it. All the poor of the island – including those who were now technically free – knew of it as a living hell that was never more than a magistrate's hearing away. Its "life of slavery and privation" might have remained a minority experience, and been a questionable deterrent to the poverty-stricken criminals of England, but the threat it posed undoubtedly proved effective in compelling the subservience of the unfree labour force of Van Diemen's Land.

New Policing and Interior Controls

Alongside the new forms of punishment came reforms to policing. As noted, all of the colony's governors recognised that the most effective and efficient form of policing was to get convicts to do it themselves. But it was not until Arthur established the field police in 1826, as part of his strategy to deal with the bushranger emergency, that this policy was extended to its logical conclusion: the establishment of an official convict-staffed police force.

Arthur described the background to this development in a despatch to Bathurst in March 1827:

> I was driven during the heat of bush-ranging to strengthen the
> establishment by the appointment of a field police, formed from the
> very best conducted prisoners, and stimulated to exertion by the
> hope of a mitigation of their sentence, which is promised after uni
> form good conduct for three years ... the employment of these con
> victs had a most powerful effect on suppressing bushranging by
> creating distrust and division among the prisoner population.[40]

A high proportion of the field police were seasoned warriors – former soldiers in the French Wars who had fallen into poverty and crime after being decommissioned in 1815. Convict police were also cheap and this allowed a rapid expansion in numbers. By 1835 there was one policeman for every 88.7 people, which, as Stefan Petrow has observed, made "Van Diemen's Land one of the most heavily policed countries in the world." About two thirds of the police were serving convicts.[41]

Arthur's convict field police made nugatory his early plans for a gentlemen-controlled militia along English lines. Arthur had envisaged compelling "all free persons to serve in small corps in their respective districts for the defence of such district", but found that the "assistance" of the well-to-do in the bushranger struggle, "although well intended, [was] so ill directed ... I should not be disposed to avail myself again of such assistance."[42]

In early 1827 the settled districts were divided into five administrative districts, each under a district police magistrate. These officials became Arthur's right-hand men, enjoying extensive delegated powers and direct authority over the field police. Robson believed that "due to this master stroke of delegation of power, by about 1827 Arthur had town and country in the island colony in a state of tranquility suitable for further land settlement and consolidation."[43]

[13]

IMPOSING DEPENDENCE

T HROUGH THE NEW SYSTEMS OF PUNISHMENT, Arthur was able to refine the servant identity first promulgated by Lieutenant Governor Collins. Convicts were presented with a daily choice – to conform and maintain their rights and freedoms as unfree servants on assignment, or be treated as criminals within a brutal punishment regime.

There were striking similarities between the assignment system as it operated by the late 1820s and the system in place on rural estates in pre-industrial England. B.A. Holderness has described the latter: "the farm servants, men and women ... had their food and working clothes provided and received a small money payment at the end of their term of service. Hired usually at special fairs, they performed most of the specialist services of the farm."[1] The "life chances" of these and other members of "the small communities, the villages, and tiny towns of the old society in which the average individual lived" were, as Harold Perkin has put it, "controlled by a paternal landlord, employer or patron," so that "resentment had to be swallowed."[2] Unpaid farm servants were rapidly replaced by wage labourers during the nineteenth century, but during the 1820s and 1830s this way of life continued in many regions of England and would have been familiar to all in Van Diemen's Land.

One paradox of Arthur's penal system was that convicts on assignment had rights and privileges not enjoyed by prisoners in British gaols. Many visitors to the colony were baffled by this. Jane Roberts noted in 1830 that convicts in private families are without any mark of disgrace, but apparently the same as hired servants in England; they are fed and clothed but receive no wages … It is said that they never forgive a person who accidentally calls them "convicts"; they denominate themselves "servants of the crown" and settlers invariably do the same.[3]

Arthur and his key allies in the colonial office, however, understood that this arrangement both improved productivity and made it easier to control the rapidly increasing convict population. Those who rebelled or misbehaved could be punished not only with hard labour or solitary confinement, but also with the loss of their dignity and identity. The authorities in London, hoping to control the poor in a time of rapid economic and social upheaval, painted Australia as a land of degraded and brutalised exiles. In reality, however, to make such extreme suffering a permanent or universal part of convict life would have been difficult, costly and counterproductive.

The convict Richard Dillingham expressed the thinking behind the assignment system in a letter to his parents in September 1836:

As to my living, I find it better than ever I expected, Thank God I want for nothing in that respect. As for tea and sugar I almost could swim in it. I am allowed two pound of sugar and quarter pound of tea per week and plenty of tobacco and good white bread and sometimes beef, sometimes mutton, sometimes pork. This I have every day. Plenty of fruit in the season of all sorts … and I want for nothing but my liberty but though I am thus situated it is not the case with all that come … For some through their misconduct get into road partys and some into chain gangs and live a miserable life.[4]

The practice of Arthur's penal system between 1828 and 1836 probably came closer to matching the ideals of the policy underpinning it than in any other period of Van Diemen's Land history, but complete realisation was prevented by the extreme and paranoid nature of the Van Diemonian caste system. The social structures of rural England were incompletely reproduced in Van Diemen's Land not only because of convict resistance, but also due to free-settler snobbery. Many convicts were willing to accept the status and condition of farm servants, but few settlers were happy to be their supervisors. The English social pyramid had far more people in the middling ranks than at the apex, but in Van Diemen's Land most of the land grantees were scrambling for a place at the top. Octavia Dawson, who arrived in 1829, did not like Van Diemen's Land because "the people ... are very *high* or very *low*."[5]

Arthur perceived the problem. He argued that the very wealthy "are not the most likely masters to succeed in reforming their servants, but such as, having but few, are daily over them and with them." He advocated the immigration of a "description of yeomen-middling agriculturalists and independent men of good character and education – if possible married – who would be the most likely to carry into effect the object of reform."[6] But the lieutenant governor's own land policy, which saw so much of the best land given to so few, meant that while Van Diemen's Land had aspiring gentry enough, it always lacked the very men that Arthur saw as the key to moral reformation.

In place of a yeomen class, there were overseers, usually serving or former convicts, and invariably of a similar background and class to the convicts themselves. This did not mean that convict discipline was lax, just that more space existed for alternative values, relationships and customs. While Van Diemen's Land continued to have two distinct settler societies – the convict-derived majority and a small group of privileged free settlers obsessed with avoiding all contact with them – the people's culture enjoyed a significant degree of autonomy. Though the convict world was increasingly confined and legally ordered by the elite, within these boundaries there remained a surprising level of freedom.

Churches, Schools and Press

In the early nineteenth century, the Church of England was widely understood to be the foundation of the nation's social hierarchy and the most effective counter to insurrectionist and revolutionary sentiments crossing the English Channel. The church was particularly associated with the privileges of the landed gentry: "I know nothing better calculated to fill a country with barbarians ready for any mischief," wrote Arthur Young, the agricultural propagandist, in 1799, "than extensive commons and divine service only once a month."[7]

Despite this, Robert Knopwood was the only minister in Van Diemen's Land until 1818, when John Youl – an evangelical former missionary to the Pacific Islands – was appointed as chaplain at Port Dalrymple. And, as in the home country, the inability of the Church of England to meet the challenge of social and economic change meant that it soon faced competition.

The first Catholic chaplain, Phillip Connolly, was appointed in 1821. The support of the British government for the post was part of a church–state partnership to control the Irish convicts, and the Catholic Church did not let its patrons down. In Van Diemen's Land, as in Ireland itself, the priests, while confronting the worst aspects of religious discrimination, generally preached co-existence and submission to the imperial power. Connolly sought an active partnership with the civil authorities, seeing them as a buffer to the influence of the church's English Benedictine hierarchy. Patrick O'Farrell's conclusion that "from early in its Australian history [the Catholic Church] developed a view of English authority as repressive, unjust, brutal, persecuting, immoral, the sort of shackles from which the real Australia must escape," has very little application in Van Diemen's Land.[8] As the Irish political prisoner John Mitchel reflected from his exile in the colony, Catholic priests may "dislike British power," but "they hate revolution worse."[9]

More significant to the protestant convict majority was the arrival of the Methodists. Soon after his arrival in Sydney in 1815, Samuel Leigh, the first Methodist missionary to New South Wales, wrote a plea to his superiors to send a missionary to Van Diemen's Land, wherein were "many thousands of British souls, many of whom are sunk almost upon a level with the Aboriginal inhabitants of the country."[10]

A number of Methodist missionaries visited from 1820, but none stayed on until the 21-year-old William Horton in 1822. The Wesleyans' commitment to working with convicts meant that Arthur became a powerful patron. Arthur also worked closely with the new Church of England chaplain, William Bedford, who arrived in 1823, and together they embarked on a moral crusade. "The last year has not only added to the number of genteel people, but Mr Bedford's decisive measures and perseverance has greatly improved the morality of the people," wrote Bedford's friend William Parramore in October 1824. Parramore optimistically conjectured that due to "Mr Bedford's vigilance ... I expect to see the people sober as well as chaste in another year."[11] The chaplain's measures included putting in the gaol or the factory every convict who lived in adultery. Unmarried convict women who became pregnant, whatever the circumstances, were punished with a return to confinement at an institution and early separation from their children. In these circumstances it is not surprising that pregnancies were concealed, and that the first woman executed in Van Diemen's Land was for infanticide (Mary MacLauchlan was reputedly talked out of a public denunciation of the father by Bedford, because he was believed to be a gentleman).[12]

The impact of such measures was summarised by Arthur in an 1828 letter to the bishop of London:

> The moral habits of the inhabitants of this colony are greatly improved within the last two years and the reformation in the character of the wretched convicts especially, is so striking that I may venture to speak ... of the advantages of transportation over every other species of punishment, where suitable arrangements are perfected for the reception and the treatment of convicts in the colony.[13]

An equally noticeable change occurred in the public behaviour of the elite. As Parramore pointed out, after Arthur's arrival it was in the "interest of all who would stand well with the governor to *seem* moral." The young evangelical observed that "the Church from being nearly empty is now so well filled that it has become necessary to add additional pews."[14]

Schools, closely linked to the church, were another critical means of social control. Convict schoolmasters maintained the early haphazard, but not always ineffective, education system, but in 1821

P.A. Mulgrave was appointed superintendent of schools, and a non-denominational curriculum known as the "National" education system in Britain was introduced.[15]

The churches and schools were largely uncritical supporters of state policy. Matters were more complex in relation to the press. In the early and mid 1820s, Van Diemen's Land enjoyed a remarkable period of press freedom, in which Andrew Bent figured prominently. As Joan Woodberry has reflected, "Bent must have been one of the few men in history ... able to print the notice of his own conditional emancipation in his own newspaper."[16] Certainly this former convict's takeover of the government paper, the *Hobart Town Gazette*, must rank as one of the most remarkable episodes in the history of the Australian media and the ongoing struggle for a free press. Parramore summarised events in early 1825: the *Hobart Town Gazette* was the "organ of government" until it

> threw off the shackles of the censorship nine months ago and boldly dismissed the government editor. The printer being in possession of the only type in the island, government have no alternative but to submit tamely to publish the government notices in his paper till a supply of type can be obtained from England.[17]

The *Hobart Town Gazette* was eventually brought back under government control, but Arthur remained in constant conflict with other budding newspaper entrepreneurs, including Henry Melville and Gilbert Robertson. The lieutenant governor argued that a free press was incompatible with a penal colony, and he was not afraid to imprison proprietors to prove it. But, in comparison with later years, a lively if not always well-informed public debate persisted. This debate remained, however, very largely the preserve of the free, and, in contrast to New South Wales, former convicts had little public voice.

Undermining Economic Independence

The high price of labour (compared with Britain) was seen as a major problem by the authorities and free settlers because of both its economic and social implications. Not only did it raise production costs and reduce profits, but workers who could pick and choose employers, and earn a living with less than full-time labour, were seen to be a threat to social order.

Wages fell so rapidly in the late 1820s because of the increased labour supply and tighter regulations that by early 1829 the *Colonial Times* could trumpet that

> the great decrease in the annual payment of wages is really amazing ... Formerly it was impossible to employ a free farm servant under 40 or 50 pounds per annum, with provisions. Now mark the contrast. There are many who are now glad to be employed for their food and 10 pounds a year.[18]

As wages fell, the resources of the bush and the sea became only more important. Nature could be called on for "free" food, clothing, shelter and heating, as well as being a source of supplementary income. Increasingly it was only the difficult-to-privatise bounty of the land that stood between Van Diemonian workers and the dependency and subservience sought by their masters.

If the vision of the landed gentry and colonial authorities was to be realised, access to the resources of the bush had to be restricted and regulated. The ending of small land grants was integral to this. In the new regime, even smallholder survivors from an earlier era were seen by the authorities and free settlers as a "serious evil." The land commissioners argued that "by means of these small grants the system of sheep stealing is fully organized" and "the evil does not rest here, were all these small grants done away with and stock runs prohibited, labour could be obtained at a much more moderate price."[19]

Concentrating ownership was a start, but restricting access to land that was as yet without any British title was a far more challenging task. Arthur's impounding laws, which required stock to be fenced in, were aimed at the control of wandering people as much as animals. As Castles concludes, they were intended "to stamp on the independent entrepreneurial activities of emancipists and convicts, as well as controlling animal thefts."[20] The laws represented a direct attack on the old pastoral system, which in turn underpinned the social freedom of the bush.

The land commissioners were strong advocates for the new regulations, asking in May 1828, "so long as the colony remains a common, and it is at the option of every one whether he chooses to fence or not, how can any man count upon being repaid for his labour by agriculture, or how is the breed of sheep to be improved?"[21] The commissioners praised Arthur's laws but also called for even more reform. Regulations were progressively tightened and, along with the shift to a wool-based economy, ensured that by the mid-1830s, what David Burn termed "cattle-hunting" – the unrestricted droving of cattle – had become "nearly an obsolete story."[22]

It was more difficult to restrict access to crown lands for those without stock. But as settlement increased, and licence systems began to be enforced, those who looked to the bush for resources without official sanction were increasingly forced onto more remote and marginal land. The exclusion of the poor from public lands was relentless, but the process was not without its contradictions. A number of the new industries paradoxically perpetuated the old way of life. For example, those who held the rights to strip wattle bark (used to tan leather) rarely did the labour themselves, preferring to contract the work out to workers who received, in lieu of a wage, a set price per volume. This guaranteed high margins for the licence holders, but it also offered the possibility of independence and a life of relative freedom in the bush for ex-convicts and their families.

As his hand was strengthened both by underlying economic change and the plethora of penal reforms, Arthur grew intolerant of settlers who allowed assigned convicts to engage in independent economic activity. In September 1826 he warned, "if it shall be ascertained any settler makes payment to convict servants in stock, or apportions to them land for their exclusive benefit, or suffers them to be employed in any other than his immediate service, every support and indulgence of the crown will be withdrawn." This warning was reinforced by similar proclamations in October 1827 and June 1828.[23]

Controlling the trade in meat and skins was a particular priority. As had been the case since 1804, dog-control remained the central means of achieving this long-sought-after end. The first colonial tax introduced in Van Diemen's Land (other than excise duties) was an annual levy on canines. The 1830 Dog Act and its 1834 successor were in part aimed at controlling the wild dog population, but they were also intended to "to keep a check on dogs used by the back-areas fraternity in their depredations."[24] Nevertheless, the tax was only effective because as forester kangaroos became rarer, and the open dog-friendly country was privatised, the economics of hunting with dogs became increasingly marginal anyway.

Changes to Poor Relief

As in Britain, where the Poor Laws were radically reformed in the early 1830s, social control in Van Diemen's Land was seen to require a harsher and more restricted system of charity. The comparatively generous systems of assistance from before 1820, when the aged and infirm were simply placed on the government store, were replaced by more limited aid conditional on behaviour.

After 1825, New South Wales and Van Diemen's Land parted ways on this question. In the former, relief was increasingly administered by charities, but in Van Diemen's Land the charitable sector was small and the government continued to be the chief provider.[25] People often petitioned the governor directly – especially single mothers struggling to feed their children. Maria Harrington's appeal to Arthur in 1835 was based on her Aboriginality:

> I am a native born some part of my existence having sprung from the Aboriginal possessors of the soil, I have an infant depending upon me for support in which I have great difficulty to obtain. I am desirous of providing better for my child, and pray that Your Excellency will take into your humane consideration my birth and the right my forefathers had to the land, and in such humanity be pleased to grant me an order to locate a piece of land as in Your Excellency's wisdom shall seem meet.

Less unusual was the rejection of this petition, with the police magistrate at Launceston condemning Maria to poverty with his judgment that "this applicant is a very immoral character, now living with a man to whom she is not married, and undeserving any indulgence."[26]

Arthur also had little time for sentiment when judging applicants for relief. In May 1833 it was recommended to him that the destitute whistleblower of the Risdon massacre, the former stock-keeper and hunter Edward White, be allowed rations as the colony's oldest resident, but the lieutenant governor even rejected this claim "unless he is in such a state as to be admitted into the invalid establishment."[27]

The largest single social welfare institution established by the government in the late 1820s also had explicit social-control objectives. Arthur, believing that "the colony is overrun with illegitimate children ... born to no certain provision of inheritance but the vices of their parents and their consequent misery," proposed the establishment of an orphan school in 1825, arguing that it should be "a school of industry, where labour as well as learning is taught."[28] Only a small minority of the residents of the institution, which was built adjoining St John's Church, New Town, were actually orphans, and the "orphan school" is more accurately characterised as Van Diemen's Land's first children's home. David Burn, writing in 1840, described the clientele as comprising "the Aboriginal native, the illegitimate offspring of the wretched female convict, and the children of the reduced and bankrupt settler."[29] Children saw little of their parents, who were regarded as a bad influence likely to undermine a regime of discipline designed to mould the boys and girls into labourers and domestic servants respectively. The committee of management recorded in 1828 that "the following days be publicly advertised for parents seeing their children – the first Monday in the month of January, April, July and October from eleven till two in the presence of the master or matron."[30] At the age of 14 children were apprenticed out and forced to work for no money until they reached the age of 18. In the intervening years they were at the mercy of their masters.[31]

The power the authorities wielded over the children of convicts was a small part of a sophisticated penal system which, along with economic and social reforms, resulted in an increasingly dependent, fearful and submissive labour force. However one serious threat remained to the profits and property of the free settlers. Their attempt to assert monopoly rights over the best hunting grounds of the island affected above all the Aborigines, whose defence of their territory proved fierce and effective. A complacent government took some time to acknowledge the new reality, but before the decade was out, even Arthur had to admit that Van Diemen's Land was at war.

[14]

FIGHTING THE ABORIGINES

SINCE PERMANENT EUROPEAN SETTLEMENT began in 1803, Van Diemen's Land had never known peace. Temporary understandings reached between Aborigines and individuals or small groups of whites had led to a degree of shared land use, but sporadic fighting continued. This was always a highly charged, sometimes violent, cultural encounter. However, the fighting was localised, and for the majority of free settlers, as for the government, the Aborigines were of little concern.

Historians since Henry Melville have dated the beginning of sustained Aboriginal resistance to the year 1824.[1] There is some evidence that the Aborigines also dated the end of their old way of life, if not as precisely as this, at least to a general period in the early 1820s. In several instances the Aborigines travelling with George Augustus Robinson on his extended conciliation mission (or "Black Embassy," as it was widely known[2]) in the early 1830s referred to nations and leaders as they had been in 1820 or 1826, with an emphasis on the changes that had occurred in the interim. It is likely that "1820" served as shorthand for how life was before the radical disruption, and "1826" for the beginning of a harried life of resistance.

Perhaps the last large-scale (and at the time surprising) visit of over 60 Aborigines to Hobart Town in November 1824 also needs to be understood in this context. Was this a final delegation to the increasingly intrusive invaders? William Parramore documented the event:

On the 10th of November we were visited by a tribe of 66 Natives
... I met ... on the Sunday after the 10th while walking from
Church with Mrs. Bedford, 3 of them with great long coats, but nor
a particle of covering before ... The Lt.Gov. on their arrival had
them immediately provided with food and old clothes – and the
second night they were conducted to the road men's hut four miles
from town ... The third day they were rather sullen and refused to
sing the Kangaroo song, and moved off early the next morning.[3]

The Aboriginal visit was in the first year of Lieutenant Governor
Arthur's term of office. Given Arthur's evangelical Christian conver-
sion in 1811 and his record of support for Indigenous people as governor of Honduras, such a large and unexpected visit from the
Aborigines to the main British settlement so early in his tenure might
have been seen as a heaven-sent opportunity. Yet the Aborigines were
quickly removed from the town and taken to a convict hut four miles
away. This blatantly unfriendly and undiplomatic move was probably
why they soon moved off, never to return in such numbers.

Arthur may have belatedly realised his mistake, for within a few
days he called a public meeting to discuss founding an "institution
for the civilization and instruction of the Aborigines of the Island"
which involved the Anglican chaplain, William Bedford, and the
Wesleyan missionary Ralph Mansfield. This meeting was also
described by Parramore: "it was proposed to institute a school for the
education of the natives' children and to grant 2000 acres of land to be
cultivated by the adults if they can be brought to any sense of the benefits of a settled life."[4] The rules and regulations were drawn up, but
the scheme was forgotten, and another attempt to found a native
institution by Arthur in 1825 also failed. As Mansfield informed the
Missionary Society in London in June 1825, this was undoubtedly in
part because "the formidable ravages of a banditti of convicts" had by
then "completely absorbed the public attention."[5]

It was at any rate probably already too late for such cross-cultural
experiments. Two months after the Hobart Town visit, a group of
Aborigines was fired upon as they attempted to approach Launceston.[6] At Birch's Bay (where there was a government logging station) a

large group of Aborigines was given better treatment – rugs, blankets and bread were reportedly provided – but there can be little doubt that, overall, relations were rapidly deteriorating.[7] This was most clearly seen in the heartland of the cultural encounter, the grassy woodlands.

The Demand for Exclusivity

By 1825, a large proportion of the best Aboriginal hunting grounds of Van Diemen's Land had a newly issued British title. The new land-owners generally assumed that their legal grant implied that the rights of other land users, including the Aborigines, had been extinguished, and that they had a right to defend their private property against trespassers. Most would have agreed with Curr's statement to the Aborigines Committee: "the Crown sells us lands, and is therefore bound to make good our titles and possessions against previous occupants and claimants."[8]

However, the increasing conflict with the Aborigines was not so much the result of changes in land title as in land use. In contrast to the first wave of British settlement, the free settlers built permanent homes, planted crops and gardens, and imported valuable stock. Aboriginal land management and hunting practices, which involved both dogs and, above all, fire, posed a direct threat to this investment. In this context, shared land use and co-existence required compromises that few free settlers were prepared to contemplate. Moreover, the new immigrants had far greater power, thanks to their assigned convicts, paid workers, arms and capital. The difference between the new settlers' and earlier white occupants' responses to Aborigines was not, then, primarily a question of law or character. Rather, it was a consequence of the use made of the land and of a change in the balance of power at the frontier.

Not surprisingly, it took some time for Aborigines to realise the extent of the change. According to J.C. Sutherland's diary, Aborigines visited his estate in March 1824 (five months after Sutherland had arrived), expecting to receive the customary payment of provisions, but they were "forthwith ordered away." In December, Sutherland "received a visit of 31 natives" who were also "instantly ordered away."

While Sutherland gave no information about how he achieved such a summary dismissal, it is unlikely that it could have been achieved without at least a show of force. Perhaps conflict was only averted by a more co-operative neighbour: Sutherland reports that the Aborigines "went to Gatenby's where they had some bread."[9]

The diary of one of the most respected east-coast settlers, Adam Amos, provides another account of the changed relations. In May 1823, Amos reported that

> My house was surrounded by natives, one a woman came to the door. I made signs for her to go away – she did and in a short time about six made their appearance amongst the brush in the river close to my hut. I fired small shot at about 50 yards distance they run off. I fired another piece loaded with ball over their head to let them know I had more pieces than one – I durst not leave the house as none of my oldest sons were at home nor my servant man … the natives made no more appearance.[10]

In December of the same year, when the Aborigines attempted to burn the bush, Amos sent his "oldest son to shoot them again but missed by minutes." On the following day, when "the natives who has been of late in the woods near my hutt … set the grass on fire near my farm, [Amos] thought it prudent to frighten them, having heard that they had thrattened to Mr Talbot's to burn my corn when sircumstances gave them opportunity." Amos reported that he "sent my eldest son who was joined by two of Mr Meredith's men who fired on them and wounded one," and that "the mob, who appeared numerous, fled over the hill" where they were pursued "for some time."[11] By the following year east-coast settlers were forcibly evicting Aborigines from the Oyster Bay district wherever they were seen, despite it being one of the most important regional food sources and seasonal gathering places.

It is not surprising that the Aborigines retaliated and the conflict escalated. Amos reported that a stockman of his neighbour, George Meredith, was killed on 6 June 1824, and on 26 July Meredith informed Arthur that he had distributed arms "amongst our various stockmen."[12] Meredith made it clear that he was prepared to kill Aborigines unless a military force was stationed on the east coast,[13] and the lieutenant governor made no protest against this threat of criminal behaviour towards what were, under British law, fellow British subjects. Indeed, no one in Van Diemen's Land was ever prosecuted for killing an Aborigine (despite recent claims to the contrary[14]) and Arthur seemed sympathetic to the settlers' position, despite his many differences with them on other issues. He informed Lord Bathurst, the colonial secretary, as part of a call for military reinforcements, that "the fears of the settlers have been much, and certainly justly excited, by the late unusual hostile proceedings of the natives, who have committed several murders."[15]

Conflict was not confined to the east coast. Wallace wrote from Port Dalrymple in September 1825 that "we are very often troubled by the Aborigines of the colony in the bush and in the different townships. They travel in gangs of 300 to 200."[16]

Initially, most of the blame for the growing hostility was slated to Musquito, a New South Wales Aborigine who had been transported to Van Diemen's Land in 1813 after eight years' exile on Norfolk Island. Following his pivotal role in the capture of Michael Howe, Musquito had failed to receive his promised passage home and had gradually resumed the active resistance to the British that he had begun in his homeland. By 1823–24, he was a central figure in the conflict, especially in southern and eastern regions of the island. He was eventually tracked down and wounded by an Aboriginal youth called Teague, then living with the surgeon Edward Luttrell. Musquito and a Tasmanian Aborigine known to the British as Black Jack were then taken to Hobart, where both were tried and convicted of murder, and hanged in February 1825.

It was convenient for the settlers to blame Musquito for the increase in hostilities. Not only did the explanation deflect concerns about the consequences of the free settlers' land grab, but, as a New South Wales Aborigine who had spent much time with the British, his actions could be characterised as those of an individual criminal – a far less threatening prospect than an uprising by the Indigenous people. More thoughtful settlers, however, knew that the resistance had far deeper sources than any individual grievance, especially as it grew in strength after Musquito's death.

A few settlers even questioned the legality of the conquest. In May 1826, the *Colonial Times* reported that as Matthew Brady and his gang were sent to their death, "two black Aboriginal natives ... are confined to the gaol, on the charge of spearing a man to death ... one ... very old, has a long beard, long hair in ringlets, and is coloured with red ochre; he is ill and feeble, so much so, that he is only able to move about in the prison by crawling on his hands and knees."[17] The paper was critical of the imprisonment and sentencing of these men and published a detailed article citing "Vattel, Grotius and other writers on international law" in support of the claim that "the conquerors [of land] become subject to the territorial laws of the conquered."[18]

Such philosophical and legal niceties were of little interest to the authorities, and the two were executed in September 1826. Nevertheless, perhaps there were doubts about the legal status of Aborigines engaged in resistance, as these were the last to be hanged. Aboriginal prisoners were thereafter treated (and mistreated) more as prisoners of war than as criminals.[19] Nor were prosecutions for murder ever again pressed, although Aborigines were frequently detained in gaol without charge for indefinite periods.

By December 1826, the *Colonial Times* had become even more critical of government policy towards Aborigines, which it saw as

impowering a class of people, so notoriously ignorant and uneducated as the generality of stock-keepers are, to hunt down and destroy their fellow man, for such the natives most assuredly are ... That the Aboriginals, or original possessors of the soil, have much cause to regret our settling amongst them, must be allowed by all; the kangaroo and other animals from which they derive their subsistence have greatly decreased and daily decreasing in number; and ought we not to endeavour to compensate for these and other evils which they have experienced at our hands?[20]

But as fighting spread, public opinion hardened. There were 72 documented incidents involving Aboriginal attacks or raids in

1827, compared with 29 in 1826, and the number of British killed or wounded increased from 30 to 52.[21] In response, free settlers pushed hard for greater government military support for their private campaigns. In November 1827, 21 inhabitants of farms on the banks of the Macquarie and Elizabeth Rivers warned Arthur that they believed Aboriginal attacks were no longer about revenge, but part of "a plan for the extirpation of the white inhabitants with whom they doubtless consider themselves at war."[22] The land commissioner Roderick O'Connor, who was to become the largest landholder in Van Diemen's Land, wrote a personal letter to the government in December 1827, asking, "Can we live in a wilderness surrounded by wretches who watch every opportunity, and who take delight in shedding our blood?"[23] And the police magistrate of the Oatlands district, Thomas Anstey – also a large landowner, who in February 1830 was to be given overall command of the government "roving parties" sent out to capture or kill Aborigines – informed Arthur that "there seems to be no probable end to the destruction of lives and property which may arise from the desperation of these bloody-thirsty barbarians." Anstey claimed that "the outsettlers and stockmen are in a dreadful state of alarm and will not drive the stock sufficiently from home to afford them sufficient pasturage – the consequence of this will be ominous in the extreme."[24]

From the settlers' perspective, matters worsened during 1828. That year the number of Aboriginal attacks doubled from 72 to 144, and the number of whites killed or wounded increased to 78.[25] In early spring the *Hobart Town Courier* concluded that the Aborigines "have formed a systematic organised plan for carrying on a war of extermination against the white inhabitants of the colony."[26] For his part, Anstey, incensed by the killing of "defenceless women and children," believed that the Aborigines "have withered their war whoop and that it is to be a war of extermination."[27]

Even settlers sympathetic to the Aboriginal cause became advocates for stronger action. The *Colonial Times*, the same paper that had queried the legality of the conquest and acknowledged Aboriginal grievances, now argued that nothing but a removal can protect us from incursion similar to the Caffrees in Africa or the back-woodsmen in North America ... We make no pompous display of philanthropy – we say unequivocally, SELF DEFENCE IS THE FIRST LAW OF NATURE. THE GOVERNMENT MUST REMOVE THE NATIVES. IF NOT THEY WILL BE HUNTED DOWN LIKE WILD BEASTS AND DESTROYED.[28]

The End of Co-existence

As fighting engulfed the island, virtually everyone became entrapped by the fearful logic of war. Even "Black Robert," who had lived with the British since he was an infant and worked on farms all his life, was captured and put in gaol in 1830, before Robinson arranged for him to be sent to the new Aboriginal establishment at Flinders Island.[29]

One of the few refuges for the harassed Aborigines visiting the rich Oyster Bay region after 1823 had been the 700-acre land grant held by an Irishman, John de Courcy (Paddy) Harte. Harte had even given refuge to Musquito when pursuers were closing in on him in late 1823. The Aborigines seem to have continued to visit his farm, which was situated inland of the other early settlements, for many years, but in 1829 Harte's stores were burnt. After this incident, his men reported that acts of barbarity had been committed upon the Aborigines who had been in the habit of calling at Harte's property, "the mere relation of which makes humanity shudder."[30]

In the summer of 1826–27 another man well known to the Aborigines, William Knight, a convict stock-keeper, had been visited by Aborigines in the "westward country" (the land around present-day Westbury and Deloraine). They stayed the day, probably conversing with the stock-keeper, as contact had been sufficiently frequent for Knight reportedly to speak their language. Yet just three months later Knight was involved in an attack on Aborigines and shortly after was himself killed.[31] An Irishman known as McHaskell, resident in the area since 1825, had also "made friends with a tribe of natives who were ... often supplied with provisions," but he too was later killed.

The surveyor, John Helder Wedge, visited another stockman in this same region who informed him that "when he first came the natives were very peaceable, but they have been drove to commit outrages on the whites." This sympathetic man, described by Wedge as living "with a half-caste female, a stout well made person by whom he has had two children,"[32] was Thomas Johnson. The woman was Dalrymple "Dolly" Briggs, daughter of George Briggs. Yet even they were to become unavoidably embroiled in the violence. When Johnson petitioned to marry Briggs in 1831, the magistrate commended her "courageous defence lately against the Aborigines – she is a capital markswoman never I am told missing her aim." The marriage was approved, and Johnson received his freedom and 20 acres of land in recognition of the "resolute conduct" of his new wife.[33]

Fire as a Weapon

The key to understanding what seems an otherwise exaggerated settler fear that the Aborigines could ultimately triumph is the dread of that defining feature of the Van Diemonian environment – fire. Given the vulnerability of crops and houses to almost instant combustion, the Aborigines' fire sticks and war cries seemed to mock the property and pretensions of the invaders. The firing of estates increased in 1828–29 and generated hysteria among the settlers. Several stacks (comprising the year's harvest), huts and standing crops were burnt, and in March 1828 the settlers near Swanport sent Arthur "a statement of the danger ... of being ultimately exterminated by the black natives" because of the "new system which these people are adopting, namely, burning our stacks as well as our houses and making their attacks in the night." These methods, the settlers complained, "render it impossible even for the largest establishment to protect itself ... so great is the horror which they create."[34] James Hobbs complained in May 1830 that it was "either the fifth or sixth time I have been burnt out by the natives ... My loss has been very severe ... In fact it is nothing less than having to commence again as a new settler ... I know not what is to be done."[35] John Allen reported that he had lost his crops, house and three wheat stacks, "being the total loss of Your Petitioners first year hard labour and outlay as well as property to the amount of £300."[36]

These attacks had a drastic effect on public opinion and settler morale. After one 1830 attack, a settler of the Clyde, John Sherwin, testified that the Aborigines had called out "Parrawa Parrawa – Go away you white b-g-rs. What business have you here?" as they burned his property. He warned that if "something is not speedily done, no one can live in the bush."[37] This account was widely publicised, and the settlers of the Clyde drew up a petition for strong government action, arguing that the Aborigines threatened the "extinction of the Colony itself by firing our crops and dwellings."[38] By this time even the most moderate of the press, the *Tasmanian,* believed that "there seems to be something like a determination to destroy all before them [the Aborigines]. Extermination seems to be the only remedy. It is a dreadful one."[39]

Aboriginal advantages in the conflict, emphasised by settlers at the time, have been reinforced by Lyndall Ryan in *The Aboriginal Tasmanians* (1981) and, especially, by Henry Reynolds in *The Fate of a Free People* (1995). The hilly and forested Van Diemonian terrain, the inaccuracy of contemporary guns and their limitations in an environment where rain and river crossings so often rendered powder useless, and the ever accessible retreats that surrounded the open country, all made killing Aborigines a challenging affair. Furthermore, the inability of the British military – trained for the next conventional European conflict and expecting to be involved only in convict guard-duty – to adapt to a guerrilla war has been well documented.[40] Another benefit that has not been given the attention it deserves was superior communications – Aborigines could send quite detailed information quickly over long distances through smokes. Robinson detailed this and other advantages enjoyed by the defenders in his journal in December 1831:

> The natives have the advantage in every respect, in their sight, hearing, nay, in all their senses, their sense of smell also. They can smell a smoke at long distance … scenting a kangaroo roasting … They are at home in the woods; the whole country with few exceptions affords them concealment … They can perceive the smallest trace, much less the plain footmarks of white men. They can trace small animals. They can also do with small fires, the smoke of which is scarcely perceptible … They can subsist on roots and

small animals and they know the passes and are well acquainted with the topography of the county. They will travel over the rocky ground where no traces are to be seen ... Their mode of attack is by surreption. They lay in ambush for some time before they make their attack.[41]

These were real advantages, but their significance has been over-stated.

The Two Phases of War

Despite their heightened state of fear, in reality the British were fighting an already defeated enemy at the height of the documented conflict between 1828 and 1831. When Robinson met with the survivors of the Big River and Oyster Bay tribes in the new year of 1832, their combined population numbered only 26. Historians, relying on settler testimony and official reports, have exaggerated Aboriginal power. While Van Diemen's Land was an unusually equal arena of struggle compared to other regions of Australia, this is mainly true only of the guerrilla stage of the conflict. The final resistance was quite distinct from the earlier stage of the fighting, in which whole communities had been in the firing line.

It is understandable that there is such an overwhelming bias in the literature towards the comparatively "equal" final phase of the war, even though almost all the Aborigines were already dead. The fighting between 1828 and 1831, is, in contrast to the years preceding it, extraordinarily well documented. The 13-volume collection of Colonial Secretary Office records pertaining to Aborigines, first collated on the orders of Arthur, largely relates to this time. Furthermore, it was not until martial law was declared in late 1828 – effectively providing legal immunity for killing Aborigines – that much of the killing began to be reported. The limitation of this rich record is that most of the opportunities for "easy" slaughter (outside of the newly settled north-west) had passed by this time. In the midlands and east coast there are no records of more than three Aborigines being killed in any one encounter after September 1829.[42] But does this mean, as is now broadly accepted, that massacres were also limited before this?

Deadly Knowledge

Settler accounts of Aborigines suggest that even as late as 1824 most Aboriginal groups had a full demographic – including the elderly and young children – and that Aborigines continued to follow established paths and visit traditional resource-rich gathering spots at predictable times of the year. By early 1830 there were no such groups surviving outside of the west coast, with the small bands of warriors almost exclusively comprising fit and agile adults. Their radically new lifestyle of resistance marked the end of a sustainable community life. What had happened in the intervening years?

The lack of *any* observation of Aborigines dying from disease means it is highly unlikely that large groups of Aborigines were killed off by epidemics before they were confined and exiled (although there may have been a significant population decline before British settlement began), as occurred in other regions of Australia. Although significant numbers may have still died from disease, other explanations must be sought for the speed of the Aborigines' demise after 1824. In particular, the proportion likely to have been killed in massacres – significantly reduced by historians in the twentieth century on the basis of evidence overwhelmingly pertaining to the 1828–31 period – must be re-evaluated.

The unusually long period of peaceful contact provides the key to understanding why large numbers of Aborigines may have been massacred in the settled districts despite the well-documented Aboriginal advantages in the conflict.

Although the military was of limited use against the Aborigines, the experienced Van Diemonian bushmen were another matter altogether. By 1824 these men knew the Aborigines' seasonal gathering places, camping sites and movements, and the paths that ran between them. Aboriginal communities that still included small children, pregnant women and the elderly were highly vulnerable to armed parties guided by such men. And Tasmanian topography, although an advantage in the later guerrilla war, restricted the Aborigines' ability to find alternative food sources and meeting sites. While small groups could find indefinite refuge in the rugged interior, a whole band could not. As Roderick O'Connor told the government-appointed Aborigines

Committee in 1830, Douglas Ibbens alone had killed half the "eastern mob" by "creeping upon them and firing amongst them." Far from being concerned about this behaviour, the land commissioner presented it as evidence for his claim that "some of the worst characters would be the best to send after them."[43]

This view seems to have been privately shared by many settlers well before their activities were effectively sanctioned by the declaration of martial law on 1 November 1828 and official roving parties were established. Hamilton Wallace had led an expedition of such bushmen in a retaliatory party in 1825, and wrote to his father on 10 September that "on the second day under the Ben Lomond Tier we fell in with about 250 Aborigines." Wallace reported that fighting occurred, and that a stock-keeper was speared, but gave no estimate of the number of Aboriginal fatalities.[44] A settler of the north-east, Michael Steel, wrote to his brother in February 1827 that when Aborigines were seen, "I instantly armed all my men, some on horseback and some on foot," and set off in pursuit. The next day "we fell in with them on the top of a mountain and poured a strong fire into them and killed their leader and one more ... had the country been even and clear we should have killed or taken the whole of them."[45] In December 1827, after one of his splitters was speared by Aborigines, George Hobler similarly "armed four men who I hope will get sight of their night fires and slaughter them as they be around it."[46] A stock-keeper told Robinson that in retaliation for an attack on his camp at the Western Marshes in which one Aborigine was killed, he and other stock-keepers shot nine Aborigines around their camp.[47] Another stock-keeper related how a "whole tribe ... except an old man and a woman who begged for mercy and were suffered to go away" were killed at Middle Plains in this same region after being driven by men on horses into a lagoon.[48] Robinson heard similar stories of mass slaughter in the upper reaches of the Emu and Jordan rivers.[49]

Arthur was well aware of how capable the Van Diemonian bushmen were in the struggle against the Aborigines. Since the bushranger emergency of 1824–26 the lieutenant governor had relied on the convict field police to fight white and black rebels, and the force had a proven track record. Gilbert Robertson testified to the Aborigines

Committee that the convict field police based at Richmond killed 14 Aborigines in a single incident in 1827.[50] It is not surprising, therefore, that when the government military campaign was intensified in late 1828 following the declaration of martial law, the convict police took the lead role. Nevertheless, the extraordinary decision to place soldiers in the roving parties under the command of convict constables (despite predictable military resentment) provides a vivid demonstration of both the confidence Arthur placed in them and the extent to which an effective military response was dependent on their expertise. Far from being an ineffectual force in the pursuit of Aborigines, as the roving parties have usually been described, they soon killed, or broke up through sustained pursuit, the few remaining large groups of Aborigines still to be found in the settled districts.

Consider, for example, the quick success achieved by the six armed parties sent out in the first weeks following the declaration of martial law. On 26 November 1828 a party of nine soldiers, two field police and "John Danvers, guide" left Oatlands. Eleven days later Aborigines were seen on the Macquarie River, "about two miles" from Tooms Lake. Danvers and Holmes, a convict constable with the Oatlands field police, reported that they "got near as possible to them that night" and on the

> twelfth day … at daybreak we formed ourselves to surround them, one of them getting up from a small fire to a larger one discovered us and gave the alarm to the rest, and the whole of them jumped up immediately and attempted to take up their spears in defence and seeing that, we immediately fired and repeated it, because we saw they were on the defensive part, they were about twenty in number, and several of whom were killed, two only unfortunately, taken alive.[51]

The *Hobart Town Courier*'s Oatlands informant claimed that ten Aborigines were killed in this incident.[52]

The mass killing of the Aborigines was clearly seen by the authorities as a welcome success, as a day after returning to Oatlands, Danvers and his party were again sent out. Meanwhile, another party of soldiers, convicts and ex-convict bushmen shot an Aborigine on 6 December "which we have reason to think took effect,"[53] while yet another reported that on 7 December, near Hobbs Hut in the Black Hills, they had surrounded 30 Aborigines and "thought it best to watch them till night to surprise them by their fires." A massacre was averted on this occasion – the Aborigines began using fire sticks, so "we could not distinguish one fire from the other and then we lost them." It is possible, however, that this was the same group that was killed the very next day near Tooms Lake, and similarly possible that it was the last surviving inter-generational clan group of the Oyster Bay people.

The final opportunities to kill large groups of Aborigines on the east coast or in the midlands occurred in 1829. Police Magistrate Lascelles of Richmond reported in June that "eight or ten of the natives were severely wounded" in a skirmish.[54] And in September of that year the "founder of Melbourne," John Batman, gave a final vivid account of the level of indiscriminate slaughter that was possible while whole communities of Aborigines, not small bands of warriors, remained the main enemy:

> In pursuit of the Aborigines who have been committing so many outrages in this district … I fell in with their tracks and followed them with the assistance of the Sydney native blacks until we came to a number of huts … we proceeded in the same direction until we saw some smoke at a distance. I immediately ordered the men to lay down; we could hear the natives conversing distinctly, we then crept into a thick scrub and remained there until after sunset … and made towards them with the greatest caution. At about 11 o'clock P.M. we arrived within 21 paces of them the men were drawn up on the right by my orders intending to rush upon them, before they could arise from the ground, hoping that I should not be under the necessity of firing at them, but unfortunately as the last man was coming up, he struck his musket against that of another party, which immediately alarmed the dogs (in number about 40), they came directly at us the natives arose from the ground, and were in the act of running away into a thick scrub,

when I ordered the men to fire upon them, which was done, and a rush by the party immediately followed, we only captured that night one woman and a male child about two years old ... next morning we found one man very badly wounded in the ankle and knee, shortly after we found another 10 buckshot had entered his body, he was alive but very bad, there were a great number of traces of blood in various directions and learnt from those we took that 10 men were wounded in the body which they gave us to understand were dead or would die, and two women in the same state had crawled away, besides a number that was shot in the legs ... We shot 21 dogs and obtained a great number of spears, waddies, blankets, rugs, knives, a tomahawk, a shingle wrench etc etc. on Friday morning we left the place for my farm with the two men, woman and child, but found it impossible that the two former could walk, and after trying them by every means in my power, for some time, found I could not get them on I was obliged to shoot them.[55]

The captured woman was later sent on to Campbell Town gaol and separated from her son, Rolepana, whom she had faced death to protect.[56] Batman's own estimate was that the band they had fired on had numbered 60 to 70 men, women and children, and about 15 had been killed or would die from the wounds. This incident was reported to Arthur, who noted the shooting of the injured. Later Arthur wrote of Batman's sympathy for the Aborigines, but also observed that he "had much slaughter to account for."[57]

The documented success of armed parties in surrounding the last surviving bands of Aborigines in the midlands and east coast during 1828–29 suggests that killing Aborigines in the first phase of the conflict was far easier than has been claimed. The roving parties' later failure is evidence of the difficulty of finding small groups of guerrilla fighters, but no measure of the British capacity to kill larger clan groups. It is also clear that, facing this level of sustained threat and harassment, any sort of normal community life would have been impossible, regardless of how many Aborigines were directly killed. The cumulative effect on health and spirit of the forced abandonment of traditional food sources, meeting places and cultural practices would have been very large. Whatever their immediate cause of death, the physically vulnerable members of the community would have had little chance of survival.

In the north-west the period of maximum slaughter occurred a little later. With British settlement concentrated in the grassy wood-lands, coastal bays and offshore islands, the Aborigines of the west coast and north-west still enjoyed, even in late 1827, not only a full age and gender demographic but a largely unchanged traditional cultural and community life. The British capacity to massacre Aborigines would be fully demonstrated on this new frontier. In only two years most of those Aborigines unfortunate enough to live on what had become, by royal charter, the private property of the Van Diemen's Land Company, were dead, and the way of life of the survivors had been radically transformed.

The Van Diemen's Land Company and the Aborigines of the North-west
The Van Diemen's Land Company surveyors arrived in the north-west of the island in 1826 to select the 250,000-acre grant the com-pany had received (this was increased in 1828 to 350,000 acres in several blocks and the company thereafter effectively monopolised the whole north-west corner of the island). Like other settlers of Van Diemen's Land, they were searching for relatively open grassland, but having arrived comparatively late on the scene, were forced to con-duct their search in a largely forested region. The surveyors found the Aborigines to be "entirely peaceful" throughout their explorations, even as late as 1827.[58] The remoteness of the district meant that the Indigenous people had not been caught up in the fighting already escalating in the settled districts.

The surveyors found the open country they were looking for at Woolnorth and the Hampshire and Surrey Hills, but, as Ian McFarlane points out, these were not "naturally occurring features of the landscape; they were Aboriginal hunting grounds created over many generations."[59] The Aborigines were dependent on these reasonably confined areas and the coastal bays and estuaries for their survival. It is not surprising, then, that in the summer of 1827–28, 118 ewes were reported to have been speared in the vicinity of Cape Grim, one of the best hunting grounds and sheep pastures available. The company's reprisal, co-ordinated and led by its chief agent, Edward Curr, was ruthless.

The only independent report of the first armed foray that followed the killing of the ewes is from Rosalie Hare, a young ship-captain's wife on board the *Caroline*, which had come direct from England to the new Van Diemen's Land Company holdings in January 1828 and remained there until March. She wrote in her journal that

> Natives are terrible robbers and do all the mischief they can to the settlers … Burning the huts of the shepherds and stealing their dogs are also the works of these incendiaries … But we are not to suppose the Europeans in their turn take no revenge. We have to lament that our own countrymen consider the massacre of these people an honour. While we remained at Circular Head there were several accounts of considerable numbers of natives having been shot by them [the Company's men], they wishing to extirpate them entirely if possible. The master of the Company's Cutter, *Fanny*, assisted by four shepherds and his crew, surprised a party and killed 12. The rest escaped but afterwards followed them. They reached the vessel just in time to save their lives.[60]

In a report to the company's directors on 14 January, Curr put forward a different version of events, admitting that the crew of the ship had gone in pursuit of the Aborigines and had come across them sitting around their fires, but that, on deciding to wait until the morning to attack, "not a musket would go off" because of overnight rain. As McFarlane suggests, it seems unlikely that the men would not have followed usual practice and attacked the Aborigines while they were vulnerable around their fires, or have allowed their muskets to so readily and universally get wet.[61]

Whatever the truth of Curr's claims, even he had not sought to deny the murderous intent of the expedition. He was open about his belief that killing Aborigines was justified to defend stock, telling the government that while he would not sanction Aborigines being fired on for stealing flour, if they attacked sheep or cattle, "I should consider the case to be quite different … [as] if they should commit a wholesale slaughter of our stock it can have no other motive than our expulsion."[62] Moreover, Curr's domain was effectively an autonomous administrative region within the colony: as he himself acknowledged, he was "both master and magistrate, party and judge."[63] Given Curr's policy towards the killing of sheep, and his near absolute power to put this into practice, it is unsurprising that further retaliation was not long in coming. Curr told the company directors in February 1828 that six Aborigines had been killed and several wounded at Cape Grim, and that "I have no doubt that this will have the effect of intimidating them and oblige them to keep aloof." He openly predicted more killings, on the basis that "strife once begun with any of these tribes, has never yet been terminated, nor will, according to present appearances, but by their extermination."[64]

Despite Curr's official status, it was November 1829 before Arthur finally heard an account of what had occurred at Cape Grim nearly two years before.[65] The lieutenant governor asked Robinson to look into the incident, and one of the shepherds involved in the killing informed the emissary that they threw the Aborigines' bodies "down the rocks where they had thrown the sheep." An Aboriginal woman claimed that the shepherds had taken "by surprise a whole tribe" and "massacred 30 of them and threw them off a cliff." The Van Diemen's Land Company superintendent, Alexander Goldie, separately confirmed to Arthur that the Aboriginal losses were "very high."[66]

Goldie's admission came after it had become widely known that he had been involved in the shooting and butchering with an axe of an Aboriginal woman on a north-west beach in September 1829. Unaware that the solicitor-general would advise Arthur not to prosecute (to ensure that "the effect of the proclamation [of martial law] was not to be forever afterwards destroyed" and the general "pursuit of these now sanguinary people" not be disrupted[67]), Goldie informed Arthur of other incidents involving the company, including the Cape Grim massacre, so as to legitimise his claim that he had killed Aborigines with the sanction of his employer. He also informed the company directors that even while supposedly conducting the inquiry into the woman's death, Curr had personally encouraged the killing of other

Aborigines – offering rum to any man who could bring him an Aboriginal head.[68] Curr freely admitted this charge, and defended his determination to kill Aborigines in a letter to the company's directors:

> My whole and sole object *was* to kill them, and this because my full conviction was and is that the laws of nature and of God and of this country all conspired to render this my duty ... it would have done good, it would have alarmed the natives ... prevented them from attempting our huts again, made them keep aloof, given them a lesson they would have long remembered ... As to my expression of a wish to have three of their heads to put on the ridge of the hut, I shall only say that I think it certainly would have the effect of deterring some of their comrades, of making the death of their companions live in their recollections, and so extend the advantage the example made of them.[69]

Curr's failure to get his head probably reflected the fact that by 1830 the surviving north-west Aborigines had largely ended their armed resistance and withdrawn to remote areas. By the time Robinson returned to the region to bring about the final removal between 1832 and 1835, the number of Aborigines in the region had dropped from an estimated 600–700 before the company arrived to about 100. Only three Europeans had been killed during this time.[70]

Van Diemonians and War

Almost all of the killing of Aborigines was done by convicts and former convicts, and since the 1820s they have been widely blamed for the tragedy that ensued. But these men can never be charged with the same level of responsibility as those whose interests they served, and their scapegoating by both the government and the free settlers is too obviously self-serving to be taken as seriously as it often has been. The opposing temptation, to assume a solidarity between poor whites and the Aborigines – because of a mutual experience of oppression by the landowning class and officialdom – must also be avoided.[71] The forms of co-existence possible before 1825 reflected the realities of the frontier, not any enduring sense of solidarity.

The longstanding fear of white officialdom and many settlers that runaway convicts and Aborigines would form an alliance found expression in the novel by Charles Rowcroft, *The Adventures of an Emigrant in Van Diemen's Land,* but real life afforded very few examples of this.[72] Arthur had published the testimony of a man taken by a group of Aborigines purportedly under the command of an escaped convict to prove that the Aborigines have "had more than savage instinct for their guide in the various murders and robberies which they have perpetrated."[73] But few other escaped convicts seem to have lived with Aboriginal groups in Van Diemen's Land or sought refuge with them.

Perhaps if the Van Diemonian bushmen had realised the implications of British victory for their own freedom, Arthur might have had more to worry about. From 1832, the social and economic control of frontier lands by the elite was greatly strengthened, and the independence and autonomy of stockmen, shepherds, hunters and squatters was curtailed in all but the most isolated regions. These men could now be much more easily evicted or brought under closer supervision. The old economy and society did not disappear during the 1830s, but it was increasingly forced to the social and geographical fringe, and the dispossession of the Aborigines proved crucial to achieving this.

The Land after War

What happened to the land when the people who had managed, created and renewed it for more than 30,000 years were almost all killed or removed?

The most immediate and obvious consequence was that wild dog numbers exploded. Although the Aborigines took many dogs into exile, even more were left behind, or had belonged to those now dead. Many wild dogs were shot, but, as George Robson of Surrey Hills complained in 1832, "notwithstanding the numbers which are destroyed" they "harass and scatter our flocks in spite of every exertion." He reported being "overrun by dogs," but "comparatively free of hyena [thylacine]."[74] In 1833, Arthur received a letter from 21 landowners of Campbell Town claiming that "they were daily suffering several losses from the country being infested with wild dogs [and] that the ravages committed by them were becoming so alarming, as to threaten the entire destruction of the flocks."[75]

Another environmental effect of Aboriginal dispossession was that some cleared or lightly wooded areas soon became overgrown. The Hampshire and Surrey hills, for example, rapidly returned to forest when Aboriginal burning ceased, and when smallholders colonised the north-west during the 1840s they found many of the previously cleared areas were already reforested. According to James Fenton, Gunns Plains, discovered in 1859–60, was covered in trees only 20 years old.[76]

From the 1850s, large bushfires also became a part of Tasmanian life. Immense fires across Mt Wellington were recorded by Lieutenant Governor William Denison in 1847, "extending through the whole neighbourhood to New Norfolk ... and to Browns River."[77] The Quaker traveller Frederick Mackie, visiting the Huon district in 1854, was pushed back by a bushfire in which eight lives were lost, and "houses and property were also destroyed." Mackie claimed that "such a conflagration has not been known before in the colony."[78] These bushfires, which reached the outskirts of Hobart, led to the Bush Fires Act, but in the absence of regular burning, new laws were unable to prevent serious fires periodically recurring.[79]

The environmental impact of dispossession was perhaps most pronounced in the last large area of grassy woodlands that had remained in Aboriginal control – the north-east. This region had become the final stronghold of the Tasmanian emu[80] and the forester kangaroo that elsewhere had been so devastated by hunting. Once the Aborigines had been removed, hunting increased sharply in this region, sealing the extinction of the emu and threatening the kangaroo with the same fate. Early in 1836, the keen amateur botanist Ronald Gunn wrote to Joseph Hooker[81] that "many of our animals and birds will become extinct or nearly so ... emus are now extremely rare and in a few years will be quite gone" and "persons may live in Van Diemen's Land for months without seeing one" kangaroo.[82] On the east coast, Louisa Meredith, who lived at Great Swanport from 1838 and was a keen observer of wildlife, never saw a black swan at the estuary named in honour of their early abundance.[83]

A more subtle but long-lasting impact of Aboriginal dispossession was that it encouraged a more intensive use of the land, contributing to the long-term decline of the ecological diversity of the grassland regions, now the most threatened and transformed ecosystem in Tasmania. Sheep could be safely moved into more marginal and remote lands, and native annual grasses and introduced weeds increasingly replaced more palatable perennial grasses on many estates as soil was compacted and erosion increased.[84] Nor was it only the grasses that were affected. Jane Williams looked back to her arrival in 1822 and wondered where all the flowers had gone: "since the large flocks and herds ... were introduced, the flowers have become comparatively rare."[85]

Perhaps the oddest environmental change was that the trees began to die. Robinson first described this phenomenon near Oatlands in late 1831: "the trees in the low land and small hills are fast decaying ... in a few years there will be no trees left. I am informed that at the Clyde and Shannon it is the same and that the settlers say they commenced falling into decay about three years ago."[86] In April 1832, between Entally and Westbury, Robinson observed that "the trees here were like the trees that I had observed in other parts of the colony, were falling fast to decay."[87] Jane Williams also found that in some of the "fine sheep country" in the northern districts, "all the trees [were] dead but the wattles."[88] And in 1844, the wife of the new bishop of Tasmania (as he was prematurely titled), Mrs Nixon, wrote of the Oatlands district: "we observed one of those frequently recurring tracts of dead timber – large trees in which every branch and their trunks perfect, only leafless ... The effect is most melancholy, as though the locust has passed over the land."[89] Robinson attributed the deforestation "to the entire exhaustion of the subsoil,"[90] but this seems unlikely to have occurred so quickly, despite the erosion brought about by over-stocking. The surveyor, John Helder Wedge, blamed "a very severe frost in 1825, or possibly ... the drought of one very hot summer," but, as Mrs Nixon observed, "no one has satisfactorily accounted for it."[91]

The most likely explanation is that the trees had been killed by possums, which increased in number with the removal of the Aborigines who had been their main predator (the Europeans did not begin to trap possums for skins in significant numbers until many years later). George Lloyd recalled that after the Aborigines were gone, brushtail possums "soon became so numerous" that farmers even had to keep packs of dogs to protect their wheat.[92] In the main Aboriginal hunting ground of the grassy woodlands, a possum population explosion would have had a noticeable impact, as many of today's landowners of the midlands, still defending remnant trees from possum damage, can testify.

Ultimately, though, the environmental impact of Aboriginal dispossession cannot be fully grasped, and perhaps belongs to another realm of understanding. The removal of the people who had been central to the ecology of the island for such a long period – three times the length of the human occupation of Britain – must have had multifarious impacts which are beyond the capacity of history, and even science, to explain.

PART IV

VAN DIEMEN'S LAND
OR TASMANIA?
1839–56

[15]

THE TRIUMPH OF
LITTLE ENGLAND

IN JANUARY 1834 THE SETTLER MICHAEL STEEL wrote to his
brother encouraging him to immigrate to Van Diemen's Land:
"This country is now getting very much improved as we have now no
blacks or any *bushrangers* to fear, with a soil most beautiful and climate the finest in the world."[1] Peace prevailed on the island, and with
the export wool market booming Steel and other free settlers could
pursue unhindered the economic and social benefits of monopoly
ownership of some of the finest pasture-lands in the empire.

Land ownership remained the goal of most settlers, and with increased demand, prices soared. Fortunes were made in the land boom
of the early 1830s. In the autumn of 1835 David Burn was offered £3000
for 1300 acres that had cost him £1300 less than a year before.[2] In September 1834 Ellen Viveash assessed that, on the basis of a few years'
capital gain, "If we were to leave now we should have an income *more
than double* what we had in London." The following year Ellen and her
husband did just that, retiring "on an income from this country of
about £540 a year"[3] and joining the growing group of newly upper-
class Britons living off the monies from their Van Diemonian land
handouts in provincial Britain, London, Sydney and Calcutta.

For the small group of wealthy landowners who stayed in Van
Diemen's Land, the capital gain, wool profits and increased supply of
convict labour available during the 1830s led to an enthusiastic – even
celebratory – building program in the towns and on rural estates. In
Lloyd Robson's words, "equipped with free convict labour virtually to

be had for the asking and fuelled by an apparently inexhaustible income from wool, the flock masters of Van Diemen's Land established great houses and gardens and parks and equipped themselves in a style of life that drew gasps of wonder from the visitor."[4]

It was in the northern midlands that the dream of reproducing the social and natural environment of late-eighteenth-century rural England was first realised. Jane Williams was surprised by the extent to which these districts had been transformed when she travelled from her home in the south to visit the Archer family in 1836: "the people here are very *gay looking* ... they dress in great style, and their houses are so large and so handsomely furnished that really it does not seem as if we were in this country." She found that Woolmers (one of the Archer family properties) "looked lovely – the plains are beautiful and more *English* than anything I've seen."[5]

By the mid 1840s the transformation of Van Diemen's Land also encompassed the capital. Lieutenant Governor William Denison recorded in his journal in 1847, shortly after arriving in Hobart Town, that "the whole air of this place, the streets, the shops, the very gardens ... are so exactly like those of a country town in England, that it is very difficult to realise the fact of being nearly at the Antipodes."[6] The town now had its own park, the "Government demesne" (or domain), described by another observer as "a most delightful place of recreation for Tasmanians ... the scene of all kinds of open-air amusements, cricketing, horse riding, etc."[7] Even the English Sabbath had belatedly arrived. William Adeney recorded in his diary that "This town on the Sabbath is a pattern which any other would do well to copy. Every shop being closed and no vehicles about except such as are necessary for conveyances to places of worship and all the streets quiet and well ordered during the whole day."[8]

Similar changes could be observed in all the townships between Hobart Town and Launceston. When Louisa Meredith took a carriage between the two in 1846, she recorded "passing through on our way the populous settlements and towns of Brighton, Bagdad, Green Ponds, Cross Marsh, Oatlands, Ross, Campbell Town, and Perth, all containing good churches and inns, and the greater number displaying shops of various kinds, and many substantial houses; whilst nearly the whole length of road traverses inclosed and cultivated land, and constantly leads us past comfortable country houses, farms and cottages."[9] Introduced plants and animals added to the effect. Many plants were privately introduced, but in the 1840s the first superintendent of the Royal Society's gardens (now the Royal Tasmanian Botanical Gardens) introduced "over 250 species in sixty genera."[10] Rabbits – which were recorded by Knopwood as early as May 1816 – were common by the mid 1820s.[11] Bees had been imported as early as 1821, and by the 1840s had gone wild in many parts of the island.[12] A number of English birds were also introduced.

Accompanying this was the accelerated destruction of those native birds and marsupials considered a threat to agriculture or sheep. Rosellas, eagles, devils and, increasingly, thylacines were among those killed – sometimes, as Louisa Meredith observed, on the basis of nothing more than prejudice.[13]

The remaking of the land did not always go according to plan. The first and most obvious problem to emerge was weeds. The Quaker "traveller under concern" Frederick Mackie noted in 1852 that "Many of our common weeds ... are spreading alongside the roadsides and waste places."[14] A bigger economic problem was the impact on native pastures. Over-grazing depleted the most palatable native perennial grasses and a mixture of annual grasses and introduced weeds soon colonised the compacted and eroded soil in many districts, reducing carrying capacity.[15] Scotch thistle ("a terrible plague" to the first settlers of the north-west), blackberry and gorse also emerged as early problems. James Fenton bravely admitted to the introduction of the blackberry to the Forth district in 1843, but asked farmers to remember "that it would have come one way or another soon, as the thistles and the docks and the sorrel, and an infinite variety of farmers' pests came."[16]

The speed with which rabbits reproduced meant that they too soon became "troublesome and mischievous." Feral cats could also be "terribly destructive," and by the 1840s were "wild in the colony in considerable numbers and are as fully as destructive among poultry as the native vermin."[17] At least they could assist with the rat plagues, which were reported in Hobart Town as early as 1816.[18]

Nor were the aesthetic changes to the landscape always appreciated. Ringbarking made for a desolate appearance in some settled districts from the 1840s, and when Mackie crossed to the east coast in late 1852 he saw thousands of dead trees "covering the ground in all directions."[19] For her part, Louisa Meredith lamented that the charge of barrenness was "usually so well merited by colonial farms" and even recorded an early precursor of a twenty-first-century tourist problem: the fern glades at the foot of Mount Wellington "oft frequented ... beloved of sketching and picnic parties" had been ruined by "empty champagne bottles which bristled besides the rocks, and the corks and greasy sandwich papers ... lurking among the moss."[20]

As in the 1820s, the desire to "improve" the land according to the reference point of rural England did not preclude appreciation of the beauty of the native environment. Just as becoming Tasmanian was not usually understood to involve becoming any less British (indeed, a central argument for self-government was that it would make colonists even more loyal to the empire), nor was any contradiction perceived in remaking an admired landscape. Burn, for example, waxed lyrical about the Tasmanian lakes in a whole chapter devoted to them but closed his commentary with an early statement of the world-view that would seal their fate: "The floral mead – the pearly stream – the goodly grove, however they delight the eye, or ravish the imagination – what are they all? – a worthless waste, until the genius and industry of man converts and fits them all for the welfare and enjoyment of his kind."[21]

Policing the Poor

In the new society, wrote Lieutenant Governor Denison, "Life and property were as secure, I may indeed say with truth more secure, than in England: there were no shutters to the windows, no locks to the doors."[22] Meredith wrote that she knew "of no place where greater order and decorum is observed by the motley crowds assembled on any public occasion than in this most shamefully slandered colony: not even in an English country village can a lady walk alone with less fear of harm or insult than in this capital of Van Diemen's Land."[23]

A brutal policing and legal apparatus, now directed at former convicts as much as those still under sentence, underpinned the order and decorum. In 1847 there was one policeman for every 135 people (compared with one for every 324 people in New South Wales).[24] Denison was full of praise for the "active and efficient police, thoroughly organised."[25] J.F. Mortlock, who became a convict constable in April 1847, observed that the field police were "stationed on spots commanding all the cross and byroads; foot travellers must exhibit their 'pass' and satisfy enquiries on pain of apprehension, so that a network of 'traps' (the slang term for constable) is everywhere spread out."[26]

Published government statistics show that in 1841, out of a population of around 53,000, a staggering 8732 free people and 11,458 convicts were before the courts (just under 3000 of these were fined for drunkenness in each group). More than 4000 people were fined under colonial acts – including for "insolence," "idleness" and "insubordination" – and these offences were so loosely defined that in practice anyone who lacked the protection afforded by wealth or privilege could be arrested at whim.[27] The legal system was backed up by the now fully operational fortress of Port Arthur, which reached a peak population of 1200 in 1846, the hell of Norfolk Island (a new site of secondary punishment and part of Van Diemen's Land from September 1844), and various forms of punishment and forced labour in government work-stations across the island.

There could be little room for doubt about whose interests the law was designed to uphold. The wealthy were rarely prosecuted, and few of the vulnerable – including women – were protected (there was only one rape conviction in Van Diemen's Land through 1845 and 1846).[28] Former convicts living independently in the bush were particularly targeted by the law. The Kangaroo Hunting Act of 1846, which required hunters to have a licence from a police magistrate, was designed more to control kangaroo hunters than to protect the threatened forester kangaroo.[29] The licensing and taxation of dogs – the most effective means of restricting hunting rights – was also tightened (although there was a vigorous dispute about the legality of the dog tax introduced in 1846). Even the right to kindle a cooking fire in the bush was regulated.[30]

Vagrancy law was another effective means of targeting those who sought to live apart from the rigid discipline demanded by employer or landlord. During the 1840s the English practice of "moving on" was increasingly employed, and in the second half of the nineteenth century regulations to clamp down on "idle or disorderly persons," mainly directed at "old hands" (former convicts), were strengthened far beyond the provisions provided in the English Acts.[31]

Welfare reforms were made with the same expressed purpose, although here budgetary considerations were perhaps more important. From the mid 1830s, one of the major public debates in Van Diemen's Land centred on social assistance and who should pay for it. Convict paupers were comparatively fortunate in that their sustenance was paid for by London through what was known as the imperial fund. By contrast, former convicts in distress were dependent on a colonial government more and more reluctant to provide any relief at all. The gap was supposedly filled by new voluntary societies, but these organisations had criteria so restrictive as to deny aid to all but a select group of the morally "deserving."

Many of the most desperate, particularly the mothers of dependent children, continued to appeal directly to the lieutenant governor for emergency assistance. For example, in May 1848 Mrs Amy Gould, wife of an emancipist artist,[32] sought the help of Denison on the basis that her husband was in gaol and she was "totally destitute with five helpless young children without any means of support." Mrs Gould's allowance from the Dorcas Society of two shillings a week had been stopped "in order to mark the Ladies' disapprobation of her conduct in refusing to allow her daughter to enter the service of Mrs Dry ... and also in consequence of there being at the time no funds," and she had been "left without a hope to suffer the pinching pangs of starvation." Even the police magistrate supported her application, and the colonial secretary lamented that "I wish the humane people would attend to such cases but they will not." Despite this, Denison – the most explicitly committed Christian lieutenant governor since Arthur – rejected the application, noting that helping "the families of criminals is in fact almost an encouragement to crime."[33]

In 1845 the Dorcas Society reported that it "regret[ted] the increasing demands of pauperism [and] the growing difficulties of repelling the impositions of the undeserving poor."[34] The *Launceston Examiner* in 1851 even praised the Evandale Benevolent Society for how effectively they denied assistance, noting that

> nearly every corner of our principal settlements is obstructed by the halt or blind, upon many of whom pecuniary relief is thrown away. It is in these cases that the Benevolent Society is especially useful. Private individuals may be imposed upon by the base whilst a public institution whose officers are bound to make inquiry before rendering assistance is scarcely liable to similar deception.[35]

Policing the poor also involved a cultural clampdown. In late 1848, Denison was petitioned by 14 Hobart musicians who claimed that "repeated attempts have been made to deprive them of their only means of subsistence by the interference of the police." They pointed out that "the only recreation [the] mechanic and labourer" has after his "daily toil is the innocent one of music and a dance." The matter was referred to the police magistrate for comment, who responded:

> I have with much pains and opposition succeeded in putting a stop to fiddling and dancing in public houses, which have been much improved in conduct and character in consequence. The practice of fiddling in public houses was the means of congregating together vicious and dishonest characters of both sexes, and was the source of much evil to the community.[36]

The war on fiddling was part of a widespread attack on convict culture. The Licensing Act of 1833 made it an offence for "a publican to allow ticket of leave holders to play skittles, bowls, ninepins or any game of chance in a public house, or even to remain on the premises while they were being played."[37] In the 1840s, it was the "noise and confusion" of dancing houses that, according to John West, "compelled their suppression."[38]

The pub was, however, ultimately saved by the revenue it gen-erated. The colonial government's dependence on the duties paid on imported liquor only increased in the 1840s with the decline in land sales and the successful resistance of the propertied class to any taxation of their wealth. The two lieutenant governors after Arthur, Sir John Franklin (1837-43) and Sir John Eardley-Wilmot (1843-46) both faced a persistent budget crisis. The colonial government, having given away so much of the crown's assets for so little public return, was forced to tolerate, even encourage, heavy drinking. Nor was this the only unintended contradiction resulting from the concentration of the colony's wealth in so few hands.

By the mid 1830s it was not only former convicts who were denied a share of the profits from the native pasture-lands. Most new free immigrants were locked out too, and by 1839 the economic boom was over. Free settlers then stopped coming and the colony's future effec-tively became mortgaged to a small group of very wealthy landowners whose major investment was to expand their already large landhold-ings. The gentry used their control over water sources and transport routes, and their ready access to capital, to secure control over remain-ing crown land surrounding their properties, as well as progressively buying up that of smaller neighbours.

Even when heavily forested country began to be leased and sold in the 1840s, the same men largely monopolised ownership, accruing profits from land they often never saw. James Fenton, an unusual free-settler resident of the forest lands of the north-west, was critical of the absentee landowners, whom he called "pompous country gentlemen … the lord of the wastes."[39]

Without further immigration, the society of the landowners became increasingly closed. Such was their wealth and status that if they chose to – and most did – it was now possible to live a quaran-tined existence, scarcely impinged upon by the social and environ-mental realities of the island. Yet the extent of their success also ensured that Van Diemen's Land would remain an overwhelmingly convict-dominated society with few middle-sized farms and only a small middle class. It was not necessary to go far from the gentry estates and principal settlements to discover a very different society from that celebrated in Hobart Town or provincial England. The paradox of the 1840s is that at the very time at which the economic and cultural vision of Little England was being realised, Van Diemonian culture also found an enduring foundation.

[16]

THE SURVIVAL OF
VAN DIEMEN'S LAND

UNLIKE THE DISPLAYS OF WEALTH favoured by the colonial elite, convict culture was never ostentatious. This was not a well-publicised rebellion against an unjust social order, but rather a silent withdrawal from the centres of dependence to the back-blocks, forests and "waste lands" of the island. The key to understanding the resilience of this alternative way of life is that the geography of Van Diemen's Land meant such land – and its inhabitants – was everywhere.

Even today both major Tasmanian cities and the prized sheep country of the midlands are framed by tree-covered hills, mountains and highland plains. Hobart is the only Australian capital city from which bush is visible in almost every direction from the CBD. Mount Wellington, which overlooks the capital, is but the best-known example of this. It may be, as Trollope put it, "just enough of a mountain to give excitement to ladies and gentlemen in middle life,"[1] but its very moderation, its near-perfect balance between accessibility and remoteness, made it invaluable to the poor. Sister hills of the Wellington Range, the Eastern and Western tiers, frame the midlands. Tourists venturing even a short distance off the "heritage" (midland) highway can still find a very different cultural and environmental landscape from the "English" villages and hedgerows described in their guidebooks. In the nineteenth century, the difference between the main road and the by-ways was far more pronounced. The hills, mountains and highland plains served as "human wildlife corridors" penetrating across the gentry's main domains. They provided an enduring refuge for the poor, and ensured that the geographical and cultural reach of Little England was a restricted one.

What changed during the 1840s was the nature and intensity of the occupation of the "waste lands." For the first time, this environment became a permanent home, including for women and children, rather than the domain of transient single men. Much of it was even farmed on a subsistence or small-holder basis, with supplementary income earned from seasonal work on the estates or in town, or from the sale of products sourced from the bush.

It was more difficult to survive off this country than off the grassy woodlands or rich coastal estuaries that the convicts had colonised a generation before. The forester kangaroo, emu and swan were now extinct or greatly reduced in numbers, and for most people it was not worth the expense of keeping a kangaroo dog, which was best adapted to the now-surrendered habitat of the gentry estates. The staples of mutton and wallaby were supplemented with almost any edible animal that could be shot (guns were now more accurate), snared or trapped (trap technology had also improved), or killed by smaller hunting dogs. Mortlock described "capital dumplings ... made with small green parrots, more common than sparrows," white cockatoos which were "good eating," rabbits "numerous in some localities," "many excellent sorts of fish, strange to Europeans" and the "very plentiful" old staple, oysters. Meredith suggested that even "large white grubs" in "old dead or dying trees" that "taste like nuts or almonds" were now being eaten, that "porcupine" (echidna) was appreciated by those "partial to sucking pig," and that wombat, "fatter and coarser, with a strong rank flavour," was "eaten and relished by some persons." The native hen was eaten "skinned and nicely stewed," but required "good cooking to render it palatable." Some people even ate the "black magpie" (black currawong), although the "bronze-winged pigeon ... being plump, tender and well flavoured" was preferred.[2] Only possum, widely eaten by the Aborigines, was still generally spurned. Mortlock believed that the flesh had "a strong disagreeable flavour" due to the "peppermint leaves upon which they chiefly subsist."[3]

Potatoes, less likely to be eaten by native animals and able to return a high yield on small holdings, became more important with the permanent colonisation of the forests, wheat less so. Certainly there were fewer "extras" as wages and other sources of cash income declined – rum sales in particular suffered. Farming methods also did not "improve" as had been expected in the 1830s. It must have been a matter of some irony to the 332 "swing" rioters (machine breakers and arsonists) transported in the early 1830s for their part in rural protest against the Agricultural Revolution that the new technology remained in such limited supply in their new home.[4] Most farmers still reaped and threshed by hand, and crop rotation and manuring remained uncommon.

Most of the new residents of the bush were self-sufficient small-holders. Others were semi-nomadic labourers. More so even than in previous decades, almost all were convicts or their children. The net effect of the internal migration was that as the Industrial and Agricultural Revolutions accelerated in Britain, and transportation to New South Wales ended in 1840, the differences between Van Diemen's Land and the societies that founded it became ever more pronounced. As the mother country was being rapidly transformed into the first modern industrial society (with her people becoming both a wage-labour force and a mass consumer market), and as mainland Australia was being transformed by free immigration, the pre-industrial and convict character of Van Diemen's Land was radically affirmed.

Demographic Change

The numbers tell part of the story. After being the favoured destination for much of the 1820s and 1830s, from 1838 to 1850 Van Diemen's Land received only 3 per cent of free immigrants to the Australian colonies. The comparison with the 1830 to 1837 period, when Van Diemen's Land received 60 per cent of arrivals from the United Kingdom, is dramatic.[5] For much of the 1840s virtually no one arrived in Van Diemen's Land but convicts,[6] and they now came in much larger numbers than ever before, with the number still under sentence reaching an all-time high of more than 30,000 in 1847.

By 1851, three-quarters of the adult males of Van Diemen's Land (which was still home to 17 per cent of the European Australian population) were or had been convicts. By contrast, in 1846 the figure was about one-fifth in New South Wales (and one-tenth in Sydney).[7] When the prisoners' children are included in this figure, the supposedly convict-free Tasmania that was coming into being can be seen for what it truly was and so long remained: an overwhelmingly convict-derived society.[8]

Of almost equal significance was the fact that during the 1840s this enlarged convict population also changed in character. During this fateful decade that would have such long-term repercussions for the social, economic and political fabric of the island colony, the convicts transported to Van Diemen's Land became proportionally both more Irish and more female.

The Irish Influx

In earlier decades the majority of Irish convicts had been sent to New South Wales, but between 1840 and 1853 almost 10,000 convicts arrived in Van Diemen's Land from Ireland.[9] Moreover, most of these men and women were sentenced during the Irish famine of 1845–49, one of the most appalling human tragedies of the nineteenth century. Of the eight million people living in Ireland in 1845, about one million died in the famine and another million more emigrated (even today the population has not recovered to its pre-famine levels).[10] The famine was worse in the rural districts, particularly the very poorest regions of Munster and Connaught, where more than half the total number of deaths occurred. Most of Van Diemen's Land's convicts came from these districts, reflecting the fact that many folk resorted to crime to survive.[11]

The Irish convicts sent to Van Diemen's Land during the 1840s were unique. They were indisputably the poorest sizeable group of emigrants to leave the old world for any Australian colony, or indeed for any other part of the new world, in the nineteenth century, distinguished from other Irish and European emigrants by their inability to raise or borrow even the cheapest passage. They were the only emigrant group who had been left with no choices – not even the option to flee.

These men and women came from rural regions of one of the most "primitive" countries in Europe, suffering from starvation and living under oppressive colonisation. They were a pre-industrial people in almost every sense of the word, culturally closer to their ancient Celtic forefathers than to their political overlords.

Famine transformed rural Ireland, and thus the cultural background of emigrants, to an extent that has often been overlooked. Even the allegiance to the prescribed practices of the Catholic Church only emerged in the aftermath of the famine. In 1850, only between 30 and 40 per cent of the population attended mass (by 1900 it was over 90 per cent), and in rural areas, especially in Irish-speaking regions, regular church attendance in the pre-famine era could be as low as 20 per cent.[12] It was this level of Catholic practice – not the later nineteenth-century norm – that was reproduced in Van Diemen's Land.

The low level of attendance did not mean that the Irish people were not Christian or Catholic. Rather, in the rural regions of Ireland a 1500-year-old Irish Celtic tradition balanced the place of the institutional church with its own customary teachings and practices. The sacred infused almost every aspect of everyday life, and formal religious practice was but one component of this. As was to be the case in Van Diemen's Land, births and deaths were marked by priests, but marriage practices varied and confirmation was widely ignored.[13]

The Irish language embodied Celtic spirituality, and most of the Van Diemen's Land convicts had Irish as their first language. Their spirituality and culture were also oral, making it a challenge for historians to penetrate. Of the Irish Catholics transported to Van Diemen's Land, only 5 per cent of women and 40 per cent of men were literate.[14]

Irish work practices were also pre-modern. E.P. Thompson suggests that by the 1840s the English industrial worker was distinguished from the Irish "not by a greater capacity for hard work, but by his regularity ... and perhaps also by a repression ... of the capacity to relax in the old uninhibited way."[15] Consistent with this, Lieutenant Governor Denison found Irish convicts to be "ignorant and insubordinate"[16], with a "want of industry," and the women "from the rural districts ... unfitted to engage in domestic service."[17] Richard Davis concludes that the Irish were considered "both too rebellious and too feeble as the result of the famine to provide a good colonial work-force," but perhaps they were simply too old-fashioned.[18]

What these famine refugees did not know about the discipline and conformity demanded by modern work was more than compensated for by their experience of surviving on small land-holdings.[19] The potato had been their main crop, but pastoral activities using communal land also had a long history. Both farming traditions were to be of great utility in Van Diemen's Land.

Irish Women

The Irish convicts of the 1840s were also the first group to include a high proportion of women.[20] Many of these were to become the pioneer colonisers of the hill and forest country and the matriarchs of large clans. In *Notorious Strumpets and Dangerous Girls*, Philip Tardif calculated that their average age on arrival was 27, with two in five aged from 18 to 24. Tardif notes that "57 per cent of the women" were "known to have married in Van Diemen's Land" – a "surprisingly high" figure given the incompleteness of the records and the number of women already married or living in relationships which were not legalised.[21] Settler accounts speak often of the difficulty of keeping domestic servants, given the competition from prospective partners. Louisa Meredith, for instance, reported that all her "prisoner women-servants have had suitors in plenty."[22]

Once children were born, convict couples were both less likely to join in the widespread emigration to mainland Australia and more ready to take on the hard labour involved in home-making in forest country. Thanks to their backgrounds, the women had the knowledge and experience of self-sufficiency, and their modest cultural and material expectations eased the transition to such a life. Moreover, the unique dynamic of the convict colony – the readiness to trade the security (and subservience) of the settlements for the hazards (and freedom) of bush life – was reinforced by the increasingly repressive regime of the 1840s, the widespread anti-Irish prejudice and a decline in wages and conditions. No matter how hard life in the bush was – and it could never approach the suffering most of the Irish had endured in their mother country – an independent and remote situation proved an increasingly attractive alternative to the English society on offer in the settlements. It is not surprising that many women in particular sought a life far from the *Anson* (the hulk moored in the Derwent which long served as the female probation station), the "factories," the orphan school – where their children were compulsorily placed during their parents' servitude – and the potential for sexual and physical abuse ever-present in domestic service. In doing so, this remarkable group of pioneer women ensured that John West's view that convicts rarely reproduced, and would thus "melt from the earth, and pass away like a mournful dream," remained nothing more than free-settler fantasy.[23]

Economic Change

Around 1840 Van Diemen's Land entered an economic recession that persisted (with the exception of a few good years during the Victorian gold rushes) until the west-coast mineral boom of the 1870s. Although all Australian colonies shared in the crisis of 1844–47, only Van Diemen's Land experienced ongoing hardship. The usual consequence of this – external migration – was evident, and many single men left for Port Phillip, South Australia and New South Wales. However, the principal effect of economic decline was to encourage a large-scale *internal* migration.

In essence, the bush became a lifeline for many thousands of unemployed. In 1841 the convict William Gates (one of the group known as the "Canadian patriots" who had been sent to Van Diemen's Land for their part in an uprising against British rule[24]) wrote that "day after day" he was turned away by employers:

> What little food we were able to procure was obtained from roots and occasionally from potato and turnip fields ... when we secured a potato or two, or accidentally found a kangaroo snared or succeeded in capturing one ourselves, we sought the most secluded place possible and cautiously built a fire wherewith to roast them. This too was in violation of the law, for the prisoner, or ticket of leave man, was not allowed to kindle even the slightest fire ... yet

we did because we could not well do without it. Almost every night we were forced to lie in the bush.[25]

Gates was not describing his experience *after* servitude, but as a serving convict still under sentence. Penal reform meant that convicts were now expected to sell their labour to survive. From 1840 convicts usually served an initial period of "probation" in government work gangs, before becoming "passholders" who competed in the labour market. In the context of high unemployment, this meant that thousands of serving convicts joined ticket-of-leave holders and emancipists to roam the island in search of work. The sight of these workers, who by necessity or choice often lived rough in the bush, horrified and frightened the free settlers: "How melancholy and deplorable it is in travelling up the country to see large bodies of men wandering about in total idleness," lamented the bishop of Tasmania's wife, Mrs Nixon. "God only knows when the present system will end or what can become of the free population if this fine country is to be thus swamped."[26]

The probation system had other unintended consequences. As many contemporary critics pointed out, the government work gangs were very effective in inculcating a convict sub-culture of shared norms and values in new arrivals. Moreover, the Colonial Office thought it integral to the supposed rehabilitative effect of probation that the stations be isolated. This did not always prove possible, but the majority of the 73 probation and punishment stations were in the bush. Many were also in locations rich in accessible resources. For example, at Southport in the far south, Lieutenant Governor Latrobe inspected "130 of the greatest scoundrels in the world; young villains from 16 to 25 years of age, and of most incorrigible habits" who lived at the "bottom of a little bay open towards the south-east to the sea; with a beautiful white, sandy beach; fish plentiful; oysters innumerable and very good." Many stations were only accessible by sea or foot, and convicts travelling to and from them often made long journeys overland. Whatever else such isolation produced, there can be little doubt that the convicts soon became familiar with the environment around them.

J.F. Mortlock provided a rare view of the probation system from the convict perspective. Arriving in Van Diemen's Land in 1844, he was shipped to a "narrow, shallow inlet, hemmed in by almost impervious, thickly wooded, broken ranges" (the Cascades on the Tasman Peninsula), where he

> soon found myself hard at work, felling an enormous gum tree, 200 feet high, whose hollow base would have sheltered a dozen men. This, with digging up potatoes, and the carrying bundles of shingles (a small, narrow, thin piece of wood, used instead of slates, for roofing) some miles, through the rugged bush down to the jetty, was my first experience of Van Diemen's Land.[27]

Another convict chronicler, William Derrincourt, engaged in clandestine hunting. Dogs and guns were not easily concealed, but they were not the only means to kill animals. Derrincourt constructed his own traps (and, if his account is to be believed, one day caught more than he bargained for when Mrs Nixon stumbled into one of them).[28]

Free settlers complained loudly about the probation system, but many also profited from it. With such an oversupply of labour, landowners found that hiring labour on a casual basis was more profitable than being responsible for the year-round housing and feeding of permanent servants (even when they went virtually unpaid). Competition and regulation ensured that wages were now very low, and that workers could be laid off as soon as they were no longer needed. In effect the gentry tolerated the social costs of itinerancy in exchange for economic gain. The Irish convict Patrick O'Donohue lambasted the landowners' commitment "to keep on foot a shifting population of blue-shirted kangaroo knapsacked labourers, whom they could feed like beasts, stye like pigs, work like horses, and get rid of like they would any other worn-out animals."[29] But for some convicts at least, the relative freedom afforded by casual employment and life outside of the estates must have had its advantages. Many made their homes in the bush country fringing the sheep lands, with seasonal employment providing a cash supplement to their simple but comparatively independent existence. Sometimes the land on which their huts were built was leased from the estate owners (who benefited twice over, as both employer and landlord).

Colonising the Forests

Necessity and opportunity were thus driving increasing numbers of convicts into the bush. Once their sentences expired, many opted to push on into more remote and inaccessible country. The island's rivers provided a highway into the otherwise impenetrable wet sclerophyll forests of the Huon Valley and north-west (a new zone for Britons in Van Diemen's Land), and colonisation spread by foot deep into the more open dry sclerophyll forests of the eastern half of the island. Some of the forest migrants of the 1840s joined the long-established itinerant wattle-bark collectors and sawyers. The great attraction of collecting wattle bark for tanning – an industry that emerged in the 1820s to fill an export market created by the shortage of tannin for leather-making in Britain[30] – was that there were few barriers to entry for those seeking an independent source of income. The only capital required was an axe. Independent sawyers and splitters soon followed.[31]

From the late 1830s, however, and accelerating in the 1840s, settlers also began to prepare land for agriculture, using new methods which meant forests could be cleared, for the first time, by the poor.

The traditional methods had been very slow. In July 1827 the Van Diemen's Land Company surveyor Henry Hellyer observed that "it took four men 20 days to fall 500 trees when they did their utmost to get through the work. They dig the roots up to one foot below the level of the ground. At this rate it would cost £40 to £50 an acre."[32]

Such laborious techniques had been used to clear the English forests over millennia, but stood in marked contrast to well-developed North American methods of girdling or ring-barking. James Fenton, having being given advice by a Canadian, used ring-barking at Forth in 1841 and – largely because he publicised his claim through his own books – is often given credit for introducing it, even though he admitted he saw a ring-barked tree at "Wesley Dale" before this.[33] Given the early and continuing North American contact with Van Diemen's

Land, it would be very surprising if some of the island's residents had not always known of this simple method of killing trees. It is even possible that the Aborigines knew about ring-barking given Robinson's intriguing journal entry: "Here was a tree about a foot diameter notched round about two inches done by the natives. I had seen a similar thing at the Surrey Hills."[34]

The main obstacle to introducing the North American methods was probably not lack of knowledge, but rather lack of need or motivation. Only when settlement shifted to more heavily forested regions, and another class of settler appeared, did the necessity arise. From 1840 there was a surplus workforce not only desperate enough to undertake the labour required, but, if it meant freedom and independence, even prepared to pay rent for the "privilege" of doing so. During the 1840s and 1850s, the forests became the cultural and economic refuge of the poor, although the products of their labour and enterprise were once again concentrated elsewhere.

Most residents of the forests lived on small holdings of 10 to 20 acres, and survived with little cash income. The title of their land was usually held by an absentee landowner. Much of the vast Van Diemen's Land Company holdings were leased to small farmers in 1843, and many of the larger estates followed the same policy. By 1858 two out of three farmers in the northern region were tenants. In forested regions there were frequently clauses in the tenancy requiring the tenant to clear the land, so that the landowner achieved both an annual return and a significant capital gain. Subservience was reinforced by the tenants' dependence on their landlord's good grace during drought or times of low prices, although even this guaranteed no protection. It was common for tenants to face eviction when they had finally completed the task of clearing their land, or else be forced to pay much-increased rents.[35]

Louisa Meredith lived for a time among the suffering tenants of the north-west and saw a level of poverty which she had never before experienced:

the only variety of scene was afforded by a few wretched-looking huts and hovels, the dwellings of "cockatooers," who are not as it might seem, a species of bird, but human beings; who rent portions of this forest from the proprietors of their mortgagees on exorbitant terms ...

The common course is this: – some industrious servant who has saved a few pounds ... agrees to pay a high annual rent for a piece of dense forest ... he builds a hut for his family, and then goes on clearing a field ... rent-day comes round, and if the remaining savings are enough, they pay the rent; if not the cart, plough or bullocks must go as well. The coming crop is offered as security for other inevitable debts, and is swept off when harvested ... the sad finale being that the wretched family goes forth again, bereft of every shilling they possessed, and the place where there all lies buried is let as an improved property to some other adventurer at an advanced rental. Until I came into the district of Port Sorell I could not conceive such poverty as I saw there, to be possible in this land of plenteousness.[36]

As had traditionally been the case in England, crown or common lands formed the final refuge for the evicted tenant or landless vagrant (as late as 1900 over three-quarters of Tasmania remained without a private title,[37] most of it deemed to have no commercial value). The Central Plateau was a particularly important sanctuary. As Burn noted in 1840, it was "so far beyond the pale of the settlement of civilisation, that few, save bushrangers, stock-keepers, or flock-masters have visited."[38] And as Tim Jetson has documented, the isolation meant that "the shepherds adopted many unique habits and customs" and the "beginnings of a regional dialect were observed."[39] After 1850 many of the occupants of the plateau stayed throughout the year, concentrating on snaring in winter (when the animals had their thickest coats) to complement the shepherding and stock-keeping duties undertaken in the warmer months. These shepherd-hunters lived off wallaby, mutton and rabbit, and in diet, clothing and accommodation pursued a way of life that remained largely unchanged until the region was transformed by hydro-electric developments in the 1950s.[40]

Wandering Van Diemen's Land

The internal migration of the poor during the 1840s did not generally result in the displacement of prior occupants. Drawn from the same social class, the settlers intermixed with the motley of hunters, shepherds and stock thieves already resident, just as the Norfolk Island and emancipist farmers had done a generation before.

Oral and written history attest to the close communities which formed. When in the early 1980s Peter MacFie interviewed a number of the older residents of the hill country of the Meehan Range near Hobart, he found the one recurring theme of those who grew up before World War One was the "unity of the district." The physical expression of this was a network of bush footpaths, enabling family and friends to visit one another and creating "shortcuts to home and work."[41] Throughout the back blocks of Van Diemen's Land, such way-marks connected a community of people vastly different from those who relied on horsepower and the roads and bridle paths that joined the midlands estates to the main settlements.

The tracks (many of them no doubt originally Aboriginal) and the availability of fresh water meant that the island continued to be far more easily traversed on foot than most regions of mainland Australia. Given that ordinary folk could still not afford to purchase or maintain a horse, this remained a great boon. Bishop Nixon noted that when convicts were released, "they cast off their religious ordinances and loved to lead solitary lives, wandering away from towns and settlements, forming little groups in the bush where they could remain unnoticed and unreproved."[42] As a ticket-of-leaver, Mortlock "indulged in a 200-mile ramble along the eastern coast to the Fingal diggings." So attractive did he find this way of life that he purchased an "opossum rug" made up of "60 skins together" that formed "a seven foot square ... easily carried on the knapsack [for] 30 shillings – the price demanded by the shepherds from whom they are procured ... henceforward any pleasant spot became a temporary home."[43]

The cultural bonds that bound emancipist communities to each other, and to their shared past of servitude, are more difficult to identify. Convicts, particularly the Irish convicts of the 1840s, had commonly experienced a depth of trauma comparable with refugee communities today. It is now thought that recovery from such trauma is for most people a quiet process, with healing to be found in the everyday tasks of work, family and home-making. Perhaps this was easier for former convicts in small communities in which most people were "old hands." Regardless, the fact that most emancipists seemed rarely to talk about their former lives is not in itself evidence of an unhealthy repression of the past. The public denial of the island's convict heritage, so central to the colony's identity from 1850, was, however, another matter altogether.

THE END OF TRANSPORTATION

The FREE SETTLERS' SOLUTION TO living in a convict colony was to construct a separate society of their own, enforced through strict social conventions and brutal controls over the majority population. However, the ideological foundation of the caste system received a mortal blow with the publication of the report of the House of Commons Select Committee on Transportation, chaired by Sir William Molesworth, in 1838.

Drawing a comparison with the moral contamination of society by slavery, the Molesworth Inquiry found that the evil of convictism could not be quarantined: "there belongs to the [convict] system [the] monstrous evil of calling into existence, and continually extending, societies or the germs of nations, most thoroughly depraved, as respects both the character and degree of their vicious propensities."[1] Others took this argument even further. The English Benedictine and former senior cleric of the Catholic Church in Australian colonies, William Ullathorne, wrote one of the most widely publicised anti-transportation tracts:

> We have been doing an ungracious and ungodly thing. We have taken a vast portion of God's earth and made it a cesspool ... we have poured down scum upon scum and dregs of the offscourings of mankind, and, as these harden and become consistent together, we are building up with them a nation of crime, to be, unless something is speedily done, a curse and a plague, a by-word to all the

peoples of the earth. The eye of God looks down upon a people such as, since the deluge, has not been ... The removal of such a plague from the earth concerns the whole human race.[2]

The free settlers were outraged at the suggestion that the moral degeneracy of convictism had corrupted their carefully constructed society, and much of the considerable literary output of the colony in the 1840s represented their counterattack. David Burn's aim, for example, was "to show Tasmania and the Tasmanians in their *true light*, and to render justice to a portion of Her Majesty's Subjects not less loyal, not less enterprising, and, assuredly *not less moral*, than any of their fellow Britons, be they located where they may." But imperial judgments were not easily countered, and it was increasingly accepted that if Tasmania were to be "the Britain of the south," it would need to be convict-free.[3]

Sodomy and Shame

From 1844 concern with the moral consequences of transportation escalated dramatically after a connection was made between the concentration of convicts in remote probation gangs and homosexuality. This topic aroused such emotion and hysteria that its implications were seen to go far beyond penal policy, with convict sex in the Van Diemonian bush becoming a matter of the highest imperial concern. With the biblical warning of Sodom vividly in mind, the politically influential evangelicals claimed that the fate of the whole society, indeed possibly the whole empire, was at stake.

William Gladstone was a powerful apologist for this view during his stint as colonial secretary. Having removed Lieutenant Governor Eardley Wilmot on the basis of rumours about his private life in 1846, Gladstone requested that the acting lieutenant governor, Charles Latrobe, investigate accounts that convicts in gangs had "fallen into habits of life so revolting and depraved as to make it nothing less than the most sacred and imperious duty to adopt, without the necessary loss of a single day ... measures ... to arrest the progress of pollution." Despite his limited knowledge, Gladstone was certain about the need for urgent action: "Unhappily there appears to be no doubt of the wide prevalence of an evil so hateful in its character and so formidable in its penal consequences, not merely to the actual victims of vice, but to all who tolerate such evils."[4] While Latrobe also considered the operation of the probation system more generally, much of his time in Van Diemen's Land between October 1846 and January 1847 was spent gathering information on the question his political master had identified as the immediate priority.[5] An inquiry was held at every probation station, with medical officers examining clothing and bedding for semen, researching medical records for symptoms that might indicate "habitual perpetration" and conducting cross-examinations.[6]

Enclosure Number Five on the "prevalence of unnatural crime" was not included in Latrobe's published report because "some may well be permitted to hesitate before they concede that the imputation of the wide prevalence of such fearful pollution is justly cast upon the colony." But the secrecy that surrounded the inquiry only increased public interest in it, as few in Van Diemen's Land could have been unaware of an issue being so actively investigated. Latrobe was himself concerned that the "crime" was "common talk with the lower classes" and these people were "consequently tainted," but he ignored the obvious contribution the government's own investigations were making to this.[7] One anonymous contributor to the anti-transportationist mouthpiece the *Launceston Examiner* asked:

> *Shall Tasman's Isle so fam'd*
> *So lovely and so fair*
> *From other nations be estrang'd*
> *The name of Sodom bear?*[8]

Enclosure Number Five concluded that "vice of every description is to be met with on every hand, not as isolated spots, but as a pervading stain." Latrobe found that as long as convicts were "congregated in the gangs, whether 'probation,' 'hiring' or 'punishment,' it is impossible to resist the conclusion, that in spite of every effort from within or without, the general tendency is to deeper degradation." While he stepped back from a direct condemnation of the upper echelons of

Van Diemen's Land society, Latrobe believed that "neither individuals nor communities can escape from the knowledge and contemplation of such abominations without moral injury," and feared the "demoralizing influence, which ... this detestable vice amongst the convicts, does and must exercise upon the character of the colony in general." Homosexuality was, in short, a "stigma upon the [whole] colony."[9]

The problem was, in part, environmental. Latrobe found that "*Within doors*, so to say, the commission of the crime is hardly possible ... But no such security can be felt in regard to the conduct of the prisoners comprising detached parties at a distance from the station ... There can be no doubt but to whatever extent the crime in question be perpetrated, it is, at this time, perpetrated in the bush."[10] To overcome this problem, Latrobe successfully recommended that the first period of sentence be served in British or Irish gaols, since the mild Van Diemonian climate was "provocative to idleness and crime" and at "Millbank or Parkhurst [British prisons] ... nature herself would be a powerful ally in restraining the passions."[11] The penal policy of the British government was thus substantially modified to counter the sexual freedom afforded by the benevolent Van Diemonian bush.

Within Van Diemen's Land itself, the contrast between the "pure" and "innocent" land and a "polluted" society was given greater prominence. Dr (later Sir) Robert Officer wrote: "I have always thought that of all the British colonies, the beautiful island of Van Diemen's Land is the last which ought to have been subjected to this cruel degradation: from its climate, its scenery, and its whole physical character, it is calculated more than any other to maintain in all its vigour the character of the race to which we are descended."[12]

Given the contents of Latrobe's report and the publicity it received, it is not surprising that in 1846 the British government decided to suspend male transportation to Van Diemen's Land. When the decision was taken to resume it two years later (in response to the pressure on the penal system caused by the Irish famine and the economic and political turbulence of 1848), this only intensified the public campaign against what James Bonwick termed the colony's "Sodom infamy."[13]

Despite the celebrated natural beauty of the island, the consequence of the anti-transportation campaign was that the mid-nineteenth-century evangelical view of homosexuality became inextricably associated with Van Diemen's Land and instilled an enduring sense of shame. The pervading "stain" of convictism arguably had its origins more in shame about sex than in memories of servitude.[14]

New Political Institutions

Concurrent with the debate about transportation, free settlers began to demand trial by jury, political representation and other rights held by members of their class in Britain. However, the British government's long-held view that these rights were inconsistent with the colony's primary status as a penal colony meant it was slow to surrender power. When New South Wales achieved a partially elected legislature in 1842 (following the end of transportation), Lord Stanley explained that the "sole reason" Van Diemen's Land did not receive equivalent rights was "the incompatibility ... between the grant of such a form of constitution and the continuation of transportation to the colony."[15]

The free-settler campaign was not a movement for democratic reform. It was assumed that greater liberties could only be safely secured if the majority of the free population – that is, former convicts – were explicitly excluded from their enjoyment. Indeed, London's commitment to upholding the rights of emancipists was (like the earlier tokens of concern for the Aborigines) a source of tension with the colonial ruling class.

The possibility that some former convicts might gain the vote was particularly horrifying. "Ten pounds to give the right of franchise!" exclaimed David Burn. "Why, this would be licence not liberty ... the choice of Legislative Councillors would fall into the hands of the worst class of emancipists ... ten pounds may become a fitting qualification; at the present moment, 50 would hardly be enough."[16] Sharing this concern, Lieutenant Governor Denison noted that "there is an essentially democratic spirit which actuates the large mass of the community; and it is with the view to check the development of this spirit, of preventing its coming into operation, that I would suggest the formation of the upper chamber" whose members "should be appointed or elected for life."[17]

A partially elected legislature with a limited franchise was eventually established in Van Diemen's Land through the Australian Colonies Government Act of 1850. The resulting Legislative Council, dominated by landowners, then drafted the Tasmanian constitution, which came into effect with self-government in 1856. Two houses of parliament were established. The upper house (still to be known as the Legislative Council) was to comprise 15 members elected by males above the age of 21 who owned a freehold estate worth £50 in annual value, or who were graduates, solicitors, doctors, clergy or retired officers. In the lower house (called the House of Assembly), the franchise was extended to men over 21 who possessed a freehold estate worth £100 clear, to householders paying £10 annual rent, to salary earners on incomes of £100 pounds a year or more, and to those with the same professional qualifications required to vote for the Council.[18] The restrictions on voting rights were effective. As late as 1881, only about 10 per cent of males over 21 were enrolled to vote in the Council, and just over 50 per cent in the Assembly. In the many small rural seats, the proportion of the male population eligible to vote was far lower – in George Town it was only 14 per cent even in the Assembly, and elections were "primarily local affairs."[19]

The new arrangements did not simply mirror those of other British colonies. When Alpheus Todd compared various colonial upper houses in 1880, he found that only Tasmania and Victoria had upper houses elected through a voting system based on regional electorates (where local patronage could exercise its greatest influence). Moreover, only in Tasmania did the powers of the upper house remain undefined, which meant that it could and did exercise a veto power over all areas of government revenue and expenditure.[20]

As in the old "rotten boroughs" of rural England, the social and economic power wielded by large landowners through much of country Tasmania led to political representatives conducive to gentry interests. There was only one election where the "essentially democratic spirit" that had worried Denison found expression: the January 1853 municipal elections in Hobart. The public denigration of convicts and former convicts led to an uncharacteristic backlash and the emergence of an emancipist voting bloc. In the background was the attempt by the Legislative Council to force on former convicts the stigma of presenting proof positive of their status as free men before being eligible to vote. This would have disenfranchised many emancipists.[21] Muted or actual discrimination in the right to apply for hotel licences, public service and teaching positions, and the election to magistracy, had also been issues for some years. As the lieutenant governor was the main bulwark against their implementation, many former convicts understandably feared the potential consequences of self-government.[22]

The Tasmanian Union, founded in October 1850 as the Prisoners Protection Society, co-ordinated the successful election campaign in support of the "people's candidates." William Carter, prominent in the union, became mayor, proclaiming, "I will take you from the senate to the church – from the church to the bench – from the bench to the bar – and from that to the merchant, and from him to the shopkeeper, and I would ask you if they [the convicts] are not as respected as any free men who ever came to this country."[23] In opposition, the *Colonial Times* rallied against "beings who claim the country as the sole inheritance of all who have been or may hereafter be in trouble" and described the election result as a victory for "slumocracy."[24]

As it happened, the elected aldermen were moderate influences and the focus on the rights of ex-convicts, like the Tasmanian Union itself, did not even last to self-government. Even so, a significant victory had been won – explicit legal discrimination against former convicts was not pursued any further. Indeed, once the provocation of the anti-transportation campaign ended, earlier custom, which viewed emancipists as free servants provided they stayed quietly within their proper domain, seemed quickly to reassert itself.

A New Future and a New Past
In December 1852, the British government finally decided to end transportation. The discovery of gold in Victoria meant that the authorities no longer saw transportation as an effective deterrent to crime. The last transport arrived in May 1853 and in the following

year the British government accepted a request from the Legislative Council that the name of the colony be changed, given that "Van Diemen's Land" was "connected to the former condition of the colony as a penal settlement."[25] On 1 January 1856, the first day of self-government, Van Diemen's Land officially became known as Tasmania. Externally the name change caused confusion for decades,[26] but on the island "Van Diemen's Land" seemed to be rapidly forgotten. The amnesia was reinforced by an interpretation of the island's history that downplayed the significance of its convict foundation. Not surprisingly, it was the leading anti-transportationist, soon to become the long-serving editor of the *Sydney Morning Herald*, John West, who put this view most persuasively.

West published his eloquent *History of Tasmania* in 1852. Over a century later, a state-government-supported publication celebrating the centenary of self-government sustained the anti-convict theme: "The colonists had demanded the end of the convict system, and it had ceased. They had demanded self-government and got it. Van Diemen's Land, with its tyranny and cruelty, with its leg-irons and the flagellator's lash, was dead, and Tasmania rose from the ashes."[27]

[18]

VICTORIA'S VAN DIEMONIAN
FOUNDATION

IN 1856 TASMANIA WAS NOT THE ONLY newly self-governing
Australian colony embarrassed by its Van Diemonian heritage.
But whereas the Tasmanian establishment reinterpreted its personal
and communal history, the squatter and merchant elite of the booming gold-rich colony of Victoria chose a simpler path: outright denial.
Even today the inconvenient truth that Victoria was first settled by
ex-convicts from Van Diemen's Land is not widely known.

For at least its first decade of existence, the Port Phillip district
was primarily an economic and social outpost of Van Diemen's Land
(even though in an administrative sense it was soon confirmed by
London to be part of New South Wales). As Marie Fels has noted, we
now tend to think of Bass Strait "as a barrier separating Tasmania
from the mainland ... a hindrance to trade and social interaction. It
was not so in the early colonial period ... Bass Strait functioned like
a highway to Port Phillip. The sea was not an obstacle, but an open
road."[1]

Port Phillip was in effect much closer to Launceston than to Sydney, and had long been visited by sealers, whalers and wattle-bark
cutters from Van Diemen's Land. John Hart, who traded in the region,
recalled that "the fame of the place was spread far and wide by the
returned bark cutters." A small settlement established at Westernport
in 1826–27 had also increased awareness of the vast grassland plains
of western and northern Victoria. And from the mid 1830s, a number
of land-hungry squatters – predominantly made up of a cross-section

of the landowners of Van Diemen's Land – employed experienced and bush-wise Van Diemonian labour to move sheep into this new frontier. Ronald Gunn's prediction that Port Phillip was "sure to thrive astonishingly fast from the knowledge of the settlers, with the colonial management, their wealth and its vicinity to Van Diemen's Land" was almost immediately fulfilled, and the contrast with the failed Port Phillip settlement of 1803 could not have been more complete.[2]

Edward Henty was the first to become an illegal squatter, transporting sheep, workers and supplies across the strait in late 1834. However, much of the initial impetus came from the Port Phillip Association, which was formed in Hobart Town in 1835 with the intention of establishing a permanent settlement with land purchased from the Aborigines. The key figure in this enterprise was John Batman, who undertook the treaty negotiations in June 1835 on the banks of Merri Creek in present-day Northcote in Melbourne, using legal advice from the former Van Diemen's Land attorney-general, Joseph Gellibrand, and with the support of his Aboriginal companions from New South Wales and Van Diemen's Land. Another significant figure was the clearly ambivalent William Buckley – the convict runaway from the 1803 settlement party, who had lived with the Aborigines ever since and remained committed to defending them to the limited extent he was able. Gellibrand wrote that Buckley was "not at all desirous of occupying any land or having sheep but is highly pleased at the idea of being appointed Superintendent of the Natives."[3] The association sought London's approval for its land grab on the grounds that they had legally purchased the land,[4] but the British government advised Governor Bourke in April 1836 that the treaty could not be recognised, as "such a concession would subvert the foundation on which all proprietary rights in New South Wales at present rest."[5] In other words, the legal recognition of prior Aboriginal land ownership would render void all previous land grants.

Once it was clear that London did not recognise the association's monopoly claims over Port Phillip and was doing nothing to prohibit settlement, the land rush from Van Diemen's Land accelerated. As *Bents News* reported in 1836, "the only feeling existing among men of capital here appears to be that of jealousy who shall have the first and best hold of land and stock at Port Phillip."[6] The work involved in settling the new land was done by the employees of these "men of capital," overwhelmingly former convicts. Up until the end of 1837, "virtually the whole population [of Port Phillip] had come from across the Bass Strait" and even in 1839 there were twice as many new arrivals from Van Diemen's Land as from New South Wales.[7]

The open grassland plains of the Port Phillip district proved to be even more profitable than the hill-buttressed grassy woodlands of Van Diemen's Land. Thomas Winter wrote in 1837, "it is very rarely that we find the steep, thickly-wooded hills which abound here [in Van Diemen's Land]. On the contrary I should say that the largest quantity of land – perhaps one-half the country already explored – is plain, generally without trees, nearly flat, and often stony." There were few hills "either too steep or too woody to prevent a horse trotting up to the top." In these circumstances, Winter reported, "the sheep, cattle, and horses … thrive in an extraordinary manner."[8]

For settlers, the principal obstacle to realising spectacular profits from wool exports was the Aborigines. As Winter observed, "the natives are numerous and troublesome; indeed, they are the greatest drawback to the colony." It was not surprising, therefore, that from 1836 Port Phillip effectively became the new frontier in the Tasmanian War. The final clearances of the Tasmanian Aborigines from the west and north-west coast during 1834–35 coincided almost exactly with the invasion of Port Phillip, and settler attitudes and strategies – and, even more significantly, seasoned and bush-wise Van Diemonian warriors – were carried across the strait. A number of former Tasmanian squatters described, in reminiscences collected in 1853, how they had so quickly achieved the exclusive possession of the pasturelands. John Hepburn acknowledged that there "were several … times I turned out the men to drive them [the Aborigines] off the run." Charles Wedge recalled that at Portland Bay the Aborigines began to attack sheep as early as 1836 and that these "depredations did not cease till many lives were sacrificed, and, I may say, many thousands of sheep destroyed." Hugh Murray, the first of eight squatters from Van Diemen's Land who settled the Colac region in 1837–38, claimed the Aborigines "never lost an opportunity of stealing our sheep … in such cases the settlers assembled and pursued them, and when their encampment was discovered they generally fled, leaving behind them their weapons, rugs etc, which, together with their huts, were destroyed." William Clarke recalled that in his first run on the East Wimmera "a number of blacks, I am sorry to say, was shot" and a "Mr Francis, the overseer of the station, was many times engaged in the fights with them." George Faithful recalled a ferocious fight around present-day Benalla on 11 April 1838 in which between ten and 14 servants and a very large number of Aborigines were killed in an all-day fight.[9]

Port Phillip even inherited Van Diemen's Land's emissary: George Augustus Robinson took up the position of chief protector of Aborigines in 1838, and Faithful blamed him for exacerbating the violence of a necessary war. Faithful argued that the threat to hang those who shot Aborigines and the search for information on these matters

> did much evil. People formed themselves into bands of alliance and allegiance to each other, and then it was the destruction of the natives really did take place … we were all branded as murderers of the blacks, they readily deprived us of portions of our runs to give them to the other squatters who were considered peaceful men, as they well might be after the war was ended. Ours was the danger, theirs the reward.[10]

Another Tasmanian squatter documented how far the government could be directly implicated in the violence. Edward Curr, son of his notorious namesake who led the conquest of Van Diemen's Land Company lands, moved north from Melbourne in mid 1841 with his former convict shepherds. When troops arrived to "apprehend all troublesome blacks and restore quiet," they took an Aboriginal hostage, who was shot dead when he fled rather than lead the troops to his tribe. When Curr challenged the officer on the accuracy of his official report of this incident, the response was illuminating: "persons unconnected with the public service know nothing of reports; indeed civilians from first to last are ill fitted to describe collisions of this sort, being apt to blurt out sentiments more properly held in reserve."[11]

Curr also noted the fear of Aborigines instilled in Van Diemen's Land convicts: "On my men, all of them old hands, unoccupied country had a very depressing effect, their idea being that we should be all killed by the Blacks." When the Aborigines arranged a meeting in July 1841, "Their approach caused some little trepidation in my old Tasmanians," who wanted to "to kid them over and shoot the lot." But, as in Van Diemen's Land, it was easy for the privileged to sit in judgment on former convicts and avoid facing up to their own responsibility for the inevitable tragedy consequent to the invasion of Aboriginal territory. When Curr reported that his neighbour, a lone, highly vulnerable, former convict hut-keeper, had shot an Aborigine,[12] did the primary responsibility lie with the worker, the settler whose land and property he defended, or the government, which ultimately sanctioned the squatter's illegal seizure of the land in the first place?

Despite the ferocity of the fighting in some districts, Aboriginal resistance scarcely affected the pace of settlement, and the first census of Port Phillip, taken on 12 September 1838, recorded that in only three years sheep numbers had increased to 310,946. Critical to the speed and ease of the conquest were the same geographical features that made the land so favourable to sheep. With even the hills and woodlands largely open to the horse, Aborigines could find few refuges from guns or germs. By 1853 only 53 Aborigines of the Yarra and Westernport tribes were thought to survive.[13]

As in Van Diemen's Land, the environmental impact of the conquest was soon apparent. For the first few years the botanical bounty of the Aboriginal hunting grounds replicated the early years in Van Diemen's Land, before over-grazing and weeds took their toll. As John Robertson recalled: "I could neither think nor sleep for admiring this new world to me who was fond of sheep. I looked among the 37 grasses that formed the pasture of my run. There was no silk-grass which had been destroying our Van Diemen's Land pastures." But by 1853 Robertson had already observed a decline and suggested "every year it will get worse as it did in Van Diemen's Land," as "many of our herbaceous plants begin to disappear" and give way to the "silk grass and the little annuals." Already "the long deep-rooted grasses" had "died out," and erosion was resulting.[14] Other familiar consequences of conquest were also soon evident. George Armytage recalled in 1853 that "emus and kangaroos, on our arrival were plentiful in all parts of the district," but "are now nearly extinct in the district; the country is almost void of game."[15]

By 1853 the European population of the new territory was more than 100,000 and increasing rapidly with the impetus of the gold rush. The new colony of Victoria (which had been established in 1851) had not only outgrown its mother island, but now sought to quarantine itself from any further influence. By an 1852 Act, the Victorian government sought to exclude former convicts emigrating from Van Diemen's Land by providing that those possessing only a conditional pardon (that is, the large majority of them) were to be treated as felons at large and imprisoned with hard labour in irons for three years. Lieutenant Governor Denison in Hobart considered this Act "ten times more objectionable" than an earlier New South Wales Vagrant Act, also targetted at former convicts, which had been deemed illegal by the British government, and he ensured that London again intervened.[16] Victorian lawmakers did not easily give up, however, coming up with new legislation that put the onus of proof on apprehended Van Diemonians to prove that they were free. Despite London's orders, the discriminatory Act continued to be applied until 1856.[17]

There were vigorous protests against the Victorian laws in Hobart Town. This included a public meeting attended by about 800 people in which members of the Anti-Transportation League were hissed at and had to leave. John Davies, proprietor of the *Mercury* and a former convict, outed the prominent Victorian John Pascoe Fawkner as the son of a convict and "stirred the crowd into a state of frantic excitement as he kept on naming names in connection with those who had the temerity and the gall to support an Act in Victoria aimed at ex-convicts."[18]

In practice the laws had little success in preventing the migration of former convicts across Bass Strait. Unlike the road blocks which were set up on the overland route from Sydney, the sea highway was almost impossible to police, and Victoria continued to provide a refuge for those seeking fortune or freedom away from social and economic controls. About 8000 people, mainly former convicts, left Van Diemen's Land in the three years from 1847 to 1850 alone, and the large majority went to Port Phillip.[19] Some, like "Red" Kelly, an Irish convict who left Van Diemen's Land in 1848, probably passed on stories of convict life (his son Ned knew it as "that land of bondage and tyranny"), but it is not surprising that, given the degree of prejudice, in 1851 only about 3000 residents of Port Phillip admitted to having a convict past.[20] Such was the anti-convict sentiment that amnesia concerning the colony's first settlers became even more pronounced and persistent in Victoria than in Tasmania. The role played by Van Diemonian convicts as the founding fathers of Victoria still remains largely hidden, and the truth that former convict shepherds and bushmen did the main work of settlement – including the violence consequent to it – is little known. Forgetting the immigrants from Van Diemen's Land and concealing their bloody deeds have, it seems, gone hand in hand.

CONCLUSION

[All countries] bear some mark of their origin; and the circumstances which accompanied their birth and contributed to their rise affect the whole term of their being. —DE TOCQUEVILLE[1]

STORED IN THE VAULTS OF the Bird Collection of the British Natural History Museum since 1838 have been two Tasmanian emus, the only complete specimens of what was the island's largest land animal.[2] Like the distinct King Island and Kangaroo Island subspecies, the Tasmanian emu fell victim to a predator unknown before British settlement: the dog. The eggs, chicks and adult birds provided food for the human invaders and their canine companions who settled Van Diemen's Land and its offshore islands from 1798.

Few Tasmanians now know there was once a Tasmanian emu. The emu and forester kangaroo (which also narrowly escaped extinction on the island and is confined to regions far from the capital) on Hobart's coat of arms are seen as quaint decorations, not as a representation of the city's birth. The motto beneath the posing animals, *Sic Fortis Hobartia Crevit* ("Thus in strength did Hobart grow") – first used by Robert Knopwood in his diary on the last day of 1804 when the chaplain, with evident pride and gratitude, tallied the number of animals his convict hunters had killed during the first year of settlement – has been reduced to an obscure piece of Latin unrelated to the bounty to which it refers.[3]

The ignorance about the Tasmanian emu is one example of the pervasive influence of a pernicious national narrative. In this, the early British colonists of Australia are assumed to be ignorant strangers in a hostile land, and their difficult, hungry existence but a prelude to the time when free settlers arrive and real development begins (whether this be judged positively, as in traditional "progress" histories, or negatively, as in most contemporary environmental history). Although this narrative is more fully expressed in Australian culture than in serious history, the failure of historians to recognise the implications of the continent's diverse environment on early British settlement underpins its continuing vitality.

Even Manning Clark, who believed that the "subject on which every historian of this country should have something to say [is] the influence of the spirit of place in the fashioning of Australians," seemed to overlook Australia's obvious geographic diversity. With "that first cry of horror and disappointment of the Dutch seamen," he believed, there arose the belief that "here, indeed, was a country where the Creator had not finished his work. Here nature was so hostile, so brutish that men in time believed God had cursed both man and the country itself, and hence its barrenness, its sterility, its unsuitability for the arts of civilised human beings."[4]

Clark is far from alone in ascribing to harsh geography a profound influence on the Australian national character. More recently, Tim Flannery has argued that "many of the great differences between American and Australian cultures" have their origin in the fact that "the Australians found themselves facing adversity almost from the moment they entered the continent."[5] And William Lines has stated that, unlike in North America, "no antipodean invader ever entertained a sentimental vision of Australia as nature's garden, a prelapsarian Eden – quite the opposite. To the British, Australia stood in need of redemption."[6]

The British conquest of Van Diemen's Land challenges us to hear an alternative settler experience. The country around both the southern and northern settlements was dramatically different from that of Port Jackson. Ready access to cleared grasslands, fresh water, rich coastal resources and fresh meat and skins in a land that had never known the dingo – all of these ensured that the grassy woodlands of Van Diemen's Land were the first Australian environment that Britons made home. Moreover, nowhere else in the New World, including North America, did Britons adapt so quickly or so comprehensively to the demands of the new environment. For the majority of the population the land soon became not a cursed place of darkness but a refuge from the horror inflicted by "civilised human beings." For convicts and their families the land became their hope, a place of redemption from the servitude of a penal colony. The story of the convict settlers of Van Diemen's Land, then, differs dramatically from the accounts which still fill Australian history books and set the terms for debates about national identity. And it is not just a story from the fringe.

By the early 1830s, Van Diemen's Land had a third of the European population of Australia, a majority of the sheep, and was receiving more new immigrants than the rest of the Australian colonies combined. At the time some commentators believed it would soon become the principal colony. This was not to be, but Van Diemen's Land remained the second most important site of British colonisation in Australia – after New South Wales – until the gold rushes transformed Australia in the 1850s, and it was the base from which the colonisation of southern Australia, from King George Sound to Port Phillip, largely proceeded.

While there is no longer silence about Tasmania's or Australia's convict past (indeed, the packaging of this "cultural heritage" is essential to the tourist industry), elements of the old public amnesia remain in the reluctance to acknowledge the convicts as the true founders of the nation. Despite new directions in convict studies (that have integrated convicts into Australian history, banished many stereotypes and highlighted the independent enterprise of convict men and women[7]), convicts are still usually seen through the lens of the penal apparatus, while a much smaller group of free settlers is given credit for shaping the land and conceiving the new society. Just as the Aborigines were for so long, the convicts are largely remembered as victims; passive prisoners in a world created by their masters. Too often they are assumed to be without culture or enterprise – that was something possessed only by those with authority over them.

The Van Diemonians of southern Australia are undoubtedly difficult founding fathers with whom to come to terms. However, their way of life poses an alternative to the widely publicised vision of their masters – which is the only early settler perspective most Australians have ever heard. In 1824 Edward Curr wrote that "our highest aim is to exhibit on a small scale something like the beauties which rise at every step in the land to which we have bade adieu."[8] These and similar sentiments have often been used to summarise the aspirations of British immigrants. Yet statements like Curr's need to be given a context. The years in which he wrote were watershed years for Van Diemen's Land, when a new class of immigrant was arriving, men who were granted private property title over the grassy woodlands and self-consciously aspired to reproduce the environment and socio-economic hierarchy of rural England. But Curr was writing about what he hoped the colony would become, not what it was. As he lamented: "alas!, with all its inviting beauties, its riches and verdure, it is still Van Diemen's Land, – still the abode of felons; a moral evil, which, in spite of other advantages, will compel many to forgo the little less than paradise which it presents."[9]

The aspirations of most residents of this "abode of felons" were a world apart from Curr's. Most came from a life of poverty in what was in many respects a pre-industrial society. As E.P. Thompson reminds us, the biggest change that came with industrialisation was in needs and expectations. Ordinary Britons in the early nineteenth century (and the Irish for much longer still) did not expect to have much in the way of possessions; meeting the essentials of life on a day-to-day basis was their primary aim. In Van Diemen's Land, where environmental imperatives meant that many imported products – clothes, tents, tools, guns and salted foods – were commonly discarded, needs were simplified still further. The transportation of this raw human material to a land that offered a degree of free access to the essentials of life which was unknown in Britain (where even wild animals were private property) led to rapid, environmentally induced changes in lifestyles and culture.

For a surprising number of current and former convicts, food, clothing and shelter were to come not from the payment of wages, prescribed rations or charity, but to be the gift of the land itself. For men and women who had known poverty, harsh penal discipline, and autocratic masters and officials, success was not to be gauged by the accumulation of capital but rather by self-sufficiency and the extent to which one could preserve life and freedom.

There is abundant evidence, then, that the Van Diemonian poor were not the wealth-maximising units commonly postulated by economic theory. Freedom, not profit, drove their colonisation of the frontier. Nevertheless, most Australian historians remain uncritically wedded to the assumptions of orthodox economics about human nature and are guilty of what E.P. Thompson described as "crass economic reductionism, obliterating the complexities of motive, behaviour and function."[10] Such reductionism has consequences for how we think about the present as well as the past. It is not, as Thompson points out, that it is possible or desirable to "return to pre-capitalist human nature", but that in the context of the ecological crisis, "a reminder of its alternative needs, expectations and codes may renew our sense of nature's range of possibilities."[11] The aim is not to idealise pre-industrial society, least of all the rough culture of the back-blocks of Van Diemen's Land, but to break out of intellectual straitjackets that constrain the national imagination.

Simon Schama is another who points to the hope for a sustainable society that may be found in forgotten memories:

> though it may sometimes seem that our impatient appetite for produce has ground the earth to thin and shifting dust, we need only poke below the subsoil of its surface to discover an obstinately rich loam of memory. It is not that we are any more virtuous or wiser than the most pessimistic environmentalist supposes. It is just that we are more retentive. The sum of our pasts, generation laid over generation, like the slow mould of the seasons, forms the compost of our future. We live off it.[12]

Van Diemen's Land surely provides a particularly fertile ground for contemplation for a nation belatedly facing up to environmental reality.

The ordinary settlers of Van Diemen's Land were not any more sensitive to the land or its people than is usually assumed in Australian history (the sorry fate of the forgotten emu is but one reminder of that). They were simply more mutable, and more pre-modern in their view of the world and their aspirations for themselves and their families, than our history books generally recognise. Their economic and cultural background, combined with the experience of servitude in a penal colony, made them open to enduring the hardships and isolation required in living with the land. It was this environmental encounter, not enlightened attitudes, that ensured adaptation and change.

The way of life of the poor came to pose a potent threat to the elite, and this needs to be remembered when reading contemporary descriptions of early colonial society. The many complaints of the land grantees and the colonial government about current and former convicts living in their bark huts, combining hunting with farming, reluctant to work beyond the minimum hours or grow more than they needed, and drinking to the moment rather than saving for tomorrow, can no longer be unthinkingly repeated as if these critics were free of self-interest or their own cultural blinkers. The great challenge of the free settlers and colonial authorities in the 1820s was not to subdue the environment, as is widely assumed, but rather to see off competitors for the native pastures and develop a docile labour force that would work the land and respect and defend the property of their masters. This conflict within the ranks of the British invaders, as with the struggle to dispossess the Aborigines from their traditional lands, was for a long time far more equal and unresolved than it appears seen from the perspective of the twenty-first century, where tangible icons of the victor's spoils, from Georgian houses to Port Arthur, are such visible features of Tasmania's landscape.

At one level, the vision of reproducing the environmental, social and economic relations of rural England undeniably and unambiguously triumphed, with almost all matters in contention seemingly resolved in favour of the elite. The penal system was refined, the grassy woodlands converted to gentry estates, and itinerant stock thieves were locked up in the many gaols that were built across the island, eventually underpinned by the fortress of Port Arthur. Most Aborigines were captured or killed, and the survivors forced into exile. There was no negotiated settlement in Van Diemen's Land: the victor's terms were unconditional. James Ross concluded his 1836 account of free-settler pioneer struggles on an understandable note of triumph: "my flocks and herds were rapidly increasing ... every day was adding something to the value of my estate, and the efforts which the government was making to put down the aggressions of both black and white invaders of life and property ... proved triumphantly success-ful." So well did a small group of landowners cement their victory that by 1875, 92 of the largest 100 rural estates were owned by families that had acquired land before 1832 (accounting, with the Van Die-men's Land Company, for almost half of all alienated land); and the gentry exercised more political power through parliament and the arms of government (largely devolved in nineteenth-century Tasma-nia to a local level where the landowners' influence was paramount) than had been the case even in Van Diemen's Land.[13]

On the other hand, what remained distinctive was that, unlike on the open plains of much of the Australian mainland, geographical realities continued to pose a challenge to hegemony. As the land com-missioners noted in 1827: "land, composed of no particles but miser-able sand and gravel, unfit for any purpose, and covered with wood, which can never be of any value, is extremely difficult to put a price on."[14] This type of country was everywhere, ensuring that the frontier existed as a perpetual patchwork rather than a continuous line retreat-ing to ever more remote and far-off places. In the disturbingly close and "useless" mountains, thick scrub, threatening forests, windswept coasts and the multitude of offshore islands, the common always beckoned, posing a challenge to the pretensions of those who would prematurely celebrate the triumph of the new order.

Although the convict settlement story is one of deep resilience, it must never be forgotten that much blood, human and animal, was spilt in Van Diemen's Land. Far from historians having exaggerated the suffering caused by British settlement to the island's Indigenous people, the truth of the crimes committed is still to be faced. The years of open warfare may be comparatively well known today, but there is considerably less awareness of the massacres which preceded this time than there was in the nineteenth century. And even when the killing was finally over, the tragedy only intensified in Tasmania's trail of tears, the west-coast clearances. The silence about the government's ethnic clearances – arguably the least defensible official action against an Indigenous people committed anywhere in the British empire during the nineteenth century – has been maintained for over 170 years. This subject is worthy of its own book. A beginning is made in the appendix of this one.

If there is no place of easy reassurance in the island's creation story, there is a sense of something new being born in the ash, something that has existed and struggled to survive ever since: a genuine experience of home. As Peter Hay points out, there has remained a "potent divide through subsequent phases of Tasmanian history" between this tradition and that of "an elite (perhaps an interlocked series of elites) that remains profoundly out of whack in time and space." A central challenge of the early twenty-first century is to reconnect this cultural heritage to the great environmental and social questions of our day. There remains in the back-blocks of Tasmania and in collective memory an experience of homemaking that will be important to honour if the constructed divisions between environmentalists and "ordinary people" (particularly evident in the debate over the forests) are to be overcome. Perhaps these long-forgotten folk can also remind the nation that there have always been many settlement stories in Australia, and that it is not only Marxists and postmodernists who need to recognise the importance of class and power in shaping environmental experience. The first step might even be, as Hay suggests, to reclaim the "tainted nomenclature" of Van Diemen's Land.[15] With local politicians talking once more of a "new Tasmania" (and acting ominously like their colonial predecessors), with national leaders sanitising Australian history for political ends, and with global forces seeking to privatise all that remains common, it may be more important than ever to remember Van Diemen's Land.

TOWARDS GENOCIDE: GOVERNMENT POLICY ON THE ABORIGINES 1827–38

[1]

PARTITION OR EXILE?

LIEUTENANT GOVERNOR ARTHUR showed surprisingly little concern for the escalating conflict with the Aborigines before 1828. Other than seeking military reinforcements (which arrived in 1826), he made almost no mention of Aborigines in his dispatches to London before January of that year, despite the British government being potentially his most powerful ally in defending Aboriginal interests. Arthur's previous record as governor of Honduras, which has often been cited to show his humanitarian concern for Indigenous peoples, has confused historians on this issue: Arthur's advocacy for the Indians in that country was not about land but slavery, the evangelical priority of the time.[1]

The most serious cause for doubt about the priority Arthur gave to the welfare of the Aborigines was the speed with which he alienated land. Over a million acres were granted in a frenzy of land handouts to free settlers between 1824 and 1831, yet no concern was expressed about the obvious implications of this for the Indigenous people. Even when Arthur was involved in an extended dispute with the Van Diemen's Land Company and the Colonial Office during 1826–27 over the amount of territory that should be handed to the company, he did not bring into the debate the immediate implications for the Aborigines of the company's inflated claims (which, he warned, would see it exercise effective control over a quarter of the island). Instead, he only highlighted the potential "exclusion" of "future settlers" should the company's position be upheld.[2]

There is no doubt that Arthur *understood* the link between land alienation and conflict with the Aborigines. In January 1828 he informed London that the Aborigines "already complain that the white people have taken possession of their country, encroached upon their hunting grounds, and destroyed their natural food, the kangaroo."[3] It was simply that with the rapid increase in the population of both convicts and free settlers, and the booming wool exports, he had other priorities. Indeed, as fighting intensified from 1828 to 1830, the amount of land granted *increased*. Not even growing criticism within evangelical circles in Britain (the influential Church Missionary Society's 1830–31 annual report wrote of the "scarcely credible" extent to which "the ancient proprietors have been deprived forcibly and without compensation") seemed to make any difference to the land policy of the evangelical lieutenant governor of Van Diemen's Land.[4]

The Policy of Partition

The intensification of the conflict in 1827–28 did, however, produce one innovative policy recommendation which, given its potential as an alternative model of Australian land settlement, deserves greater attention. Arthur's January 1828 memo to the new Colonial Office secretary, Lord Goderich, set out his proposed response to this "exceedingly perplexing" subject:

> The measure which I rather incline to attempt, is to settle the Aborigines in some remote quarter of the island, which should be strictly reserved for them, and to supply them with food and clothing, and afford them protection ... on condition of their confining themselves peaceably to certain limits ... The Commissioners have recommended the north east coast as being the most advantageous situation for such a purpose ... this plan also had its difficulties ... [including the] migratory habits of the Aborigines ... but it is but justice to make the attempt, and notwithstanding the clamour and urgent appeals which are now made to me for an adoption of harsh measures, I cannot divest myself of the consideration that all aggression originated with the white inhabitants, and that there-

fore much ought to be endured in return before the blacks are treated as an open and accredited enemy by the government.[5]

Arthur's plan for a formal partition of the island was expanded further in an April 1828 dispatch: he was "convicted of the absolute necessity of separating the Aborigines altogether from the white inhabitants, and of removing the former entirely from the settled districts until their habits shall become more civilized."[6]

This policy was outlined in a government notice entitled "Proclamation Separating the Aborigines from the White Inhabitants." Published on 19 April 1828, it aimed to "regulate and restrict the intercourse between the white and the coloured inhabitants" by confining Aborigines to non-settled regions of the island (including those containing "remote and scattered stock huts"). The difficulty raised by the nomadic nature of Aboriginal society was to be dealt with through negotiations:

> Nothing herein contained shall prevent the Aborigines from traveling annually (according to their custom), until their habits have been rendered more regular and settled, through the cultivated or occupied parts of the island to the sea coast ... on condition of their respective leaders being provided with a general passport, under my hand and seal, arrangements for which form a part of the intended negotiation.[7]

The goal of colonial government policy from April 1828 was thus to reach an agreement with the Aborigines on the division of Van Diemen's Land, with the right of Aborigines to travel across the resulting border guaranteed. This proposal had much merit. The open country of the north-east of the island which Arthur was considering as setting aside as Aboriginal territory had many advantages for refugees from the midlands and east coast. It was an area traditionally visited on a seasonal basis by a number of different groups for its food reserves and mild climate. It was still largely unoccupied by the British (and its comparatively poor soils and lower-quality grassland meant that it was not much sought after by land claimants), and it was

rich in game. The region was the last stronghold of the forester kangaroo and the emu and, with rivers, estuaries and sheltered bays, it
contained abundant bird life and shellfish. George Augustus Robinson noted that it was "well suited to the natives" and described it as
"altogether the finest country I have seen."[8] Furthermore, as the negotiations conducted by Robinson were to prove, key Aboriginal leaders
in the settled districts were eager to negotiate a peace settlement on
remarkably similar terms.

However, despite its positive potential, the formal proclamation
of the partition of Van Diemen's Land had only one practical outcome: it provided the first official sanction for the use of force against
Aborigines for no other reason than that they were Aboriginal. From
April 1828, any Aborigine visiting midlands, east-coast or north-
west hunting grounds (now deemed "settled districts"), regardless
of their purpose for doing so, was deemed a criminal. The executive council was told of the necessity "to arm the civil and military
authorities with additional power, and thereby enable them to expel
from, and keep out of the settled districts, the native tribes becoming so difficult and troublesome." The proclamation advised that
"the coloured population should be induced by peaceful means to
depart, or should otherwise be expelled by force from all the settled
districts therein."[9] The result was that the previously illegal private
vendettas were now sanctioned, with Arthur authorising the settlers to resort to "whatever means a severe and inevitable necessity
may dictate," albeit with six impossible-to-enforce provisos. This
policy received London's endorsement in early 1829, when the secretary of state sanctioned "confining the haunts of the natives to
particular limits" on the basis that no alternative existed, particularly given "the idea which they [the Aborigines] appear to entertain
in regard to their own rights over the country, in comparison with
those of the colonist" (although, it should be noted, the belief that
Aborigines had *some* rights over settled country was, in London, still
entertained).[10]

Both the Colonial Office and the lieutenant governor knew the
effect of the April 1828 proclamation. During the executive council
meeting that debated this issue over three consecutive days, Chief

Justice Pedder unsuccessfully sought changes to it with regard to the use of force. And, having lost the argument (with his main points preserved in the minutes that were forwarded to London), Pedder wrote to Arthur once more to document that "the object of this proclamation is their [the Aborigines'] expulsion wherever they may appear in the settled districts and however harmlessly they may be conducting themselves."[11] Thus, 25 years after first settlement, the chief justice of the colony confirmed that the legal pretence that had been maintained since 1803 – that the Aborigines were British subjects under the protection of the crown – had formally been abandoned. Any Aborigine could now be legally killed for doing no more than crossing an unmarked border that the government did not even bother to define.

Even so, Arthur continued to hope that the Aborigines could be confined to defined districts (he claimed that negotiations had been held up by a "spirit of dissention … amongst the tribes[12]), and he supported conciliation as a complementary strategy towards this end. In the winter of 1829, George Augustus Robinson, the overseer of the failed government settlement on Bruny Island (in which most of the surviving Neunonne people and many Aborigines from the west coast died), was authorised "to proceed on an expedition to Port Davey for the purpose of endeavouring to effect an amicable understanding with the Aborigines in that quarter, and, through them, with the tribes in the interior."[13] The embassy, comprising the Aborigines who had survived the Bruny Island settlement, and a few of those captured in the war, along with a number of bush-wise convict assistants, began its nine-month traverse of Van Diemen's Land on 30 January 1830. Over the next five years Robinson was to conduct a number of other expeditions to different regions of the island, and much historiographical confusion about the nature of his work has arisen because of a failure to recognise the extent to which these missions differed from each other. Undoubtedly the first expedition was, by any measure, an extraordinary journey of cultural and geographical discovery. There were many peaceful meetings with the Aborigines, and none was forced into exile. However, unlike the less benevolent expeditions to come, other than building up relationships of trust (which were to be exploited some years later), this expedition had little political effect and no obvious outcome.

While Robinson wandered the west coast, out of touch with his employer for months at a time, the main emphasis of government policy continued to be on the successful waging of war.

Legalising the War

The remaining legal limits on using force against Aborigines in the poorly defined "settled districts" were removed with the declaration of martial law. The fateful decision was made by the executive council on 30 October 1828 on the basis that "the outrages of the Aboriginal natives amount to a complete declaration of hostilities against the settlers generally" and that "to inspire them with terror ... will be found the only effectual means of security for the future." Hope for a negotiated settlement was largely abandoned at this point, with the council claiming that the "treachery" and "lack of government" of the Aborigines meant that they doubted "if any reliance could be placed upon any negotiations which might be entered into."[14] By this declaration settlers were given not only legal immunity but active encouragement for their campaign against the Aborigines, and official roving parties were formed to pursue, capture or kill them.[15]

The new measures inevitably escalated and geographically extended the conflict. While remote, largely unoccupied districts in the north-east, west and south of the island were supposedly excluded from martial law, and the public proclamation of 6 November 1828 asked that "bloodshed be checked as much as possible" and "defenceless women and children be invariably spared," its popular interpretation and overall effect was to provide legal immunity and state sanction for the killing of Aborigines wherever they could be found.[16] As Edward Curr triumphantly informed his British-based directors in January 1829, Arthur's "bias to philanthropy" had "ended in what I can only consider a war of extermination. The recent proclamation of martial law does not speak this out in very clear terms but it is to be the practical effect of it," as there is now "no safety for the white man but in the destruction of his black opponent."[17]

Arthur knew that treating the fight with the Aborigines as if it were a war with "an accredited state"[18] would lead to an increase in violence, but, he informed his military officers, he hoped that by such "energetic and decisive means ... an end will be put to that lawless and cruel warfare which is now carrying on, and which must terminate in the total annihilation of the natives."[19] The executive council considered that the alternative was a continued "war of private persons,"[20] although if this was genuinely believed, there is surely some irony in the sanction and encouragement that martial law gave to the settlers' private campaigns.

The Aborigines Committee

In late December 1829 Arthur requested that the "committee for the care and treatment of the captured Aborigines" conduct an inquiry into the "the origin of the hostility displayed by the black natives of this island against the settlers" and "consider the measures expedient to be adopted with a view of checking the devastation of property and the destruction of human lives occasioned by the state of warfare which has so extensively prevailed."[21] The establishment of the committee (which became known as the Aborigines Committee) was a wise move politically – it ensured broad ownership for government action, guaranteed shared blame for its failings, and deflected both the settlers' anger and London's concern. As Arthur noted, it "would afford a most satisfactory exposé, to answer any objections which hereafter be raised to the proceedings of the government in this very anxious matter."[22]

The Aborigines Committee's report of March 1830 was to provide a detailed justification for extending the reign of terror into every region of Van Diemen's Land. The methodology for its inquiry, which largely involved a consultation with an elite group of landowners, meant that the report ignored the direct correlation between the outbreak of sustained resistance and the alienation of the best Aboriginal hunting grounds of the island to the free settlers. Indeed, in what amounted to a classic whitewash, all the wrongs endured by the Aborigines were presented as *past* events, while all responsibility for the *present* violence lay with the Aborigines. The committee found that current "acts of violence on the part of the natives are generally to be regarded, not as retaliating for any wrongs which they conceived themselves collectively or individually to have endured, but as proceeding from a wanton and savage spirit inherent in them." Furthermore, responsibility for the "universal and permanent excitement of that spirit" rested solely with "dissolute and abandoned characters" (that is, convicts). It was their actions that had caused the Aborigines indiscriminately to attack "a different and totally innocent class."[23]

It was undoubtedly true that "miscreants who were a disgrace to our name and nation, and even to human nature" had played their part in the violence. But to suggest that "outrages" were past history, and that the current violence of the Aborigines reflected their inherent savagery rather than legitimate grievances, was, even to London, unsubstantiated speculation. When the report was forwarded to the secretary of state, Sir George Murray, he noted that the committee did not establish its central conclusion that the violence emanated from a "wanton and savage spirit inherent in them,"[24] even though the recommendation that force would be necessary to end the fighting relied on this claim.

Even some settlers were less willing than the committee to absolve the British of responsibility for the hostilities. Nonetheless, few would have disagreed with the editor of the *Tasmanian* that "the question of who was the aggressor is lost in the fact of our being at war." The government's flirtation with conciliation, negotiation and treaties was widely seen to have undermined the firm resolve and consistent application of brute force which was seen to be necessary to end the fighting. The Aborigines, it was argued, could not now be reconciled, individually or collectively, and the final proof of this was how many Aboriginal children raised by the settlers had now joined the resistance. Roderick O'Connor cited the example of the resistance leader "Black Tom," who had spent much of his childhood with the British, and asked how "is it possible to conciliate those who become more brutal in proportion to the kindness shown?"[25]

The War in 1830
The Aborigines Committee Inquiry was conducted in the context of a further escalation in hostilities. There were 30 separate incidents in

which seven Europeans were killed during February alone.[26] Even before the committee had reported, Arthur informed the executive council that the Aborigines would "derive fresh courage" from "any hesitancy in the show of force."[27] He now proposed to increase the armed parties in pursuit of them, including "every soldier that could be spared" with "as many as possible mounted."[28]

Moreover, the executive council now adopted a new policy with implications nearly as dramatic as the declaration of martial law. A five-pound reward was to be paid for every adult Aborigine and two pounds for every child delivered alive to the authorities.[29] This initiative represented the lieutenant governor's most blatant attempt to enlist former convicts in the fight – the sum of five pounds per adult was insignificant to the wealthy elite but a large amount of money for the Van Diemonian workers, hunters and the motley collection of bush vagrants who had the most experience of living on Aboriginal lands.

Colonial Secretary Burnett's opinion, expressed in the council meeting, that the reward should only be paid for uninjured Aborigines to minimise cruelty to them, was rejected by Arthur with the observation that "it would scarcely be possible to capture any of the blacks without in some way wounding them."[30]

The decision to pay a reward, without qualification, for the capture of Aborigines represented the end of any residual official concern for the private actions of British settlers against the Indigenous people of Van Diemen's Land. It was clear to all that the Aborigines most likely to be captured were not the guerrilla bands operating within the settled districts but members of the remote and intact Aboriginal communities that had not yet been broken up by the fighting. Yet the proclamation of February 1830 made not even a token attempt to distinguish, as British policy up to this point had done, between Aborigines in the settled regions and those living outside of them. Moreover, any stock-keeper, shepherd, sealer, bushranger or hunter who still had peaceful contact with Aborigines beyond the settled districts was effectively being bribed to betray and capture them. These men were encouraged to roam remote areas of Van Diemen's Land where traditional Aboriginal community life survived and capture any Aborigine they could, regardless of how many were killed in the process. It was a vicious and cruel policy designed to intensify the war on the cheap, with just enough of a veneer of humanity to satisfy the Colonial Office: while the captives would be visible and "protected," those Aborigines inevitably killed or wounded in private raids could be forever forgotten.

Along with enlisting former convicts in the struggle, Arthur set out to increase the total number of convicts living in frontier areas. In September 1829 he had advised London that "a very considerable augmentation of convicts" would be "most useful in affording protection to the settlers from the attacks of the Aboriginal natives,"[31] and in April 1830 requested that all convict transports be diverted to Van Diemen's Land to help in the fight:

> I would anxiously hope that ... you will be pleased to recommend that all the transports about to sail with convicts *from England* ... may be ordered to proceed to this Colony – at once two thousand convicts might be assigned away ... and by distributing them principally among the settlers *in the most remote parts of the Colony*, very great protection would be afforded at a very trifling expense to the Government.[32]

Arthur rightly recognised that the bush knowledge that some possessed, combined with the sheer number of convicts and former convicts engaged directly or indirectly in the struggle, amounted to a potent (and, just as importantly, largely unaccountable) British force.

In March 1830, Arthur largely accepted the Aborigines Committee's analysis and informed Murray that although

> lawless convicts ... together with the distant convict stock-keepers in the interior and the sealers ... acted with great inhumanity towards the black natives ... on the other hand it is increasingly apparent the Aboriginal natives of this colony are, and ever have been, a most treacherous race; and that the kindness and humanity which they have always experienced from the free settlers has not tended to civilize them in any degree.[33]

Efforts at conciliation were now largely abandoned, and while Robinson's party continued its isolated journey up the west coast, the level of fighting elsewhere remained intense. There were 222 documented incidents during 1830, up from 148 the year before, with 76 whites killed or wounded.[34] The number of Aboriginal casualties is as hard to estimate as ever, with the few official reports focused solely on actions against the small groups of guerrilla fighters remaining in the settled districts. Not one Aborigine was reported as killed during the most intense period of fighting in the first seven months of 1830; officials did not even make a cursory attempt to find out how many died outside of the operations of the official roving parties. What is clear is that remorseless British pursuit of Aborigines throughout Van Diemen's Land caused the Aboriginal population to decline very rapidly. Only in the remote west coast, where even Van Diemonian bushmen feared to wander, were communities intact. Ever-smaller groups of Aboriginal warriors continued to conduct raids on the stock huts and estates, but the end was clearly in sight.

Nevertheless, during 1830 the level of hostilities followed their usual seasonal pattern of reducing in winter and this, combined with Robinson's positive reports on his meetings with Aboriginal people, led Arthur to adopt a more conciliatory tone in government notices of 19 and 20 August 1830. The first requested settlers and servants "to abstain from all acts of aggression" because of Robinson's success, and the second, more significantly, placed restrictions on the payment of the reward for captured Aborigines. Arthur belatedly advised that "no violence or restraint" was to be used against friendly Aborigines, and that the reward was only intended for the capture of Aborigines who had committed aggression.[35]

The settlers were not impressed by the government's softer tone. The Van Diemen's Land Company superintendent George Robson noted that it was "decidedly contradictory to former proclamations on the same subject" and "has a bad effect on such persons as those by whom I am surrounded."[36] The Jericho jury at the inquest of James Hooper, killed by Aborigines, sent a protest letter to the lieutenant governor claiming that the new restrictions had led to feelings of "gloom, misery and apprehension" among the settlers. Thomas

Anstey, who had overall operational command of the government's military operations against the Aborigines, argued against complacency, warning that the "coming spring will be the most bloody we have yet experienced."[37] With unfortunate timing a series of Aboriginal attacks in the days following the order seemed to vindicate the settlers' stand, and within a week Arthur had backed down. By government notice, he advised that, "It is not expected, much less required, that the settlers are calmly to wait in their dwellings to sustain the repeated and continued attacks of the tribes ... They are, *by every possible means*, to be captured, or driven beyond the settled districts."[38] Arthur unconvincingly suggested to Murray that the Aborigines had – during the one critical week in which he had reversed government policy – "attacked and plundered in a more systematic manner than they had hitherto done." But even Arthur had to acknowledge the predominant influence of free-settler opinion on the almost immediate reversal of policy: "so great was the alarm created by the promulgation at such a moment of the government notices in question, that ... I felt it necessary to issue a further notice."[39]

In August 1830 Arthur received a dispatch from his increasingly concerned superior, Sir George Murray, which, paradoxically given its emphasis on peace, was to escalate the government's commitment to all-out war.

"One Great and Enduring Pursuit": The Black Line

Murray's dispatch of 23 April 1830 arrived in Hobart Town on 12 August 1830 and was read in the executive council on 27 August. The secretary of state advised Arthur that "nothing, I am certain, will tend more effectually to check the evil than to bring before a court of justice any person who may have been instrumental to the death of a native," and ordered that "you will take care that this be distinctly understood by all classes of person in the colony and that they may be made duly aware of the serious consequences which will result to any person against whom a criminal prosecution may be undertaken."[40]

This dispatch made Arthur choose between ending his endorsement of the settlers' actions – which the British government had now classed as murder – or disobeying the instructions of the secretary of state. Given the response to his recent call for restraint, Arthur well knew the likely reaction to the proclamation of Murray's orders, and, in an extraordinary gamble, he chose to ignore them. The executive council found on 27 August 1830 that to issue Murray's instructions would be "exceedingly impolitic and would lead to the most unhappy results." Exploiting the fact that the dispatch had taken only four months to arrive from London and six could be considered standard, the council instead decided to launch a final all-out assault on the Aborigines. Arthur's hope was that by the time he was forced to respond to Murray's dispatch and carry out his instructions, the policy conundrum would have been permanently resolved.

While there is some doubt about the council's deliberations at the crucial 27 August meeting because of the decision to modify the minutes before forwarding them to London, the surviving record shows that the colonial government essentially chose to declare war on all the Aborigines of Van Diemen's Land. The council found that "the wanton and barbarous murders committed by the natives indiscriminately … can be considered in no other light than as acts of warfare against the settlers generally, and that a warfare of the most dreadful description." It was considered necessary to bring to "decisive issue a state of warfare which there seems no hope of ending by any other means, and which, if much longer continued … will become a war of extermination." The council therefore resolved on an all-out attempt to drive "these miserable people" from the settled districts once and for all through a military operation of an unprecedented scale.[41]

Arthur never sought Colonial Office permission for the military operation that became known as the Black Line; his first dispatch advising of it was not written until November.

During early September 1830, Arthur, as both lieutenant governor and commander-in-chief, developed his plan. Arguing that this was "a cause of the most important and serious kind, in which the lives and property of the whole community are more or less at stake," he made it his stated goal to drive the Aborigines into long-term captivity on the Tasman Peninsula where they could be permanently confined beyond the narrow isthmus known as Eaglehawk Neck. In a government order dated 9 September 1830, Arthur called on every settler,

> whether residing on his farm, or in a town, who is not prevented
> from some over-ruling necessity ... to place himself under the
> direction of the police magistrate ... [so] that in combination with
> the whole disposable strength of the military and police, and by
> one cordial and determined effort, will afford a good prospect of
> either capturing the whole of the hostile tribes, or of permanently
> expelling them from the settled districts.[42]

Advice was given that the "general movement shall commence on Thursday the 7th of October next, and in the meantime, every settler is enjoined to state to the police magistrate of his district, the number of men he can furnish properly equipped for the service." All ticket-of-leave holders "who are capable of bearing arms" were "required to report themselves ... in order that they may be enrolled" and "all minor objects must for a time give way to this one great and engrossing pursuit."[43]

The men were to be divided into groups of ten, each "with experienced guides for directing the marches" and with closely co-ordinated local command structures.[44] On 9 October 1830, martial law was extended beyond the settled districts to cover the whole island and to all Aborigines "until the cessation of hostilities." Arthur argued that as it was "scarcely possible to distinguish the particular tribe or tribes by whom such outrages have been in any particular instance committed," there was no alternative to "an active and extended military operations against the natives generally throughout the island and every portion thereof, whether actually settled or not."[45]

There was strong public support for the Black Line, although at a public meeting in Hobart Town in late September there was a vigorous debate about its legality and intent. The former attorney-general and strident critic of Arthur, Joseph Gellibrand, spoke against what he termed "a war of extermination," and argued that the killing of Aborigines under the "present state of law" amounted to "murder." The solicitor-general, Alfred Stephen, was reluctantly drawn into the debate and, according to the *Tasmanian*, speaking in what he said was a private capacity, argued that the government had a legal duty to protect convicts. "And if you cannot do so without extermination," he reportedly declared, "then I say boldly and broadly, exterminate."[46]

The senior government official G.T.W.B. Boyes put his private views in a letter of 31 October 1830:

> it has become apparent that unless means were devised for making them prisoner ... in some well adapted part of this country, or, otherwise exterminating the race, that the country must be abandoned. All other means having been tried unsuccessfully, the Government found itself reduced to the second and third of the experiments just mentioned, and with that object in view the most vigorous and extensive measures have been taken that the resources of the colony could be put into operation.[47]

Some 2200 men were enlisted for the six-week campaign, and until 24 November, a line, or more accurately, lines, of men worked their way towards the Tasman Peninsula. A map published by the House of Commons in September 1831 illustrates the extent of the "military operations against the aboriginal inhabitants of Van Diemen's Land." The direct cost of the campaign was estimated at the time to be £30,000, half the colonial government's annual budget.

An Aboriginal perspective on evading the Black Line was given by Luggernemenner in November 1830. He told Robinson that the soldiers extended "for a long way and that they kept firing off muskets. Said plenty of Parkutetenner horsemen, plenty of soldiers, plenty of big fires on the hills."[48] The scale of the operation must have been a profoundly shocking and frightening experience even for those Aborigines who were not direct witnesses to it. Robinson informed the Aborigines with him on 26 November "of the operations carrying on against the blacks, and the whole of them [were] in tears throughout the whole of the day."[49]

In the short term, however, the Line failed to achieve its objectives, and Arthur's gamble seemed to have failed. Only two Aborigines were captured and none was confined on the peninsula. The lieutenant governor had defied London without result and now prepared to face the consequences. He bought some time by finally replying to Murray's August dispatch a few days before the Line was complete. He was thus able to leave open the assessment of its impact – even though it was already quite clear that it had failed to achieve its objectives – and focus instead on matters of more dubious relevance. Arthur outlined to the secretary of state what he saw as the betrayal of the Aboriginal leader of the Port Dalrymple or Stoney Creek people, Eumarrah, during the Line's operations, citing this as evidence of the "treacherous character of these savages" and proof that "conciliatory measures are not likely to succeed, and cannot, in prudence, be any longer pursued."[50]

The failure of the Line left the government with few options. The executive council meeting of 30 November faced what seemed an impossible dilemma – how to prosecute the war while belatedly fulfilling the instructions of the British government. The council resolved to place small armed parties in remote huts and strengthen the resistance of convict workers through an increase in indulgences, including pardons and tickets of leave, for all who rendered effective service.[51] The killing of Aborigines by convicts in "defensive" operations was to be rewarded, in the apparent hope that the matter would be quietly resolved on the frontier without the need for further government-sponsored military operations.

As the lieutenant governor and colonial authorities awaited Murray's judgment on the Black Line, unbeknown to them their reputations, and possibly Arthur's career, were salvaged by an unexpected event – the demise of their monarch. King George IV's death led to elections in Britain and, in November 1830, as the Black Line came to an end, a new British government was installed, with the ineffectual and disinterested Lord Goderich replacing Murray in a second stint as colonial secretary. Goderich did not question Arthur's actions, and at some point the decision was made to cover up the whole affair by omitting the ignored directive from the September 1831 House of Commons parliamentary paper which purported to provide *Copies of all Correspondence between Lieutenant Governor Arthur and His Majesty's Secretary of State for the Colonies on the subject of the Military Operations lately carried on against the Aboriginal inhabitants of Van Diemen's Land.* Arthur's November 1830 dispatch was included, but was censored to remove all references to the conflict between his actions and the advice he had received. In short, the colonial authorities were never to be held accountable for their defiance of Murray's instructions, and the tampering with the documentary record meant that the sanction that was ultimately given to their actions by the Colonial Office largely escaped both parliamentary and historical scrutiny.[52]

However, even before Goderich resumed the flow of reassuring dispatches from London, a resolution to the government's policy conundrum emerged. Arthur was elated to hear in late November 1830 that, following the Line's overwhelming show of force, Robinson had taken his first captives. In consequence, on 26 November 1830 Arthur issued a public notice which, for the first time, publicly expressed support for the policy favoured by the press since 1826[53] – enforced island exile:

> it would be in vain to expect any reformation in these savages while allowed to continue in their native habits. It will, therefore, become an immediate subject of anxious consideration with the Government, whether it is not proper to place those who are now secured, and who amount about thirty, together with any others who may be captured, upon an island from whence they cannot escape, but where they will be gradually induced to adopt the habits and feelings of civilized life.[54]

A relieved Arthur informed Murray (whom he still believed to be the secretary of state) on New Year's Day 1831 that 13 Aborigines had "sought protection" and that "I shall not relax in resorting to every practicable means of endeavouring to conciliate these deluded beings, which it is no less my anxious desire than it is the wish of His Majesty's Government to effect."[55] The captured Aborigines were portrayed to London as voluntary exiles, with their rights as British subjects intact. In his instructions to Robinson, however, Arthur was less sanguine, warning his emissary of the "utmost importance" of keeping these Aborigines in captivity.[56] At no time during the next five years was the actual policy of forced removal ever presented to, let alone sanctioned by, the Colonial Office. This crime was to be primarily a local affair.

[11]

THE REMOVAL OF THE ABORIGINES
IN A TIME OF WAR

B Y NOVEMBER 1830 ROBINSON had been travelling through
Aboriginal-controlled areas of Tasmania for the best part of
a year and, despite many meetings, had not persuaded any Aborigines to place themselves under his protection. He was well aware
that events were moving towards a final resolution with the Black
Line and that time was running out for his work of conciliation. It
was in this context that Robinson abandoned honest negotiations
and used deceit to ensure much-needed "success." Robinson reported
to Arthur that he had informed the Aborigines he met in the north-
east of

the military plans that were in operation against them and the
desire of the government to better their condition. I then described
to them the nature and formation of the line by tracing it on the
ground with a stick, and further informed them that the mighty
enemy who were at that time engaged in capturing their countrymen to the southward would shortly appear in formidable array in
front of their own territory. In reply to this preamble they complained in bitter terms of the injuries to which they and their pro-
genitors had been exposed through the medium of the whites, and
seemed fully to appreciate the sympathy I expressed on their
behalf. I then made known to them my intention of visiting the
islands in the straits and the determination of the local Government to emancipate the female Aborigines ... I proposed to them

to accompany me to Swan Island as a place of security and to remain there whilst I repaired to the islands referred, to which they cheerfully assented ... On this occasion I affected to be quite unconcerned as to their concurrence, but at the same time adduced a variety of arguments bearing upon their own most immediate interests and which had the effect, winning their unanimous assent. Having packed up their little property we set forward on our journey accompanied by their dogs, twenty-three in number.[1]

From Robinson's journal it is clear that the "variety of arguments" included offering the opportunity of collecting the eggs of the short-tailed shearwaters (mutton birds) that nest in great numbers in Bass Strait islands during November. Visits to these islands had been an established part of cross-cultural relations in the north-east for 20 years before the war. No doubt the Aborigines were eager to take up Robinson's culturally familiar offer and escape the soldiers, but the conciliator's journal makes it clear that having got "hundreds of eggs," they were eager to return home.[2] It was never to be, and this group of Aborigines became the first to be permanently exiled from their homeland.

Robinson's Testimony

This first betrayal and capture of Aborigines need not have been of long-term consequence. In November 1830, Robinson noted that he "spent some time in conversation with Mannerlelargenne and Worter-lettelarnnenne ... The two chiefs said they wanted to go to Hobart Town, that they did not want to leave me behind, but wished me to go with them."[3] However, this request – which recognised Robinson's status as an emissary – was never communicated to Arthur. Robinson's fatal character flaw, a craving for recognition and a corresponding fear of being cheated of full public credit for "saving" the Aborigines and rescuing the settlers ("I may sow the seed and there are not a few who would readily and greedily gather in the harvest," he was wont to complain[4]), became evident when he chose to travel to Hobart Town alone for his February meetings with the Aborigines Committee and the executive council. If Robinson had facilitated direct negotiations at this juncture, or even passed on the Aborigines' request, a different policy might have been adopted, given Arthur's urgent need to placate the Colonial Office. Instead, Robinson's self-serving actions set back the final opportunity for negotiations by a critical year, during which time the government's drift towards a policy of permanent exile for *all* the Aborigines of Van Diemen's Land, regardless of the part they played in the fighting, became inexorable.

In January 1831 Arthur was resolved to place all captured Aborigines on a secure island for a considerable length of time. However, removing all Aborigines on a permanent basis was not yet government policy, and the justification for the radical policy change was provided by Robinson's testimony to the Aborigines Committee on 4 February. The minutes of this meeting record that Robinson "felt confident of the possibility of effecting the voluntary removal of the entire black population," and urged the committee to select "the most eligible place for the immediate formation of an establishment to receive those that have been taken, and for the future reception of the whole of the Aborigines."[5]

The committee's decision to support the removal of all Aborigines was based explicitly on Robinson's assurances that the Aborigines would go into exile voluntarily. However, even a cursory analysis of the circumstances of the Swan Island removal would have made clear to the committee that he was in no position to give assurances of this kind.

The scrutiny became more rigorous when the issue passed to the executive council, which considered the committee's recommendations. Robinson was now cross-examined "at great length." The minutes record that under more critical questioning, he gave ever more outlandish assurances: "Mr Robinson is of opinion that the natives generally would not object to be removed to an island in Basses Strait" and does not believe they would "feel themselves imprisoned there, or pine away in consequence of the restraint, nor would they wish to return to the mainland or regret their inability to hunt or roam about in the manner they had previously."[6]

Not all members of the executive council were persuaded. Chief Justice Pedder supported the removal of the Aborigines held on

Swan Island and any other Aborigines captured "during any hostile incursion made by them" to Gun Carriage Island, but believed that they should only be "detained there until some satisfactory negotiation could be concluded with the tribes to which they belong." Pedder "could not recommend the adoption of measures tending to induce the natives ... to consent to expatriation and imprisonment ... for notwithstanding Mr Robinson's opinion to the contrary ... they would soon begin to pine away when they found their situation one of hopeless imprisonment." The chief justice also pointed out the contradiction of the committee abandoning support for a negotiated settlement at the very time when negotiations were achieving success:

> Until Mr Robinson had gone upon his mission, scarcely any hope had been entertained of opening an amicable intercourse with these people, but Mr Robinson's success justified a hope that more was attainable, and before His Honor could concur in the advice of the rest of the Council, he wished it to be ascertained whether some treaty could not be made with these people, by which their chiefs should engage for their tribes not to pass certain lines of demarcation which might be agreed upon, and that it should be proposed to them to allow a European agent to reside with or accompany each tribe.[7]

Robinson argued that it would be "a very long time" before such arrangements could be made. He rejected the possibility of having a white person "reside constantly" with the Aborigines to "protect them ... and escort them safely from one district to another, and enable them to make known their wants and complaints to the government, and negotiate them for them whenever it might be necessary," even though this was exactly the model Robinson himself was employing in his travels.

Robinson did, however, concede that the "tribes to the westward" might accept the chief justice's proposal, and even this could have been a significant concession.[8] The "westward" included the northwest region as well as the west coast, and by 1831 it was the home of the large majority of surviving Tasmanian Aborigines. The formal adoption by the government of a different policy towards these Aborigines could therefore have moved government policy very close to Pedder's position, but this does not seem to have been recognised by even the chief justice.

Robinson's testimony makes it clear why he had privately vetoed Mannalargenna's proposal to travel to Hobart Town. Aborigines had given evidence to the executive council before, and both the council and Arthur generally showed themselves willing to accommodate requests for direct meetings. As will be seen, Robinson knew Mannalargenna to be an articulate and charismatic leader whose evidence would both contradict his own account of the circumstances of the Swan Island removal and counter his assurances "that the natives generally would not object to be removed to an island in Basses Strait." Mannalargenna, whom Robinson liked to call "the Chief," and Chief Justice Pedder had similar negotiating positions. The tragedy was that because of the actions of the emissary, neither knew this.

The potential outcome of Mannalargenna's presence at the executive council is easily imagined. The chief justice's arguments were in broad terms consistent with the position set out by Arthur in 1828, which was still the policy endorsed by London. It was Robinson and the Aborigines Committee proposing a radical change in government policy, not Pedder, and Arthur remained very nervous about the ethics and implications of removing all Aborigines. Arthur needed to be particularly careful both in relation to the legality of putting a large group of British subjects (many of whom had not been part of the fighting) into exile contrary to the chief justice's advice, and in dealing with a concerned and observant secretary of state in Sir George Murray (whom even now Arthur believed to be still in office). Arthur knew that for the removal of the Aborigines to be sanctioned by the Colonial Office, it would have to be presented as in accord with the Aborigines' own aspirations. Robinson's confident testimony to the executive council (whose minutes, it must always be remembered, were forwarded to London) was thus absolutely central to the change of policy, and it provided an easy way out for the bewildered colonial authorities. We can now only lament the consequences of Robinson ensuring that there was no conversation between Chief Mannalar-genna and Chief Justice Pedder, as such a meeting might well have changed the course of Van Diemen's Land history.

The Removal Policy: March–April 1831

Arthur took nearly three weeks to consider the issues debated in the executive council before announcing his new policy on 14 March 1831. First, he formally abandoned support for a treaty. The lieutenant governor repeated his belief "that no terms which could now be entered into with the natives inhabiting this portion of the country could be depended on," before adding a new justification for his position: while the "respectable class of settlers might be depended on" to uphold a treaty, "it would be hopeless to contemplate that it would be observed by their servants, runaway convicts, stock-keepers and all that class of characters, who, being free by servitude, are under no special control."[9] Thus, the character deficiencies of both Aborigines and poor whites, having already being blamed for the fighting, were now also to bear responsibility for the government's refusal to negotiate a peace.

The lieutenant governor then stated his support for the removal of hostile Aborigines. He could "no longer doubt the propriety as well as the policy of allowing 200 to 300 hostile natives to be encouraged to proceed with their own consent to any island in the Straits." The Aborigines could go to the straits *or* "bind themselves to commit no further outrages on the condition of receiving food and clothing, and protection from all aggressions."[10] But this policy never bore any relation to practice, and seems to have been designed more to reassure (and mislead) London. No interest at all was shown, then or later, in obtaining the views, let alone the "consent," of the 34 Aborigines by then on Swan Island as preparations were made to move them to the more remote and secure Gun Carriage Island. No attempt was ever made to differentiate between "hostile natives" and Aborigines from remote or pacified regions (even farm workers and other Aborigines integrated into white society were removed). Nor, most crucially, were any Aborigines ever given the choice to receive supplies and protection in their own lands if they desisted from violence. Arthur repeated this inaccuracy in his April 1831 dispatch to Murray, in which he claimed that Robinson had offered the removed Aborigines "food and clothing, and protection from injury, on condition of their being peaceful and inoffensive *or* of their going to the Aboriginal establishment." Even Robinson had never suggested that he had made such an offer.[11]

Arthur's misrepresentation almost certainly arose from his awareness that, as the *Tasmanian* had once recognised, it was "out of the power of the government to remove them [the Aborigines], except as prisoners of war or by treaty,"[12] and that this would almost certainly have been the view of Sir George Murray. But Murray's replacement as secretary of state for the colonies, Lord Goderich (described by the eminent historian G.S.R. Kitson Clark as "the most feeble prime minister the country has ever had"),[13] was a much less critical observer. Even so, it is likely that the policy communicated in the April 1831 dispatch would have received much closer scrutiny but for the fact that during 1831 the secretary of state's attention, along with that of the rest of the government, parliament, press and civil society, was consumed by the political and social crisis that engulfed Britain before the passing of the Reform Bill.[14]

Negotiations and Deceit: August 1831–January 1832

After concluding his meetings in Hobart Town, Robinson spent much of the first six months of 1831 wandering the bush with a few of his Aboriginal companions, endeavouring to persuade other Aborigines to go to the islands. With the mutton birds not yet returned from their annual migration, his efforts were a failure, and in August, with his inflated ego sufficiently humbled, direct negotiations were finally resumed with Mannalargenna:

> This morning I developed my plans to the chief Mannalargenna and explained to him the benevolent views of the government towards himself and people … I informed him in the presence of Kickerterpoller that I was commissioned by the governor to inform them that if the natives would desist from their wonted outrages upon the whites, they would be allowed to remain in

their respective districts and would have flour, tea and sugar, clothes &c given them; that a good white man would dwell with them who would take care of them and would not allow any bad white man to shoot them, and he would go with them about the bush like myself and they then could hunt. He was much delighted.[15]

Robinson gave an unequivocal commitment that if hostilities ceased, Aborigines would be protected and have their essential needs met by the government while being able to live and hunt within their own districts. These concessions, combined with the promised return of their women from the sealers, were the documented terms under which Mannalargenna joined the embassy. There were, however, two potential pitfalls for the Aborigines: the only record of the agreement was in a private journal, and its implementation was explicitly dependent on an end to the fighting, with Aborigines to be removed to the islands until peace had been achieved. The Aboriginal leadership had struck what seemed a good deal, but would need to persuade all Aborigines to surrender before it would be implemented.

Robinson was elated to have achieved Mannalargenna's co-operation, believing that his

influence amongst his people was great. He was universally admitted by all the native tribes who knew him as being the most able and successful warrior of all the Aborigines. Thus in him my hopes centred, in full anticipation of a favourable issue to my endeavours.[16]

So dependent was Robinson on Mannalargenna, that "the Chief" now took over day-to-day decision-making to the point where even Robinson referred to it as "Mannalargenna's mission."[17]

Robinson must have been well aware that the agreement he had reached with Mannalargenna contradicted his own undertakings to the Aborigines Committee and the executive council. Given this, it is not surprising that the emissary took the precaution of informing Arthur of the position he had taken on the government's behalf one day after the deal had been struck:

> [I] gave them [Mannalargenna and Kickertpoller] to understand
> that provided their countrymen would be pacific and desist from
> their wonted outrages that a person would be sent among them who
> would accompany them in their migratory excursions, that they
> could follow their usual recreations and that they would be allowed
> food and clothing and would receive other encouragement.[18]

Arthur could thus have been under no illusion that an agreement
had been reached for the Aborigines to leave the main island of Van
Diemen's Land voluntarily.

During Robinson's travels with Mannalargenna during August
and September 1831, the terms under which the Aborigines were
engaged in the embassy were regularly reiterated in his journal. On
27 August, he noted:

> I omit no opportunity of impressing upon the mind of the chief
> and the other natives that they are to remain in their own country;
> and that I am anxious to get to them for the purpose of going to
> others, and I will leave a man to take care of them and that some of
> the Tyrelore women shall stay with them.[19]

This negotiating position then became the basis for a meeting on
29 August with seven Aborigines of the Stoney Creek people (including Eumarrah, the familiar English-speaking resistance leader personally well known to both Arthur and Robinson): "I made known to
them the wish of the Government: that if they would not spear white
men they might remain and hunt, and they seemed glad and lifted up
their hands." On 8 September, after a number of Aborigines nearly
absconded when it became clear to them that Robinson was heading
for Swan Island rather than Hobart Town (these Aborigines had also
sought a direct meeting with Arthur), the conciliator again assured
one of the Aborigines that "the blacks should stay in their own country … [with] a white man to take care of them."[20]

Robinson was entangled in a web of deceit, and with the return
of the mutton birds providing the lure he needed, the lies only
grew worse. In September 1831 he recorded that, "I proposed to the

strangers to accompany me to Waterhouse Island where they could get eggs, and that I was going to George Town to remove the natives there in gaol to this situation." Tootetitteyerlargener was "very reluctant to go," but "after some persuasion they reluctantly proceeded me to the boat." Once on Waterhouse the Aborigines were persuaded to remain "until such time as I should return from George Town" but, like the Swan Island group, they were never to see their homeland again. Robinson justified the deceit in his journal as "the most humane as being the only way to save their lives," and suggested that the promised return to their homeland might still eventually occur: "Here they can remain and when by a proper discipline their ferocious dispositions are subdued, they can be brought on the main, should it be proper to do so, and placed under the protection of a missionary."[21]

Robinson was Arthur's ambassador, and the removals could not have proceeded without his complicity. During his August negotiations with Robinson, Mannalargenna had wisely reiterated his insistence on a direct meeting with Arthur. Robinson now finally passed on the request, and on 23 September received an affirmative response:

> It having been represented to the lieutenant governor that the native chief Leminabunger [Mannalargenna] has expressed a very strong desire to have an interview with His Excellency and that he obtained a promise from you that the wish should be gratified, I am directed to inform you that as it is not desirable that the aborigines should be brought to Hobart Town, His Excellency will meet you with any natives you may wish to bring with you.

Robinson noted in his journal that the "letter from the government stated that the governor would meet me at Campbell Town or St Pauls Plains or Launceston to meet the natives." The meeting eventually occurred in Launceston.[22] Why was it so important to keep the Aborigines out of Hobart Town? Was this related to public anger and possible vengeance towards the Aborigines, or was the real worry the difficulty of avoiding an awkward minute-taking meeting with an executive council which included a concerned and critical chief justice?

Any remaining possibility that the lieutenant governor was open to honest negotiations had been removed by an unfortunate contemporaneous event. On 31 August 1831, Captain Bartholomew Thomas and his overseer, William Parker, were killed by Aborigines near Port Sorell. No other incident had such a dramatic impact on public opinion or government policy. Unfortunately for the Aboriginal cause, Thomas was not just a landowner but the brother of the colonial treasurer, Jocelyn Thomas, who also happened to be the chair of the Aborigines Committee and the only official to sit on both this body and the executive council. But the key to understanding the impact of this killing goes deeper than family connections. The killing of Thomas was final confirmation of the negative view of Aboriginal character set out by the committee in its March 1830 report. Thomas was widely believed to have been a friend of the Aborigines (the jury at the inquest found that Thomas and Parker were killed "whilst endeavouring to carry into effect the conciliatory measures recommended by the government"[23]), and his killing was seen as final proof of what the committee now termed the "rancorous inveteracy of these savages" towards all Europeans, no matter how they were treated. From this time the view that there could be no safety for the British while any Aborigine remained on Van Diemen's Land was taken for granted by the government and by the press.

From an Aboriginal perspective, the timing of this act of resistance was almost as unfortunate as the choice of victim. While the number of British dead and injured in 1831 had dropped dramatically to 33 (including the latest killings), the fact that ten of these had been landowners (a much higher proportion than in any other year of the conflict) meant that press agitation for the removal or extermination of the Aborigines remained high.[24] The peaceful winter was interpreted as nothing more than a seasonal pause, with the death of Thomas signalling another bloody spring to come.[25] In fact, no killings were ever to follow this incident (an indication of just how few Aborigines were left to carry on the fight). The fighting largely ended just as Arthur's lingering hesitancy gave way to an absolute commitment to the forced and permanent removal of all Tasmanian Aborigines by any means.

Following the death of Thomas, Arthur informed the Aborigines Committee that he was "exceedingly anxious" to receive their final recommendation "with regard to the future station for the reception of the Aborigines." On 28 September 1831, the committee decided on Great (Flinders) Island. The Church of England chaplain, William Bedford, supported Maria Island to the last, as he believed it offered the best hope of civilising the Aborigines, but it was rejected by the majority because of the probability that "many of the natives would escape from Maria Island to the main." On Flinders Island, "escape is quite impossible."[26] There was no doubt that the committee understood the reality of the situation – the Aborigines were captives and Flinders Island was to be their prison.

What of Arthur's imminent meeting with the Aboriginal leaders? In a letter to the Aborigines Committee, he requested that they "state what presents they would recommend be forwarded for the Aborigines who have been recently conciliated, and also whether any presents should be given to the Sydney Blacks, and whether Mr Robinson should be provided with a horse." The committee, "having considered these several points," was "of [the] opinion that a few articles of a gaudy description should be purchased ... a few knives be given to the Sydney Blacks," and that Robinson should get his horse. In other words, there was no interest, or curiosity even, in finding out what Aboriginal views on permanent exile to Flinders Island might be. There can surely be little doubt that neither the Aborigines Committee nor Arthur believed in the impression consistently given in the dispatches to London that the Aborigines voluntarily agreed to go into exile. Voluntary removal had become a charade maintained for the sake of imperial sensitivities. Yet following their meeting with the lieutenant governor, the Aborigines clearly believed that Mannalargenna's original agreement with Robinson had been endorsed, and that its terms would be fulfilled once the most feared enemy of all, the Big River Tribe, had been conciliated.

There are no minutes of the October 1831 meetings between the Aborigines and the lieutenant governor. Nor does Robinson give any information in his journal except to note on 5 October that "in the afternoon [I] had a conference with the governor and the whole of the natives waited on him."[27] Most revealing is that Arthur did not mention the meeting at the critical executive council meeting of 10 October 1831. No doubt Chief Justice Pedder, who even at this meeting continued to advocate a treaty with non-hostile Aborigines, would have been interested to hear the content of Arthur's discussions with Mannalargenna, as would the Colonial Office, who still shared the chief justice's preference for a negotiated settlement.

Arthur's silence about his meeting with Mannalargenna is all the more striking in light of the rest of the 10 October executive council meeting. A proposal for a reserve at Campbell Town was put forward by Arthur, and agreed to by the council, as if it were purely Robinson's idea and bore no relation to the Aborigines' own aspirations or commitment to conciliation: "Mr Robinson was ... of opinion that some central situation should be established ... so as to constitute a home for the Chiefs Manna Langana 'Eumarrah,' and the rest of the natives who form Mr Robinson's party, and whom he considers perfectly conciliated."[28]

Establishing a reserve at Campbell Town remained government policy for the rest of the year. Given how central Campbell Town was to some of the best wool country in Van Diemen's Land, and that government policy had previously focused on the removal of Aborigines from settled areas, this proposal makes little sense except in the context of an agreement with the Aborigines. It is therefore most probable that the proposed reserve was an attempt to honour the letter – if not the spirit – of Arthur's understanding with Mannalargenna, and so to ensure the Aborigines' continued co-operation. However, even this token acknowledgment of the agreement with the Aborigines was to be forgotten once the remaining fighters had been captured.

There is further evidence that Mannalargenna's meeting with Arthur confirmed his earlier understanding with Robinson: Robinson continued to use the agreement to motivate the often wavering Aborigines. Many times he feared that they would abscond or were only leading him on an extended hunting trip, and it is not surprising that he did not attempt to use the promise of permanent exile to inspire their trust. Rather, there are exchanges like the one of 23 November 1831: "Tom said the people did not like going back and forward. I replied that I did not like it and the governor would not like it, that if they had attended to my orders when they were at Lake Echo all our troubles would be at end, and we and the Lairmairrener natives might go and hunt among the settlers." On 28 December, Robinson again "urged them on and told them the governor only wanted me to get to the Big River Tribe and then our troubles would be over, we should no have to go after any more and they could then hunt." On 30 December, Robinson, "heartily tired of this sort of life," reached an agreement "that we should follow them [the Big River people] up and get to them. I told them the governor only wanted me to get to the natives and then we had done."[29]

The long-sought-after meeting with the Big River people eventually came after Robinson received an impatient letter from Arthur, which Robinson suggested to the Aborigines meant that if the meeting did not occur soon, the agreement with the governor was off.[30] Immediately following this threat, a meeting with the principal remaining members of the Aboriginal resistance was finally arranged.

The End of the War

There is no record in Robinson's journal of the momentous encounter that occurred on New Year's Eve 1831 in a small plain above Lake Echo in the central highlands. But there is no reason to doubt that the agreement he reached with the 26 survivors of the Big River and Oyster Bay people, which ended the Tasmanian War and led them freely to accompany Robinson into Hobart Town, was based on assurances any different from those previously set out in the journal. On 5 January – the day after he arrived with the Aborigines at Bothwell, en route to the capital – Robinson wrote in his official report:

> I have promised them a conference with the lieutenant governor and the governor will be sure to redress all their grievances. I earnestly hope that every possible kindness and attention may be shewn to these people for they cannot and ought not to be looked upon as captives. They have placed themselves under my protection and are desirous for peace.[31]

But Arthur, having already heard of the events, wrote to Robinson on the same day, making it clear that the government viewed the Aborigines as captives:

> The Big River and Oyster Bay tribes of Aborigines having surrendered themselves to you I am directed by the lieutenant governor to request you will forthwith bring them to Hobart Town ... every possible degree of humanity is to be exercized towards them, but at the same time *every precaution should be taken to prevent their escape*.[32]

The Aborigines, unaware of their true status, walked confidently into Hobart Town to meet the lieutenant governor on the morning of 7 January 1832. According to the *Hobart Town Courier*, they "walked very leisurely along the road, followed by a large pack of dogs ... Soon after their arrival they walked up to the Government House and were introduced to His Excellency." The band played and the Aborigines performed feats of dexterity in a cross-cultural celebration of peace, but what the *Courier* most rejoiced in was the reclamation by the settlers of "the large tracts of pasture that have been so long deserted" and the "very sensible relief" that would "be afforded to the flocks of sheep that had been withdrawn from them and pent up on inadequate ranges."[33]

Predictably, the content of the meetings held between the Big River and Oyster Bay people and Lieutenant Governor Arthur at government house has also not been recorded. But again there is no reason to doubt that Arthur gave his sanction to Robinson's promise and undertook "to redress all their grievances." Certainly there is no evidence to suggest that the Aborigines agreed to the extraordinary, and surely almost inexplicable, notion of a *permanent* exile to a Bass Strait island. What was involved here was not only a personal betrayal by Robinson, but a violation of undertakings given by the colonial government.

Given the quantity of evidence on the matter, it is surprising that there has been contention about Henry Reynolds' claim in *Fate of a Free People* that there was a negotiated agreement with the Aborigines.

Reynolds, in his analysis, leaves open the possibility that the Aborigines may have agreed to their permanent removal from the mainland of Van Diemen's Land in return for occasional seasonal returns (although he considers this unlikely). There is no evidence for this possibility except for an admission by Robinson in a report written in July 1838, shortly before he left Flinders Island, that "it was guaranteed by me on behalf of the government that ... as far as practicable they were in the summer months under proper protection to occasionally visit their native districts."[34] But this promise doesn't suggest that the Aborigines expected that the visits would occur from exile in Bass Strait. It is quite consistent with the earlier documented understanding – reserves would be established on Van Diemen's Land and Aborigines would have the right to visit their ancestral lands from them. As the Aborigines sailed from Hobart Town in early 1832, they undoubtedly believed that their time on Flinders Island would be short.

[III]

THE REMOVAL OF THE ABORIGINES
IN A TIME OF PEACE

THE LANDMARK LAKE ECHO AGREEMENT, which ended the Tasmanian wars, was not typical of the circumstances under which the large majority of Aborigines were removed from Van Diemen's Land. Remarkably, although Aboriginal–settler relations in Van Diemen's Land have been extensively written about for more than 170 years, it is still almost universally accepted that the removals were undertaken without the use of arms, in the context of a terrible conflict. No less an authority than Henry Reynolds, in his groundbreaking study *Fate of a Free People*, writes that "the Friendly Mission itself was not accompanied by force."[1] Moreover, since the publication of Reynolds' work it has become widely accepted that Tasmanian Aborigines were removed as a result of political negotiations to end the war, and that this amounted to a "treaty ... which was then dishonoured."[2]

The reality for most Aborigines was very different. Most were removed by either force or trickery from lands of no interest to the British, after they had already given up the fight. There was no economic or security justification for the forced removal of Aborigines from western Tasmania during 1832 and 1833. This fact alone arguably makes the removal unique among the tragedies experienced by Indigenous peoples during the nineteenth century. Even the infamous and almost exactly contemporaneous "trail of tears" in the United States (which saw Native Americans living east of the Mississippi River forcibly removed and thousands die in their long march west) had a purpose (the acquisition of land). Moreover, only in Van Diemen's Land was the immediate mortality rate so high that government officials had openly to acknowledge the fact that their policy was likely to result in the "extinction" of a distinct race.

The sense of inevitability about what occurred to the Aborigines that still pervades Tasmanian history is a distortion of the historical record. It disguises the fact that the colonial government made a policy *choice*. The decision to remove *all* Tasmanian Aborigines after 1832 and to pursue this relentlessly to its tragic end was, even by the standards of its own time, an extraordinary and extreme policy position. Robinson's public lies and absurd journal self-justifications, along with Arthur's carefully worded dispatches, have disguised the truth for too long. The colonial government from 1832 to 1838 ethnically cleansed the western half of Van Diemen's Land and then callously left the exiled people to their fate. The black hole of Tasmanian history is not the violence between white settlers and the Aborigines – a well-recorded and much-discussed aspect of the British conquest – but the government-sponsored ethnic clearances which followed it.

The Context of the Removals

Most of the Aborigines taken to Bass Strait were removed between 1832 and 1835. In 1830–31, a total of 46 Aborigines from three main groups had been taken into exile,[3] but during the subsequent period, Robinson or members of his mission captured 148 Aborigines in 11 groups.[4]

From January 1832 there was virtually no conflict between settlers and Aborigines in Van Diemen's Land. In the Van Diemen's Land Company holdings of the north-west, the only settled district where Aborigines remained, there was only one violent incident in 1832 and probably none in 1833. No Briton was injured or killed.[5] The dramatic change was evident to the executive council when it resolved in May 1832 to end the bounty paid for captured Aborigines, noting that it "was no longer necessary as no outrages had been committed by the natives since Mr Robinson brought in the Oyster Bay and Big River tribes [in the New Year]." The council believed "that only one hostile tribe now remained at large and Mr Robinson was at this moment with the conciliatory mission endeavouring to communicate with it."[6] At the time of the executive council meeting, Robinson was still on his way to Cape Grim. The next phase of the conciliation work thus began *after* the government had acknowledged that peace prevailed.

The almost complete absence of conflict from 1832 had much to do with topography: the surviving Aborigines lived on land that was of little interest to the British. There were almost no white settlers in the west and south-west regions, and even these few left during the early 1830s. Since the winter of 1830, when most of the Van Diemen's Land Company sheep on the exposed west coast had died and it had become clear that the region was unsuitable for wool production or grazing, the company had begun to remove sheep (and their shepherds), completing the evacuation by early 1834 (except for a much-reduced population at Cape Grim itself). Robinson documented the evacuation, even as he finished the work of removing the native peoples: "It is now ascertained after repeated losses that Cape Grim ... is not suited for fine wool nor even the crossbreed of the colony, for these have died ... Hence they were obliged to remove the sheep both from West Point and Studland Bay."[7] Meanwhile, the decision to close Macquarie Harbour penal station, the only other British outpost in this region, was made in early 1833. The departure of the British and the removal of the Aborigines from the west coast of Van Diemen's Land thus proved to be almost exactly contemporaneous.

The Phases of Removal, 1832–35

Robinson's work from 1832 was completed in two main phases (followed by a third and final "clean-up" phase in which the last small groups of Aborigines, desperate to be reunited with their families and communities, were located and removed).

In the first phase, during the winter and spring of 1832, most of the people living north of Arthur River were tricked into going to Hunter Island, where they were held captive for many months before being herded onto a Royal Navy vessel which took them to Flinders

Island. Although negotiations occurred to bring the Aborigines into Cape Grim, it is clear from Robinson's journal that restoring access to this lost hunting ground was as far as any "deal" went. Not even Robinson's longest-serving Aboriginal companions knew the truth about what Robinson called his "*ruse de guerre*." The plan was simple but effective. First, in order "to inspire the natives with confidence," they were promised the right to hunt and roam freely at Cape Grim.[8] Second, to make up for the awkward fact that the planned "inducement" for them to travel to Hunter Island (that is, mutton birds) had not turned up,[9] they were offered a pleasant family day out on a sealers' boat: "I promised to the natives to let their children have a ride ... They were much pleased with the excursion. The boat appeared an object of curiosity among them."[10] Then, after "divine service" on 22 July (during which, as had become usual, "the strangers burst out into an involuntary fit of laughter"), they were fatefully persuaded to go on a longer "excursion" to Hunter Island (and here it was again made clear that Pevay, Woorady and other Aborigines accompanying the mission were as much deceived as anyone else):

> Being informed that both the sealers boats was at the jetty, I thought I would try the experiment of the getting the natives removed to the islands ... I proposed to Jack [Pevay] to go with me and look at the boats, to which he readily assented. On arriving at the boats I began to praise them, and said what an excellent opportunity it would be to go to the islands, Jack readily assented and wanted to go alone, but this was not what I wanted. My object was to remove the whole of the strangers if possible. I said that we would all go ... I would get them some dogs ... I now went back to the encampment with Peevay and with an air of indifference proposed to the natives to make an excursion to the islands. Jack capered about quite delighted at the idea, but the strangers stared and gaped, appeared quite indifferent about going, and proposed to go and hunt for kangaroo. (I was much annoyed at Woorady [a Bruny Island Aborigine who had been with Robinson since the beginning] who objected to going on the grounds that there was no kangaroo on the islands). I appeared careless and said I should go without them; they might come if they

chose. They soon followed after me, though but slowly … I was now in the boat with the people and afloat.[11]

The mortality rate at the Hunter Island detention centre was terrible. Previously healthy people began to die within days. A mother who "had an infant sucking at her breast" was the first to succumb. Others to die in the first weeks included her baby and "one old man who was very much deformed."[12] The people continued to die through the early spring, but it was not until the end of October that the survivors were removed by the Royal Navy to Flinders Island.

In the following year, during the winter and spring of 1833, the second phase began and the work of the "friendly mission" degenerated further as most of the remaining west-coast Aboriginal people were captured by force before being imprisoned for lengthy periods at the Macquarie Harbour penal station. Robinson exploited relationships formed during his 1830 expedition to arrange meetings with Aboriginal groups, at which armed convicts exposed their weapons.

The Macquarie Harbour penal station was centred on Sarah Island, but there were many outlying stations on and around Macquarie Harbour. Confinement on Grummet Island, one of the smallest islands in the harbour, was used to discipline the worst convict offenders. Little more than a rocky outcrop, Grummet Island was described by the commandant in 1827 as

A very small barren island, of about a quarter of an acre in its utmost extent and about 500 yards from the nearest point of this island and more in the centre of the bay … the weather for the greater part of the year is generally wet and windy, and occasionally violently boisterous, which materially increases the punishment and inconvenience of a residence upon this solitary rock. All turbulent and permanently bad characters, I necessarily place upon this island … producing the best effect … as it makes them at all extents assume an appearance of reformation and good conduct in order to get removed and then a continuation of the same to prevent being sent back.[13]

In 1833, "five women, two men and one boy"[14] were imprisoned for 100 days in this remote corner of the most notorious gaol in the British empire for no reason other than that they were Aboriginal. Not surprisingly, the child died on this "solitary rock."[15] These people had been captured by Robinson's assistant, Anthony Cottrell, in February 1833. While Robinson was not personally involved in the capture and detention of this group, he had personally authorised the use of arms. Cottrell reported to him that as the group had "evinced such a hostile feeling, and there is no probability of their being taken but by force, I purpose adopting the plan you at one time pointed out, and have procured some firearms."[16]

Moreover, after Robinson returned to the west coast from Hobart Town in the autumn of 1833, he used the same methods, and the same detention facility. When he left Macquarie Harbour on 9 May, his party included ten whites. Nervous of sharing credit for his work and tired of supervising convicts, Robinson had employed fewer and fewer white assistants on his expeditions of the previous two years. But this was a military foray, and Robinson knew that convict bushmen, seeking privileges and freedom, would be central to its success.

Thanks to relationships established during the genuinely "friendly mission" to the west-coast Aborigines in 1830, and to the desperation of Robinson's Aboriginal companions to see the work completed and the promises made to them finally fulfilled, a meeting with a group of Indigenous people was quickly arranged. Robinson reported the subsequent events in his journal:

> The strangers were told that we only awaited their acquiescence to proceed on our journey to the settlement. At this information they appeared quite astonished ... I made use of every argument as did my people which appeared to have little effect ... The wild natives said it (the settlement) was a stinking place ... I now ordered the two white men and my sons to uncover their fusees and to file off on each side. [17]

Robinson himself was also armed. He reported that the convicts became increasingly rebellious after the Aborigines were captured (did they perhaps sympathise with the Aborigines' plight?), and on the night of 23 May he drew "a small pistol in my pocket which I had carried to intimidate the natives" on one of his convict assistants.[18]

There was no attempt to pretend that the captured Aborigines were anything but prisoners. The captives were

> very dissatisfied ... the friendly natives told them that Tymedeen and the rest had gone a long way off [to Flinders Island] and how they also would have to go. They cried at this and said they would try all they could to escape. Under the circumstances I judged it most advisable to remove them back to the hospital at the large island [Sarah Island] ... and doubled my guard and made the place more secure.[19]

Subsequent expeditions followed a similar pattern. Even the husband of Dray (a local woman who had come to trust Robinson in 1830 and now supported his work in good faith) was not spared. When he expressed reluctance to accept imprisonment at the penal station, Robinson recorded, "I told the white man to uncover his fusee, for I could not be trifled."[20] A summary of the gruesome work undertaken by Robinson during July and August 1833 alone should be sufficient to dispel persistent misconceptions about the nature of the "conciliator's" work with the Aborigines at this time.

On 11 July 1833, Robinson left Macquarie Harbour and the very next day met with 16 Aborigines (aided again by knowing some of them from the friendly encounters of 1830). The members of this group, like all the others Robinson met up with in the west and northwest between 1833 and 1835, were showing no signs of the diseases that some historians claim (without direct evidence) were decimating the Aboriginal population: "The whole of the strangers were in good health."[21]

Unusually, it seemed force might not be required to capture this group; it was hoped that they would not "want to stop alone seeing all the rest had gone." But by 13 July Robinson found the Aborigines "reluctant to come" and soon "ordered the white men to uncover their fusees, and my son who had a pistol without a cock also exhibited it."[22]

Once these people were securely detained, the expedition again left Macquarie Harbour and walked north along Henty Beach. By 22 July "9 strangers of the Pieman River Tribe, viz two men, one boy, two girls, and four women," including the Aboriginal leader Wyne and his family, had been captured: "they had tried to flee but were surrounded, and hadn't realised until too late that there were white men in the group ... In the course of the night they made several attempts to escape but were foiled."[23]

The different strategies chosen by the two Aboriginal men in this group reveal the terrible conundrum that fatally divided the Aboriginal cause. Wyne favoured resistance to the end, but the other man, Tartoyenruc, was "extremely anxious to come" as his "wife was at the settlement." Two other men remained in the bush; Robinson was confident that they would soon come, as "I had their two wives," but was also "apprehensive they might go to the Sandy Cape natives, which would have militated against my removal of them, as they would then be on their guard and watch my approach."[24]

In his private journal, Robinson justified the forced removal on the grounds that it was "for their own good ... for all the love they bear their country the aboriginal settlement will soon become their adopted country and they will find that protection which they cannot find in their own land."[25] As the Aborigines began to die at Macquarie Harbour, however, this belief could only be sustained through increasing self-delusion. The gaol, Robinson argued, "was well adapted in my opinion for the natives. It was both warm and comfortable and secure and afforded abundant room and had a large yard attached and secured by a high fence and yet still the Aborigines were in a sickly state." Quite how he reconciled this statement with the admission that convicts were "pouring down water through the boards, urinating upon them and hammering on the floor" is not clear.

Increasingly, Robinson avoided contact with the imprisoned Aborigines. Not until 25 July did he report that he "visited the Aborigines at the penitentiary." Two Aborigines died that day. They were followed on 27 July by a 19-year-old woman, Reeheleepan, and on

31 July by Wyne. Robinson noted that the latter maintained his resistance to the end: "when he first went to the penitentiary he threatened to burn the door and attempted to break the door with a billet of wood" and "the night previous to his death, walked to the gate; the watchman brought him back ... he wanted to abscond. Poor man, he was in a delirious state and little knew what he was about."[26]

Despite the terrible death toll, Robinson was "anxious to proceed after the few natives at Sandy Cape," and on 1 August he "sent away the invalid Aborigines to the small island" with a white man to guard them. That night Robinson recorded the death of Penenebope, a "fine young man about 20 years of age," on Grummett Island. He

> had fallen over the rocks in front of the penitentiary on the small island in a fit of delirium ... he was quite insane ... he ought to have been confined in a strait waistcoat ... It was a dangerous place for these poor people. The building ... stands on top of the rock and almost covers it. The people are no sooner out of the door then they are on the verge of the precipice.[27]

On 2 August, Robinson sent his son and a doctor to Grummett Island "to examine the sick and sent over a man to block up the door to prevent accident." They returned that evening with the body of another man who had died the previous night, Tartoyenruc, a "fine young man and in health when arrived at the settlement ... about 22 years of age ... my son said they were greatly dissatisfied at being there." The doctor recommended bringing them back to Sarah Island and this was done.[28]

On 3 August, Robinson sent away five children "to avoid the contagion" (some form of respiratory disease, presumably either influenza, pneumonia or tuberculosis), noting, apparently without irony, that "in removing the children I first obtained their consent to the measure, for nothing ought to be done contrary to their wishes." On the same day a pregnant 21-year-old woman, Wyyener, died at the hospital. Her grief-stricken husband, Warrertarerer (a "fine young man ... about 22," who had come "to the settlement in good health"), lay beside her before dying the same afternoon. Their bodies were "enclosed as the rest in neat coffins."[29] Finally on this day, 3 August 1833, more than a week since his last visit, Robinson again visited the Aborigines and personally witnessed the extent of their mental and physical breakdown. He recorded that "the people became troubled in mind" and were so desperate to get out that "even the sick that was able to crawl, when they saw me ... packed up all their things and walked out." This encounter sparked his first journal entry to acknowledge the scale of the horror: "the mortality was dreadful, its ravages was unprecedented, it was a dreadful calamity."[30]

Robinson's visit also revealed that the imprisoned Aborigines were treated even worse than the convicts. They had not been given "sustenance or medicine" because they had not been officially "admitted as patients."[31] In other words, the Aborigines had not been entitled to rations or medications because they were not legally prisoners. Robinson expressed outrage at this, but the fact that such neglect could have continued for so long highlighted what little attention he had given his sick captives, as well as the illegality of their confinement.

Meanwhile the deaths continued. On 4 August the 12-year-old son of Wyeree died, and later that day his mother followed. Only then, at last, did Robinson act. Eight of the surviving Aborigines were immediately sent from the penal station, and on 6 August four more followed, including the "widow of Wyne, who was very ill and far advanced in pregnancy." Robinson documented the Aborigines' relief: "their impatience would scarcely allow the men to carry the things down to the boat, and shed tears from fear of their not going." The survivors clearly wanted nothing more to do with white people and "refused tea and even water when offered."[32]

On 7 August, another woman died at Sarah Island and Robinson now resolved to send all the remaining adult Aborigines to the pilot's station, an outlying building near Macquarie Heads from which ships were guided in and out of the harbour. This plan met some opposition: "My son George opposed ... saying they would abscond ... Still I ordered them and him off, the only thing likely to save their lives."[33] Robinson neglected to note that with the children still being detained (it is not clear exactly where), the likelihood of their parents absconding was slim.

On 10 August, Naydip, Wyne's widow, gave birth to a baby girl, who soon died. The same day a little girl who had "absconded" to find her mother arrived at the pilot's station and "was in tears nearly the whole time she remained with her mother." She was not allowed to stay.

The people remained prisoners, locked in a hut, but on 11 August, the day that Naydip followed her baby to the grave, Robinson allowed a life-saving concession. He permitted the women to go "with my people" to get "mutton fish" (abalone) and "crawfish." This decision brought an almost immediate end to the deaths. On 12 August over 100 crayfish were eaten, and the very next day Robinson reported: "people all well."[34]

Robinson, as he himself made explicit, knew that the removal of the Aborigines from Macquarie Harbour penal station was "the only thing likely to save their lives." This had been the case at each site where Aborigines had been confined or detained, including Bruny, Flinders and Hunter islands. Yet no action had been taken until the casualty rate was more than 75 per cent. Even then, the children continued to be separately detained to ensure the adults' compliance, despite the risk to their lives. As a direct consequence, on 27 August, Towterer's little girl died. That same day Robinson heard of the continuing deaths at Flinders Island – another 13 Aborigines had recently died there.[35]

Back in Hobart Town with some of his captives, Robinson soon met with Arthur. Shortly after, on 20 October 1833, the lieutenant governor had a two-hour interview with the captured Aborigines at government house and a second meeting the next day. Any ambiguity left by Robinson's regular dispatches was surely dispelled by these interviews. Arthur could have been in no doubt as to the circumstances of the Aborigines' capture, the events at Macquarie Harbour, and the Aborigines' reluctance to go into exile.[36] Yet even now, the pretence that the removals were done voluntarily was not corrected. Robinson's official report claimed that the Aborigines' removal had occurred "in almost every instance with their own free will and consent." He expressed hope, moreover, that the "time is not far distant when the same humane policy will be adopted towards the aboriginal inhabitants of every colony throughout the British Empire."[37]

On 20 November, the west-coast Aborigines left Hobart Town for Flinders Island. Three days later the British evacuation of Macquarie Harbour (except for a small boat-building party) was complete. As Robinson had well known, if the Aborigines could have maintained their freedom for a few more months, their capture would have become virtually impossible and they almost certainly would have been left in uncontested possession of the west and south-west regions of Van Diemen's Land, which even today remain largely wilderness.

Why?

In the context of heavy fighting and the settlers' thirst for revenge, Robinson's earlier work in the settled districts had an obvious purpose and rationale. But in 1832–33 there was neither a political imperative to act, nor land, property or lives to defend. The people removed by Robinson were not in terminal decline. On the contrary, their population was demographically diverse, including young men and women, babies, children and the elderly.

Why, then, was the policy of removal pursued? Robinson's personal agenda is certainly one part of the answer. He seems to have insisted on the reward of £900 (along with the smaller up-front fee, salary, land grant and pension), to be paid if he could bring in every Aborigine during his negotiations with the Aborigines Committee in early 1832. There was also the lure of fame: "I did well to engage with the government for the capture of all the natives ... By taking the whole I gain not only the reward but celebrity."[38]

But Robinson was a colonial government employee, whose actions were sanctioned, directed and rewarded by the government. In this case, the "government" had become Lieutenant Governor George Arthur. Arthur's motives remain uncertain. It is clear that he knew that his superiors would regard the forced removal of non-hostile Aborigines living outside the settled districts as both illegal and wrong, since he went to considerable efforts to disguise the truth of what occurred. Even today, we would know almost nothing of the reality of the removals were it not for Robinson's private journal. After dominating executive council meetings during 1830–31, government policy regarding the Aborigines was not discussed by the council between 25 January 1832 (when the rewards to be paid to Robinson were ratified) and 28 May 1832, when the bounty on captured Aborigines was scrapped. Flinders Island received brief mention in June, but Aboriginal policy was not discussed again until 18 October 1833 (by which time the removals were all but complete), when "the chief justice undertook to prepare a proclamation declaring the cessation of martial law against the Aborigines." Moreover, the only two meetings of 1832 to consider the Aborigines coincided with the unusual absence of Chief Justice Pedder, the only council member prepared to take an independent view.[39]

Arthur personally determined the council's agenda, and fully controlled the issues that came before it. Why would Arthur have kept Aboriginal policy off the council's agenda? His authority would not have been compromised by a debate about the Aborigines – the council was, after all, only an advisory body – but council minutes were forwarded to the secretary of state in London. The fact that the council never discussed the removal of the Aborigines, and that no matter concerning the Aborigines came before it when Pedder was present, meant that Arthur was able to control the information passed to London.

However deliberate Arthur's actions were, it is a fact that the actual policy of removing *all* Aborigines from Van Diemen's Land without their consent was never put to either the executive council or the Colonial Office. On paper, the removals were restricted to captured Aborigines "belonging to hostile tribes" (and those living with sealers "contrary to their wishes" or in gaol), as had been decided at the executive council meeting of 10 October 1831 and communicated to London in a dispatch two days later.[40] The deportation of most of the Aborigines of Van Diemen's Land proceeded in circumstances that were in direct contravention of official government policy. Questions could and should have been asked, especially by the British government. Unfortunately, after the tenure of Sir George Murray ended in 1830, not even cursory scrutiny occurred.

Nevertheless, Arthur exercised full personal control of this policy area, and the primary responsibility for the forced deportation of the Aborigines between 1832 and 1835 must lie with him. The question remains: why did he pursue it?

In part, because it had become the easiest administrative and political path to follow. To question the basis of the west-coast clearances would have cast doubt on the justification for the previous removals, which paradoxically became more difficult to defend as the mortality at Flinders Island exposed what a disaster the policy had been.

Arthur also seems to have accepted the widely held belief that the Aborigines of Van Diemen's Land were inherently savage, so that even the end of hostilities did not remove the threat they posed. It was also thought that the Aborigines themselves would benefit from removal to Flinders Island, where they might receive the twin gifts of civilisation and Christianity.

But what is most disturbing and most hard to fathom is the pervasive psychological appeal – to Arthur, Robinson and, it seems, the colonists generally – of a "native-free" Van Diemen's Land. Clearly this in part reflected the strains of a long war, and the desire to resolve the legal, ethical and practical complexities of settlement once and for all. The desire for an ethnically cleansed island, however, seems to have gone beyond such considerations. The removal of all Aborigines came to be seen as a good in itself, its benefits taken for granted. Few would have disagreed with the observation made by Charles Darwin (who visited in February 1836) that "Van Diemen's Land enjoys the great advantage of being free from a native population."[41]

No Agreement, Treaty or Deal

The Aborigines who travelled with Robinson between 1832 and 1835 were undoubtedly integral to the expeditions' "success," but these men and women had already lost everything and their bargaining power had been greatly diminished by the end of armed resistance. The only options available to them were to leave a large group of their countrymen in indefinite exile or continue to co-operate in the hope that the promises made to them would be honoured when the work was complete. The friction, resistance and division that were increasingly plain show that they understood the terrible dilemma they were facing. They were no longer free agents or the arbiters of genuine negotiations.

Furthermore, although the Aboriginal negotiators succeeded in arranging meetings between Robinson and groups of Aborigines, the deal they put forward was almost universally rejected. Without the threat of war, only a very small number of Aborigines agreed to leave their ancestral lands even temporarily, and this co-operation reflected a desperate desire to be reunited with wives, children and other community members already removed to Flinders Island, rather than any endorsement of a negotiated agreement.

Flinders Island

Robinson delayed going to Flinders Island for as long as he could – 16 months elapsed between his return from his last mission in 1834 (the final removals were undertaken by others, including his son) and beginning his work as commandant of the Flinders Island Aboriginal Establishment in October 1835. He even sought to get out of his promise to take up the post altogether, seeking a life-long pension instead, but at the executive council meeting of 15 June 1835, Arthur forced the issue, observing that Robinson "had agreed to go to Flinders Island when the contract was originally made."[42]

Before leaving for Flinders Island, Robinson advocated that the Aborigines be removed from there to New Holland (mainland Australia). It is difficult to explain this odd proposal other than as a means of partially honouring his commitment to the Aborigines that they would only be detained until the mission's work was complete. The proposal had Arthur's support, although with the war over the lieutenant governor was no longer particularly concerned about the issue. He certainly did not press the Colonial Office on the matter, perhaps because such pressure would have exposed the fact that the Aborigines did not want to be on Flinders Island and the falsity of previous assurances to the contrary.

In late October 1835 Robinson, still hopeful that the New Holland plan would be agreed to, finally returned to the Aboriginal establishment. The Aborigines greeted him joyfully, clearly believing that the end of their exile was at hand. But once the celebrations were over, the truth had to be faced. Robinson recorded that he "spent some time in conversation relative to a removal to New Holland ... The natives complain and say why keep us here to starve. We don't want to live here. Let us go to our own country and we can live. There is plenty of kangaroo in our own country."[43] After this, Robinson once more put the New Holland plan to Arthur, with a new macabre twist that he hoped would spark official concern and encourage the government to act. He openly put the view that the extinction of the Aborigines was inevitable given the high mortality rate, and argued that feelings of "excitement" about this would be lessened if the people were first to amalgamate with the Aborigines of New Holland.[44]

Robinson made no further reference in his journal to what must have been the main topic of discussion and dissent within the Flinders Island community until August 1836, when a positive Aboriginal comment about exile is noted. Robinson reported that one Aborigine told him, "he was like me, he had put away his country."[45] Nevertheless, Robinson seems to have prolonged hope and probably stifled open rebellion by continuing to suggest that the exile would end. He made forceful appeals to Arthur as he prepared to leave Van Diemen's Land in 1836 for the Aborigines to be allowed to return to their homeland.[46] But these were ignored (or not received in time) and Robinson seems to have thereafter harboured resentment that an understanding he had reached with the lieutenant governor had not been honoured. While grieving Tongerlongter's[47] death in mid 1837, Robinson noted that "Time would fail nor is this the time for me to dwell largely upon these topics. Hereafter I trust they will be made fully known."[48]

Robinson nevertheless remained hopeful about the New Holland plan, but in 1838 the British government gave Sir George Gipps, governor of New South Wales (which still included the Port Phillip district), full discretion to decide the matter. Gipps referred it to a Legislative Council committee, who gave Robinson a hearing but proved to be "unanimously, and very decidedly, opposed to the introduction of these natives of Van Diemen's Land into any part of New South Wales."[49] Not surprisingly, it was felt that Van Diemen's Land should take responsibility for its own Aborigines.

Robinson was present at the executive council meeting at which the implications of this decision were considered, and was asked "to state what course he thinks should now be taken with respect to them [the Aborigines] by the [Van Diemen's Land] government."

He argued that if the Aborigines "remain two years longer in Flinders Island, they will at the end of that time almost all be dead." He pointed out that there were now only 78 Aborigines left, 35 of whom were his companions (including their wives and children). He argued that the group of 35 should go with him to Port Phillip and that the others be sent to a family property in the north-west of Van Diemen's Land. He noted that the two groups were of "different tribes" (the former were mainly west-coast people and the latter from the settled districts) and would "not so much feel the separation." Robinson also belatedly acknowledged that the Aborigines could not be legally detained on Flinders Island or be denied the right to live in New South Wales (or, by implication, Van Diemen's Land): "if the natives of this country are free subjects, they have a right to occupy the soil of New South Wales, the same as any other foreigner, for it is most unjust to be kept for the remainder of their lives upon that island."

Three days later, on 14 December 1838, the executive council considered the issue again. In this short time, Robinson's message had changed. He now reassured the lieutenant governor that "the rate of mortality at Flinders Island had diminished by more than a half since the Aborigines were removed to a more sheltered situation" and that there had been only four deaths since August. Even at that rate, all the Aborigines would be dead in six years, but Robinson's new assurances gave the council the justification it needed to do nothing and allowed the lieutenant governor to leave the Aborigines where they were. Why did Robinson change his position so markedly between the two council meetings of 11 and 14 December 1838? Perhaps the executive council minutes of 8 January the following year provide the answer. It was noted that

His Excellency and Council have under consideration Mr Robinson's letters of 24 December 1838 and 6 [January] instant: submitting that an award of 3000 acres of land sometime since made to him by the Governor as a compensation for the services he had rendered in the "subjugation" and removal of the hostile Aborigines – that he has not yet been put in possession of this location: that he has addressed the Secretary of State upon the subject, but has not as yet received any answer, and that he is upon the eve of taking his departure from the colony.[50]

Robinson had already received all of the generous rewards specified in his January 1832 contract. At an earlier executive council meeting, Arthur had rejected his claim for an additional 3000 acres,[51] but a grateful Lieutenant Governor Franklin and executive council now resolved to provide him with it. Robinson got his land, and the Aborigines were left to their fate.

In choosing to leave the Aborigines on Flinders Island, the colonial government accepted that the Aborigines of Van Diemen's Land would probably become "extinct." Franklin himself had predicted this at the executive council in June 1838:

The Lieutenant Governor observes in reference to the Aborigines Establishment at Flinders Island, that the removal of the Aborigines to some situation more congenial to their constitutions seems to be now of indispensable necessity. The climate of Flinders Island appears to excite diseases of the lungs amongst them. The mortality is most distressing, and some change is indispensable. An effort to save them from extinction must be made. It would be better to adopt some arrangement even though it may be liable to many objections, than to allow them to remain where they are notwithstanding the anxious attention which is by the commandant and catechist devoted to their welfare and comfort.[52]

This was not a new insight. As early as 1831, Chief Justice Pedder had warned that the removal of the Aborigines would probably lead to their demise, and even Arthur acknowledged the likelihood of this. His argument to London was that even if the Aborigines "should pine away in the manner the Chief Justice apprehends, it is better that they should meet with their death in that way, while every act of kindness is manifested towards them, than that they should fall a sacrifice to the inevitable consequences of their continued acts of outrage upon the white inhabitants."[53] The logic of this argument obviously collapsed with the end of the hostilities, but no other justification for the appalling mortality consequent to the removal of the Aborigines was ever developed. The likelihood of extinction could be used by Franklin to support a removal of the Aborigines to New South Wales, but it was never considered a strong enough reason to bring the Aborigines back to Van Diemen's Land. As the lieutenant governor frankly informed Robinson in a private interview on 18 December 1838, "respectable settlers ... would not hear of it ... if the natives were brought [back]. Property would immediately fall in value very considerably."[54]

In January 1839, Robinson returned to Flinders Island from Hobart Town and the next month departed for Port Phillip to take up his new post as chief protector of Aborigines. A group of Robinson's closest Aboriginal companions accompanied him to Port Phillip, five of whom were to be arrested for murder after conducting raids on the Mornington Peninsula. Robinson obtained clemency for the three women, including Truganini, but the two men, one of whom was Pevay (who had played a critical role in the north-west expedition), became the first people to be executed in the new territory after Robinson effectively condemned them with his assurance to the court that "They have a knowledge of the principles of religion and the existence of a Supreme Being and know right from wrong." At the well-attended public hanging on 20 January 1842, the *Port Phillip Herald* reported that when Pevay went to the scaffold he "seemed perfectly unconcerned, even gay," and that he stated that after "his death he would join his father in Van Diemen's Land and hunt kangaroo; he also said he had three heads, one for the scaffold, one for the grave, and one for Van Diemen's Land."[55]

POSTSCRIPT: THE FINAL CONQUEST

I N 1854, DURING THE SECOND-LAST YEAR of existence of the
crown colony of Van Diemen's Land, the Church of England
bishop Francis Nixon accompanied the surveyor-general on a visit to
the former sealing communities of Bass Strait. It seems timely that in
these final months before self-government and the establishment of
the new Tasmania, the two men bearing official responsibility for
communal ethics and land title should have visited the refuges of the
island's dispossessed first peoples.

Bishop Nixon wrote an account of this voyage, published as *The
Cruise of the Beacon*. The first stop was the old Aboriginal settlement
at Wybalenna on Flinders Island, where the Aborigines captured and
removed by George Augustus Robinson had lived and died. Although
the settlement had been abandoned only seven years before, with the
surviving residents transferred to a condemned convict probation
station at Oyster Cove south of Hobart, "desolation" now "stared in
the face wherever the eye was turned."[1]

A very different scene met the bishop at his next port of call, Gun
Carriage Island, where many of the 200 or so descendents of the
Aboriginal women taken to the strait by the sealers had come to meet
him. Nixon was impressed: there was an "air of quiet domestic union
– the men appeared sober, active and intelligent; the women were
unmistakably modest and retiring." The bishop judged one of the
leaders of the community, Lucy Beedon, the "greatest lady it has ever
been my good fortune to encounter."[2]

While the bishop celebrated divine service, married couples

(including Edward Mansell, one of the few remaining sealers, to his long-time Aboriginal partner, Judy Thomas) and baptised infants, the surveyor-general was busy formalising land title.[3] He ominously informed Lieutenant Governor Denison that "by their acceptance of tickets of occupation on the payment of nominal rent, the right of the Crown has been fully established to the lands which up to the period of my visit they considered their own."[4] That is, with the stroke of a pen, the Crown had transformed the island's residents into precarious lease-holders.

After returning to Hobart, Nixon became a supporter of Lucy Beedon's determined efforts to secure a teacher for the Aboriginal children. Nixon's advocacy was directly based on his belief that, having "dispossessed these poor people of this fair land," Tasmanian society bore some responsibility for the Aborigines' fate.[5] There was little public or government support but despite, or perhaps because of, this neglect, the population continued to increase. By the time Archdeacon Thomas Reibey (grandson of a notorious convict and later to be Tasmanian premier) visited the Bass Strait in 1862, there were 66 islander children "scattered over the various islands."[6]

Thus, even as the new self-governing colony of Tasmania awaited the final "extinction" of the Aborigines at Oyster Cove, the islander community was increasing in numbers and asserting rights based on historical obligations. Yet the respite afforded by the remoteness of Bass Strait was short-lived. Facilitated by the Waste Land Acts of 1861 and 1870, which encouraged European occupation of "empty" land, the people soon faced dispossession from even this final frontier. By 1883 Europeans owned or leased 28 islands in the strait, and only one was held by an Aborigine.[7] Many of these leases were in the name of the absentee landlord Robert Gardiner, known grimly to the Aborigines as "Resurrection Bob" for his habit of digging up Aboriginal bones and selling them as scientific specimens.

Once more the Aborigines called on clerical support in their campaign to have some land reserved for them,[8] and on 14 February 1881 the Tasmanian government gazetted a reserve of some 6000 acres at the western end of Cape Barren Island. This prompted an angry backlash, with one correspondent to the *Examiner* writing:

"we and our children have more right to own land on these islands than the half-castes ... [who] combine the lowness of the black, and the cunningness of the whites."[9] To which the Aborigines replied: "We are under no obligation to the government. Whatever land they have reserved for us is a token of their honesty, in as much as it has been granted in lieu of that grand island which they have taken from our ancestors."[10]

From the outset white Tasmanians and Aborigines had different ideas about the new reserve.[11] For Bishop Bromby it was a means of overcoming what he called the "moral weakness" and "vulnerability to drunkenness and sloth" caused by Aboriginal ancestry. On a reserve, Aborigines could "relinquish the pursuit of mutton birds, properly attend to the soil and receive tuition in the sober virtues of respectable white society."[12] The Aborigines, by contrast, wanted a reserve not to change their way of life, but to protect it.

The conflict was to be regularly repeated over the next century, but this small area of land nevertheless proved crucial to the survival of Aboriginal identity and culture. Even after the reserve was terminated in the 1950s, and the government pressured islanders to move to the mainland and assimilate, Cape Barren Island remained the cultural centre of the Aboriginal community and was finally returned to Aboriginal ownership in 2005.

With the death of Truganini in 1876, "full-blood" Aborigines were widely thought to be "extinct" and their story deemed over.[13] The fact that Truganini's death was contemporaneous with the takeover of the last remaining Aboriginal lands went unnoticed. Colonists could both publicly ponder the tragic consequences of the British conquest and allow its final chapter to proceed almost without comment. Questions about the invasion of Van Diemen's Land were now deemed to be of purely historical interest. Nevertheless, as the next 130 years would demonstrate, for both white and black Tasmanians, the conquest of Van Diemen's Land was by no means resolved.

CHIEF EXECUTIVES OF VAN DIEMEN'S LAND, 1803–61

Lt. John Bowen, R.N.	Sept. 1803–Feb. 1804
Col. David Collins, R.M., Lt.-Gov.	Feb. 1804–Mar. 1810
Lt. Edward Lord, R.M.	Mar. 1810–July 1810
Capt. John Murray, 73rd Regt.	July 1810–Feb. 1812
Lt.-Col. Andrew Geils, 73rd Regt.	Feb. 1812–Feb. 1813
Col. Thomas Davey, R.M., Lt.-Gov.	Feb. 1813–Apr. 1817
Col. William Sorell, Lt.-Gov.	Apr. 1817–May 1824
Col. George Arthur, Lt.-Gov.	May 1824–Oct. 1836
Lt.-Col. K. Snodgrass, Acting Lt.-Gov.	Oct. 1836–Jan. 1837
Sir John Franklin, R.N., Lt.-Gov.	Jan. 1837–Aug. 1843
Sir John E. Eardley-Wilmot, Lt.-Gov.	Aug. 1843–Oct. 1846
C.J. Latrobe, Administrator	Oct. 1846–Jan. 1847
Sir William Denison, Lt.-Gov.	Jan. 1847–Jan. 1855
Sir Henry Fox Young, Gov.	Jan. 1855–Dec. 1861

ACKNOWLEDGMENTS

This book owes much to two men. It would never have been written but for Pete Hay, my PhD supervisor and friend, whose generous soul, broad intellect and passionate care for this island have sustained and profoundly shaped my work. On the other side of the Van Diemonian frontier, Melbourne-based Chris Feik has been much more than a skilful and supportive editor. His enduring interest in and considerable knowledge of the subject matter have benefited the book's content as much as its style. My thanks are also due to Robert Manne and Morry Schwartz for their faith, and for everyone else involved in Black Inc.'s dynamic and friendly team.

The University of Tasmania provided the environment in which the ideas in the book could emerge and develop. Michael Roe, who supervised my honours thesis in History, contributed greatly to the early development of my thinking about Van Diemen's Land. Students and staff at the School of Geography and Environmental Studies, where I completed my PhD and am now an honorary associate, have offered years of stimulation and support. I owe particular thanks to Andrew Harwood, Patricia McKay, Aidan Davidson and Elaine Stratford.

Tom Griffiths, Alan Atkinson, John Hirst, Richard Flanagan and Margaret Glover provided helpful comments and corrections. Every conversation with Hamish Maxwell-Stewart seemed to lead to a new insight.

I am also in the debt of Tony Marshall and the staff of Tasmaniana in the State Library, who provide with unfailing courtesy an outstanding example of an increasingly endangered environment – a space for quiet study and reflection.

Practical help of another form was given by the Literature Board of the Australia Council in the form of an emerging writers grant.

Work on this book began when my daughter, Clare, was still a toddler, and my son, William, was not even born. Given that Clare is now pushing double digits and William will soon be able to kick a footy as far as his dad, it hardly needs saying that the work could not have been done without the help of many family members and friends. I owe particular thanks to my parents and sisters. Above all, the journey could never have been completed without the love and generosity of my wife, Emma.

NOTES

Abbreviations

AOT   Archives Office of Tasmania
CSO   Colonial Secretary's Office
HRA   Historical Records of Australia
ML   Mitchell Library
SLV   State Library of Victoria
THRA Tasmanian Historical Research Association

INTRODUCTION

1. Terry Newman, *Becoming Tasmania: Renaming Van Diemen's Land* (Hobart: Parliament of Tasmania, 2005): 134–135.

2, For a comprehensive discussion of the influence of Clarke, see Roslyn D. Haynes, *Tasmanian Visions: Landscapes in Writing, Art and Photography* (Hobart: Polymath Press, 2006): Ch. 5.

3. Marcus Clarke, *For the Term of His Natural Life* (Melbourne: Hallcraft Publishing, 1953): preface.

4. Readers seeking more detail of how the arguments of this book relate to Australian historiography should consult the introduction to the author's PhD thesis: James Boyce, "An Environmental History of Van Diemen's Land," University of Tasmania, 2006.

5. Ann Young, *Environmental Change in Australia Since 1788* (Melbourne: Oxford University Press, 2000): 1.

6. White to Skill, 17 April 1790, in Alec Chisholm, *Land of Wonder: The Best Australian Nature Writing* (Sydney: Angus and Robertson, 1964).

7. N.G. Butlin, *Forming a Colonial Economy: Australia 1810–1850* (Cambridge: Cambridge University Press, 1994): 181.

8. Glen McLaren, *Beyond Leichhardt: Bushcraft and the Exploration of Australia* (Fremantle, WA: Fremantle Arts Centre Press, 1996): 33, 36–37.

9. These grasslands are of two types: lowland silver tussock grassland and kangaroo grass tussock grasslands. There may be as many as 50 different species in 10 square metres. For a description of the various types of grassy woodland in Tasmania, including the now threatened *Eucalyptus ovata* (black gum) grassy woodland "so favoured by the graziers and agriculturalists," see James Reid *et al.*, *Vegetation of Tasmania: Flora of Australia Supplementary Series Number 8* (Canberra: Australian Biological Resources Study, Environment Australia, 1999): 274–282.

323

10. For an analysis of the role played by hunting dogs in the early settlement of Van Diemen's Land, including their contribution to cross-cultural relations, see James Boyce, "Canine Revolution: The Social and Environmental Impact of the Introduction of the Dog to Tasmania," *Environmental History* 11(1) (2006): 102–139; and James Boyce, "A Dog's Breakfast ... Lunch and Dinner: Canine Dependency in Early Van Diemen's Land," *THRA Papers and Proceedings* 51(4) (2004): 194–214.

11. David Collins, *An Account of the English Colony in New South Wales, 1788–1801* (London: Whitcombe and Tombs, 1910): 77, 169.

12. *Sydney Gazette*, 17 May 1822.

13. D.N. Jeans, ed., *Space and Society* (Sydney: Sydney University Press, 1987): 6.

14. Tom Griffiths and Libby Robin, eds, *Ecology and Empire: Environmental History of Settler Societies* (Melbourne: Melbourne University Press, 1997): 4. Tom Griffiths, "The Nature of Culture and the Culture of Nature" in Hsu-Ming Teo and Richard White, eds, *Cultural History in Australia* (Sydney: UNSW Press, 2003): 70.

15. William Lines, *Taming the Great South Land: A History of the Conquest of Nature in Australia* (Sydney: Allen and Unwin, 1991): 26.

16. E.P. Thompson, *Customs in Common* (London: Penguin, 1993): 1.

17. Thompson, *Customs in Common*: 64, 127.

18. John Mannion, *Irish Settlements in Eastern Canada* (Toronto: University of Toronto Press, 1974): 56.

19. John West, *The History of Tasmania* (Sydney: Angus and Robertson, 1971): 272–273.

20. Sharon Morgan, *Land Settlement in Early Tasmania: Creating an Antipodean England* (Cambridge: Cambridge University Press, 1992): 2. For a critique of Morgan's thesis see M.A. Staples, "Comparative Landscape, European Settlement, and the Myth of Little England in Tasmania," *THRA Papers and Proceedings* 49, no. 3 (2002): 194–195.

21. Robert Hughes, *The Fatal Shore: A History of the Transportation of Convicts to Australia, 1787–1868* (London: Collins Harvill, 1987): Ch. 11.

22. For an exploration of this, see for instance J.B. Hirst, *Convict Society and Its Enemies: A History of Early New South Wales* (Sydney: Allen and Unwin, 1983), especially chapter 2; Hamish Maxwell-Stuart, "The Bushrangers and the Convict System of Van Diemen's Land, 1803–1846," PhD thesis, University of Edinburgh, 1990; Stephen Nicholas, ed., *Convict Workers: Reinterpreting Australia's Past* (Cambridge: Cambridge University Press, 1988); Ian Duffield and James Bradley, eds, *Representing Convicts: New Perspectives on Convict Forced Labour Migration* (London: Leicester University Press, 1997).

23. West, *The History of Tasmania*; Lloyd Robson, *A History of Tasmania*, vol. 1, *Van Diemen's Land from the Earliest Times to 1855* (Melbourne: Oxford University Press, 1983).

PART I

1. *Van Diemonian Sea-Wolves*

1. Leslie Norman, *Sea Wolves and Bandits: Sealing, Whaling, Smuggling and Piracy, Wild Men of Van Diemen's Land, Bushrangers and Bandits, Wrecks and Wreckers* (Hobart: J. Walch, 1946): 96.

2. Tim Jetson, "An Island of Contentment? A History of Preservation Island," *THRA Papers and Proceedings* 43, no. 1 (1996). Traces (including a brick hearth) of the settlement at Preservation Island were excavated in 2002.

3. David Day, *Claiming a Continent: A New History of Australia* (Sydney: HarperCollins, 2001): 49.

4. Eric Rolls, "Flowers and the Wide Sea: China and Australia with Special Reference to Tasmania," *THRA Papers and Proceedings* 36, no. 4 (1989): 133.

5. Edward Duyker, *François Péron: An Impetuous Life – Naturalist and Voyager* (Melbourne:

The Miegunyah Press, 2006): 156.

6. Statement of Southern Whale Fishery, Mitchell Library [ML], CY 1747, Brabourne papers, vol. 4.
7. Stephen Murray-Smith, "Beyond the Pale: The Islander Community of Bass Strait in the 19th Century," *THRA Papers and Proceedings* 20, no. 4 (1973): 169.
8. *Sydney Gazette*, 5 April 1817, cited in Stephen Murray-Smith, "Beyond the Pale": 170.
9. *Hobart Town Gazette*, 10 December 1824.
10. The east coast settler George Meredith made an agreement in 1824 to provide his boat for a season in return for a quarter of the takings. Meredith papers, Archives Office of Tasmania (AOT) NSA 123/1.
11. *Historical Records of Australia*, series 3, vol. 2 [*HRA* 3/2]: 575–576.
12. Will Lawson, *Blue Gum Clippers and Whale Ships of Tasmania*, facsimile edition (Launceston, Tas.: D&C Book Distributors, 1986): 23.
13. The sites where bay whaling occurred are described in Michael Nash, *The Bay Whalers: Tasmania's Shore-Based Whaling Industry* (Hobart: Navarine Publishing, 2003).
14. John Hart's recollections, found in Thomas Francis Bride, *Letters from Victorian Pioneers* (Melbourne: Lloyd O'Neil, 1983): 51–53. J. S. Gumpton, *Kangaroo Island 1800–1836* (Canberra: Roebuck Society, 1970): v.
15. Brian Plomley and Kristen Anne Henley, "The Sealers of Bass Strait and the Cape Barren Island Community," *THRA Papers and Proceedings* 37, nos. 2 and 3 (1990): 37–127.
16. Ronald Worthy Giblin, *The Early History of Tasmania*, vol. 2, *1804–1828* (Melbourne: Melbourne University Press, 1939): 645.
17. *HRA* 3/5: 827.
18. Day, *Claiming a Continent*: 51.

2. The Settlement of the Derwent

1. A comprehensive account of the French visits is given in Colin Dyer, *The French Explorers and the Aboriginal Australians 1772–1839* (St Lucia, Qld.: University of Queensland Press, 2005), and Frank Horner, *The French Reconnaissance: Baudin in Australia* (Melbourne: Melbourne University Press, 1987). The Baudin expedition in Van Diemen's Land was discussed by the author in James Boyce and Peter Hay, "Nicolas Baudin: The Bicentenary of the Expedition to Van Diemen's Land of an Extraordinary French Explorer," *40 Degrees South* 24 (2002).
2. Dyer, *The French Explorers*: 9.
3. Horner, *The French Reconnaissance*: 271–273.
4. Nash, *The Bay Whalers*: 35.
5. Bowen to King, 20 September 1803, *HRA* 3/1: 197–198.
6. West, *The History of Tasmania*: 262.
7. N.J.B. Plomley, ed., *Friendly Mission: The Tasmanian Journals and Papers of George Augustus Robinson 1829–1834* (Hobart: Tasmanian Historical Research Association, 1966): 375.
8. Amas Delano, *A Narrative of a Voyage to New Holland and Van Diemen's Land*, facsimile edition (Hobart: Cat and Fiddle Press, 1978): no page numbers; *Van Diemen's Land: Copies of All Correspondence between Lieutenant Governor Arthur and His Majesty's Secretary of State for the Colonies on the Subject of the Military Operations Lately Carried on against the Aboriginal Inhabitants of Van Diemen's Land (Including Minutes of Evidence Taken before the Committee for the Affairs of the Aborigines, 1830)* (Hobart: Tasmanian Historical Research Association, 1971): 259.
9. Phillip Tardif, *John Bowen's Hobart: The Beginning of European Settlement in Tasmania* (Hobart: Tasmanian Historical Research Association, 2003): 142.
10. Bowen to King, 27 September 1803, *HRA* 3/1: 193.

11. Who these original 49 settlers were is not totally clear. For a description of those we know of, or who were likely to have been in the group, see Tardif, *John Bowen's Hobart*: appendix 2, 200–214.

12. Margaret Glover, *History of the Site of Bowen's Settlement Risdon Cove* (Hobart: National Parks and Wildlife Service, 1978): 1, 10.

13. Charles Jeffreys, *Van Diemen's Land : Geographical and Descriptive Delineations of the Island of Van Diemen's Land* (London: J.M. Richardson, 1820): 111.

14. Rhys Jones, "Fire-Stick Farming," *Australian Natural History* 16 (1969): 224–228.

15. Edward Curr, *Recollections of Squatting in Victoria (from 1841 to 1851)* (Adelaide: Libraries Board of South Australia, 1968): 188–189.

16. John Rickard, *Australia: A Cultural History* (London: Longman, 1988): 54.

17. *Van Diemen's Land: Copies of All Correspondence*: 259.

18. David Burn, *A Picture of Van Diemen's Land*, facsimile edition (Hobart: Cat and Fiddle Press, 1973): 134.

19. Stonehenge wrote in 1867 that this animal "claimed his descent from the most ancient race in Britain," but reported that they were then little used. W. Beilby, *The Dog in Australasia* (Melbourne: George Robertson, 1897): 125.

20. Boyce, "A Dog's Breakfast": 194–214 and Boyce, "Canine Revolution": 102–139.

21. Louisa Meredith, *My Home in Tasmania* (New York: Bunce and Britain, 1883): 171–172.

22. Barbara Hamilton-Arnold, ed., *Letters and Papers of G.P. Harris, 1803–1812: Deputy Surveyor-General of New South Wales at Sullivan Bay, Port Phillip, and Hobart Town, Van Diemen's Land* (Sorrento, Vic.: Arden Press, 1994): 54–64.

23. Benjamin Bensley, *Lost and Found or Light in the Prison: A Narrative with Original Letters of a Convict Condemned for Forgery* (London: W. Wells Gardner, 1859): 143–144.

24. The abundant availability of food outweighed the problem of Risdon's doubtful water supply. Although the creek's summer flow was inadequate to sustain a large settlement, it was sufficient for a small military post.

25. Maxwell-Stewart, "The Bushrangers and the Convict System of Van Diemen's Land": 230.

26. M. Tipping, *Convicts Unbound: The Story of the Calcutta Convicts and Their Settlement in Australia* (Melbourne: Viking O'Neill, 1988): ix, 67–69.

27. Tipping, *Convicts Unbound*: 18, 25–27, 79.

28. Bensley, *Lost and Found or Light in the Prison*: 36–37, 129.

29. Tipping, *Convicts Unbound*: 33.

30. Tipping, *Convicts Unbound*: 19.

31. Hamilton-Arnold, ed., *Letters and Papers of G.P. Harris*: 27.

32. John Currey, *David Collins: A Colonial Life* (Melbourne: Melbourne University Press, 2000): 195.

33. Collins to Hobart, 14 November 1803, *HRA* 3/1: 36.

34. John Pascoe Fawkner, *Reminiscences of Early Settlement at Port Phillip*, Fawkner papers, State Library of Victoria [SLV], cited in Currey, *David Collins*: 218.

35. Collins to Sullivan, 3 August 1804, *HRA* 3/1: 264; Tipping, *Convicts Unbound*: 72.

36. Hamilton-Arnold, ed., *Letters and Papers of G.P. Harris*: 44–46.

37. Hamilton-Arnold, ed., *Letters and Papers of G.P. Harris*: 77–78.

38. J.M. Tuckey, *General Observations of Port Phillip*, Brabourne papers, vol. 3, ML CY 1747.

39. Tipping, *Convicts Unbound*: 80, 99.

40. Tipping, *Convicts Unbound*: 80, 94.

41. Tipping, *Convicts Unbound*: 72, 88.

42. James Backhouse Walker, *Early Tasmania: Papers Read before the Royal Society of Tasmania During the Years 1888 to 1899* (Hobart: Government Printer, 1973): 96.

43. Currey, *David Collins*: 203.

44. Currey, *David Collins*: 214.

45. Collins to King, 28 February 1804, in Clark, *Select Documents in Australian History*: 75–76.
46. Tipping, *Convicts Unbound*.
47. Government order, 31 December 1803. David Collins, *General and Garrison Orders, 1803–1808*, ML, AK 341.
48. Government order, 29 January 1804. Collins, *General and Garrison Orders 1803–1808*, ML, AK 341.
49. Government order, 29 January 1804. Collins, *General and Garrison Orders 1803–1808*, ML, AK 341.
50. Hamilton-Arnold, ed., *Letters and Papers of G.P. Harris*: 54–64.
51. Tardif argues that credit for their choice rightfully belongs with the convict surveyor already resident at Risdon, James Meehan. Tardif, *John Bowen's Hobart*: 108–109.
52. Mary Nicholls, ed., *The Diary of the Reverend Robert Knopwood, 1803–1838: First Chaplain of Van Diemen's Land* (Hobart: Tasmanian Historical Research Association, 1977): 46.
53. Currey, *David Collins*: 86.
54. Inga Clendinnen, *Dancing with Strangers* (Melbourne: Text Publishing, 2003): 56, 251.
55. Currey, *David Collins*: 250–252.
56. Collins, *An Account of the English Colony*: 45, 107, 349.
57. Collins, *An Account of the English Colony*: 327.
58. James Backhouse, *A Narrative of a Visit to the Australian Colonies* (London: Hamilton, Adams and Co., 1843): 21; and Tipping, *Convicts Unbound*: 123. This is given a broader context in Alan Atkinson, *The Europeans in Australia: A History*, vol. 2, *Democracy* (Melbourne: Oxford University Press, 2004): 11.
59. James Bonwick, *The Last of the Tasmanians; or, the Black War of Van Diemen's Land* (Adelaide: Libraries Board of South Australia, 1969): 38–39.
60. This possibility is further suggested by the fact that the botanist Robert Brown had an interview with what he described as "the same party of natives that are generally in the neighbourhood of Sullivans Cove" at Simpsons Bay, South Bruny, in 1804.
61. James Meehan, notebook, AOT LSD 355/3. H. Ling Roth, *The Aborigines of Tasmania* (Halifax: F. King and Sons, 1899): 2.
62. Hamilton-Arnold, ed., *Letters and Papers of G.P. Harris*: 66.
63. Bensley, *Lost and Found or Light in the Prison*: 145–146, 148, 152.
64. Harold Perkin, *The Origins of Modern English Society 1780–1880* (London: Routledge and Kegan Paul, 1969): 20–22.
65. Tim Bonyhady, *The Colonial Earth* (Melbourne: Melbourne University Press, 2000): 34.
66. Hamilton-Arnold, ed., *Letters and Papers of G.P. Harris*: 65.
67. See, for example, diary entries for 26–27 October and 3 November 1804.
68. William Thornley (edited by John Mills), *The Adventures of an Emigrant in Van Diemen's Land* (Adelaide: Rigby, 1973): 13–14. This book, by Charles Rowcroft (who wrote under the pseudonym William Thornley), is a novel, but is largely based on personal experience, and offers much of interest to the historian.
69. Government orders, 27 February and 9 March 1804, Collins, *General and Garrison Orders 1803–1808*, ML, AK: 341.
70. Bonyhady, *The Colonial Earth*: 3.
71. K.R. Von Stieglitz, *The Story of the Pioneer Church in Van Diemen's Land* (Hobart: Fullers Bookshop, 1954): 67–69.

3. How Shall We Sing the Lord's Song in a Strange Land?

1. Bensley, *Lost and Found or Light in the Prison*: 152.
2. Knopwood sermon, Ps 137 verse 5, Sullivans Cove, 13 May 1804, Knopwood papers, ML A259.
3. Collins to Banks, 20 July 1804, ML CY 1747.

4.   Warren R. Dawson, ed., *The Banks Letters: A Calendar of the Manuscript Correspondence of Sir Joseph Banks Preserved in the British Museum (National History) and Other Collections in Great Britain* (London: British Museum, 1958): letter, 20, July 1804: 248.

5.   The purveyor from the Naval Board, R. Mart, believed in 1819 that all the trees of Van Diemen's Land were the same as in New South Wales, except the "Huon River pine tree and the Adventure Bay pine tree." (R. Mart, Purveyor, *Extract from the Report of the Purveyor of the Naval Board on the Timber of New South Wales and Van Diemen's Land* in Barron Field, ed., *Geographical Memoirs of New South Wales; by Various Hands ... Together with Other Papers on the Aborigines, the Geology, the Botany, the Timber, the Astronomy, and the Meteorology of New South Wales and Van Diemen's Land* (London: J. Murray, 1825): 315–316.

6.   Collins to Hobart, 3 August 1804, *HRA* 3/1: 264.

7.   Collins informed London that they were almost out of clothes and were very short of blankets. Collins to Hobart, 10 November 1804, *HRA* 3/1: 388.

8.   For the most comprehensive review of the evidence pertaining to this incident see Tardif, *John Bowen's Hobart*: 144–148; also Phillip Tardif, "Risdon Cove," in Robert Manne, ed., *Whitewash: On Keith Windschuttle's Fabrication of Aboriginal History* (Melbourne: Black Inc., 2003): 218–225.

9.   *Van Diemen's Land: Copies of All Correspondence*: 259.

10. Nicholls, ed., *The Diary of Reverend Robert Knopwood*: 51.

11. "Robert" was still living in Hobart Town in November–December 1805 when he was listed among the children inoculated with the smallpox vaccine. It is perhaps most likely that he was thereafter returned to Port Dalrymple and the care of his godfather, Jacob Mountgarret, who had obtained an official appointment there, and died sometime before 1818 (an era when few records were kept). See James Boyce, "Robert May: Real Name Forever Lost," *40 Degrees South* 35 (2004): 45–52.

12. Collins to King, 11 September 1804, *HRA* 3/1: 281.

13. Currey, *David Collins*: 220; Tardif, *John Bowen's Hobart*: 137–140.

14. Collins to King, *HRA* 3/1: 238.

15. Nicholls, ed., *The Diary of the Reverend Robert Knopwood*: 78, 109, 126, 128 (entries for 5 March 1805, 16 June 1806, 14 February 1808 and 2 March 1808).

16. Government order, 8 May 1804. David Collins, *General and Garrison Orders 1803–1808*, ML AK 341; Tardif, *John Bowen's Hobart*: 61, 152.

17. Knopwood reported seeing 250 to 300 Aborigines at Brown's River on 9 October 187, mostly women and children, the "men out a hunting." Nicholls, ed., *The Diary of the Reverend Robert Knopwood*: 145. Brown's River is on the western shore of the Derwent, south of Hobart, at the present day suburb of Kingston.

18. Paterson to King, 26 November 1804, *HRA* 3/1: 605–607.

19. Collins, *An Account of the English Colony*: 247.

20. Paterson to King, 8 January 1805, *HRA* 3/1: 629.

21. Dawson, ed., *The Banks Letters*: 656.

22. Paterson to Banks, 7 January 1806, Banks papers, vol. 20, ML CY 1753.

23. Dawson, ed., *The Banks Letters*: 656.

24. Paterson to King, 8 January 1805, *HRA* 3/1: 629.

25. Paterson to King, 10 March 1806, *HRA* 3/1: 658–659.

26. Paterson to Castlereagh, 12 August 1806, *HRA* 3/1: 661.

27. Paterson to King, 10 March 1806, *HRA* 3/1: 658–659.

28. Collins to Hobart, 3 August 1804, *HRA* 3/1: 257–264. Surgeon Anson's medical returns for November 1804 show that three marines, five free settlers and 28 convicts were sick and 21 in all still had scurvy, including John Pascoe Fawkner. Cecil Billot, *The Life and Times of John Pascoe Fawkner* (Melbourne: Hyland House, 1985): 37.

29. Government order, 10 September 1804, Collins, *General and Garrison Orders 1803–1808*, ML AK: 341.

4. A Kangaroo Economy

1.   Government order, 27 September 1804. Collins, *General and Garrison Orders 1803–1808*, *ML AK*: 341.
2.   Government order, 27 December 1804, Collins, *General and Garrison Orders 1803–1808*, ML AK 341.
3.   Paterson to King, 8 January 1805, *HRA* 3/1: 629.
4.   Paterson to King, 14 November 1805, *HRA* 3/1: 645.
5.   King to Paterson, 20 November 1805, *HRA* 3/1: 648.
6.   Government order, 5 July 1805, Collins, *General and Garrison Orders 1803–1808*, ML AK: 341.
7.   Hamilton-Arnold, ed., *Letters and Papers of G.P. Harris*: 72–73.
8.   Nicholls, ed., *The Diary of the Reverend Robert Knopwood*: 88, 91, 92.
9.   Nicholls, ed., *The Diary of the Reverend Robert Knopwood*: 80.
10. Nicholls, ed., *The Diary of the Reverend Robert Knopwood*: 85.
11. Government order, 31 December 1803, Collins, *General and Garrison Orders 1803–1808*, ML AK: 341. Glover, *History of the Site of Bowen's Settlement*: 20.
12. Tipping, *Convicts Unbound*: 129.
13. Examination of J. Gordon, 4 March 1820, *HRA* 3/3: 252.
14. Nicholls, ed., *The Diary of the Reverend Robert Knopwood*: 98–99.
15. Nicholls, ed., *The Diary of the Reverend Robert Knopwood*: 88–98.
16. Hamilton-Arnold, ed., *Letters and Papers of G.P .Harris*: 56.
17. Thompson, *Customs in Common*: 189, 263.
18. George Meredith, "On the expediency of encouraging distillation in the settlements of New South Wales," 28 June 1820, Meredith papers, AOT, NS 123/15.
19. Hamilton-Arnold, ed., *Letters and Papers of G.P. Harris*: 87, 95.
20. Nicholls, ed., *The Diary of the Reverend Robert Knopwood*: 94.
21. Hamilton-Arnold, ed., *Letters and Papers of G.P. Harris*: 85.
22. Government order, 7 January 1805. Collins, *General and Garrison Orders 1803–1808*, ML AK: 341.
23. Thompson, *Customs in Common*: 2, 6, 36–37.
24. Nicholls, ed., *The Diary of the Reverend Robert Knopwood*: 99.
25. See, for example, Knopwood's diary entries for 3 November 1804, 17 February 1805, 24 June 1805, 26 September 1805 and 27 November 1806. Nicholls, ed., *The Diary of Reverend Robert Knopwood*: 65, 77, 86, 96.
26. *Memoirs of Joseph Holt, United Irishman*, quoted in the preface to Collins, *An Account of the English Colony in New South Wales, 1788–1801*: xxx.
27. The estimate that approximately 110 average-sized forester kangaroos would have been required each week to maintain the ration is based on the European population of 481 in January 1805. The number of full rations required, allowing for the smaller ration granted women and children, is estimated at 400. The average kangaroo weight of 66 2/3 pounds, and the proportion of each animal taken in by the store, 65 per cent, are based on figures given in M. Fels, "Culture Contact in the County of Buckinghamshire, Van Diemen's Land, 1803–1811," *THRA Papers and Proceedings* 29, no. 2 (1982): 51–52.
28. AOT CO 201/43.
29. AOT CO 201/43.
30. Government order, 6 October 1806. Collins, *General and Garrison Orders 1803–1808*, ML AK: 341.
31. Nicholls, ed., *The Diary of the Reverend Robert Knopwood*: 117.

32. In British currency during this period, there were twelve pence (12d) in a shilling, and twenty shillings (20s) in a pound (£1). Prices were generally written as £-s-d – thus two pounds, four shillings and sixpence would be written as £2-4s-6d. A guinea was equal to one pound, one shilling (£1-1s).

33. Government order, 8 December 1806. Collins, *General and Garrison Orders 1803–1808*, ML AK: 341

34. Paterson to Windham, 29 August 1808, *HRA* 3/1: 672–673.

35. Nicholls, ed., *The Diary of the Reverend Robert Knopwood*: 120.

36. Tipping, *Convicts Unbound*: 112–113.

37. Nicholls, ed., *The Diary of the Reverend Robert Knopwood*: 116.

38. Nicholls, ed., *The Diary of the Reverend Robert Knopwood*: 121–122.

39. Hamilton-Arnold, ed., *Letters and Papers of G.P. Harris*: 99.

40. Fels, "Culture Contact in the County of Buckinghamshire": 53.

41. Nicholls, ed., *The Diary of the Reverend Robert Knopwood*: 146.

42. Government order, 15 September 1807. Collins, *General and Garrison Orders 1803–1808*, ML AK: 341.

43. Nicholls, ed., *The Diary of the Reverend Robert Knopwood*: 141.

44. Paterson to Sullivan, 21 April 1807, *HRA* 3/1: 668.

45. Paterson to Sullivan, 25 August 1807, *HRA* 3/1: 671.

46. Paterson to King, 5 April 1805, *HRA* 3/1: 634–635.

47. Paterson to King, 5 April 1805, *HRA* 3/1: 634–635.

48. Paterson to King, 14 November 1805, *HRA* 3/1: 646–647.

49. Paterson to Banks, 13 November 1807, ML CY 2456.

50. *Sydney Gazette*, 18 March 1804.

51. Nicholls, ed., *The Diary of the Reverend Robert Knopwood*: 109–146.

52. Conflict between the Aborigines and these groups will be considered in detail in the next chapter.

PART II

5. *Access without Conquest*

1. Nicholls, ed., *The Diary of the Reverend Robert Knopwood*: 160.

2. Hamilton-Arnold, ed., *Letters and Papers of G.P. Harris*: 98.

3. For a discussion of this issue see James Boyce, "Fantasy Island," in Manne, ed., *Whitewash*. Keith Windschuttle concludes that almost all other Aborigines died from disease, without providing one piece of direct evidence of this (other than those who were confined or detained after 1828), even though he argues that no claims about the number of Aborigines who died from violence can be made beyond those definitively documented. Keith Windschuttle, *The Fabrication of Aboriginal History*, vol. 1, *Van Diemen's Land* (Sydney: Macleay Press, 2002).

4. *HRA* 3/3: 418.

5. *HRA* 3/3: 501.

6. John Barnes, "A Few Remarks on the Natives of Van Diemen's Land," unpublished paper given to the Royal College of Physicians (London), 23 February 1829, R. Coll. Phys. archives 3058 (1). This paper was unearthed and edited by Dr Ian Gregg, Royal College of Physicians, London, who consulted dermatologists to inform his opinion that the skin disease was "most likely" to have been canine scabies. I am grateful to Professor Campbell Macknight for bringing this paper to my attention and providing me with a copy of it.

7. Rhys Jones, "Tasmanian Aborigines and Dogs," *Mankind* 7, no. 4 (December 1970): 70, 263.

8. Jones, "Tasmanian Aborigines and Dogs": 644.

9. Bonwick, *The Last of the Tasmanians*: 44–45.

10. Macquarie to Geils, 8 February 1812, *HRA* 3/1: 466.
11. Fels, "Culture Contact in the County of Buckingamshire": 60.
12. *Van Diemen's Land: Copies of All Correspondence*: 53.
13. Bonwick, *The Last of the Tasmanians*: 43–44.
14. For example, Peter Harrison mentions never being troubled by Aborigines (AOT NS 690/23). A group of Aborigines also visited the farm of William Barnes two or three times a year (AOT CSO 1/323/7578, 300). Cited in Maria Monypenny, "Going out and Coming in: Co-operation and Collaboration between Aborigines and Europeans in Early Tasmania," *Tasmanian Historical Studies* 5, no. 1 (1995–96): 69–70.
15. Nicholls, ed., *The Diary of the Reverend Robert Knopwood*: 232, 277, 293–294.
16. Knopwood records the firing of the bush on 15 January 1818, noting "the country on fire by the natives."
17. *HRA* 3/1: 761.
18. Fels, "Culture Contact in the Country of Buckinghamshire": 66. In addition to these animals, the government owned 122 sheep and 322 cattle, of which 252 had arrived just six weeks before.
19. Curr, *An Account of the Colony of Van Diemen's Land*: 85–87.
20. Semmens, "Food and Agriculture in the New Colony of Van Diemen's Land 1803 to 1810": 28.
21. Brown, *The Narrative of George Russell*: 402.
22. Curr, *An Account of the Colony of Van Diemen's Land*: 71.
23. McKay, *Journals of the Land Commissioners for Van Diemen's Land*: 84–85.
24. R.M. Hartwell, *The Economic Development of Van Diemen's Land, 1820–1850* (Melbourne: Melbourne University Press, 1954): 11.
25. Robson, *A History of Tasmania*, vol. 1: 70.
26. Butlin, *Forming a Colonial Economy*: 204.
27. Curr, *An Account of the Colony of Van Diemen's Land*: 65.
28. Ross, *The Settler in Van Diemen's Land*: 65–66.
29. Butlin, *Forming a Colonial Economy*: 98, 140.
30. G.J. Abbot and N.B. Nairn, *Economic Growth in Australia 1788–1821*: 327. Cited in Canteri, "The Origins of Australian Social Banditry": 327.
31. Butlin, *Forming a Colonial Economy*: 204.
32. Burn, *A Picture of Van Diemen's Land*: 107; Hamilton-Arnold, ed., *Letters and Papers of G.P. Harris*: 65.
33. T.O. Curling, letter to Sir T. Mantell from Guilton on the Lake River, 14 November 1823, cited in Giblin, *The Early History of Tasmania*, vol. 2: 321–323.
34. William Williamson, letter, 16 December 1820, AOT NS 14/1/1.
35. Curr, *An Account of the Colony of Van Diemen's Land*: 35, 38.
36. James Lord, who died in 1824, was particularly successful, and left a fortune of £50,000. His son David was to become the richest man in Van Diemen's Land. See Richard Lord, *The History of the James Lord (c.1757–1824) Family in Tasmania*, vol. 1, *James Lord* (Hobart: R. Lord, 1966): 5–11.
37. G.M. Webb, "Twenty Men of Fortune," *THRA Papers and Proceedings* 45, no. 3 (1998): 151.
38. Burn, *A Picture of Van Diemen's Land*: 10; Curr, *An Account of the Colony of Van Diemen's Land*: 77–78.
39. These men and women owned 6 per cent of the cattle and 22 per cent of the sheep. Maxwell-Stewart, "The Bushrangers and the Convict System of Van Diemen's Land": 171–173.
40. *HRA* 3/3: 250.
41. *HRA* 3/4: 575–577.
42. *Hobart Town Gazette*, 6 November 1819.
43. *Colonial Times*, 19 May 1826.

6. *The Lieutenant Governor of the Woods*

1. West, *The History of Tasmania*: 44. The main memorial to Collins was to be St David's Church. In the manner of saints of old, a small wooden church was initially erected where Collins was buried, with its altar directly over the late lieutenant governor's grave, and the church named in his honour.
2. West, *The History of Tasmania*: 356–367.
3. West, *The History of Tasmania*: 358.
4. Robson, *A History of Tasmania*, vol. 1: 82.
5. West, *The History of Tasmania*: 358.
6. *HRA* 3/3: 253.
7. *HRA* 3/4: 495.
8. James Calder, *The Circumnavigation of Van Diemen's Land in 1815 by James Kelly and in 1824 by James Hobbs, Edited from Their Own Accounts by James Calder* (Hobart: Sullivans Cove, 1984): 23.
9. Macquarie to Davey, 30 January 1813, *HRA* 3/2: 13
10. Robson, *A History of Tasmania*, vol. 1: 81.
11. Canteri, "The Origins of Australian Social Banditry."
12. Maxwell-Stewart, "The Bushrangers and the Convict System of Van Diemen's Land": 159–160.
13. *HRA* 3/3: 701–702, 957.
14. Discussed in Maxwell-Stewart, "The Bushrangers and the Convict System of Van Diemen's Land": 161.
15. George Mackaness, "Introduction," in Thomas E. Wells, *Michael Howe, the Last and Worst of the Bush Rangers of Van Diemen's Land* (Hobart: Platypus Publications, 1966): 10.
16. Wells, *Michael Howe*: 29.
17. For more information about Lord, see E.R. Henry, "Edward Lord: The John Macarthur of Van Diemen's Land," *THRA Papers and Proceedings* 20, no. 2 (1973).
18. K.R. Von Stieglitz, *Tasmanian Bushrangers* (Evandale, Tas.: Telegraph Printery, 1951): 28.
19. *HRA* 3/3: 246, 310.
20. Humphrey to Bathurst, AOT CO 201/79 in Eustace Fitzsymonds, *Mortmain: A Collection of Choice Petitions, Memorials, and Letters of Protest and Request from the Convict Colony of Van Diemen's Land* (Hobart: Sullivan's Cove, 1977): 43–44.
21. Robson, *A History of Tasmania*, vol. 1: 82, 84, 89.
22. *Hobart Town Gazette*, 30 November 1816.
23. James Erskine Calder, *Some Account of the Wars, Extirpation, Habits etc of the Native Tribes of Tasmania*, facsimile edition (Hobart: Fullers Bookshop, 1972): 46.
24. Canteri, "The Origins of Australian Social Banditry": 153; Wells, *Michael Howe*: 13. The fact that Howe singled out Knopwood makes it less, not more, likely that any contacts Knopwood had were of consequence.
25. Canteri, "The Origins of Australian Social Banditry": 152.
26. *Hobart Town Gazette*, 14 March 1818.
27. Sorell had sent Mary to Sydney initially for her safety. Bonwick, *The Last of the Tasmanians*: 46.
28. Wells, *Michael Howe*: 37–38.
29. Wells, *Michael Howe*: 15.
30. Nicholls, ed., *The Diary of the Reverend Robert Knopwood*: 292.
31. Wells, *Michael Howe*: 38.
32. The *Hobart Town Gazette* reported on 3 July 1819: "on Tuesday died in the Colonial Hospital the native woman usually called Black Mary ... one time the partner of Michel Howe."
33. Von Stieglitz, *Tasmanian Bushrangers*: 28.
34. Canteri, "The Origins of Australian Social Banditry": 31.

35. Wells, *Michael Howe*: 36–37.
36. West, *The History of Tasmania*: 364.
37. Tim Jetson, *The Roof of Tasmania: A History of the Central Plateau* (Launceston, Tas.: Pelion Press, 1989): 23.
38. This fascinating and significant historical document is dated 13 November 1816. A copy made in 1817 is held in the AOT CSO 1/223/5399. It is reproduced in Fitzsymonds, *Mortmain*: 44. According to Canteri, the original is held in the Public Record Office, London. Canteri, "The Origins of Australian Social Banditry": 336.
39. Wells, *Michael Howe*: 10.
40. *HRA* 3/2: 794.
41. The *Hobart Town Gazette* of 31 October 1818 noted that extra payments had been made to "parties of the 46th regiment in secret service to August 1817" as well as an "amount advance to crown prisoners employed on secret service."

7. Cross-Cultural Encounters

1. Fels, "Culture Contact in the Country of Buckingamshire": 65.
2. Plomley, ed., *Friendly Mission*: 109.
3. James Boyce, *God's Own Country? The Anglican Church and Tasmanian Aborigines* (Hobart: Anglicare Tasmania, 2001): 26.
4. Brabyn to Paterson, 18 February 1809, *HRA* 3/1: 694–697. The rebel administration in New South Wales pardoned the convict Richard Dry, who subsequently became a large northern landowner and the father of Tasmania's first native-born premier.
5. Inquest, 24 October 1817, *HRA* 3/3: 707.
6. *Hobart Town Gazette*, 7 February 1818.
7. *Colonial Times*, 27 August 1830.
8. *Hobart Town Gazette*, 29 March 1817.
9. *Hobart Town Gazette*, 28 November 1818.
10. AOT CSO1/317–8. Plomley, ed., *Friendly Mission*: 740–741.
11. Keryn James in Anne Chittleborough, Gillian Dooley, Brenda Glover and Rick Hosking, eds, *Alas, for the Pelicans! Flinders, Baudin and Beyond: Essays and Poems* (Adelaide: Wakefield Press, 2002): 177. James explores how the slavery mindset contributed to the abduction of Aboriginal women, but her analysis is equally pertinent to the removal of Aboriginal children.
12. Plomley, ed., *Friendly Mission*: 109.
13. *Van Diemen's Land: Copies of All Correspondence*: 36.
14. *Hobart Town Gazette*, 13 March 1819.
15. Plomley, ed., *Friendly Mission*: 249.
16. Plomley, ed., *Friendly Mission*: 93.
17. Nicholls, ed., *The Diary of the Reverend Robert Knopwood*: 182; Bonwick, *The Last of the Tasmanians*: 41; *HRA* 3/4: 645–647.
18. *HRA* 3/3: 251, 380.
19. It must also be kept in mind that Gordon, a wealthy stockowner and merchant, would have been concerned to ensure that access to the grasslands was not threatened by philanthropic concern about native rights in London. Barrett, a former convict, had no obvious vested interest.
20. Lyndall Ryan, *The Aboriginal Tasmanians* (St Lucia, QLD: University of Queensland Press, 1981): 69.
21. Rebe Taylor, *Unearthed: The Aboriginal Tasmanians of Kangaroo Island* (Adelaide: Wakefield Press, 2002): 34.
22. Giblin, *The Early History of Tasmania*, vol. 2: 652.
23. Taylor, *Unearthed: The Aboriginal Tasmanians of Kangaroo Island*: 35.

24. Ryan, *The Aboriginal Tasmanians*: 71.
25. Keryn James in Chittleborough *et al.*, *Alas, for the Pelicans!*: 175–176.
26. Plomley, ed., *Friendly Mission*: 82.
27. *Van Diemen's Land: Copies of All Correspondence*: 49–50.
28. The term "native born" is used as it was in colonial times – to mean someone born in one of the Australian colonies.
29. K.M. Bowden, *Captain James Kelly of Hobart Town* (Melbourne: Melbourne University Press, 1964): 23; Tipping, *Convicts Unbound*: 66.
30. Calder, *The Circumnavigation of Van Diemen's Land*: 13.
31. Calder, *The Circumnavigation of Van Diemen's Land*: 13.
32. Calder, *The Circumnavigation of Van Diemen's Land*: 16.
33. Calder, *The Circumnavigation of Van Diemen's Land*: 18.
34. Calder, *The Circumnavigation of Van Diemen's Land*: 19–21.
35. Calder, *The Circumnavigation of Van Diemen's Land*: 26.
36. Calder, *The Circumnavigation of Van Diemen's Land*: 26.
37. Calder, *The Circumnavigation of Van Diemen's Land*: 27.
38. Calder, *The Circumnavigation of Van Diemen's Land*: 28.
39. Calder, *The Circumnavigation of Van Diemen's Land*: 30–34.
40. Rebe Taylor suggests that Kelly's depiction of Briggs and sealing generally may have been overly benign. As a trader, Kelly had a vested interest in not exposing high levels of violence and brutality. Taylor, "Savages or Saviours: The Australian Sealers and Aboriginal Tasmanian Survival," *Journal of Australian Studies*, no. 66 (2000): 76. But, if this is so, Kelly's claim that the sealers assisted in Aboriginal disputes to aid the abduction of women seems odd. Kelly was also open with Commissioner Bigge in 1820 (despite still being involved in the industry) that sealers sometimes forcibly abducted women.
41. *Hobart Town Gazette*, 28 March 1818. Plomley, ed., *Friendly Mission*: 55.
42. Williamson, letter, AOT NS 14/1/1.

8. The "Savage Life" of the Van Diemonians

1. An account for goods purchased for Tom and Woorady in early 1832 from a merchant in Launceston included jackets, trousers, waistcoats, handkerchiefs, tobacco, plums, pipes, sugar, tea, red ochre, marbles, fish hooks and fishing line. Plomley, ed., *Friendly Mission*: 687.
2. *Sydney Gazette*, 5 April 1817, cited in Murray-Smith, "Beyond the Pale: The Islander Community of Bass Strait in the 19th Century": 170. In 1832, this quote was incorrectly attributed to Captain Sutherland in 1819 by the South Australia Land Company, and their mistake has been commonly reproduced since.
3. Plomley and Henley, "The Sealers of Bass Strait and the Cape Barren Island Community": 55.
4. 9 December 1830. Plomley, ed., *Friendly Mission*: 95, 290.
5. For a discussion of this issue see Shayne Breen, "Tasmanian Aborigines: Making Fire," *THRA Papers and Proceedings* 39, no. 1 (1992): 40–43. Most people in Van Diemen's Land believed that the Aborigines knew how to make fire even though they often carried it with them. The only significant evidence that they did not is that an Aborigine once told Robinson this was the case. However, as Shayne Breen has pointed out, there were many examples of Aborigines withholding cultural information from Robinson by giving him a misleading answer, and, taken alone, this evidence counts for little.
6. Diary of Adam Amos, 17 March 1824, AOT NS 323/1.
7. Maxwell-Stewart, "The Bushrangers and the Convict System of Van Diemen's Land": 117; West, *The History of Tasmania*: 360.

8. While in the bush in 1839, Fenton had "to be careful to preserve my newly invented Bryant and May matches from the wet." James Fenton, *Bush Life in Tasmania Fifty Years Ago* (London: Hazell, Watson and Viney, 1891. Reprinted in Launceston, Tas.: Mary Fisher Bookstore, no date): 40.

9. James Ross, *The Settler in Van Diemen's Land*, facsimile edition (Melbourne: Marsh Walsh Publishing, 1975): 57.

10. Thornley, *The Adventures of an Emigrant in Van Diemen's Land*: 106, 13.

11. Aboriginal fire-management was much more sophisticated than an annual burn off, and over time this was recognised by some of the British. Robinson recorded on Bruny Island on 3 April 1829 that he "traversed a vast extent of clear country interspersed with clumps" that he believed was "intended as a cover for kangaroo," and that this had "been done by the natives: when burning the underwood they have beat out the fire in order to form these clumps." Plomley, ed., *Friendly Mission*: 54.

12. Meredith, *My Home in Tasmania*: 83.

13. West, *The History of Tasmania*: 263, 355–357.

14. M.C.I. Levy, *Governor George Arthur: A Colonial Benevolent Despot* (Melbourne: Georgian House, 1953): 271.

15. Robson, *A History of Tasmania*, vol. 1: 79, 86.

16. Clark, *Select Documents in Australian History*: 408; Maxwell-Stewart, "The Bushrangers and the Convict System of Van Diemen's Land": 154.

17. Hamilton-Arnold, ed., *Letters and Papers of G.P. Harris*: 99.

18. Clark, *Select Documents in Australian History*: 408.

19. A vineyard had been planted by G.W. Gunning at Coal River as early as 1826. Eustace FitzSymonds, *A Looking-Glass for Tasmania: Letters, Petitions and Other Manuscripts Relating to Van Diemen's Land 1808–1845* (Adelaide: Sullivan's Cove, 1980): 42.

20. *HRA* 3/1: 763.

21. *Hobart Town Gazette*, 29 June 1816.

22. Curr, *An Account of the Colony of Van Diemen's Land*: 34–35.

23. Lachlan Macquarie, *Lachlan Macquarie, Governor of New South Wales: Journals of His Tours in New South Wales and Van Diemen's Land, 1810–1822* (Sydney: Trustees of the Public Library of New South Wales, 1956): 59.

24. Clark, *Select Documents in Australian History*: 399; Giblin, *The Early History of Tasmania*, vol. 2: 263; Morgan, *Land Settlement in Early Tasmania: Creating an Antipodean England* (Cambridge: Cambridge University Press, 1992): 78.

25. Curr, *An Account of the Colony of Van Diemen's Land*: 119.

26. Jeffreys, *Van Diemen's Land*: 55, emphasis in original.

27. William Barnes, letter to his brother, 15 March 1824, in Brown, *The Narrative of George Russell*: 402–406.

28. Curr, *An Account of the Colony of Van Diemen's Land*: 58.

29. Ross, *The Settler in Van Diemen's Land*: 67–68, 82.

30. Hamish Maxwell-Stewart has calculated from the March 1817 tender list "that only 7 per cent of those proprietors cultivating under five acres of wheat negotiated a government contract in that year." Among those who had 5 to 9 acres cultivated, the proportion fortunate enough to sell any wheat to the commissariat was still only 24 per cent, even though 60 per cent of the 212 farms cultivated in the southern county had fewer than 10 acres under wheat. Maxwell-Stewart, "The Bushrangers and the Convict System of Van Diemen's Land": 170.

31. Of the 88 land grants detailed in the *Hobart Town Gazette* on 14 February 1818, 77 were for less than 100 acres, with 52 of them for 50 acres or less. *HRA* 3/3: 247.

32. *HRA* 3/3: 320–322.

33. *HRA* 3/3: 221, 311.

34. Maxwell-Stewart, "The Bushrangers and the Convict System of Van Diemen's Land": 165–166.
35. *HRA* 3/3: 421–426.
36. Maxwell-Stewart, "The Bushrangers and the Convict System of Van Diemen's Land": 175.
37. Brown, *The Narrative of George Russell*: 403.
38. Canteri, "The Origins of Australian Social Banditry": 105.
39. Nicholls, ed., *The Diary of the Reverend Robert Knopwood*: 407.
40. Maxwell-Stewart, "The Bushrangers and the Convict System of Van Diemen's Land": 189–190.

9. Food, Clothing and Shelter

1. Clark, *Select Documents in Australian History*: 170–171.
2. Peter Mathias, *The First Industrial Nation: An Economic History of Britain 1700–1914* (London: Methuen, 1969): 218–222. John Rule, *The Labouring Classes in Early Industrial England, 1750–1850* (London: Longman, 1986): 54–60.
3. Williamson, letter, AOT NS 14/1/1.
4. Jeffreys, *Van Diemen's Land*: 69.
5. Michael Roe, "Mary Leman Grimstone: For Women's Rights and Tasmanian Patriotism," *THRA Papers and Proceedings* 36, no. 1 (1989): 19.
6. Frank Crowley, *A New History of Australia* (Melbourne: William Heinemann, 1974): 10.
7. Williamson, letter, AOT NS 14/1/1.
8. Williamson, letter, AOT NS 14/1/1.
9. George William Evans, *A Geographical, Historical, and Topographical Description of Van Diemen's Land: With Important Hints to Emigrants, and Useful Information Respecting the Application for Grants of Land* (London: J. Souter, 1822): 57.
10. Thomas James Lempriere, *The Penal Settlements of Early Van Diemen's Land* (Launceston, Tas.: First published 1839; Sequicentenary edition published by the Royal Society of Tasmania, Northern Branch, 1954): 44, 64, 72.
11. For a comprehensive history of mutton birding, see Irynej Skira, "Tasmanian Aborigines and Mutton Birding," PhD thesis, University of Tasmania, 1993.
12. Charles Maclean, *Island on the Edge of the World: The Story of St Kilda* (New York: Taplinger, 1980): 90.
13. Williamson, letter, AOT NS 14/1/1. Thornley, *The Adventures of an Emigrant in Van Diemen's Land*: 24.
14. Curr, *An Account of the Colony of Van Diemen's Land*: 71–73.
15. Pamela Statham, *The Tanner Letters: A Pioneer Saga of Swan River & Tasmania, 1831–1845* (Nedlands, WA: University of Western Australia Press, 1981): 106–108.
16. John Broxup, *Life of John Broxup: Late Convict of Van Diemen's Land* (Hobart: Sullivans Cove, 1973): 12.
17. T. Jordan and M. Kaups, *The American Backwoods Frontier* (Baltimore, MD: John Hopkins University Press, 1989): 118.
18. *HRA* 3/1: 762.
19. Elizabeth Fenton, *The Journal of Mrs Fenton* (London: Edward Arnold, 1901): 381.
20. Alexander Pearce, *Confessions of Murder and Cannibalism*, ML A1326.
21. Evans, *A Geographical, Historical, and Topographical Description of Van Diemen's Land*: 54, 57.
22. Lempriere, *The Penal Settlements of Early Van Diemen's Land*: 62–63. This is presumably the vigorous climber now known as the Macquarie Vine (*Muehlenbeckia Gunnii*), which the Plants of Tasmania nursery at Ridgeway near Hobart recommends for its excellence in disguising chook sheds!
23. Jeffreys, *Van Diemen's Land*: 133.

24. Jetson, *The Roof of Tasmania*: 4–5.
25. William Breton, "Excursion to the Western Range, Tasmania," *Journal of Natural Science* vol. 2, 1846: 125, in T.E. Burns and J.R. Skemp, *Van Diemen's Land Correspondents 1827–1849: Letters from R.C. Gunn, R.W. Lawrence, Jorgen Jorgenson and Others to Sir William J. Hooker* (Launceston, Tas.: Queen Victoria Museum, 1961): 99.
26. Plomley, ed., *Friendly Mission*: 534.
27. *Hobart Town Gazette*, 26 September 1818.
28. William Williamson, letter, 16 December 1820, AOT NS 14/1/1.
29. William Barnes, letter, 5 May 1824; Brown, *The Narrative of George Russell*: 406–409.
30. Jeffreys, *Van Diemen's Land*: 133.
31. Wells, *Michael Howe*: 38.
32. Ross, *The Settler in Van Diemen's Land*: 107.
33. Burn, *A Picture of Van Diemen's Land*: 67.
34. Calder, *The Circumnavigation of Van Diemen's Land*: 21.
35. James Dixon, *Narrative of a Voyage to New South Wales, and Van Diemen's Land: In the Ship Skelton, During the Year 1820; with Observations on the State of These Colonies, and a Variety of Information, Calculated to Be Useful to Emigrants* (Hobart: Melanie Publications, 1984): 85.
36. Lempriere, *The Penal Settlements of Early Van Diemen's Land*: 54–55.
37. J. Crawford, W.F. Ellis and G.H. Stancombe, eds, *The Diaries of John Helder Wedge 1824–1835* (Hobart: Royal Society of Tasmania, 1962): 46.
38. G.F. James, ed., *A Homestead History*, cited in Henry Reynolds, "Australian Nationalism: Tasmanian Patriotism," *New Zealand Journal of History* 5, no. 1 (1971): 19.
39. Robson, *A History of Tasmania*, vol. 1: 14.
40. Wells, *Michael Howe*: 29.
41. Canteri, "The Origins of Australian Social Banditry": 358.
42. Diary of Adam Amos, 1822–1825, AOT NS 323/1.
43. McKay, *Journals of the Land Commissioners for Van Diemen's Land*: 6; Robson, *A History of Tasmania*, vol. 1: 197.
44. Plomley, ed., *Friendly Mission*: 206.
45. Plomley, ed., *Friendly Mission*: 200, 207.
46. Burn, *A Picture of Van Diemen's Land*: 112.
47. Jeffreys, *Van Diemen's Land*: 129.
48. For example, in the evening of 19 September 1830, Robinson recorded: "whilst my servant was erecting the huts or shelters, I sent Mutteellee and Peevay to endeavour to discover the tracks of the natives." But on a later mission Robinson records that "although I was without servants they [the Aborigines] scarcely would render me assistance in the construction of my hut." Plomley, ed., *Friendly Mission*: 214, 530.
49. Ross, *The Settler in Van Diemen's Land*: 58.
50. Jeffreys, *Van Diemen's Land*: 132–133.
51. Curr, *An Account of the Colony of Van Diemen's Land*: 105.
52. Ross, *The Settler in Van Diemen's Land*: 58–60.
53. Burn, *A Picture of Van Diemen's Land*: 112–113.
54. Jordan and Kaups, *The American Backwoods Frontier*: 35–37, 62, 165, 209.
55. *HRA* 3/3: 278–279, 324–326.
56. *HRA* 3/3: 323.
57. Peter Chapman, ed., *The Diaries and Letters of G.T.W.B. Boyes*, vol. 1, *1820–1832* (Melbourne: Oxford University Press, 1985): 267.
58. Curr, *An Account of the Colony of Van Diemen's Land*: 8–9.
59. George Thomas Lloyd, *Thirty-Three Years in Tasmania and Victoria* (London: Houlston and Wright, 1862): 8.

60. *HRA* 3/3: 278–279.

61. *HRA* 3/3: 278–279.

62. Macquarie, *Journals of His Tours in New South Wales and Van Diemen's Land, 1810–1822*: 59–60, 69.

63. Giblin, *The Early History of Tasmania*, vol. 2: 263.

64. Curr, *An Account of the Colony of Van Diemen's Land*: 42, 14–16.

65. Mary Morton Allport was the first female artist of note in Australia. Much of her work, including her portrayal of the family's early residences, can be found in the Allport Library and Museum of Fine Arts, which is part of the State Library of Tasmania.

66. The retrospective assessment that Van Diemonian architecture was "provincially British" reflects both the bias of those who recorded it and a practical reality: most of the early shelters have long since burnt down or rotted back into the earth, leaving the grander homes of the elite as the main architectural record. Clive Lucas, "The Architecture of Van Diemen's Land to 1850," in Gillian Winter, ed., *Tasmanian Insights: Essays in Honour of Geoffrey Thomas Stillwell* (Hobart: State Library of Tasmania, 1992): 127.

67. Cited in Morgan, *Land Settlement in Early Tasmania*: 53.

10. *Wine, Women and Song*

1. Westminster Archdiocese archives, cited in W.T. Southerwood, "New Light on the Foundation of Australian Catholicism," *Australasian Catholic Record* 61, no. 2 (1984): 165.

2. John Henderson, *Observations on the Colonies of New South Wales and Van Diemen's Land*, facsimile edition (Adelaide: Libraries Board of South Australia, 1965): 18.

3. Ross, *The Settler in Van Diemen's Land*: 29. Thornley, *The Adventures of an Emigrant in Van Diemen's Land*: 61. Meredith, *My Home in Tasmania*: 229.

4. Thompson, *Customs in Common*: 444–445.

5. West, *The History of Tasmania*: 38, 48.

6. Southerwood, "New Light on the Foundation of Australian Catholicism": 38.

7. Patrick O'Farrell, *The Catholic Church in Australia: A Short History 1788–1967* (London: Chapman, 1969): 10.

8. Robson, *A History of Tasmania*, vol. 1: 59.

9. Tipping, *Convicts Unbound*: 118.

10. Tipping, *Convicts Unbound*: 105–106. See also Alison Alexander, *Governors' Ladies: The Wives and Mistresses of Van Diemen's Land Governors* (Hobart: Tasmanian Historical Research Association, 1987).

11. Lloyd Robson, *The Tasmanian Story* (Melbourne: Oxford University Press, 1987): 8.

12. Thompson, *Customs in Common*: 28, 44, 54, 405. Divorce for the poor was not possible until 1857 in England, but the rich could go through ecclesiastical courts and the House of Lords.

13. John Pascoe Fawkner, *Reminiscences of Early Settlement at Port Phillips*, SLV: 366.

14. Robson, *The Tasmanian Story*: 6.

15. Kay Daniels, *Convict Women* (Sydney: Allen and Unwin, 1998): ix.

16. See the *Hobart Town Gazette*, 28 February 1818, 15 August 1818, 22 August 1818.

17. *Hobart Town Gazette*, 31 July 1819.

18. *Hobart Town Gazette*, 22 May 1819.

19. *Hobart Town Gazette*, 28 February 1818.

20. *Hobart Town Gazette*, 20 July and 27 July 1816.

21. Letter, 7 October 1824, in D.C. Shelton, ed., *The Parramore Letters* (Sydney: D. and C. Shelton, ed., 1993): 55.

22. Letter to Mrs Taylor, Rosedale, 8 June 1833, in *Reports on the Historical Manuscripts of Tasmania, Numbers 1–7* (Hobart: Department of History, University of Tasmania, 1964): 51–52.

23. West, *The History of Tasmania*: 510.
24. AOT CSO 1/82/1871, reproduced in FitzSymonds, *A Looking-Glass for Tasmania*: 35.
25. Commissioner Bigge learnt of the use of the iron collar on Alice Blackstone of George Town. Macquarie's subsequent inquiry into this incident found it to have been without legal sanction. Alex Castles, "The Van Diemonian Spirit and the Law," *THRA Papers and Proceedings* 38, nos. 3 and 4 (1991): 112.
26. Anne Bartlett, "The Launceston Female Factory," *THRA Papers and Proceedings* 41, no. 2 (June 1994): 116. See also Tony Raynor, *Female Factory Female Convicts: The Story of More than 13000 Women Exiled from Britain to Van Diemen's Land* (Dover, Tas.: Esperance Press, 2004): 69–74.
27. Castles, "The Van Diemonian Spirit and the Law": 112. Married women in Van Diemen's Land could be a party to legal actions, while English law said that their rights were essentially subsumed by their husbands'. At this time women even acted as legal agents, usually, but not only, for their spouses. This right then lapsed for a century or more.
28. Henderson, *Observations on the Colonies of New South Wales and Van Diemen's Land*: 19–21.
29. Castles, "The Van Diemonian Spirit and the Law": 113.
30. Samuel Guy, letter to Thomas Guy, 4 August 1823, AOT NS 381.
31. Lindy Scripps, "Women's Sites and Lives: Historical Research" (Hobart: Hobart City Council, 2000): 86–87.
32. *Hobart Town Gazette*, 2 January 1819.
33. Dianne Snowden, "Women and Work in Van Diemen's Land", BA Honours thesis, University of Tasmania, 1982: 1–30.
34. Tipping, *Convicts Unbound*: 114.
35. For a detailed and sympathetic account of Maria Lord, see Daniels, *Convict Women*.
36. Harris to Paterson, 14 February 1809, in Hamilton-Arnold, ed., *Letters and Papers of G.P. Harris*: 111–112.
37. William Williamson, letter, 16 December 1820, AOT NS 14/1/1.
38. Patricia Clarke and Dale Spender, *Life Line: Australian Women's Letters and Diaries 1788–1840* (Sydney: Allen and Unwin, 1992): 152.
39. Shelton, ed., *The Parramore Letters*: 61. Emphasis original.
40. From March 1804 to the end of 1819, Knopwood christened 685 children, of whom 524 had married parents. Von Stieglitz, *The Story of the Pioneer Church in Van Diemen's Land*: 36. John Youl, appointed as Port Dalrymple chaplain in 1819, christened 67 children and married 41 couples on his first visit to Launceston. *Hobart Town Gazette*, 6 February 1819.
41. Pearce, *Confessions of Murder and Cannibalism*, ML A1326.
42. For example, one settler, William Allison, had a notebook which contained lists of herbal treatments and sacred charms. AOT NS 261/1.
43. The Tasmanian Devil was termed the "Devil" from the commencement of British settlement, and, as today, was heard far more often than it was seen.
44. Robson, for example, wrote of Van Diemen's Land as a "virtually pagan population, which in some areas had lost count of which day was the Sabbath." Robson, *A History of Tasmania*, vol. 1: 122.
45. Hamilton-Arnold, ed., *Letters and Papers of G.P. Harris*: 59–60.
46. F. Gray, "Music of the Early Settlements of the 1800s," *THRA Papers and Proceedings* 43, no. 2 (1996): 62.
47. Daniels, *Convict Women*: 153.
48. Daniels, *Convict Women*: 264; Phillip Tardif, *Notorious Strumpets and Dangerous Girls: Convict Women in Van Diemen's Land, 1803–1829* (Sydney: Angus & Robertson, 1990): 27, 1024.
49. Journal of Mrs Nixon, 30 September 1844, in Anna Nixon and Norah Nixon, *The Pioneer*

Bishop in Van Diemen's Land, 1843–1863: Letters and Memories of Francis Russell Nixon, D.D., First Bishop of Tasmania: 32–33.

50. Gray, "Music of the Early Settlements of the 1800s": 61.
51. Jorgenson to Anstey 29 July 1829, AOT CSO1/320/7578, cited in Bronwyn Desailly, "The Mechanics of Genocide: Colonial Policies and Attitudes Towards the Tasmanian Aborigines 1824–1836," MA thesis, University of Tasmania, 1977: 41.
52. Gray, "Music of the Early Settlements of the 1800s": 61–62.
53. West, *The History of Tasmania*: 425.
54. McKay, *Journals of the Land Commissioners for Van Diemen's Land*: 62.
55. West, *The History of Tasmania*: 357.
56. Burn, *A Picture of Van Diemen's Land*: 97. The land commissioners had also noted that the "River Styx or Sticks" was "so called by the bushrangers on account of the immensely long spars to be found on its banks." McKay, *Journals of the Commissioners for Van Diemen's Land*: 38.
57. *HRA* 3/3: 952.
58. Macquarie, *Journals of His Tours in New South Wales and Van Diemen's Land*: 64.
59. McKay, *Journals of the Land Commissioners for Van Diemen's Land*: 74.
60. *HRA* 3/3: 321.
61. Curr, *An Account of the Colony of Van Diemen's Land*: 19–20.
62. McKay, *Journals of the Land Commissioners for Van Diemen's Land*: 47.
63. William Denison, *Varieties of Vice Regal Life*, vol. 1 (London: Longmans, Green and Co., 1870): 29.
64. West, *The History of Tasmania*: 59.

PART III

11. *The Coming of Little England*

1. Evans, *A Geographical, Historical, and Topographical Description of Van Diemen's Land*: 28.
2. Evans, *A Geographical, Historical, and Topogrpahical Description of Van Diemen's Land*: 26.
3. Henry Melville, *The History of Van Diemen's Land from the Year 1824 to 1835 Inclusive*, facsimile edition (Sydney: Hortivity Publications, 1965): 19.
4. West, *The History of Tasmania*: 515.
5. James Fenton, *A History of Tasmania from its Discovery in 1642 to the Present Time* (Hobart: J. Walch & Sons, 1884): 51–52.
6. William Williamson, letter, 16 December 1820, AOT NS 14/1/1; Samuel Guy, letter to Thomas Guy, 4 August 1823, AOT NS 381; Shelton, ed., *The Parramore Letters*: 19.
7. Morgan, *Land Settlement in Early Tasmania*: 22.
8. Curr, *An Account of the Colony of Van Diemen's Land*: 27.
9. Macquarie to Lord Bathurst, 22 February 1820, in Clark, *Select Documents in Australian History*: 310.
10. Robson, *A History of Tasmania*, vol. 1: 199.
11. Fenton, *A History of Tasmania from Its Discovery in 1642 to the Present Time*: 52.
12. E. Frank Lawrence, *1823 – Before and After: A Story of William Effingham Lawrence, Tasmanian Pioneer and His Family* (Melbourne: The National Press, 1973): 23–26.
13. J. Montagu, *Statistical Returns of Van Diemen's Land 1824–1836* (Hobart Town: James Ross, 1836): no page numbers.
14. *Sydney Gazette*, 21 July 1821.
15. Letter, 7 August 1827, *Lieutenant Governor: Letters and Miscellaneous Papers Passing Direct to Lieutenant Governor 1821–1837*, AOT GO 39.
16. Bathurst to Darling, 2 April 1827, *Lieutenant Governor: Letters and Miscellaneous Papers Passing Direct to Lieutenant Governor 1821–1837*, AOT GO 39.

17. Curr, *An Account of the Colony of Van Diemen's Land*: 114–115.
18. Letter, 15 March 1824, in Brown, *The Narrative of George Russell*: 402–406.
19. George Hobler, *The Diaries of Pioneer George Hobler, October 6 1800–December 13 1882* (n.p. [California]: C & H Reproductions, 1992), diary entry, 18 May 1831; W.G. McMinn, "A Pioneer Who Failed," *THRA Papers and Proceedings* 13, no. 1 (1965): 22.
20. McKay, *Journals of the Land Commissioners for Van Diemen's Land*: vi.
21. Robson, *A History of Tasmania*, vol. 1: 199.
22. Jack Richards, "Fifteen Tasmanian Letters 1824–1852" (Unpublished manuscript accessible at the State Library of Tasmania): no page numbers.
23. Williamson, letter, AOT NS 14/1/1.
24. Report, June 1828, *Lieutenant Governor: Letters and Miscellaneous Papers Passing Direct to Lieutenant Governor 1821–1837*, AOT GO 39.
25. Chapman, ed., *The Diaries and Letters of G.T.W.B. Boyes*, vol. 1: 464.
26. Levy, *Governor George Arthur*: 269.
27. McKay, *Journals of the Land Commissioners for Van Diemen's Land*: v.
28. Robson, *A History of Tasmania*, vol. 1: 198.
29. John Molony, *The Native Born: The First White Australians* (Melbourne: Melbourne University Press, 2000): 45.
30. Robson, *A History of Tasmania*, vol. 1: 204.
31. On 1 January 1825, Bathurst instructed New South Wales and Van Diemen's Land to institute a comprehensive survey and valuation of alienated and crown lands. Because the Ripon regulations had been announced by the time their report was completed, the policy impact of the commissioners' work was minimal, but their now published journals remain a valuable historical document. See McKay, *Journals of the Land Commissioners for Van Diemen's Land*: 8.
32. McKay, *Journals of the Land Commissioners for Van Diemen's Land*: xxi, 81.
33. McKay, *Journals of the Land Commissioners for Van Diemen's Land*: 99.
34. McKay, *Journals of the Land Commissioners for Van Diemen's Land*: xxiii–xxv.
35. Ross, *The Settler in Van Diemen's Land*: 33–34.
36. Curr, *An Account of the Colony of Van Diemen's Land*: 62. Curr was writing here specifically of land "beyond the eastern tier," but it is equally pertinent to all accessible well-watered grassland regions.
37. *Hobart Town Gazette*, 10 October 1818.
38. Ross to R. Barker, 10 January 1818, *HRA* 3/4: 850.
39. Fitzsymonds, *Mortmain*: 159–160; AOT CSO 1/287/6834.
40. Fitzsymonds, *Mortmain*: 159–160; AOT CSO 1/287/6834.
41. McKay, *Journals of the Land Commissioners for Van Diemen's Land*: 98.
42. Perkin, *The Origins of Modern English Society 1780–1880*: 125–126.
43. Ross, *The Settler in Van Diemen's Land*: 21.
44. Curr, *An Account of the Colony of Van Diemen's Land*: 103.
45. Ross, *The Settler in Van Diemen's Land*: 29–30. Ross's first sight of these vacant pastures along the Shannon River included a "large herd of fine cattle."
46. Lois Nyman, *The East Coasters: The Early Pioneering History of the East Coast of Tasmania* (Launceston, Tas.: Regal Publications, 1990): 12–13.
47. Margaret Kiddle, "Vandiemonian Colonists in Port Phillip 1834–1850," *THRA Papers and Proceedings* 3, no. 3 (1954): 38.
48. Clarke and Spender, *Life Line*: 150.
49. Chapman, ed., *The Diaries and Letters of G.T.W.B. Boyes*: 355.
50. William Barnes, letter, 15 March 1824 in Brown, *The Narrative of George Russell*: 402–406; Evans, *A Geographical, Historical, and Topographical Description of Van Diemen's Land*: 74.
51. Giblin, *The Early History of Tasmania*, vol. 2: 306.

52. Ross, *The Settler in Van Diemen's Land*: 12–13.
53. Fenton, *The Journal of Mrs Fenton*: 351.
54. Samuel Guy, letter to Thomas Guy, 4 August 1823, AOT NS 381.
55. Fenton, *The Journal of Mrs Fenton*: 361.
56. Ross, *The Settler in Van Diemen's Land*: 24.
57. McKay, *Journals of the Land Commissioners for Van Diemen's Land*: appendix A, 105.
58. Williamson, letter, AOT NS 14/1/1.
59. Roe, "Mary Leman Grimstone: For Women's Rights and Tasmanian Patriotism": 28.
60. Fenton, *The Journal of Mrs Fenton*: 90, 388.
61. Curr, *An Account of the Colony of Van Diemen's Land*: 34–35.
62. According to Terry Newman's comprehensive coverage of this question, the map-making firm of Laurie and Whittle of London provided the first known use of "Tasmania" in their 1808 atlas. Terry Newman, *Becoming Tasmania: Renaming Van Diemen's Land* (Hobart: Parliament of Tasmania, 2005): 5–6.
63. Jeffreys noted that "Van Diemen's Land, or Tasmania, is an island of considerable extent." Jeffreys, *Van Diemen's Land*: 1.
64. See Newman, *Becoming Tasmania*: 37–54.
65. Giblin, *The Early History of Tasmania*, vol. 2: 528.
66. Melville, *The History of Van Diemen's Land from the Year 1824 to 1835 Inclusive*: 14–15.
67. Joan Woodberry, "Andrew Bent and the Proprietorship of the Hobart Town Gazette: An Examination of Some New Letters," *THRA Papers and Proceedings* 14, no. 2 (1967): 59.
68. FitzSymonds, *A Looking-Glass for Tasmania*: 172.
69. Martin Cash, *The Bushranger of Van Diemen's Land: 1843–44* (Hobart: J. Walch and Sons, 1929): 106.
70. Burn, *A Picture of Van Diemen's Land*: 28–29.
71. Chapman, ed., *The Diaries and Letters of G.T.W.B. Boyes*, vol. 1: 395.
72. Fenton, *The Journal of Mrs Fenton*: 344.
73. Letter, 22 July 1827, Meredith papers, AOT NSA 123/1.
74. Sharon Morgan, "George and Mary Meredith: The Role of the Colonial Wife," *THRA Papers and Proceedings* 36, no. 3 (1989): 126.
75. Shelton, ed., *The Parramore Letters*: 58.
76. Hamilton Wallace wrote to his father in 1825 from Launceston: "Certainly the soil is very good and the climate I really think the best in the world, but for society-comfort or happiness you cannot have it." Richards, "Fifteen Tasmanian Letters": no page numbers.
77. Curr, *An Account of the Colony of Van Diemen's Land*: 34–35.
78. Curr, *An Account of the Colony of Van Diemen's Land*: 60.
79. Chapman, ed., *The Diaries and Letters of G.T.W.B. Boyes*, vol. 1: 291.
80. Gillian Winter, "Under My Own Immediate Observation: Jane Roberts' Visit to Hobart Town in 1830," *THRA Papers and Proceedings* 48, no. 3A (2001): 189.
81. Levy, *Governor George Arthur*: 249.

12. Controlling the Convicts

1. For a comprehensive review of Sorell's tenure as lieutenant governor, see Leonie Mickleborough, *William Sorell in Van Diemen's Land 1817–24: A Golden Age?* (Hobart: Blubber Head Press, 2004).
2. Given in full as Appendix 1 in Curr, *An Account of the Colony of Van Diemen's Land*: 153–161.
3. Curr, *An Account of the Colony of Van Diemen's Land*: 154–155.
4. Arthur to Bathurst, 7 January 1827, HRA 3/5: 480.
5. Arthur to Bathurst, 11 August 1825, HRA 3/4: 318–319.
6. Arthur to Bathurst, 23 March 1827, HRA 3/5: 621.

7. Robson, *A History of Tasmania*, vol. 1: 140.
8. Arthur to Bathurst, 15 August 1824, *HRA* 3/4.
9. Arthur to Horton, 14 September 1825, *HRA* 3/4: 366–371.
10. Arthur to Bathurst, 23 March 1827, *HRA* 3/5: 624.
11. Arthur to Bathurst, 7 January 1827, *HRA* 3/5: 480.
12. FitzSymonds, *A Looking-Glass for Tasmania*: 115.
13. K.R. Von Stieglitz, *Mathew Brady: Van Diemen's Land Bushranger* (Hobart: Fullers Bookshop, 1964): 4–10.
14. *Hobart Town Gazette*, 14 October 1826.
15. Connolly to Bishop Poynter in London, 19 April 1826, cited in Southerwood, "New Light on the Foundation of Australian Catholicism": 171.
16. Meredith to Kerr, 25 October 1825, Meredith papers AOT NS 123/15.
17. Kerr to Meredith, 23 October 1825, Meredith papers, AOT NS 123/1.
18. Richards, "Fifteen Tasmanian Letters": no page numbers.
19. Clarke and Spender, *Life Line*: 139.
20. Nyman, *The East Coasters*: 59–60.
21. Robson, *A History of Tasmania*, vol. 1: 144.
22. Arthur to Bathurst, 21 June 1826, *HRA* 3/5: 294.
23. Ross, *The Settler in Van Diemen's Land*: 6.
24. Castles, "The Van Diemonian Spirit and the Law": 114.
25. Fitzsymonds, *Mortmain*: 125.
26. Maxwell-Stewart, "The Bushrangers and the Convict System of Van Diemen's Land": 99–100.
27. Hobler, *The Diaries of Pioneer George Hobler*: 10.
28. Chapman, ed., *The Diaries and Letters of G.T.W.B. Boyes*, vol. 1: 486.
29. Letter, 31 August 1826, Meredith papers, AOT, NSA 123/1. The identity of the sender is not clear.
30. Chapman, ed., *The Diaries and Letters of G.T.W.B. Boyes*, vol. 1: 486–487.
31. Chapman, ed., *The Diaries and Letters of G.T.W.B. Boyes*, vol. 1: 486.
32. Chapman, ed., *The Diaries and Letters of G.T.W.B. Boyes*, vol. 1: 486.
33. W.D. Forsyth, *Governor Arthur's Convict System, Van Diemen's Land 1824–36: A Study in Colonization* (London: Longmans Green for the Royal Empire Society, 1935): 95.
34. Rayner, *Female Factory Female Convicts*.
35. Arthur to Bathurst, 21 June 1826, *HRA* 3/5: 294.
36. AOT CSO 1/73/1559; Fitzsymonds, *Mortmain*: 28.
37. Arthur to Goderich, 2 November 1827, *HRA* 3/6: 316–318.
38. Executive council minutes, AOT EC 4/1,2.
39. Precisely because Port Arthur is so well known and studied, this aspect of the convict experience is not considered in detail in this book.
40. Arthur to Bathurst, 24 March 1827, *HRA* 3/6: 691–706.
41. Stefan Petrow, "After Arthur: Policing in Van Diemen's Land 1837–46" in Mike Enders and Benoit Dupont, eds, *Policing the Lucky Country* (Sydney: Hawkins Press, 2001): 176.
42. Arthur to Bathurst, 15 August 1824, *HRA* 3/4: 161–163.
43. Robson, *A History of Tasmania*, vol. 1: 160.

13. Imposing Dependence

1. B.A. Holderness, *Pre-Industrial England* (London: J.M. Dent, 1976): 50.
2. Perkin, *The Origins of Modern English Society 1780–1880*: 37.
3. Winter, "Under My Own Immediate Observation": 187–188.
4. Richard Dillingham, letter, 29 September 1836, AOT NS 157/1.
5. Letter, 11 August 1829 in Clarke and Dale, *Life Line*: 154–155.

6. Levy, *Governor George Arthur*: 163.
7. Thompson, *The Making of the English Working Class*: 61.
8. Patrick O'Farrell, *The Irish in Australia* (Sydney: University of New South Wales, 2000): 53.
9. Letter, August 1854, AOT NS 157/2.
10. R.D. Pretyman, *A Chronicle of Methodism in Van Diemen's Land: 1820–1840* (Melbourne: Aldersgate Press, 1970): 8, 11.
11. Shelton, ed., *The Parramore Letters*: 53–54.
12. Robson, *A History of Tasmania*, vol. 1: 184.
13. Fitzsymonds, *Mortmain*: 200.
14. Shelton, ed., *The Parramore Letters*: 53.
15. Robson, *A History of Tasmania*, vol. 1: 121.
16, Woodberry, "Andrew Bent and the Proprietorship of the *Hobart Town Gazette*": 50.
17. Shelton, ed., *The Parramore Letters*: 65.
18. *Colonial Times,* 13 February 1829, cited in Hartwell, *The Economic Development of Van Diemen's Land*: 86–87.
19. McKay, *Journals of the Land Commissioners for Van Diemen's Land*: 63–64.
20. Castles, "The Van Diemonian Spirit and the Law": 110–111.
21. McKay, *Journals of the Land Commissioners for Van Diemen's Land*: 84.
22. Burn, *A Picture of Van Diemen's Land*: 109.
23. *Hobart Town Gazette*, 30 September 1826, 24 October 1827, 23 June 1828.
24. Levy, *Governor George Arthur*: 271.
25. Joan Brown, *Poverty Is Not a Crime* (Hobart: Tasmanian Historical Research Association, 1972): 11–14.
26. AOT CSO 1/789/16844 in Fitzsymonds, *Mortmain*: 160.
27. FitzSymonds, *A Looking-Glass for Tasmania*: 228–229.
28. Joyce Purtscher, "Children in Queens Orphanage Hobart Town 1828–1863," Kings and Queens Orphan Schools records, AOT SWD 28.
29. Burn, *A Picture of Van Diemen's Land*: 31.
30. Kings and Queens Orphan Schools records AOT SWD 24.
31. Joyce Purtscher, "Children in Queens Orphanage Hobart Town 1828–1863," Kings and Queens Orphan Schools records, AOT SWD 28.

14. *Fighting the Aborigines*

1. Melville, *The History of Van Diemen's Land from the Year 1824 to 1835 Inclusive*: 30.
2. This terminology was, as James Calder pointed out, appropriate "enough in every sense." James Erskine Calder, *Recollections of Sir John and Lady Jane Franklin in Tasmania* (Adelaide: Sullivan's Cove, 1984): 24.
3. Shelton, ed., *The Parramore Letters*: 60–61.
4. Shelton, ed., *The Parramore Letters*: 61.
5. Mansfield to the Wesleyan Missionary Society, 30 June 1825, Bonwick Missionary Transcript BT53, ML, cited in Desailly, "The Mechanics of Genocide": 25.
6. Reported in the *Tasmanian*, 12 and 19 January 1825, cited in N.J.B Plomley, ed., *Weep in Silence: A History of the Flinders Island Aboriginal Settlement* (Hobart: Blubber Head Press, 1987): 5.
7. Giblin, *The Early History of Tasmania*, vol. 2: 507.
8. Ian McFarlane, "Aboriginal Society in North West Tasmania," PhD thesis, University of Tasmania, 2002: 130.
9. Diary of J.C. Sutherland, AOT NP 61/1–3.
10. Diary of Adam Amos, 1822–1825, AOT NS 323/1.
11. Diary of Adam Amos, 1822–1825, AOT NS 323/1.
12. Diary of Adam Amos, 1822–1825, AOT NS 323/1.

13. FitzSymonds, *A Looking-Glass for Tasmania*: 35.
14. The first Supreme Court trial in Van Diemen's Land related to the killing of a "black man." In *The Fabrication of Aboriginal History*, Keith Windschuttle wrongly assumes this man was an Aborigine.
15. Arthur to Bathurst, 15 August 1824, *HRA* 3/4.
16. Jack Richards, "Fifteen Tasmanian Letters."
17. *Colonial Times*, 5 May 1826.
18. *Colonial Times*, 2 June 1826.
19. Henry Reynolds, *Fate of a Free People: A Radical Re-examination of the Tasmanian War* (Melbourne: Penguin, 1995): 94.
20. *Colonial Times*, 15 December 1826.
21. N.J.B. Plomley *et al.*, *The Aboriginal/Settler Clash in Van Diemen's Land, 1803–1831* (Launceston, Tas.: Queen Victoria Museum and Art Gallery in association with the Centre for Tasmanian Historical Studies, 1992): 26.
22. AOT CSO 1/316/7578, cited in Desailly, "The Mechanics of Genocide": 38–39.
23. O'Connor to Parramore, 11 December 1827 AOT, CSO 1/323/7578 in Desailly, "The Mechanics of Genocide": 58.
24. Anstey to Parramore, 26 November 1827, Arthur papers, ML, cited in Plomley, ed., *Friendly Mission*: 43.
25. Plomley *et al.*, *The Aboriginal/Settler Clash in Van Diemen's Land*: 26–27.
26. *Hobart Town Courier*, 18 October 1828.
27. AOT CSO 1/316/7578, cited in Desailly, "The Mechanics of Genocide": 39.
28. *Colonial Times*, 1 December 1826, emphasis original.
29. Plomley, ed., *Friendly Mission*: 283, 306. Robert arrived at Flinders Island, to live with a people he hardly knew, on 1 January 1831.
30. Lois Nyman, *The East Coasters*: 36, 91.
31. Shayne Breen, *Contested Places: Tasmania's Northern Districts from Ancient Times to 1900* (Hobart: Centre for Tasmanian Historical Studies, 2001): 25.
32. Crawford *et al.*, *The Diaries of John Helder Wedge 1824–1835*: 219.
33. Hoping to boost settler morale in the face of vigorous Aboriginal resistance, the government published an account of Briggs' efforts, praising "the successful resistance of a SINGLE FEMALE to their attacks." FitzSymonds, *A Looking-Glass for Tasmania*: 199–200. Government notice of 22 September 1831, published in the *Hobart Town Gazette* on 24 September 1831 (emphasis original).
34. J.D. Harte to Arthur, 28 March 1828, AOT CSO 1/316.
35. Hobbs to Anstey, 20 May 1830, AOT CSO 1/315.
36. AOT CSO 1/359/7578.
37. Aborigine Committee minutes of evidence, 23 February 1830, AOT CBE/1.
38. Petition of 27 February 1830, AOT CSO 1/316/7578.
39. *Tasmanian*, 26 February 1830, cited in Desailly, "The Mechanics of Genocide": 43.
40. See John McMahon, "The British Army: Its Role in the Counter Insurgency in the Black War in Van Diemen's Land," *Tasmanian Historical Studies* 5, no. 1 (1995–96): 58–59.
41. Plomley, ed., *Friendly Mission*: 552–553.
42. A comprehensive tally of the documented incidents between Aborigines and settlers is provided in H.A. Wills, *A Tally of Those Killed During the Fighting between Aborigines and Settlers in Van Diemen's Land 1803–34*, at: <www.historians.org.au/discus>, published 2002, viewed August 2003.
43. *Van Diemen's Land: Copies of All Correspondence*: 54–55.
44. Richards, "Fifteen Tasmanian Letters."
45. G. Dow and H. Dow, *Landfall in Van Diemen's Land: The Steels' Quest for Greener Pastures* (Melbourne: Footprint, 1990): 45.

46. Hobler, *The Diaries of Pioneer George Hobler*.
47. Plomley, ed., *Friendly Mission*: 219; AOT CSO 28.
48. Plomley, ed., *Friendly Mission*: 218.
49. For example, Plomley, ed., *Friendly Mission*: 197–198, 503.
50. *Van Diemen's Land: Copies of All Correspondence*: 49.
51. "Statement of proceedings of an armed party of nine soldiers, two constables and John Danvers, guide, in pursuit of the Aborigines 9 December 1828," AOT CSO 1/319, correspondence file 7578, 320.
52. *Hobart Town Courier*, 13 December 1828. This incident also highlights how much research remains to be done on even the comparatively well-studied CSO records. This official report of the killing of ten Aborigines has never previously been documented. Windschuttle, who reported the *Hobart Town Courier* coverage of this incident, was also unaware of the official report. Windschuttle, *The Fabrication of Aboriginal History*: 160–162.
53. AOT CSO 1/319, correspondence file 7578, 353.
54. AOT CSO 1/320/7578.
55. Batman to Anstey, 7 September 1829, AOT, CSO1/320/7578, cited in A.H. Campbell, *John Batman and the Aborigines* (Melbourne: Kibble Books, 1987): 31–32.
56. Rolepana remained with Batman until Batman's death in Melbourne in 1839.
57. Campbell, *John Batman and the Aborigines*: 32. Keith Windschuttle's treatment of this encounter – reducing it to two deaths, sanitising the quote and omitting to mention Batman's estimate of the carnage in text or footnote – provides a telling expression of the distortions created by his methodology. Because Batman only saw two dead bodies, Windschuttle puts the figure at two dead, without reference or acknowledgment of Batman's much greater personal estimate of the number of Aborigines killed. Windschuttle, *The Fabrication of Aboriginal History*: 156–157.
58. McFarlane, "Aboriginal Society in North West Tasmania": 91.
59. McFarlane, "Aboriginal Society in North West Tasmania": vii.
60. Ida Lee, ed., *The Voyage of the Caroline from England to Van Diemen's Land and Batavia in 1827-28* (London, New York: Longmans, 1927): 40–41.
61. McFarlane, "Aboriginal Society in North West Tasmania": 104. See also McFarlane's chapter in Manne, ed., *Whitewash*.
62. Lee, *The Voyage of the Caroline from England to Van Diemen's Land and Batavia in 1827-28*: 181.
63. McFarlane, "Aboriginal Society in North West Tasmania": 91.
64. McFarlane, "Aboriginal Society in North West Tasmania": 106–107.
65. McFarlane, "Aboriginal Society in North West Tasmania": 105.
66. McFarlane, "Aboriginal Society in North West Tasmania": 109–110.
67. McFarlane, "Aboriginal Society in North West Tasmania": 126–127.
68. McFarlane, "Aboriginal Society in North West Tasmania": 121–123.
69. McFarlane, "Aboriginal Society in North West Tasmania": 125.
70. McFarlane, "Aboriginal Society in North West Tasmania": 139.
71. John Molony's evidence to support his claim that the native-born in New South Wales as early as 1806 "were conjoined to the Aborigines" and that the majority "treated the Aborigines as fellow Australians" is not convincing. Molony's book does not consider Van Diemen's Land, but there seems little evidence for its ambitious claim even in relation to New South Wales. Molony, *The Native Born*: 10–11.
72. Thornley, *The Adventures of an Emigrant in Van Diemen's Land*. The battle scenes involving Aborigines and bushrangers in an alliance against the settlers are pure fiction.
73. Government notice, 18 October 1831, published in the *Hobart Town Gazette*, 23 October 1831.

74. Robert Paddle, *The Last Tasmanian Tiger: The History and Extinction of the Thylacine* (Cambridge: Cambridge University Press, 2000): 115.

75. The lieutenant governor responded by diverting one of Robinson's conciliation missions to kill the wild dogs that had multiplied in the Eastern Tiers. Executive council minutes, 18 October 1833, AOT EC 4/3, 4.

76. Fenton, *Bush Life in Tasmania Fifty Years Ago*: 113.

77. Denison, *Varieties of Vice Regal Life*, vol. 1: 29.

78. Mary Nicholls, ed., *Traveller under Concern: The Quaker Journals of Frederick Mackie on His Tour of the Australasian Colonies 1852–1855* (Hobart: University of Tasmania, 1973): 173–175.

79. Roger McNeice, "Bushfires," in Alison Alexander, ed., *The Companion to Tasmanian History* (Hobart: Centre for Tasmanian Historical Studies, University of Tasmania, 2005): 59.

80. Robinson, for example, did not see or taste emu until he was in the north-east. In December 1830 he saw three, the first he had seen. On 13 September 1831 he found it to be "very tender and pleasant." Plomley, ed., *Friendly Mission*: 288, 425.

81. Hooker was a friend of Charles Darwin, and later became the director of Kew Gardens and the compiler of the four volume *Flora Tasmaniae*. This eminent reference work was published by the British Admiralty in 1860 with the financial assistance of the Tasmanian government.

82. Burns and Skemp, *Van Diemen's Land Correspondents 1827–1849*: v, 59.

83. Meredith, *My Home in Tasmania*: 76.

84. Neil Barr, *Greening a Brown Land: The Australian Search for Sustainable Land Use* (Melbourne: Macmillan, 1992): 13–14.

85. Morgan, *Land Settlement in Early Tasmania*: 112.

86. Plomley, ed., *Friendly Mission*: 501.

87. Plomley, ed., *Friendly Mission*: 596.

88. Philip L. Brown, ed., *Clyde Company Papers* (London: Oxford University Press, 1941): 33.

89. Nixon, *The Pioneer Bishop in Van Diemen's Land*: 34.

90. Plomley, ed., *Friendly Mission*: 596.

91. Nixon, *The Pioneer Bishop in Van Diemen's Land*: 34.

92. Lloyd, *Thirty-Three Years in Tasmania and Victoria*: 48. See also the *Hobart Town Courier*, 24 September 1831.

PART IV

15. *The Triumph of Little England*

1. Dow and Dow, *Landfall in Van Diemen's Land*: 83. Emphasis original.

2. Burn, *A Picture of Van Diemen's Land*: 118.

3. Statham, *The Tanner Letters*: 79, 82–83, 103.

4. Robson, *A History of Tasmania*, vol. 1: 360.

5. Brown, *Clyde Company Papers*: 31–33.

6. Denison, *Varieties of Vice Regal Life*, vol. 1: 20.

7. R.F. Malone, *Three Years Cruise in the Australasian Colonies* (1854), in Clark, *Select Documents in Australian History*: 424.

8. SLV MS 8520, box 991/5.

9. Meredith, *My Home in Tasmania*: 331.

10. Andrew Rozefelds, "Acclimatisation of Plants," in Alexander, ed., *The Companion to Tasmanian History*: 8.

11. Michael Steele, letter, 1826: AOT NP 41.

12. *Hobart Town Gazette*, 7 April 1821. Fenton, *Bush Life in Tasmania Fifty Years Ago*: 72. Meredith, *My Home in Tasmania*: 337.

13. Meredith described the now endangered Tasmanian species of the wedge-tailed eagle as a "noble bird" that "never molested any of our livestock," but noted that the "prejudice here is very strong against him." Meredith, *My Home in Tasmania*: 304–305.

14. Nicholls, ed., *Traveller under Concern*: 37, 39.

15. Barr, *Greening a Brown Land*: 13–14.

16. Fenton, *Bush Life in Tasmania Fifty Years Ago*: 108, 19.

17. Meredith, *My Home in Tasmania*: 17–18, 75, 208.

18. The *Hobart Town Gazette* reported on 30 November 1816 that "a very large number of rats have lately made their appearance."

19. Nicholls, ed., *Traveller under Concern*: 52–53.

20. Meredith, *My Home in Tasmania*: 118–119, 327–328.

21. Burn, *A Picture of Van Diemen's Land*: 41, 127.

22. Denison, *Varieties of Vice Regal Life*: 15–16.

23. Meredith, *My Home in Tasmania*: 35.

24. Petrow, "After Arthur: Policing in Van Diemen's Land 1837–46" in Enders and Dupont, eds, *Policing the Lucky Country*: 182, 185–186.

25. Denison, *Varieties of Vice Regal Life*: 15–16.

26. Mortlock, *Experiences of a Convict: Transported for 21 Years* (Sydney: Sydney University Press, 1966): 90.

27. *Statistics of Van Diemen's Land 1838–1841*: 20–21.

28. *Statistics of Van Diemen's Land 1838–1841*: 20–21.

29. Bonyhady, *The Colonial Earth*: 134–135. See also the *Hobart Town Courier*, 14 July 1846.

30. According to William Gates, who was granted a ticket of leave in February 1842, "the prisoner, or ticket of leave man, was not allowed to kindle even the slightest fire." Ian Brand, *The Convict Probation System: Van Diemen's Land, 1839–1854* (Hobart: Blubber Head Press, 1990): 61.

31. Breen, *Contested Places*: 120–122.

32. Gould is better known now than he was in his own lifetime, having been famously portrayed in Richard Flanagan's prize-winning novel *Gould's Book of Fish* (Sydney: Pan Macmillan, 2001).

33. Fitzsymonds, *Mortmain*: 142–143.

34. Brown, *Poverty is Not a Crime*: 33–36.

35. Fitzsymonds, *Mortmain*: 33–36.

36. Denison's comment on the petition was straightforward: "refused of course." Fitzsymonds, *Mortmain*: 139–140.

37. David Young, *Sporting Island: A History of Sport and Recreation in Tasmania* (Hobart: Sport and Recreation Tasmania, 2005): 18.

38. West, *The History of Tasmania*: 506.

39. Fenton, *Bush Life in Tasmania Fifty Years Ago*: 72. Meredith, *My Home in Tasmania*: 74.

16. The Survival of Van Diemen's Land

1. Anthony Trollope, *Australia* (St Lucia, Qld: University of Queensland Press, 1967): 530.

2. Meredith, *My Home in Tasmania*: 163, 166–167, 178–180, 208.

3. Mortlock, *Experiences of a Convict*: 85–86.

4. George Rude, *Protest and Punishment* (Melbourne: Oxford University Press, 1978): 9.

5. The raw figures can be found in Clark, *Select Documents in Australian History*: 215.

6. In 1843 there were only 24 free immigrants recorded as having arrived from Britain, and the next year only a solitary individual.

7. Molony, *The Native Born*: 159.

8. Huon, "By Moral Means Only: The Origins of the Launceston Anti-Transportation League 1847–49," *THRA Papers and Proceedings* 44, no.2 (1997): 92.

9. Richard Davis, "'Not So Bad as a Bad Marriage': Irish Transportation Policies in the 1840s," *THRA Papers and Proceedings* 47, no. 1 (2000): 10. John Williams, "Irish Convicts and Van Diemen's Land," *THRA Papers and Proceedings* 19, no. 3 (1972): 101–103.

10. Richard Davis and Stefan Petrow, eds, *Ireland and Tasmania 1848: Sesquicentenary Papers* (Sydney: Crossing Press, 1998): 38.

11. Davis and Petrow, *Ireland and Tasmania 1848*: 103, 108.

12. S.J. Connolly, *Priests and People in Pre-Famine Ireland 1780–1845* (New York: Gill and Macmillan, 1982): 88.

13. Connolly, *Priests and People in Pre-Famine Ireland*: 91–97.

14. Williams, "Irish Convicts and Van Diemen's Land": 104.

15. Thompson, *Customs in Common*: 396.

16. Davis, "'Not So Bad as a Bad Marriage': Irish Transportation Policies in the 1840s": 24.

17. Williams, "Irish Convicts and Van Diemen's Land": 105. The Comptroller-General of Convicts, J.S. Hampton, also complained that Irish women's "utter ignorance of every species of useful household labour … unfits them for domestic service." Davis, "'Not So Bad as a Bad Marriage': Irish Transportation Policies in the 1840s": 25.

18. Williams, "'Not So Bad as a Bad Marriage': Irish Transportation Policies in the 1840s": 64.

19. In 1841 nearly a million families in Ireland were supported by 820,000 land holdings (overwhelmingly tenancies), with 45 per cent of these between one and five acres only, and only 7 per cent bigger than 30 acres.

20. Of the 12,460 convict women who came to Van Diemen's Land (over half of all the convict women transported to Australia before 1853), 8673 did so from 1841 to 1853. Tardif, *Notorious Strumpets and Dangerous Girls*: 1.

21. Tardif, *Notorious Strumpets and Dangerous Girls*: 23.

22. Meredith, *My Home in Tasmania*: 318–319.

23. West, *The History of Tasmania*: 517.

24. See Cassandra Pybus and Hamish Maxwell-Stewart, *American Citizens, British Slaves: Yankee Political Prisoners in an Australian Penal Colony* (Melbourne: Melbourne University Press: 2002).

25. William Gates, *Recollections of Life in Van Dieman's Land, Australian Historical Monographs No. 40* (Sydney: D.S. Ford, 1961). Cited in Brand, *The Convict Probation System*: 61.

26. Nixon and Nixon, *The Pioneer Bishop in Van Diemen's Land*: 32–33.

27. Mortlock, *Experiences of a Convict*: 81–82.

28. William Derrincourt, *Old Convict Days* (London: Penguin, 1975): 75.

29. *Irish Exile*, 5 October 1850, cited in Richard Davis, "Patrick O'Donohue: Young Ireland Rebel and Convict Worker Advocate, Van Diemen's Land 1850," *THRA Papers and Proceedings* 46, no. 2 (1999): 100.

30. Glen McLaren, *Beyond Leichhardt: Bushcraft and the Exploration of Australia* (Fremantle: Fremantle Arts Centre Press, 1996): 13.

31. Faye Gardam, *Sawdust, Sails and Sweat: A History of the River Don Settlement* (Port Sorell, Tas.: self published, 1996): 17.

32. B.M. Thomas, "Forest to Field and Fencing the Field," *THRA Papers and Proceedings* 47, no. 2 (2000): 75–76.

33. Fenton, *Bush Life in Tasmania Fifty Years Ago*: 53.

34. Plomley, ed., *Friendly Mission*: 26.

35. Breen, *Contested Places*: 49–50, 53–54, 58.

36. Meredith, *My Home in Tasmania*: 282–283.

37. Margaret Row, "The Huon Timber Company and the Crown: A Tale of Resource Development," *THRA Papers and Proceedings* 27, no. 3 (1980): 87.

38. Burn, *A Picture of Van Diemen's Land*: 124.

39. Jetson, *The Roof of Tasmania*: 111.

40. Jetson, *The Roof of Tasmania*: 116–118. The oral history of the Central Plateau is documented in a remarkable multi-volume collection. Simon Cubit, *What's the Land For? People's Experience of the Tasmania's Central Plateau Region, Central Plateau Oral History Project* (1990).

41. Peter MacFie, "Oral History and the Demise of Folk Culture in the Richmond District, Tasmania," *THRA Papers and Proceedings* 29, no. 3 (1982): 96.

42. Robson, *A History of Tasmania*, vol. 1: 411.

43. Mortlock, *Experiences of a Convict*: 126–128.

17. The End of Transportation

1. Clark, *Select Documents in Australian History*: 152–154.

2. Patrick O'Farrell, *Documents in Australian Catholic History*, vol. 1 (London: Geoffrey Chapman, ed., 1969): 45.

3. Burn, *A Picture of Van Diemen's Land*: 54, 165.

4. Brand, *The Convict Probation System*: 63–64.

5. Robson, *A History of Tasmania*, vol. 1: 419.

6. Brand, *The Convict Probation System*: 148–152.

7. Brand, *The Convict Probation System*: 56, 59, 147.

8. The poem was signed "Chrisianos" and dedicated "to the freemen of Tasmania." *Launceston Examiner*, 5 May 1847. Cited in Brand, *The Convict Probation System*: 105.

9. Brand, *The Convict Probation System*: 11–13, 19, 52, 56, 59, 117.

10. Brand, *The Convict Probation System*: 159.

11. Brand, *The Convict Probation System*: 130.

12. Reynolds, "Australian Nationalism: Tasmanian Patriotism": 22.

13. James Bonwick, *The Bushrangers: Illustrating the Early Days of Van Diemen's Land* (Hobart: Fullers Bookshop, 1967): 7.

14. Another probable consequence of the anti-transportation campaign linking homosexuality and convictism was to increase the intolerance and vilification of gay males. Tasmania was the last place in the British empire to hang someone for sodomy (in 1867). In the twentieth century, Tasmania had the highest rate of imprisonment per capita for private consenting male homosexual sex anywhere in the world, and in 1997 was the last Australian state to decriminalise homosexuality (It should be noted, however, that it has subsequently developed some of the most progressive laws and policies in the world). Rodney Croome, "Homosexuality" in Alexander, ed., *The Companion to Tasmanian History*: 180.

15. Clark, *Select Documents in Australian History*: 345.

16. Burn, *A Picture of Van Diemen's Land*: 154.

17. Clark, *Select Documents in Australian History*: 372–373.

18. John Reynolds and W.A. Townsley, *A Century of Responsible Government in Tasmania* (Hobart: Commonwealth Parliamentary Association and the Tasmanian Historical Research Association, 1956): 63–64.

19. Reynolds and Townsley, *A Century of Responsible Government in Tasmania 1856–1956*: 69–71.

20. Alpheus Todd, *Parliamentary Government in the British Colonies* (Boston: Little, Brown, and Company, 1880): 80, 87, 474.

21. Michael Roe, "The Establishment of Local Self Government in Hobart and Launceston, 1845 –1858," *THRA Papers and Proceedings* 14, no. 1 (1966): 32.

22. Michael Roe, *Quest for Authority in Eastern Australia* (Melbourne: Melbourne University Press, 1965): 101.

23. Report of a public meeting at the Mechanics Institute, as published in the *Irish Exile* on 30 January 1850 and 2 February 1850, cited by Davis, "Patrick O'Donohue: Young Ireland Rebel and Convict Worker Advocate": 103.

24. Roe, "The Establishment of Local Self Government in Hobart and Launceston": 32–36. Roe, *Quest for Authority in Eastern Australia*: 101.

25. Newman, *Becoming Tasmania*: 134–135.

26. For example, the American editors of Louisa Meredith's *My Home in Tasmania* believed that "Tasmania was the name bestowed on Australia by the Dutch." Meredith, *My Home in Tasmania*, editor's note.

27. F.C. Green, introduction to Reynolds and Townsley, *A Century of Responsible Government in Tasmania*. In the same publication, John Reynolds, chairman of the Tasmanian Historical Research Association, chose to ignore the convict ancestry of some prominent Tasmanian premiers and political leaders. For example, while he acknowledged that Thomas Reibey was the grandson of Mary Reibey, she was only described as "a colourful personality of early Sydney." And Sir Richard Dry was described as the "elder son of Richard Dry, the most successful pioneer landowner and pastoralist in northern Tasmania, who had come from Ireland to Tasmania," although he had come from Ireland via Sydney and servitude. Townsley and Reynolds, *A Century of Responsible Government in Tasmania*: 37–40, 144–147.

18. *Victoria's Van Diemonian Foundation*

1. Marie Fels, "Congruences and Contradictions in Aboriginal–European Relations in Van Diemen's Land and Port Phillip," *Bulletin of the Centre for Tasmanian Historical Studies* 3, no. 2 (1991–1992): 73.

2. Burns and Skemp, *Van Diemen's Land Correspondents 1827–1849*: 59.

3. Bride, *Letters from Victorian Pioneers*: 16, 20. Powerless in practice to protect the Aborigines, Buckley soon fled the invasion and moved to Van Diemen's Land.

4. Port Phillip Association records, SLV MS1123

5. Clark, *Select Documents in Australian History*: 93.

6. Brown, *Clyde Company Papers*: 15–16.

7. Alan Shaw, "Van Diemonian Influences on Port Phillip Settlement," *Bulletin of the Centre for Tasmanian Historical Studies* 2, no.2 (1989–1990): 29–30.

8. Shaw, "Van Diemonian Influences on Port Phillip Settlement": 394–395.

9. Bride, *Letters from Victorian Pioneers*: 74–77, 87–88, 103.

10. Bride, *Letters from Victorian Pioneers*: 20–21, 277–280.

11. Curr, *Recollections of Squatting in Victoria*: 191–199.

12. Curr, *Recollections of Squatting in Victoria*: 77–94.

13. Bride, *Letters from Victorian Pioneers*: 396, 415.

14. Bride, *Letters from Victorian Pioneers*: 167–169.

15. Bride, *Letters from Victorian Pioneers*: 191.

16. Robson, *A History of Tasmania*, vol. 1: 508–509.

17. Robson, *A History of Tasmania*, vol. 1: 511.

18. Robson, *A History of Tasmania*, vol. 1: 509–511. John Pascoe Fawkner (whose father was a convict) was not the only prominent Victorian who seemed to have a selective memory. One of the leading families of the western districts also seemed quickly to forget where they had come from. As Marjorie Tipping notes: "The father-in-law of George Armytage, one of the best known names in the history of Victoria's western district, was not, as Henderson's Victorian families and other authorities tell us, a lieutenant in the Duke of York's regiment stationed in Van Diemen's Land. He was ... Thomas Peters ... sentenced to life transportation for grand larceny – the theft of ten silver cups." Tipping, *Convicts Unbound*: 23–24.

19. Shaw, "Van Diemonian Influences on Port Phillip Settlement": 30–31.

20. Ned Kelly, Jerilderie Letter. Accessible online at <www.slv.gov.au/collections/treasures>. In 1851, the census reported only 3409 ex-convicts in Port Phillip (including those who

had come from New South Wales), out of a total recorded population of 77,345. Roe, *Quest for Authority in Eastern Australia*: 207.

CONCLUSION

1. De Tocqueville's observation also prefaced Russel Ward's *The Australian Legend* (Melbourne: Oxford University Press, 1977).

2. The Tasmanian Museum and Art Gallery only has "an egg and some bones from the Tasmanian species, some egg shell and bones from the King Island species and also a feather from one of the King Island birds collected by Baudin in 1803." Dr Andrew Rozefelds, Deputy Director Collections and Research TMAG, personal communication, 9 September 2005.

3. I am grateful for the assistance of Brendan Lennard, Cultural Heritage Officer of the Hobart City Council, who advised that "the motto was first used by Council at the outset (ie from the 1850s), though the first 'coat of arms' was an unofficial crest. The present arms, formally granted in 1853, was largely designed by Alderman I.G. Anderson, an architect. The motto is featured on both the coat of arms and the earlier crest." Lennard pointed out that Knopwood "has adapted the famous line from Virgil's Georgics, where it is used in relation to Etruria – an important area of central Italy inhabited and governed by the Etruscans." Personal communication, 3 September 2005.

4. C.M.H. Clark, *Occasional Writings and Speeches* (Sydney: Fontana, 1980): 32, 43–45.

5. Tim Flannery, *The Eternal Frontier: An Ecological History of North America and Its Peoples* (Melbourne: Text Publishing, 2001): 291.

6. William Lines, *Taming the Great South Land: A History of the Conquest of Nature in Australia* (Sydney: Allen and Unwin, 1991): 48.

7. See J.B. Hirst, *Convict Society and Its Enemies: A History of Early New South Wales* (Sydney: Allen and Unwin, 1983); Alan Atkinson, "Four Patterns of Convict Protest," *Labour History* 37, November 1979; Atkinson, *The Europeans in Australia*; Maxwell-Stuart, "The Bushrangers and the Convict System of Van Diemen's Land"; Daniels, *Convict Women*; For a succinct, insightful overview of late twentieth-century scholarship, see Marian Quartly, "Convict History," in Graeme Davison, John Hirst, Stuart Macintyre, eds, *The Oxford Companion to Australian History* (Melbourne: Oxford University Press, 1998).

8. Curr, *An Account of the Colony of Van Diemen's Land*: 11–12.

9. Curr, *An Account of the Colony of Van Diemen's Land*: 29.

10. Thompson, *Customs in Common*: 187.

11. Thompson, *Customs in Common*: 14–15.

12. Simon Schama, *Landscape and Memory* (London: Fontana Press, 1996): 574.

13. Breen, *Contested Places*: 34; Henry Reynolds, "Regionalism in Nineteenth Century Tasmania," *THRA Papers and Proceedings* 17, no. 1 (1969): 16. One of the many paradoxes of Van Diemen's Land is that the British crown offered some level of protection to the convicts and Aborigines which was largely lost with self-government. The Aborigines never forgot that the crown offered their best, if very limited, hope of recognition and redress. They directly petitioned Queen Victoria in 1847 on the basis of their historical rights, and right through to the 1950s, when the governor was asked by Cape Barren Islanders to prevent their eviction from the reserve, there are examples of direct appeals to the governor of the day. The famous petition presented by Aboriginal activist Michael Mansell direct to Queen Elizabeth II in the 1970s, which symbolises the emergence of an assertive and confident contemporary Tasmanian Aboriginal identity, was thus a powerful expression of the historical continuity of the Aborigines' cause.

14. McKay, *Journals of the Land Commissioners for Van Diemen's Land*: 27.

15. Peter Hay, *Van Diemonian Essays* (Hobart: Walleah Press, 2002): viii–ix. For an insight-

ful and wedge-breaking analysis of the forestry debate – what could be termed a Van Diemonian perspective – see Peter Hay, "The Moral Economy of the Bush," *Arena* 83,
June–July 2006.

APPENDIX

1. *Partition or Exile?*

1. As Arthur himself explained, the attacks in Honduras were by "merchants whose inveter-
    ate hatred I brought upon myself by protecting some Indians held by them in slavery."
    Arthur to Hay, 24 September 1832, cited in Levy, *Governor George Arthur*: 282–283.
2. Arthur to Hay, 15 November 1826, HRA 3/5: 435.
3. Arthur to Goderich, 10 January 1828, *HRA* 3/7: 26–29.
4. A. Johnstone, *A History of the Church Missionary Society in Australia and Tasmania* (Syd-
    ney: CMS, 1925): 165–166.
5. Arthur to Goderich, *HRA* 3/7: 26–29
6. Arthur to Huskisson, 17 April 1828, *HRA* 3/7: 179.
7. *HRA* 3/7: 180–184.
8. Plomley, ed., *Friendly Mission*: 55, 251.
9. *HRA* 3/7: 178–184
10. Murray to Arthur, 20 February 1829, *HRA* 3/8: 261–262.
11. Cited by Desailly in "The Mechanics of Genocide": 84.
12. *HRA* 3/7: 179.
13. Robinson to Arthur, 19 December 1829, AOT CSO 1/328/7578.
14. *HRA* 3/7: 625–630.
15. Arthur relied on Bathurst's 14 July 1825 instructions to justify inspiring the Aborigines
    with "terror," quoting it in the executive council, to London and in the public proclama-
    tion. Bathurst had advised Governor Darling on 14 July 1825 that when "hostile incur-
    sions for the purposes of plunder" could not "be prevented or allayed by less vigorous
    means," the "duty" of the authorities was "to oppose force by force and to repel such
    aggression in the same manner as if they proceeded from the subjects of any accredited
    state." *HRA* 1/12, 211 and *HRA* 3/8: 846.
16. *HRA* 3/7: 631–632.
17. McFarlane, "Aboriginal Society in North West Tasmania": 117.
18. *HRA* 1/12: 21 and *HRA* 3/8: 846.
19. *HRA* 3/7: 634.
20. *HRA* 3/7: 629.
21. Plomley, ed., *Friendly Mission*: 98.
22. *HRA* 3/8: xliii
23. *HRA* 3/9: 202–236
24. Murray noted in his reply of 5 November 1830 that for the Aborigines Committee to
    establish that Aboriginal attacks emerged from the "wanton and savage spirit inherent in
    them," it would have been necessary to establish "the fact that aggressions had not begun
    with the new settlers." Murray to Arthur, 5 November 1830, in *Van Diemen's Land: Cop-
    ies of All Correspondence*: 56.
25. O'Connor to the Aboriginal Committee, 11 December 1829, AOT CSO 1/323/7578.
26. Plomley *et al.*, *The Aboriginal/Settler Clash in Van Diemen's Land*: 26.
27. Plomley *et al.*, *The Aboriginal/Settler Clash in Van Diemen's Land*: 26.
28. Desailly, "The Mechanics of Genocide": 109.
29. Desailly, "The Mechanics of Genocide": 108–110.The vacillations in colonial government
    policy are set out in Bronwyn Desailly's thesis, which still provides the most comprehen-
    sive guide to colonial government policy to Aborigines, at least in the 1827–1832 period.

30. Government order, 25 February 1830, published in the *Hobart Town Gazette*, 27 February 1830.

31. Executive council minutes, 26 February 1830, cited in Desailly, "The Mechanics of Genocide": 111.

32. *HRA* 3/8: 592–593.

33. Arthur to Murray, 15 April 1830, *HRA* 3/9: 167–168.

34. Plomley *et al.*, *The Aboriginal/Settler Clash in Van Diemen's Land*: 26.

35. *Van Diemen's Land: Copies of All Correspondence*: 61–62.

36. Robson to Robinson, 19 September 1830, in Plomley, ed., *Friendly Mission*: 238.

37. Desailly, "The Mechanics of Genocide": 126–127.

38. *Hobart Town Gazette*, 28 August 1830. My emphasis.

39. *Van Diemen's Land: Copies of All Correspondence*: 57–58.

40. *HRA* 3/9: 311–312.

41. *Van Diemen's Land: Copies of All Correspondence*: 63–64.

42. *HRA* 3/9: 617–620.

43. *HRA* 3/9: 617–620.

44. *HRA* 3/9: 628–636.

45. *HRA* 3/9: 644–645.

46. Discussed in Desailly, "The Mechanics of Genocide": 136–138. See also the *Colonial Times*, 24 September 1830. The editor of the *Tasmanian*, R.L. Murray, was a participant in the debate.

47. Chapman, ed., *The Diaries and Letters of G.T.W.B. Boyes*, vol. 1: 378–380.

48. Plomley, ed., *Friendly Mission*: 277.

49. Plomley, ed., *Friendly Mission*: 283.

50. *HRA* 3/9: 591–592.

51. Desailly, "The Mechanics of Genocide": 144.

52. The disreputable distortion of the parliamentary paper, which even today is a widely-relied-on primary source (reprinted in 1971), is documented in Desailly, "The Mechanics of Genocide": 129–131.

53. The *Hobart Town Gazette* first broached the removal of the Aborigines on 11 November 1826. Thereafter removal became the policy of the *Colonial Times*, the *Colonial Advocate* and, from its establishment in October 1827, the *Hobart Town Courier*. The *Tasmanian* did not fall into line until 28 March 1828. Thereafter, Desailly notes, "the unity of the press seemed complete" and there were articles "almost every week" on this theme, although doubts were expressed in the *Tasmanian*, the most moderate of the various journals, on 30 May 1828. Desailly, "The Mechanics of Genocide": 51. The government had prevaricated on this issue during 1830 with the standing committee on captured Aborigines even recommending the release of a group of captured women and children at its first meeting (although the hopelessly contradictory nature of government policy was exposed when these unfortunate people were soon recaptured by bounty hunters, with one woman being shot in the process). AOT CSO1/319/7578; Desailly, "The Mechanics of Genocide": 12–13. On 27 August 1830 the committee resolved that *captured* Aborigines should be sent to Maria Island "if they can be detained there in safety." AOT CSO1/319/7578.

54. Government notice, *Hobart Town Gazette*, 27 November 1830.

55. Arthur to Murray, 1 January 1831, in *Van Diemen's Land: Copies of All Correspondence*: 47.

56. Burnett to Robinson, 23 November 1830, Robinson papers, vol. 32, cited in Desailly, "The Mechanics of Genocide": 147.

11. *The Removal of the Aborigines in a Time of War*

1. Plomley, ed., *Friendly Mission*: 438–439.

2. Plomley, ed., *Friendly Mission*: 81, 261.

3. Plomley, ed., *Friendly Mission*: 280.
4. Plomley, ed., *Friendly Mission*: 519.
5. Minutes of the Aborigines Committee, 4 February 1831, in *Van Diemen's Land: Copies of All Correspondence*: 76–77.
6. Executive council minutes, 23 February 1831, in *Van Diemen's Land: Copies of All Correspondence*: 80–83.
7. Executive council minutes, 23 February 1831, in *Van Diemen's Land: Copies of All Correspondence*: 80–83.
8. Executive council minutes, 23 February 1831, Plomley, ed., *Friendly Mission*: 81.
9. Executive council minutes, 14 February 1831 in *Van Diemen's Land: Copies of All Correspondence*: 83–84.
10. Executive council minutes, 14 February 1831, *Van Diemen's Land: Copies of All Correspondence*: 83–84
11. Arthur to Murray, 4 April 1831, in *Van Diemen's Land: Copies of All Correspondence*: 78–79. My emphasis.
12. *Tasmanian*, 30 May 1828.
13. G.S.R. Kitson Clark, *An Expanding Society: Britain 1830–1900* (Melbourne: Melbourne University Press, 1967): 22.
14. Nevertheless, it is likely that key bureaucrats in the Colonial Office recognised the potential political embarrassment of the Indigenous people of Van Diemen's Land dying out on a remote island after being exiled there by the British government (voluntarily or otherwise). During this period, prominent evangelicals were bringing the suffering of the empire's native peoples to public attention. It is in this context that the decision was made to publish the official correspondence about the conflict with the Aborigines (after, as has already been noted, some careful editing). No one could now claim that the tragedy had been covered up. The timing of this show of openness, however, in the English autumn of 1831, when working-class demonstrations of over 100,000 people (seen by many as a prelude to revolution) were being held, and while the associated political crisis was dominating public and parliamentary debate, meant that the imperial government was never to be called to account. Thompson, *The Making of the English Working Class*: 888–891.
15. Plomley, ed., *Friendly Mission*: 394.
16. Plomley, ed., *Friendly Mission*: 398.
17. Plomley, ed., *Friendly Mission*: 13.
18. Plomley, ed., *Friendly Mission*: 468.
19. Plomley, ed., *Friendly Mission*: 413.
20. Plomley, ed., *Friendly Mission*: 21, 415.
21. Plomley, ed., *Friendly Mission*: 424–425.
22. Plomley, ed., *Friendly Mission*: 429–430, 476–477.
23. *Colonial Times*, 28 September 1831.
24. Plomley *et al.*, *The Aboriginal/Settler Clash in Van Diemen's Land, 1803–1831*: 27.
25. Desailly, "The Mechanics of Genocide": 157–158.
26. AOT CSO 1/319/7578.
27. Plomley, ed., *Friendly Mission*: 483.
28. Executive council minutes, 10 October 1831, AOT EC 4/1, 2.
29. Plomley, ed., *Friendly Mission*: 67, 69, 528.
30. Plomley, ed., *Friendly Mission*: 66–67, 583.
31. Plomley, ed., *Friendly Mission*: 572.
32. Plomley, ed., *Friendly Mission*: 573. My emphasis.
33. *Hobart Town Courier*, 14 January 1832.
34. AOT CSO 5/39/833, cited in Reynolds, *Fate of a Free People*: 152.

III. *The Removal of the Aborigines in a Time of Peace*
1. Reynolds, *Fate of a Free People*: 133.
2. Reynolds, *Fate of a Free People*: 156
3. Thirteen Aborigines were captured in November 1830, seven in August 1831 and 26 in the New Year of 1832.
4. During 1832, 23 Aborigines were captured in June, 36 in September and six in November. During 1833, eight Aborigines were captured in February, 12 in May, eight in June, and 27 in July. During 1834, 28 Aborigines were removed in four encounters. These figures exclude the Aborigines removed from sealers, delivered from gaol or given up by settlers.
5. Plomley *et al.*, *The Aboriginal/Settler Clash in Van Diemen's Land*: 16, 28.
6. Executive council minutes, 28 May 1832, AOT EC 4/1, 2.
7. Plomley, ed., *Friendly Mission*: 844, 914.
8. Plomley, ed., *Friendly Mission*: 622.
9. Plomley, ed., *Friendly Mission*: 625, 633
10. Plomley, ed., *Friendly Mission*: 634.
11. Plomley, ed., *Friendly Mission*: 634–635
12. Plomley, ed., *Friendly Mission*: 635–639.
13. Commandant to Colonial Secretary, 30 June 1827 *HRA* 3/6: 100. Cited by Ian Brand, Macquarie Harbour Research, vol.1, 1984 <www.dpiw.tas.gov.au/library/brand>.
14. Plomley, ed., *Friendly Mission*: 804–805.
15. Plomley, ed., *Friendly Mission*: 805.
16. Plomley, ed., *Friendly Mission*: 700, 803.
17. Plomley, ed., *Friendly Mission*: 724–726.
18. Plomley, ed., *Friendly Mission*: 729.
19. Plomley, ed., *Friendly Mission*: 732.
20. Plomley, ed., *Friendly Mission*: 743.
21. Plomley, ed., *Friendly Mission*: 752.
22. Plomley, ed., *Friendly Mission*: 753–754.
23. Plomley, ed., *Friendly Mission*: 764.
24. Plomley, ed., *Friendly Mission*: 764–765.
25. Plomley, ed., *Friendly Mission*: 725–726.
26. Plomley, ed., *Friendly Mission*: 770–773.
27. Plomley, ed., *Friendly Mission*: 773–774.
28. Plomley, ed., *Friendly Mission*: 774.
29. Plomley, ed., *Friendly Mission*: 774–775. Aboriginal custom prescribed cremation, but Robinson had earlier banned this.
30. Plomley, ed., *Friendly Mission*: 775.
31. Plomley, ed., *Friendly Mission*: 775.
32. Plomley, ed., *Friendly Mission*: 776–777.
33. Plomley, ed., *Friendly Mission*: 778.
34. Plomley, ed., *Friendly Mission*: 780–781.
35. Plomley, ed., *Friendly Mission*: 784–785.
36. Plomley, ed., *Friendly Mission*: 800–801.
37. Plomley, ed., *Friendly Mission*: 822–823.
38. Plomley, ed., *Friendly Mission*: 647.
39. AOT EC 4/1, 2.
40. Executive council minutes, 10 October 1831, AOT EC 4/1, 2.
41. Charles Darwin, *The Voyage of the Beagle* (London: J.M. Dent, 1961): 430.
42. Executive council minutes, AOT EC 4/3, 4.
43. Plomley, ed., *Weep in Silence*: 326.
44. Robinson report no. 2 (1835), in Robinson papers, vol. 22. Cited in Desailly, "The

Mechanics of Genocide": 169.

45. Plomley, ed., *Weep in Silence*: 326, 75.

46. Robinson to Colonial Secretary, 27, 28 and 29 October 1836, in Arthur papers, vol. 28. Cited in Desailly, "The Mechanics of Genocide": 169.

47. Described by Robinson as a chief of the Oyster Bay tribe, he was one of the 26 Aborigines with whom Robinson negotiated near Lake Echo in the New Year of 1832 to end the Tasmanian War.

48. Plomley, ed., *Weep in Silence*: 455.

49. Executive council minutes, 11 December 1838, AOT EC 4/5.

50. Executive council minutes, 8 January 1839, AOT EC 4/5.

51. The additional 3000 acres were to be in lieu of, not in addition to, Robinson receiving government employment at the completion of the conciliation mission.

52. AOT EC 4/5.

53. Arthur to Murray, 4 April 1831, cited in Plomley, ed., *Weep in Silence*: 455.

54. Plomley, ed., *Weep in Silence*: 608.

55. Ian McFarlane, "A Casualty of War," *THRA Papers and Proceedings* 48, no. 4 (2001): 303–305.

POSTSCRIPT: THE FINAL CONQUEST

1. Francis R. Nixon, *Cruise of the Beacon: A Narrative of a Visit to the Islands in Bass's Straits* (London: Bell and Daldy, 1857): 18–33.

2. Nixon, *Cruise of the Beacon*: 38–45.

3. Nixon, *Cruise of the Beacon*: 45–47.

4. Stephen Murray-Smith, "Beyond the Pale: The Islander Community of Bass Strait in the 19th Century," *THRA Papers and Proceedings* 20, no. 4 (1973): 181.

5. *Church News*, 20 November 1862.

6. Reibey letter, 19 August 1863, AOT NS 585/1.

7. Irynej Skira, "Always Afternoon: Aborigines on Cape Barren Island in the Nineteenth Century," *THRA Papers and Proceedings* 44, no. 3 (1997): 122.

8. See Boyce, *God's Own Country*.

9. Stephen Murray-Smith, ed., *Mission to the Islands: The Missionary Voyages in Bass Strait of Canon Marcus Brownrigg 1872–1885* (Hobart: Cat and Fiddle Press, 1979): xix.

10. Various signatories, the *Examiner*, 30 May 1883. Cited in Greg Lehmann, "Narrative, Identity and Land," BA Honours thesis, University of Tasmania, 1998.

11. Boyce, *God's Own Country*: chapter six.

12. *Examiner*, 6 February 1876, cited in Ryan, *The Aboriginal Tasmanians*: 229.

13. The view that Truganini was the last representative of her race was, however, contested in the nineteenth century. For example, in September 1882 the Tasmanian Parliament voted to increase the pension of a former Oyster Cove resident, Fanny Cochrane Smith, to £50 per annum on the basis that she was the "the last survivor of the Aboriginal race of Tasmania." The *Mercury*, 8 and 15 September 1882.

REFERENCES

Theses

Boyce, James. "An Environmental History of Van Diemen's Land." PhD thesis, University of Tasmania, 2006.

Canteri, Carlo. "The Origins of Australian Social Banditry: Bushranging in Van Diemen's Land 1805–1818." BLitt thesis, Oxford University, 1973. Original unabridged version privately distributed by the author.

Desailly, Bronwyn. "The Mechanics of Genocide: Colonial Policies and Attitudes Towards the Tasmanian Aborigines 1824–1836." MA thesis, University of Tasmania, 1977.

Lehmann, Greg. "Narrative, Identity and Land." BA Honours thesis, University of Tasmania, 1998.

Maxwell-Stewart, Hamish. "The Bushrangers and the Convict System of Van Diemen's Land, 1803–1846." PhD thesis, University of Edinburgh, 1990.

McFarlane, Ian. "Aboriginal Society in North West Tasmania: Dispossession and Genocide." PhD thesis, University of Tasmania, 2002.

Skira, Irynej. "Tasmanian Aborigines and Mutton Birding." PhD thesis, University of Tasmania, 1993.

Snowden, Dianne. "Women and Work in Van Diemen's Land." BA Honours thesis, University of Tasmania, 1982.

Published letters, diaries and other primary sources

Bensley, Benjamin. *Lost and Found or Light in the Prison: A Narrative with Original Letters of a Convict Condemned for Forgery.* London: W. Wells Gardner, 1859.

Bride, Thomas Francis. *Letters from Victorian Pioneers.* Melbourne: Lloyd O'Neil, 1983.

Brown, Philip L., ed. *Clyde Company Papers.* London: Oxford University Press, 1941.

Burns, J.R. and Skemp, T.E. *Van Diemen's Land Correspondents 1827–1849: Letters from R.C. Gunn, R.W. Lawrence, Jorgen Jorgenson and others to Sir William J. Hooker.* Launceston, Tas.: Queen Victoria Museum, 1961.

Calder, James. *The Circumnavigation of Van Diemen's Land in 1815 by James Kelly and in 1824 by James Hobbs, Edited from Their Own Accounts by James Calder.* Hobart: Sullivans Cove, 1984.

Chapman, Peter, ed. *The Diaries and Letters of G.T.W.B. Boyes*, vol. 1, *1820–1832*. Melbourne: Oxford University Press, 1985.

Clark, C.M.H. *Select Documents in Australian History*. Sydney: Angus and Robertson, 1966.

Clarke, Patricia and Spender Dale. *Life Line: Australian Women's Letters and Diaries 1788–1840*. Sydney: Allen and Unwin, 1992.

Crawford, J., W.F. Ellis and G.H. Stancombe, eds. *The Diaries of John Helder Wedge 1824–1835*. Hobart: Royal Society of Tasmania, 1962.

Dawson, Warren R., ed. *The Banks Letters: A Calendar of the Manuscript Correspondence of Sir Joseph Banks Preserved in the British Museum (National History) and Other Collections in Great Britain*. London: British Museum, 1958.

Fenton, Elizabeth. *The Journal of Mrs Fenton*. London: Edward Arnold, 1901.

FitzSymonds, Eustace. *A Looking-Glass for Tasmania: Letters, Petitions and Other Manuscripts Relating to Van Diemen's Land 1808–1845*. Adelaide: Sullivans Cove, 1980.

——*Mortmain: A Collection of Choice Petitions, Memorials, and Letters of Protest and Request from the Convict Colony of Van Diemen's Land*. Hobart: Sullivans Cove, 1977.

Hamilton-Arnold, Barbara, ed. *Letters and Papers of G.P. Harris, 1803–1812: Deputy Surveyor-General of New South Wales at Sullivan Bay, Port Phillip, and Hobart Town, Van Diemen's Land*. Sorrento, Vic.: Arden Press, 1994.

Historical Records of Australia, series 3, vols 1–6. Sydney: Library Committee of the Commonwealth Parliament, 1921–1923.

Historical Records of Australia, series 3, vol. 7. Canberra: AGPS, 1997. Edited by Peter Chapman.

Historical Records of Australia, series 3, vol. 8. Melbourne: Melbourne University Press, 2003. Edited by Peter Chapman.

Historical Records of Australia, series 3, vol. 9. Melbourne: Melbourne University Press, 2006. Edited by Peter Chapman

Hobler, George. *The Diaries of Pioneer George Hobler, October 6 1800–December 13 1882*. C. & H. Reproductions, 1992.

Lee, Ida, ed. *The Voyage of the Caroline from England to Van Diemen's Land and Batavia in 1827–28*. London: Longmans, 1927.

Macquarie, Lachlan. *Lachlan Macquarie, Governor of New South Wales: Journals of His Tours in New South Wales and Van Diemen's Land, 1810–1822*. Sydney: Trustees of the Public Library of New South Wales, 1956.

McKay, Anne, ed. *Journals of the Land Commissioners for Van Diemen's Land, 1826–28*. Hobart: University of Tasmania in conjunction with the Tasmanian Historical Research Association, 1962.

Nicholls, Mary, ed. *The Diary of the Reverend Robert Knopwood, 1803–1838: First Chaplain of Van Diemen's Land*. Hobart: Tasmanian Historical Research Association, 1977.

——*Traveller under Concern: The Quaker Journals of Frederick Mackie on His Tour of the Australasian Colonies 1852–1855*. Hobart: University of Tasmania, 1973.

Nixon, Anna and Norah Nixon. *The Pioneer Bishop in Van Diemen's Land, 1843–1863: Letters and Memories of Francis Russell Nixon, D.D., First Bishop of Tasmania*. Hobart: Walch & Sons, 1953.

Nixon, Francis R. *Cruise of the Beacon: A Narrative of a Visit to the Islands in Bass's Straits*. London: Bell and Daldy, 1857.

O'Farrell, Patrick. *Documents in Australian Catholic History*, vol.1. London: Geoffrey Chapman, 1969.

Plomley, N.J.B., ed. *Friendly Mission: The Tasmanian Journals of George Augustus Robinson 1829–1834*. Hobart: Tasmanian Historical Research Association, 1966.

Reports on the Historical Manuscripts of Tasmania, Numbers 1–7. Hobart: Department of History, University of Tasmania, 1964.

Richards, Jack. "Fifteen Tasmanian Letters 1824–1852." Unpublished manuscript, accessible at the State Library of Tasmania.

Shelton, D.C., ed. *The Parramore Letters: Letters from William Thomas Parramore, Sometime Private Secretary to Lieutenant Governor Arthur of Van Diemen's Land, to Thirza Cropper, His Fiancée in Europe and England, the Majority from 1823–1825*. Sydney: D. and C. Shelton, 1993.

Statham, Pamela. *The Tanner Letters: A Pioneer Saga of Swan River & Tasmania, 1831–1845*. Nedlands, WA: University Of Western Australia Press, 1981.

Van Diemen's Land: Copies of All Correspondence between Lieutenant Governor Arthur and His Majesty's Secretary of State for the Colonies on the Subject of the Military Operations Lately Carried on against the Aboriginal Inhabitants of Van Diemen's Land. London: Parliamentary Paper, ordered by the House of Commons to be printed 23 September 1831. Republished by the Tasmanian Historical Research Association, Hobart, 1971.

Books written before 1856 or based on personal experience of Van Diemen's Land

Backhouse, James. *A Narrative of a Visit to the Australian Colonies*. London: Hamilton, Adams and Co., 1843.

Bonwick, James. *The Last of the Tasmanians; or, the Black War of Van Diemen's Land*. Adelaide: Libraries Board of South Australia, 1969. First published 1870.

——*The Bushrangers: Illustrating the Early Days of Van Diemen's Land*. Hobart: Fullers Bookshop, 1967. First published 1856.

Brown, P.L., ed. *The Narrative of George Russell*. London: Oxford University Press, 1935.

Broxup, John. *Life of John Broxup: Late Convict of Van Diemen's Land*. Hobart: Sullivans Cove, 1973. First published 1850.

Burn, David. *A Picture of Van Diemen's Land*. Facsimile edition. Hobart: Cat and Fiddle Press, 1973. First published in the *Colonial Magazine*, 1840–41.

Calder, James Erskine. *Some Account of the Wars, Extirpation, Habits etc of the Native Tribes of Tasmania*. Facsimile edition. Hobart: Fullers Bookshop, 1972. First published 1875.

——*Recollections of Sir John and Lady Jane Franklin in Tasmania*. Adelaide: Sullivans Cove, 1984. First published in six parts in the *Tasmanian Tribune*, 1875.

Cash, Martin. *The Bushranger of Van Diemen's Land: 1843–44*. Hobart: J. Walch and Sons, 1929. First published 1870.

Collins, David (edited by James Collier). *An Account of the English Colony in New South Wales, 1788–1801*. Christchurch: Whitcombe and Tombs, 1910. First published 1802.

Curr, Edward. *An Account of the Colony of Van Diemen's Land: Principally Designed for the Use of Emigrants.* Hobart: Platypus Publications, 1967. First published 1824.

Curr, Edward (Junior). *Recollections of Squatting in Victoria (from 1841 to 1851).* Adelaide: Libraries Board of South Australia, 1968. First published 1883.

Darwin, Charles. *The Voyage of the Beagle.* London: J.M. Dent, 1961. First published 1839.

Delano, Amasa. *A Narrative of a Voyage to New Holland and Van Diemen's Land.* Facsimile edition. Hobart: Cat and Fiddle Press, 1973. First published 1817.

Denison, William. *Varieties of Vice Regal Life*, vol. 1. London: Longmans, Green and Co., 1870.

Derrincourt, William. *Old Convict Days.* Melbourne: Penguin, 1975. First published 1899.

Dixon, James. *Narrative of a Voyage to New South Wales and Van Diemen's Land: In the Ship Skelton, During the Year 1820; with Observations on the State of These Colonies, and a Variety of Information, Calculated to Be Useful to Emigrants.* Hobart: Melanie Publications, 1984. First published 1822.

Evans, George William. *A Geographical, Historical, and Topographical Description of Van Diemen's Land: With Important Hints to Emigrants, and Useful Information Respecting the Application for Grants of Land.* London: J. Souter, 1822.

Fenton, James. *Bush Life in Tasmania Fifty Years Ago.* London: Hazell, Watson and Viney, 1891. Reprinted Launceston, Tas.: Mary Fisher Bookstore, no date.

———*A History of Tasmania from Its Discovery in 1642 to the Present Time.* Hobart: J. Walch & Sons, 1884.

Field, Barron, ed. *Geographical Memoirs of New South Wales by Various Hands ... Together with Other Papers on the Aborigines, the Geology, the Botany, the Timber, the Astronomy, and the Meteorology of New South Wales and Van Diemen's Land.* London: J. Murray, 1825.

Gates, William. *Recollections of Life in Van Diemen's Land.* Australian Historical Monographs, no. 40. Sydney: D.S. Ford, 1961. First published 1850.

Henderson, John. *Observations on the Colonies of New South Wales and Van Diemen's Land.* Facsimile edition. Adelaide: Libraries Board of South Australia, 1965. First published 1832.

Jeffreys, Charles. *Van Diemen's Land: Geographical and Descriptive Delineations of the Island of Van Diemen's Land.* London: J.M. Richardson, 1820.

Lempriere, Thomas James. *The Penal Settlements of Early Van Diemen's Land.* Launceston, Tas.: Royal Society of Tasmania, 1954. First published 1839.

Lloyd, George Thomas. *Thirty-Three Years in Tasmania and Victoria.* London: Houlston and Wright, 1862.

Melville, Henry (edited by George Mackaness). *The History of Van Diemen's Land from the Year 1824 to 1835 Inclusive.* Facsimile edition. Sydney: Horwitz-Grahame, 1965. First published 1835.

Meredith, Louisa. *My Home in Tasmania.* New York: Bunce, 1853.

Montagu, J. *Statistical Returns of Van Diemen's Land 1824–1836.* Hobart: James Ross, 1836.

Morgan, John. *The Life and Adventures of William Buckley: Thirty-Two Years a Wanderer Amongst the Aborigines of the Unexplored Country Around Port*

Phillip. Canberra: Australian National University Press, 1980. First published 1852.

Mortlock, J.F. *Experiences of a Convict: Transported for 21 Years*. Sydney: Sydney University Press, 1966. First published 1865.

Ross, James. *The Settler in Van Diemen's Land*. Facsimile edition. Melbourne: Marsh Walsh Publishing, 1975. First published in the *Hobart Town Almanack*, 1836.

Statistics of Van Diemen's Land 1838–1841. Hobart: Government Printer, 1843.

Thornley, William (edited by John Mills). *The Adventures of an Emigrant in Van Diemen's Land*. Adelaide: Rigby, 1973. First published 1843.

Wells, Thomas E. *Michael Howe, the Last and Worst of the Bush Rangers of Van Diemen's Land*. Hobart: Platypus Publications, 1966. First published 1818.

West, John (edited by A.G.L. Shaw). *The History of Tasmania*. Sydney: Angus and Robertson, 1971. First published 1852.

Secondary sources published since 1856

Alexander, Alison, ed. *The Companion to Tasmanian History*. Hobart: Centre for Tasmanian Historical Studies, University of Tasmania, 2005.

—— *Governors' Ladies: the Wives and Mistresses of Van Diemen's Land Governors*. Hobart: Tasmanian Historical Research Association, 1987.

Atkinson, Alan. *The Europeans in Australia: A History*, vol. 2, *Democracy*. Melbourne: Oxford University Press, 2004.

——"Four Patterns of Convict Protest." *Labour History* 37, November 1979.

Barr, Neil. *Greening a Brown Land: The Australian Search for Sustainable Land Use*. Melbourne: Macmillan, 1992.

Bartlett, Anne. "The Launceston Female Factory." *THRA Papers and Proceedings* 41, no. 2 (June 1994).

Beilby, W. *The Dog in Australasia*. Melbourne: George Robertson, 1897.

Billot, Cecil, *The Life and Times of John Pascoe Fawkner*. Melbourne: Hyland House, 1985.

Bolt, Frank. *Old Hobart Town Today*. Hobart: Waratah Publications, 1981.

Bonyhady, Tim. *The Colonial Earth*. Melbourne: Melbourne University Press, 2000.

Bowden, K.M. *Captain James Kelly of Hobart Town*. Melbourne: Melbourne University Press, 1964.

Boyce, James. "Canine Revolution: The Social and Environmental Impact of the Introduction of the Dog to Tasmania." *Environmental History* 11, no. 1 (2006).

——"A Dog's Breakfast ... Lunch and Dinner: Canine Dependency in Early Van Diemen's Land." *THRA Papers and Proceedings* 51, no. 4 (2004).

—— *God's Own Country? The Anglican Church and Tasmanian Aborigines*. Hobart: Anglicare Tasmania, 2001.

——"Robert May: Real Name Forever Lost." *40 Degrees South* 35 (2004).

Bradley, James and Ian Duffield, eds. *Representing Convicts: New Perspectives on Convict Forced Labour Migration*. London: Leicester University Press, 1997.

Brand, Ian. *The Convict Probation System : Van Diemen's Land, 1839–1854*. Hobart: Blubber Head Press, 1990.

—— *Macquarie Harbour Research*, vol. 1, 1984. Published online by the Tasmanian Department of Primary Industries and Water at <www.dpiw.tas.gov.au/library>.

Breen, Shayne. "Tasmanian Aborigines: Making Fire." *THRA Papers and Proceedings* 39, no. 1 (1992).

—— *Contested Places: Tasmania's Northern Districts from Ancient Times to 1900*. Hobart: Centre for Tasmanian Historical Studies, 2001.

Brown, Joan. *Poverty Is Not a Crime*. Hobart: Tasmanian Historical Research Association, 1972.

Butlin, N.G. *Forming a Colonial Economy: Australia 1810–1850*. Cambridge: Cambridge University Press, 1994.

Campbell, A.H. *John Batman and the Aborigines*. Melbourne: Kibble Books, 1987.

Castles, Alex. "The Van Diemonian Spirit and the Law." *THRA Papers and Proceedings* 38, nos. 3 and 4 (1991).

Chisholm, Alec. *Land of Wonder: The Best Australian Nature Writing*. Sydney: Angus and Robertson, 1964.

Chittleborough, Anne, Gillian Dooley, Brenda Glover and Rick Hosking, eds. *Alas, for the Pelicans!: Flinders, Baudin and Beyond, Essays and Poems*. Adelaide: Wakefield Press, 2002.

Clark, C.M.H. *Occasional Writing and Speeches*. Melbourne: Fontana, 1980.

Clarke, Marcus. *For the Term of His Natural Life*. Melbourne: Hallcraft Publishing, 1953. First published 1870–72.

Clendinnen, Inga. *Dancing with Strangers*. Melbourne: Text Publishing, 2003.

Connolly, S.J. *Priests and People in Pre-Famine Ireland 1780–1845*. New York: Gill and Macmillan, 1982.

Crowley, Frank. *A New History of Australia*. Melbourne: William Heinemann, 1974.

Cubit, Simon and the Central Plateau Oral History Project. *What's the Land For? People's Experience of the Tasmania's Central Plateau Region*. Tasmania: The Oral History Project, 1990.

Currey, John. *David Collins: A Colonial Life*. Melbourne: Melbourne University Press, 2000.

Daniels, Kay. *Convict Women*. Sydney: Allen and Unwin, 1998.

Davis, Richard. "'Not So Bad as a Bad Marriage': Irish Transportation Policies in the 1840s." *THRA Papers and Proceedings* 47, no. 1 (2000).

—— "Patrick O'Donohue: Young Ireland Rebel and Convict Worker Advocate, Van Diemen's Land 1850." *THRA Papers and Proceedings* 46, no. 2 (1999).

Davis, Richard and Stefan Petrow, eds. *Ireland and Tasmania 1848: Sesquicentenary Papers*. Sydney: Crossing Press, 1998.

Davison, Graeme, John Hirst and Stuart Macintyre, eds. *The Oxford Companion to Australian History*. Melbourne: Oxford University Press, 1998.

Day, David. *Claiming a Continent: A New History of Australia*. Sydney: HarperCollins, 2001.

Dow, G. and H. Dow. *Landfall in Van Diemen's Land: The Steels' Quest for Greener Pastures*. Melbourne: Footprint, 1990.

Dupont, Benoit and Mike Enders, eds. *Policing the Lucky Country*. Sydney: Hawkins Press, 2001.

Duyker, Edward. *Francois Peron: An Impetuous Life – Naturalist and Voyager*. Melbourne: The Miegunyah Press, 2006.

Dyer, Colin. *The French Explorers and the Aboriginal Australians 1772–1839*. St. Lucia, Qld.: University of Queensland Press, 2005.

Edmonds, Penelope and Samuel Furphy, eds. *Rethinking Colonial Histories: New and Alternative Approaches*. Melbourne: University of Melbourne History Department, 2006.

Fels, Marie. "Culture Contact in the County of Buckingamshire Van Diemen's Land 1803–1811." *THRA Papers and Proceedings* 29, no. 2 (1982).

——"Congruence and Contradictions in Aboriginal–European Relations in Van Diemen's Land and Port Phillip." *Bulletin of the Centre for Tasmanian Historical Studies* 3, no. 2 (1991–1992).

Flanagan, Richard. *Gould's Book of Fish*. Sydney: Pan Macmillan, 2001.

Flannery, Tim. *The Eternal Frontier: An Ecological History of North America and Its Peoples*. Melbourne: Text Publishing, 2001.

Forsyth, W.D. *Governor Arthur's Convict System, Van Diemen's Land 1824–36: A Study in Colonization*. London: Longmans Green for the Royal Empire Society, 1935.

Gardam, Faye. *Sawdust, Sails and Sweat: A History of the River Don Settlement*. Port Sorell, Tas.: Self published, 1996.

Giblin, Ronald Worthy. *The Early History of Tasmania*, vol. 2, *1804–1828*. Melbourne: Melbourne University Press, 1939.

Glover, Margaret. *History of the Site of Bowen's Settlement Risdon Cove*. Hobart: National Parks and Wildlife Service, 1978.

Gray, F. "Music of the Early Settlements of the 1800s." *THRA Papers and Proceedings* 43, no. 2 (1996).

Griffiths, Tom and Libby Robin, eds. *Ecology and Empire: Environmental History of Settler Societies*. Melbourne: Melbourne University Press, 1997.

Hartwell, R.M. *The Economic Development of Van Diemen's Land, 1820–1850*. Melbourne: Melbourne University Press, 1954.

Hay, Peter. "The Moral Economy of the Bush." *Arena* 83, June–July 2006.

——*Van Diemonian Essays*. Hobart: Walleah Press, 2002.

Haynes, Roslyn D. *Tasmanian Visions: Landscapes in Writing, Art and Photography*. Hobart: Polymath Press, 2006.

Henry, E.R. "Edward Lord: The John Macarthur of Van Diemen's Land." *THRA Papers and Proceedings* 20, no. 2 (1973).

Hirst, J.B. *Convict Society and Its Enemies: A History of Early New South Wales*. Sydney: Allen and Unwin, 1983.

Holderness, B.A. *Pre-Industrial England*. London: J.M. Dent, 1976.

Horner, Frank. *The French Reconnaissance: Baudin in Australia*. Melbourne: Melbourne University Press, 1987.

Hughes, Robert. *The Fatal Shore: A History of the Transportation of Convicts to Australia, 1787–1868*. London: Collins Harvill, 1987.

Huon, Dan. "By Moral Means Only: The Origins of the Launceston Anti-Transportation League 1847–49." *THRA Papers and Proceedings* 44, no. 2 (1997).

Jeans, D.N., ed. *Space and Society*. Sydney: Sydney University Press, 1987.

Jetson, Tim. "An Island of Contentment? A History of Preservation Island." *THRA Papers and Proceedings* 43, no. 1 (1996).

——*The Roof of Tasmania: A History of the Central Plateau*. Launceston, Tas.: Pelion Press, 1989.

Johnstone, A. *A History of the Church Missionary Society in Australia and Tasmania*. Sydney: Church Missionary Society, 1925.

Jones, Rhys. "Fire-Stick Farming." *Australian Natural History* 16 (1969).

——— "Tasmanian Aborigines and Dogs." *Mankind* 7, no. 4 (December 1970).

Jordan, T. and M. Kaups. *The American Backwoods Frontier*. Baltimore, MD: John Hopkins University Press, 1989.

Kiddle, Margaret. "Vandiemonien Colonists in Port Phillip 1834–1850." *THRA Papers and Proceedings* 3, no. 3 (1954).

Kitson Clark, G.S.R. *An Expanding Society: Britain 1830–1900*. Melbourne: Melbourne University Press, 1967.

Lawrence, E. Frank. *1823 – Before and After: A Story of William Effingham Lawrence, Tasmanian Pioneer and His Family*. Melbourne: The National Press, 1973.

Lawson, Will. *Blue Gum Clippers and Whale Ships of Tasmania*. Facsimile edition. Launceston, Tas.: D&C Book Distributors, 1986. First published 1949.

Levy, M.C.I. *Governor George Arthur: A Colonial Benevolent Despot*. Melbourne: Georgian House, 1953.

Lines, William. *Taming the Great South Land: A History of the Conquest of Nature in Australia*. Sydney: Allen and Unwin, 1991.

Lord, Richard. *The History of the James Lord Family in Tasmania,* vol. 1, *James Lord*. Hobart: R. Lord, 1966.

MacFie, Peter. "Oral History and the Demise of Folk Culture in the Richmond District, Tasmania." *THRA Papers and Proceedings* 29, no. 3 (1982).

Maclean, Charles. *Island on the Edge of the World: The Story of St Kilda*. New York: Taplinger, 1980.

Manne, Robert, ed. *Whitewash: On Keith Windschuttle's Fabrication of Aboriginal History*. Melbourne: Black Inc., 2003.

Mannion, John. *Irish Settlements in Eastern Canada*. Toronto: University of Toronto Press, 1974.

Mathias, Peter. *The First Industrial Nation: An Economic History of Britain 1700–1914*. London: Methuen, 1969.

McFarlane, Ian. "A Casualty of War." *THRA Papers and Proceedings* 48, no. 4 (2001).

McLaren, Glen. *Beyond Leichhardt: Bushcraft and the Exploration of Australia*. Fremantle, WA: Fremantle Arts Centre Press, 1996.

McMahon, John. "The British Army: Its Role in the Counter Insurgency in the Black War in Van Diemen's Land." *Tasmanian Historical Studies* 5, no. 1 (1995–96).

McMinn, W.G. "A Pioneer Who Failed." *THRA Papers and Proceedings* 13, no. 1 (1965).

Mickleborough, Leonie. *William Sorell in Van Diemen's Land 1817–1824: A Golden Age?* Hobart: Blubberhead Press, 2004,

Molony, John. *The Native Born: The First White Australians*. Melbourne: Melbourne University Press, 2000.

Monypenny, Maria. "Going out and Coming in: Cooperation and Collaboration between Aborigines and Europeans in Early Tasmania." *Tasmanian Historical Studies* 5, no. 1 (1995–96).

Morgan, Sharon. "George and Mary Meredith: The Role of the Colonial Wife." *THRA Papers and Proceedings* 36, no. 3 (1989).

————Land Settlement in Early Tasmania: Creating an Antipodean England. Cambridge: Cambridge University Press, 1992.

Murray-Smith, Stephen. "Beyond the Pale: The Islander Community of Bass Strait in the 19th Century." THRA Papers and Proceedings 20, no. 4 (1973).

Nash, Michael. The Bay Whalers: Tasmania's Shore-Based Whaling Industry. Hobart: Navarine Publishing, 2003.

Newman, Terry. Becoming Tasmania: Renaming Van Diemen's Land. Hobart: Parliament of Tasmania, 2005.

Nicholas, Stephen, ed. Convict Workers: Reinterpreting Australia's Past. Cambridge: Cambridge University Press, 1988.

Norman, Leslie. Sea Wolves and Bandits: Sealing, Whaling, Smuggling and Piracy, Wild Men of Van Diemen's Land, Bushrangers and Bandits, Wrecks and Wreckers. Hobart: J. Walch, 1946.

Nyman, Lois. The East Coasters: The Early Pioneering History of the East Coast of Tasmania. Launceston, Tas.: Regal Publications, 1990.

O'Farrell, Patrick. The Catholic Church in Australia: A Short History 1788–1967. London: Chapman, 1969.

————The Irish in Australia. Sydney: University of New South Wales Press, 2000.

Paddle, Robert. The Last Tasmanian Tiger: The History and Extinction of the Thylacine. Cambridge: Cambridge University Press, 2000.

Perkin, Harold. The Origins of Modern English Society 1780–1880. London: Routledge and Kegan Paul, 1969.

Plomley, Brian and Kristen Anne Henley. "The Sealers of Bass Strait and the Cape Barren Island Community." THRA Papers and Proceedings 37, nos. 2 and 3 (1990).

Plomley, N.J.B., Martina Smythe and Caroline Goodall. The Aboriginal/Settler Clash in Van Diemen's Land, 1803–1831. Launceston, Tas.: Queen Victoria Museum and Art Gallery in association with the Centre for Tasmanian Historical Studies, 1992.

Plomley, N.J.B., ed. Weep in Silence: A History of the Flinders Island Aboriginal Settlement. Hobart: Blubber Head Press, 1987.

Pretyman, R.D. A Chronicle of Methodism in Van Diemen's Land: 1820–1840. Melbourne: Aldersgate Press, 1970.

Rayner, Tony. Female Factory Female Convicts: The Story of More than 13000 Women Exiled from Britain to Van Diemen's Land. Dover, Tas.: Esperance Press, 2004.

Reid, James et al. Vegetation of Tasmania: Flora of Australia Supplementary Series Number 8. Canberra: Australian Biological Resources Study, Environment Australia, 1999.

Reynolds, Henry. Fate of a Free People: A Radical Re-Examination of the Tasmanian War. Melbourne: Penguin, 1995.

————"Australian Nationalism: Tasmanian Patriotism." The New Zealand Journal of History 5, no. 1 (1971).

————"Regionalism in Nineteenth Century Tasmania." THRA Papers and Proceedings 17, no. 1 (1969).

Reynolds, John and W.A. Townsley. A Century of Responsible Government in Tasmania 1856–1956. Hobart: Commonwealth Parliamentary Association and the Tasmanian Historical Research Association, 1956.

Rickard, John. *Australia: A Cultural History*. London: Longman, 1988.

Robson, Lloyd. *The Tasmanian Story*. Melbourne: Oxford University Press, 1987.

—— *A History of Tasmania*, vol. 1, *Van Diemen's Land from the Earliest Times to 1855*. Melbourne: Oxford University Press, 1983.

Roe, Michael. "Mary Leman Grimstone: For Women's Rights and Tasmanian Patriotism." *THRA Papers and Proceedings* 36, no. 1 (1989).

—— *Quest for Authority in Eastern Australia*. Melbourne: Melbourne University Press, 1965.

—— "The Establishment of Local Self Government in Hobart and Launceston, 1845–58." *THRA Papers and Proceedings* 14, no. 1 (1966).

Rolls, Eric. "Flowers and the Wide Sea: China and Australia with Special Reference to Tasmania." *THRA Papers and Proceedings* 36, no. 4 (1989).

Roth, H. Ling. *The Aborigines of Tasmania*. Halifax, Eng.: F. King and Sons, 1899.

Row, Margaret. "The Huon Timber Company and the Crown: A Tale of Resource Development." *THRA Papers and Proceedings* 27, no. 3 (1980).

Rude, George. *Protest and Punishment*. Melbourne: Oxford University Press, 1978.

Rule, John. *The Labouring Classes in Early Industrial England*. London: Longman, 1986.

Ryan, Lyndall. *The Aboriginal Tasmanians*. St Lucia, Qld.: University of Queensland Press, 1981.

—— *The Aboriginal Tasmanians*, 2nd edition. Sydney: Allen & Unwin, 1996.

Schama, Simon. *Landscape and Memory*. London: Fontana Press, 1996.

Scripps, Lindy. *Women's Sites and Lives: Historical Research*. Hobart: Hobart City Council, 2000.

Semmens, Trevor. "Food and Agriculture in the New Colony of Van Diemen's Land 1803–1810." *Papers and Proceedings of the Royal Society of Tasmania* 122, no. 2 (1988).

Shaw, Alan. "Van Diemonian Influences on Port Phillip Settlement." *Bulletin of the Centre for Tasmanian Historical Studies* 2, no.2 (1989–90).

Southerwood, W.T. "New Light on the Foundation of Australian Catholicism." *Australasian Catholic Record* 61, no. 2 (1984).

Tardif, Phillip. *John Bowen's Hobart: The Beginning of European Settlement in Tasmania*. Hobart: Tasmanian Historical Research Association, 2003.

—— *Notorious Strumpets and Dangerous Girls: Convict Women in Van Diemen's Land, 1803–1829*. Sydney: Angus & Robertson, 1990.

Taylor, Rebe. "Savages or Saviours: The Australian Sealers and Aboriginal Tasmanian Survival." *Journal of Australian Studies*, no. 66 (2000).

—— *Unearthed: The Aboriginal Tasmanians of Kangaroo Island*. Adelaide: Wakefield Press, 2002.

Teo, Hsu-Ming and Richard White, eds. *Cultural History in Australia*. Sydney: University of New South Wales Press, 2003.

Thomas, B.M. "Forest to Field and Fencing the Field." *THRA Papers and Proceedings* 47, no. 2 (2000).

Thompson, E.P. *Customs in Common*. London: Penguin, 1993.

—— *The Making of the English Working Class*. London: Penguin, 1977.

Tipping, M. *Convicts Unbound: The Story of the Calcutta Convicts and Their Settlement in Australia.* Melbourne: Viking O'Neill, 1988.

Todd, Alpheus. *Parliamentary Government in the British Colonies.* Boston: Little, Brown and Company, 1880.

Trollope, Anthony. *Australia.* St Lucia, Qld.: University of Queensland Press, 1967. First published 1873.

Von Stieglitz, K.R. *Matthew Brady: Van Diemen's Land Bushranger.* Hobart: Fullers Bookshop, 1964.

——*The Story of the Pioneer Church in Van Diemen's Land.* Hobart: Fullers Bookshop, 1954.

——*Tasmanian Bushrangers.* Evandale, Tas.: Telegraph Printery, 1951.

Walker, James Backhouse. *Early Tasmania: Papers Read before the Royal Society of Tasmania During the Years 1888 to 1899.* Hobart: Government Printer, 1973.

Ward, Russel. *The Australian Legend.* Melbourne: Oxford University Press, 1977.

Webb, G.M. "Twenty Men of Fortune." *THRA Papers and Proceedings* 45, no. 3 (1998).

Wills, H.A. *A Tally of Those Killed During the Fighting between Aborigines and Settlers in Van Diemen's Land, 1803–34.* Published online by the Australian Council of Professional Historians Associations at < http://www.historians. org.au/discus>. Published 2002, viewed August 2003.

Windschuttle, Keith. *The Fabrication of Aboriginal History,* vol. 1, *Van Diemen's Land 1803–1847.* Sydney: Macleay Press, 2002.

Winter, Gillian, ed. *Tasmanian Insights: Essays in Honour of Geoffrey Thomas Stillwell.* Hobart: State Library of Tasmania, 1992.

——"Under My Own Immediate Observation: Jane Roberts Visit to Hobart Town in 1830." *THRA Papers and Proceedings* 48, no. 3A (2001).

Woodberry, Joan. "Andrew Bent and the Proprietorship of the Hobart Town Gazette: An Examination of Some New Letters." *THRA Papers and Proceedings* 14, no. 2 (1967).

Young, Ann. *Environmental Change in Australia Since 1788.* Melbourne: Oxford University Press, 2000.

Young, David. *Sporting Island: A History of Sport and Recreation in Tasmania.* Hobart: Sport and Recreation Tasmania, 2005.

Newspapers
Church News
Colonial Times
Hobart Town Courier
Hobart Town Gazette
Sydney Gazette
Tasmanian

Archives of Tasmania documents [AOT]
Meredith papers, NS 123.
James Meehan notebook, LSD 355/3.
William Williamson letter, PL 16/4.
Samuel Guy letter, NS 381.

References

William Allison's notebook, NS 261/1.
Journal of William Pike, MM130.
Diary of Adam Amos 1822–1825, NS 323/1.
Richard Dillingham letter, NS 157/1.
Michael Steel letter, NP 41.
Diary of JC Sutherland, NP 61/1–3.
Colonial Secretary Office (CSO) papers.
Letters and Miscellaneous Papers Passing Direct to the Lieutenant Governor
    1821–1837, GO 39.
Kings and Queens orphan schools records, SWD 24.
Joyce Purtscher, *Children in Queens Orphanage Hobart Town 1828–1863*, Kings
    and Queens orphan schools records, SWD 28.
Aborigine Committee minutes of evidence, CBE/1.

Mitchell Library documents [ML]
Brabourne papers, CY 1747.
Banks papers, Brabourne papers, vol. 4, A78–3, CY 1747.
Tuckey, M. *General Observations of Port Phillip*, Brabourne Collection vol. 3, CY
    1747.
Collins, David. *General and Garrison Orders 1803–1808*, AK 341.
Knopwood Papers, A259.
Governor King's letter book, A2015.
Pearce, Alexander. *Confessions of Murder and Cannibalism*, A1326.
Brown, Robert. *Prodromus Florae Novae Hollandiae et Van Diemen*, CY 1390.
Gregson correspondence, A245.
George Meredith pocket book, Parker transcript, Parker papers.
Arthur papers, A2161–220.

State Library of Victoria documents [SLV]
Fawkner, John Pascoe. *Reminiscences of Early Settlement at Port Phillip*, Fawkner
    Papers 366.
——— *Some account of the marriage and subsequent fate of George Watts, a pris-
    oner*, SLV 366 1/6.
Henty Papers, MS 9038.

Glamorgan–Spring Bay Historical Society records
Aborigines file, 399H.

University of Tasmania archives
Belbin diaries, RS 90.

Other
Barnes, John. "A Few Remarks on the Natives of Van Diemen's Land." Unpublished
    paper presented to the Royal College of Physicians, London, 23 February 1829.
    R. Coll. Phys. Archives 3058 (1).

INDEX